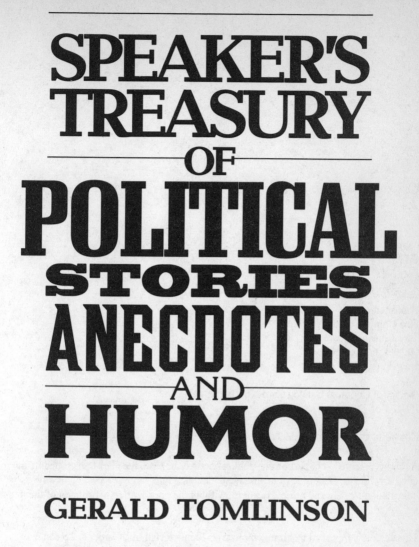

SPEAKER'S TREASURY OF POLITICAL STORIES ANECDOTES AND HUMOR

GERALD TOMLINSON

MJF BOOKS

NEW YORK

Published by MJF Books
Fine Communications
Two Lincoln Square
60 West 66th Street
New York, NY 10023

Library of Congress Catalog Card Number 95-82187
ISBN 1-56731-110-5

Copyright © 1990 by Gerald Tomlinson

This edition is reprinted by arrangement with Prentice-Hall Inc./Career & Personal Development.

Manufactured in the United States of America

MJF Books and the MJF colophon are trademarks of Fine Creative Media, Inc.

10 9 8 7 6 5 4 3 2 1

How to Use This Book

Your next speech is only as good as its stories, anecdotes, humor, quotations, analogies, examples, vignettes....

That may be an overstatement, but not much of one. A first-rate speech, an exciting speech, offers more than just facts and careful analysis. The best speeches include a story or two. They illustrate ideas with real-life incidents... or riveting language... or engaging humor. Or all three.

Few activities provide more stories, anecdotes, and humor than politics, whether local, state, national, or international. The subject is endlessly fascinating. While it may be true, as Will Rogers said, that "politics is applesauce," it's also true that the applesauce is rich and spicy. Almost any successful monologuist from Demosthenes to Jay Leno can be cited to show the popular attraction of politics.

This source book contains well over a thousand stories, anecdotes, and one-liners, all of them focused on the political arena. The entries hopscotch the world, as Walter Winchell used to say, and embrace the centuries. From the story of an ancient Greek questioning Themistocles to the thoughts of a modern Greek running for President against George Bush, the tales and aphorisms in this book are ideally suited for use in speeches.

Although the general topic of the entries is politics, the actual range is broad. Any story told by a politician, especially a renowned statesman, is assumed to be political. Abraham Lincoln, to take a single example, had an anecdote for just about every occasion. More often than not his stories dealt with life apart from statecraft. None of them has been excluded for that reason.

Certain kinds of war stories are basically political, too, for as Clausewitz said, "War... is a continuation of political relations, a carrying out of the same [policies] by other means." Eisenhower echoed the idea. "My life is a mixture of politics and war," Ike wrote to his wife Mamie in the midst of World War Two. Think, too, of Julius Caesar, Richard the Lion-hearted, George Washington, Napoleon Bonaparte, Simón Bolívar, Ulysses S. Grant, Teddy Roosevelt, and Charles de Gaulle. It's hard to separate the sword from the scepter.

The history that students learn in high school and college is by and large political—with military, social, and labor history thrown in. What this book contains is pretty much the same thing, with one important difference. Not every story here purports to be true. A few are simply tall tales, such as the one about Arthur Talmadge Abernethy's 125-year-old mountaineer (page 65), and FDR's joke about the suspected New Dealer who is a "son of a bishop" (page 154).

Even supposedly factual stories can be iffy. The difference between truth and apocrypha is not always easy to spot. Stories that appear in respected histories or collections of quotations are not, alas, always to be trusted. If you believe that old Patrick Henry story containing the line "if *this* be treason" (told in its traditional form on page 130), you may have second thoughts after reading Richard Hanser's "Of Deathless Remarks..." in the June 1970 issue of *American Heritage*. Although Hanser and others doubt that the incident had the dramatic impact ascribed to it, that doesn't detract from its effectiveness *as a story* (but it may now rate as folklore rather than history).

Similarly, the anecdote about Khrushchev banging his shoe at the UN and Prime Minister Macmillan asking to have the Soviet Premier's startling act translated into English—it's a great story (told factually on page 163). As commonly presented it fuses two separate incidents into one funnier-than-life tale. How many times this sort of fudging has occurred with stories included in the *Speaker's Treasury*, or in other collections, for that matter, is hard to tell. Anecdotes, along with many quotations, are history on the wing. They seldom appear in letters or state papers. Sometimes—who knows how often?—they are nothing more than journalistic hoaxes (pages 100 and 109), and no amount of checking is likely to verify or disprove them.

There are two common ways to organize a book of this kind. The first is by subject categories; the second is by chronology—a calendar of events. The subject-matter plan organizes stories under categories of interest to speech writers: ambition, bureaucracy, cooperation, decision, economy, and so on. That is the basic organizational plan I have used, and the book contains 76 such categories. This framework provides a clear, easy-to-use format for locating and identifying the exact story, anecdote, or comment you need for a specific purpose in a specific speech.

Many entries, as you will see, could easily fit under more than one category heading. The Fisher Ames anecdote, for example (page 50), appears under Democracy, but it might also seem at home under Comparison, Government, or Problems. The tale about a lobbyist who "corrected" his expense account (page 224) is categorized as Resourcefulness, but it could well have been put under Change, Discovery, Honesty, Mistake, Outcome, Quick-thinking, or Surprise.

Incidentally, if I had placed the lobbyist's expense account story under Honesty, it would have been categorized by its polar opposite. The tale portrays *dis*honesty. You will find many instances of that in the book. A story illustrating verbosity may appear under Brevity; one showing illogicality may show up under Logic. This may seem odd at first glance, but you will find that it works. It reduces the number of categories (which are somewhat arbitrary divisions in the first place) and simplifies the search for the exact story you need.

You will indeed find a few categories of opposites—Consistency and Inconsistency, Failure and Success—but keep in mind that the anecdote you need to illustrate nonprogress may appear under Progress.

Since there is no way to predict the exact use you will make of an entry, no attempt has been made to form specific content connections. In other words, while the joke about the wife of the ham-stealer (page 202) might be used to stress the corporate usefulness of an unpopular executive, let's say, it might also be used for a hundred other purposes. To write specifics into the story would only seem to limit the uses to which the entry could be put.

Whatever use you make of a story, there is a kind of formula you can apply. It's the old lead-in, anecdote, and wrap-up technique. Observe its use by Abraham Lincoln in a speech he gave to Congress in 1848:

"I have heard some things from New York, and if they are true, one might well say of your party [the Democrats]... END OF LEAD-IN

"...as a drunken fellow once said when he heard the reading of an indictment for hog-stealing. The clerk read on till he got to and through the words 'did steal, take, and carry away ten boars, ten sows, ten shoats, and ten pigs,' at which the drunk exclaimed, 'Well, by golly, that is the most equally divided gang of hogs I ever did hear of!' END OF ANEC-DOTE

"If there is any other gang of hogs more equally divided than the Democrats of New York are about this time, I have not heard of it." END OF WRAP-UP

That's the usual technique. The writer or speaker makes the subject-matter connections by means of the lead-in and the wrap-up. In between those two items is the story, the anecdote, the joke or comment. You may be able to use an entry verbatim, exactly as it appears in the book, or you may find that you need to revise it for your own purposes. If your speaking style is either more or less formal than that of the printed entry, you will probably want to make adjustments.

As noted earlier, there is a second method of categorizing entries in a collection like this. It is the chronological (calendar or almanac) method. The Speaker's 366-Day Calendar of Political Events, beginning on page 273, uses the chronological approach. If you are giving a speech on September 23, for instance, you might want to tie your opening, or even your whole talk, to something that occurred on or about September 23. By using the Speaker's 366-Day Calendar of Political Events you will find (page 310) that this is the anniversary day of both Franklin D. Roosevelt's "Fala" speech and Richard M. Nixon's "Checkers" speech. A cross-reference at the end of the day's entry leads you to a longer account (page 260) of the Fala story.

Many of the calendar entries have cross-references to related stories in the book. Even if they don't, you will sometimes find that a connection can be made. For example, the May 22 entry concerning the treason trial of Aaron Burr (page 293) contains no cross-reference. But if you check the index at the back of the book under Burr, you will find a story (page 75) about the Hamilton-Burr duel that cos⁺ Alexander Hamilton his life. The two stories are otherwise unrelated, but if for some reason you happen to be looking specifically for Burr stories, you will be able to find them.

Something has already been said about the veracity of the anecdotes, stories, and quotations in the book. A bit more should be said. The author cited last in the bibliography, P.M. Zall, compiled a scholarly book of Lincoln anecdotes in which he accepted nothing that lacked what he considered to be respectable origins. It's an admirable idea, but the very nature of politics (and journalism) ensures that many stories will be hearsay, garbled, or otherwise rendered suspect.

The New Columbia Encyclopedia states: "More or less apocryphal sayings and anecdotes illustrating Napoleon's character and manners are as innumerable as the books written about him." Similarly, the wording of Churchill's quip about taking Lady Astor's poison (page 215) is as varied as the sources in which it can be found. And the story itself may be fictitious. Professional historians try to be careful about such things, and so have I, to the extent possible. But this is a book for speakers, not for scholars. When Churchill was called to account for saying incorrectly that Joseph Guillotin had died beneath the blade of his own invention, Sir Winston replied, "Well, he should have." So, too, about the tales in this book: If some of the events never really happened in quite the way described, well, they should have.

The calendar is intended to be factually accurate, and if any errors appear in it (there are glaring discrepancies in some of the sources), they are unintentional. For events prior to the year 1582, dates shown are Old Style, wherever this could be determined. (That is to say, they are not adjusted for the New Style Gregorian Calendar).

The book contains 1,267 carefully chosen entries on politics. The choices are based primarily on their usefulness to speakers and speech writers. Since the motif is politics, some differences of opinion are inevitable. I have tried throughout to balance liberal and conservative sentiments, and to avoid pushing any special viewpoint.

My hope is that the reader will find in this book a politically related story for almost every kind of speech or speaking occasion. The subject matter of politics is inexhaustible, and a complete collection of political anecdotes and quotations, if such a thing were possible, would fill a large library. This distillation, I hope, is the next best thing.

Gerald Tomlinson

Acknowledgments

In putting together a collection of this kind, it takes no time at all to become awed by the abundance of sources available. Almost every biography of a political figure, no matter how dull the politician or how dry the biographer, seems to contain at least a couple of appealing anecdotes. Then there are books (although only a few) that contain nothing but anecdotes. Clifton Fadiman's *The Little, Brown Book of Anecdotes* is one of the best general collections. Paul Boller's *Presidential Anecdotes* is one of the best specific ones. Bill Adler has made a specialty of assembling stories about specific politicians. In addition, there are many fine collections of quotations and jokes, plus more than a few calendars, or almanacs, of world events. Magazines and newspapers are a rich source of anecdotes and quotations. I have made use of all these sources and more.

In his book *Too Funny to Be President*, Morris K. Udall quotes "Buchwald's Fourth Law," to this effect: "The first two times you use a joke, give your source credit. From then on, to hell with it! Be shameless—claim it as your own. After all, your source undoubtedly stole it form someone else." No claim of total originality is made for the stories or anecdotes in this book, but nearly all of them have been rewritten for use by speakers. Generally, that means they have been compressed and simplified. I have given source credit within the story itself when that seems appropriate.

A complete list of book-length sources can be found in the bibliography. Some books provided only a fact or two for a single calendar entry. Others supplied the basis for up to five stories. As Buchwald's Fourth Law suggests, a number of the entries appear in one form or another in book after book, so it is hard to know whom to credit.

I did, however, definitely receive specific stories or helpful advice from the following people, and I am most grateful to them: John Bendix, Department of Political Science, Lewis and Clark College, Portland, Oregon; Lowell L. Blaisdell, Department of History, Texas Tech University, Lubbock, Texas; Bill Bradley, U.S. Senator from New Jersey; Richard C. Crepeau, Department of History, University of Central Florida, Orlando, Florida; Dean A. Gallo, U.S. Congressman from the 11th District of New Jersey; Masaru "Massy" Ikei, Department of Political Science, Keio University, Tokyo, Japan; Jim Lightfoot, U.S. Congressman from the 5th District of Iowa; David Mills, Department of History, University of Alberta, Edmonton, Canada; Eugene C. Murdock, Emeritus Professor of History, Marietta College, Marietta, Ohio; Mayumi Otsuma, Department of Chinese, Comparative

Literature, and Slavic Languages and Literatures, Rutgers University, New Brunswick, New Jersey; my son Matthew Tomlinson, a student at Rutgers College, New Brunswick, New Jersey; and the staff of the Morris County Free Library in Whippany, New Jersey.

Every effort has been made to get the facts right, wherever the facts can be determined. If here and there I have wandered from the truth, as the truth ought to be known by the average eleventh-grader (but probably isn't), please remember that I am not alone. So have a lot of politicians, journalists, and even historians. Nevertheless, any factual or interpretative mistakes in this book are my own, not someone else's.

Contents

ACHIEVEMENT

Catherine corresponded with... Voltaire....

When Catherine the Great, Empress of All the Russias, learned of a border dispute between Manchuria and Siberia, she sent an envoy to China to resolve the issue and to reopen trade with the Celestial Empire. The two nations signed a treaty, after which camel caravans began carrying goods to and from China.

Catherine corresponded with the great French writer Voltaire, who was then living at Ferney, an estate in Switzerland, just over the border from France. One of the enterprises at Ferney was the making of Swiss watches. Voltaire asked Catherine if she would be willing to market some of these watches. She said yes, and soon Swiss watches were among the items the camel caravans carried for sale to the mandarins in Peking.

Hannah Grant's son....

Just as no man is a hero to his valet, neither are most men heroes to their immediate family. The reason is that a second aphorism applies: Familiarity breeds contempt.

After the tide turned for the Union in the Civil War, there was no greater hero in the United States than Ulysses S. Grant. After years of searching for a capable general, Lincoln had found one at last in the hard-driving Grant. Hannah Grant's son, a failure in private life, was suddenly the toast of the nation.

But Hannah was not much impressed. Once after assuming command, Grant visited her at home. Hannah came out in an old apron to greet him. She said, "Well, Ulysses, you've become a great man, haven't you?"

That's all she said. She didn't smile or make any further fuss. She just turned and went back to her household tasks.

The Little Flower was running for Congress....

Political upsets are familiar news in every election, but the one Fiorello H. LaGuardia pulled off in 1916 remains a classic. The Little Flower was running for Congress in Manhattan's 14th Congressional District. As a rule, the Democrats won that district by a five-to-one margin. LaGuardia was given little chance of overcoming those odds.

Even the Republican organization in the 14th District didn't back LaGuardia with much enthusiasm. Its leaders were beholden to Tammany Hall, and they saw no reason to cause waves on behalf of a sure loser.

The Little Flower, a Republican in a sea of Democrats, had to go it alone. He campaigned up and down the West Side district. He spoke on the stump and door-to-door, using his wide knowledge of languages to communicate with people in the ethnic neighborhoods. He charged his Irish opponent, Mike Farley, with being soft on the British. Besides, he added, "I know more about the history of Ireland than Mike Farley ever did."

On the day of the election, LaGuardia rounded up the Bowery bums at daybreak and herded them to the polls. By the time Tammany got to them they had already cast their ballots for the maverick Republican. But LaGuardia was going to get plenty of legitimate votes, too. He was sure of it.

LaGuardia and his men watched the counting process closely to make sure the Democrats didn't steal the election after the polls had closed. The outcome shocked Tammany Hall, embarrassed the Republican clique in the 14th District, and probably surprised LaGuardia himself.

The inconceivable had happened. When the votes were counted, a Republican, running with little party support, had won New York's 14th District, squeaking by with just a 357-vote margin. Fiorello H. LaGuardia, better known today as New York City's flamboyant mayor, became the first American of Italian descent ever to sit in the United States House of Representatives.

"What is past is prologue...."

After being elected to a second term as President of the United States, Ronald Reagan exclaimed, "You ain't seen nothing yet."

The Great Communicator didn't originate that line, of course. Back in 1956, in his speech accepting the Republican nomination for President, Dwight Eisenhower told the following story:

A government worker who had just arrived in Washington was passing the National Archives Building in a taxi. He noticed the motto carved on the building: "What is past is prologue."

Since cab drivers throughout the world are presumed to be all-knowing about their cities, the government worker asked what the motto meant.

"Oh," said the cabbie, "that's just bureaucrat talk. What it means is, 'You ain't seen nothing yet.'"

At a White House dinner....

One of John F. Kennedy's political heroes was Thomas Jefferson, the brilliant and versatile third President of the United States. At a White House dinner honoring Nobel Prize winners, President Kennedy said:

"I think this is the most extraordinary collection of talent, of human knowledge, that has ever been gathered together at the White House—with the possible exception of when Thomas Jefferson dined alone."

Quote/Unquote

Andrew Jackson (1767–1845)

I have only done my duty.

Stephen A. Douglas (1813–1861)

Lincoln is one of those peculiar men who perform with admirable skill everything which they undertake.

Theodore Roosevelt (1858–1919)

Far and away the best prize that life offers is the chance to work hard at work worth doing.

George Santayana (1863–1952)

In what sometimes looks like American greediness and jostling for the front place, all is love of achievement; nothing is unkindness....

ADVICE

"You, who will deserve the praise...."

When Alexander Pope, the English poet, was a young man, he wondered if he should join a political party. He asked the advice of Joseph Addison, the essayist, who told him, "No."

Addison explained: "You, who will deserve the praise of the whole nation, should not content yourself with the praise of half of it."

"Do not talk too much...."

As a young man, Benjamin Disraeli longed to become a celebrity. He wrote popular novels. He wore green velvet trousers and canary yellow waistcoats. But most of all, he tried to impress people with his dazzling conversation. He kept a journal of advice to himself. In it he wrote:

"Do not talk too much at present... But whenever you speak, speak with self-possession. Speak in a subdued tone, and always look at the person whom you are addressing. Before one can engage in general conversation with any effect, there is a certain acquaintance with trifling but amusing subjects that must be first attained. You will soon pick up sufficient by listening and observing. Never argue."

Disraeli's advice is still valid. It's much the same as Barbara Walters' advice in her book on the art of conversation.

"Squire, you have no such authority...."

A justice of the peace, a man by the name of Bolling Green, once asked Senator Edward D. Baker of Oregon for some law advice.

"Baker," said the old man, "I want to know if I have jurisdiction in a case of slander."

At the time Baker was a very young man and, according to his own admission, a very poor lawyer. But he tried to look important and wise as he replied: "Squire, you have no such authority; that is reserved to a court of general jurisdiction."

"Well," the justice of the peace said, "think again; you have not read law very well or very long. Try again. Now, have I not jurisdiction? Can I not do it?"

"No," said Baker positively, "you cannot. I know it. I have read the law from Blackstone to—well, I have read Blackstone, and I know you cannot do it."

"Now, sir," said Green with equal conviction, "I know I can. For, by God, I've done it!"

"The course I wish to deliver...."

Abe Lincoln knew a man in Springfield named Campbell. The man had served for a time as Illinois Secretary of State. One of his duties was to act as the rental agent for the state legislative hall.

One day a quiet, pallid man approached Campbell and asked about renting the place for a series of lectures he planned to give. Campbell asked the man about the subject of his lectures.

The pale man replied solemnly: "The course I wish to deliver is on the second coming of our Lord."

Campbell tried to talk him out of it. "If you'll take my advice," he said "you won't waste your time in this city. It's my private opinion that if the Lord has been in Springfield once, he will never come a second time."

"...the phrase 'a typical prairie state'...."

Even the best politician puts his foot in his mouth now and then. Jim Farley, the shrewd campaign manager of Franklin D. Roosevelt in his early campaigns, knew all the angles. But on the eve of the Republican national convention in 1936, Farley made a remark that hurt the Democrats and delighted the Republicans.

He predicted that "the Governor of a typical prairie state" would get the Republican nomination for President. Farley was referring to Alfred Landon of Kansas, but he wanted to avoid mentioning both the man and the state. In so doing, he made a worse blunder.

The phrase "a typical prairie state," and the uproar that followed, caused FDR to write one of his few letters to Farley. His tone was restrained, but the message was clear. FDR wrote: "...no section of the country should be spoken of as 'typical' but only with some laudatory adjective." He suggested that the sentence might have read, "One of those splendid prairie states." And he ended by noting, "...the word 'typical' coming from any New Yorker is meat for the opposition."

Farley admitted his mistake and took the advice to heart.

He had no cash for the voyage home.

The public tends to be fascinated with the children of American Presidents. More often than not people regard the Presidential offspring as spoiled or otherwise unworthy. That was certainly the case with Franklin D. Roosevelt's four sons and a daughter. They were often in the news, usually unfavorably. The one who got the poorest press was James, FDR's oldest son. He seemed to be in some kind of trouble most of the time.

Americans of the day who thought young Jimmy was coddled by his parents might have had a different view if they knew the aftermath of his Grand Tour of Europe. Just out of Harvard, Jimmy spent money pretty freely throughout the tour. By the time he got to Ireland he was down to his last few hundred dollars.

There he met a persuasive country gentleman who had a fine racehorse for sale. Jimmy, who never managed money well, spent his last four hundred and fifty dollars on the horse. He had no cash for the voyage home. Since this was in the pre-credit-card age, Jimmy had no recourse but to wire for money. He asked his father to please send along five hundred.

On this occasion anyway, FDR wasn't quite the pushover he was pictured as being. Jimmy must have been a bit surprised when he received his father's reply. It read: "So happy about the horse. Suggest both of you swim home."

It's doubtful that Warren Austin....

The way advice is worded can often make a difference. It's doubtful that Warren Austin got very far with his. Austin was the U.S. Ambassador to the United Nations at the time of the Middle East War in 1948. He told the Arabs and Jews that they should try to settle their differences "like good Christians."

"I am expecting a baby...."

Back in the 1950s, before the women's movement gained momentum, Congressman Harold Cooley of North Carolina received this letter from a constituent:
"Honorable Sir:

"I am expecting a baby in June. Would you advise me to name him after a Republican or a Democratic President. What I mean is, which do you think will do him the most good politically when he grows up?"

A second letter followed not long afterwards. It said:

"Never mind advising me to name my baby after a Republican or a Democratic President. The baby arrived last week and I'm calling her Marjorie."

Herblock thought about it for a while.

The Presidential election of 1968 was close, although no one had expected it to be. Early on, Richard Nixon seemed to be leading Hubert Humphrey by a comfortable margin.

Humorist Art Buchwald and editorial cartoonist Herbert Block, or Herblock, figured that Nixon had it in the bag. They weren't happy, because they both disliked Nixon intensely.

But Buchwald pointed out that the outcome might be good for both of them. There would be lots of humorous barbs, lots of vitriolic pictures.

Herblock thought about it for a while. Then he told his colleague that he was worried about a Nixon Presidency. Genuinely worried.

At which Buchwald lived up to his reputation as a humorist. He looked at Herblock quite seriously and said, "Herb, you've got to stop putting the country ahead of your work."

Quote/Unquote

Benjamin Franklin (1706–1790)

Who says Jack is not generous?—he is always fond of giving, and cares not for receiving—what?—why, advice.

Benjamin Disraeli (1804–1881)

There are exceptions to all rules, but it seldom answers to follow the advice of an opponent.

Josh Billings (1818–1885)

I never had a man come to me for advice yet, but what I soon discovered that he thought more of his own opinion than he did of mine.

Harry S Truman (1884–1972)

I have found the best way to give advice to your children is to find out what they want and then advise them to do it.

AMBITION

"Fain would I climb...."

The story goes that Queen Elizabeth I saw a line cut in the glass of a windowpane. It read:

"Fain would I climb, but that I fear to fall." The Queen knew that this was the work of Walter Raleigh, who had recently come to court to seek his fortune. After studying the line for a moment, she asked if a suitable second line might be:

"If thy heart fail thee, do not climb at all."

The Queen's courtiers applauded her effort, and she used a diamond to inscribe the words on the glass.

Some time later young Raleigh saw them and was entranced. He went on to become one of the great heroes and adventurers of Elizabethan England.

He led a 57-man private army....

William Walker was a man of restless ambition. He weighed barely a hundred pounds, but he was a "half-horse, half-alligator" type who fought his way from poverty to the Presidency... of Nicaragua.

William Walker was a filibuster. In the old days a filibuster was a private citizen who tried to take over a foreign nation by force. If the idea sounds silly, remember that William Walker—"the greatest American filibuster"—actually did take over the government of Nicaragua.

He did it in typical filibuster fashion. He led a 57-man private army against the native forces at the town of Rivas, where he won a victory. He then led a much larger force against the city of Granada, which at the time was the capital of Nicaragua. Again he won.

Seizing the moment—the date was July 12, 1856—he declared himself President of Nicaragua. As luck would have it, a friend of his, John H. Wheeler, was the American minister to Nicaragua. Wheeler immediately recognized the new government. But when this news reached Washington, the impetuous minister was recalled.

Still, the brash American filibuster remained in charge of things in the Nicaraguan capital. He had great plans, too. He wanted to relegalize slavery in Nicaragua. He wanted to build a canal connecting the Atlantic and Pacific oceans.

Unfortunately for him, there were five neighboring Central American countries that wanted no part of a gringo running Nicaragua. Add to this the fact that Commodore Vanderbilt up in New York lost patience when Walker's forces seized a number of Vanderbilt steamships in Nicaraguan waters. Before long a sizable army moved against Walker—and defeated him.

The little filibuster should have given up at that point, but he didn't. Three more times he tried to regain his Presidency. At the end of his third try, the opposition lost patience. Walker was backed up against an adobe wall and dispatched by a Honduran firing squad.

He was buried in an unmarked grave.

The American poet Joaquin Miller commemorated Walker in a poem, "That night in Nicaragua." The man was a daredevil all right, but his ambition outran his common sense by a country mile.

"...gleams of stars coruscant...."

The English loved their Virgin Queen. Subjects who lived in the countryside envied Londoners who had the Queen near them most of the time. It was a big occasion when Elizabeth I traveled to one's home county to visit.

Four times the Earl of Leicester had expected to see the Queen at his

Kenilworth Castle. Four times he had been disappointed. But finally in July of 1575 the Queen made the journey—and Leicester, an ambitious planner, was ready for her.

Determined to put on a spectacle that would show his fealty in full flower, Leicester first had the clock on Caesar's Tower deliberately stopped when she arrived. The idea was to set the tone for a fantasy midsummer night's dream.

Next came a fireworks display. The Italian who put it on had a grandiose idea. He wanted to fill a fiery dragon with live dogs, cats, and birds, then send the dragon into orbit, where it would spew out the barking, howling, and flying animals. He was persuaded to tone down his display a bit, to a simple "blaze of burning darts..., gleams of stars coruscant, [and] streams and hails of fiery sparks."

Naturally, there were grand banquets, dramatic performances, hunting, and bear-baiting. The showpiece of Leicester's welcome was a water pageant called "The Delivery of the Lady of the Lake." In the pageant Proteus rode on a massive dolphin whose fins were the oars of the boat conveying him. Inside the dolphin "a consort of music was secretly played."

Queen Elizabeth evidently enjoyed her 19-day fun-filled stay at Leicester Castle. The Earl, for his part, came out of the celebration about three million dollars poorer. But he had no complaint. Not at all. In fact, Leicester had a few "other entertainments in reserve" had the Queen chosen to extend her visit even longer.

"They think he has a trick."

On the night before his election to the Presidency, John F. Kennedy spoke at Boston Garden to a wildly cheering crowd of supporters. On the dais with him, wrote Theordore H. White, sat "a covey of the puffy, pink-faced, predatory-lipped politicians who had so dominated Massachusetts politics before he had taken over."

White could recall nothing of the speech. But he did remember a remark by Richard Donahue, one of Kennedy's so-called Irish Mafia. Donahue saw envy on the faces of local pols as they watched the young Presidential candidate in action.

"You know, they can't understand this," Donahue said. "They think he has a trick. They're listening to him because they think if they learn the trick they can be President, too."

Quote/Unquote

Edmund Burke (1729–1797)

Well is it known that ambition can creep as well as soar.

Johann Wolfgang von Goethe   (1749–1832)

Ambition and love are the wings of great actions.

Abraham Lincoln   (1809–1865)

Towering genius disdains a beaten path… It thirsts and burns for distinction.…

Ambrose Bierce   (1842–1914)

Ambition: *n.* An overmastering desire to be villified by enemies while living and made ridiculous by friends when dead.

W.L. Mackenzie King   (1874–1950)

Were man never to fall, he would be a God; were he never to aspire, he would be a brute.

ASSISTANCE

"Don't mind him; I know him.…"

Lincoln liked to tell about the time he got help on the campaign trail from a small, lame man in Cumberland County.

After Lincoln had delivered a speech there, a local celebrity, Dr. Hamburgher jumped to the platform and began making an unscheduled speech of his own. Dr. Hamburgher, a staunch Democrat, became more and more violent and insulting.

A small, lame man from the audience came up to Lincoln and said, "Don't mind him; I know him; I live here; I'll take care of him."

Dr. Hamburgher's speech went on and on. The small, lame man came back two or three times to repeat his promise.

Finally, Hamburgher concluded. The lame man made his way to the platform and began to speak. He was even more insulting to the doctor than the doctor had been to Lincoln.

After a few minutes of abuse, Hamburgher could take no more. He roared, "That's a lie!"

The lame man stopped. "Never mind," he said calmly. "I'll take that from you. In fact, I'll take anything from you except your *pills*."

That line didn't pacify the doctor at all. "You scoundrel," he shouted, "you know I've quit practicing medicine."

It was the lame man's cue. He instantly dropped to one knee, raised his hands as if in prayer, and said, "Then, thank God! The country is safe!"

"This is an insane asylum."

David Lloyd George, the British Prime Minister, was traveling through Wales. Night came on, and he began looking for a place to spend the night. In the small town where he found himself the inns were full.

Lloyd George approached a large brick building in town and knocked on the door. To the man who opened the door he asked about the chances for lodging.

"This is an insane asylum," the man said.

"Well, I have to stay somewhere," the Prime Minister replied. "Can't you put me up? I am David Lloyd George."

The man smiled. "I say, old man, we have five Lloyd Georges here already, but I suppose there's always room for a sixth."

The man asked the father of the bride-to-be....

When he needed campaign help, Adlai Stevenson liked to tell the story of a young man who was seeking the hand of a young woman in marriage. The man asked the father of the bride-to-be for his approval, but the old man was skeptical.

"I doubt that you would be able to support my daughter," he said. "I can hardly do it myself."

The young suitor was undaunted. He said, "We'll just have to pool our resources."

"Tell me, how I can help."

Richard Nixon lost the 1960 Presidential race to John F. Kennedy by a slim margin. People afterwards wondered whether outgoing President Dwight D. Eisenhower had supported Nixon, his two-term Vice President, as fully as he should have.

It was a legitimate question. Eisenhower apparently didn't like Nixon very much. Still, he hated to see his own Presidential achievements belittled, as he thought JFK was doing. So about a week before the election, he invited Nixon to the White House to have lunch with him and a group of advisers.

Ike said he realized that Nixon was in trouble in some key states. And he added, "Tell me how I can help."

Nixon, given this belated offer, flubbed it. He asked for no help at all. He turned down the prospect of what might have been decisive last-minute support from the popular President of the '50s.

In his memoirs Nixon claimed that his refusal was altruistic. He was fearful for the President's health. Ike's heart attack had frightened him badly.

But Len Hall, the Republican Party chairman of that day, had a different opinion. When Eisenhower asked Hall, "Why didn't Dick pay attention to what I was saying?," Hall replied, "He was uptight, Mr. President. "You could have fired a gun off and he wouldn't have noticed."

To which Eisenhower snapped with cruel accuracy, "Goddammit, he looks like a loser to me!"

So Nancy spoke right up....

During the 1980 Presidential primaries, Ronald Reagan poured forth a stream of amazing but suspicious-sounding facts that kept reporters off balance. In a debate in South Carolina he called marijuana the most dangerous drug in America. The next day he tried to correct his remark. But in doing so, he introduced a new fact—that a marijuana cigarette is probably a much greater cancer risk than a tobacco cigarette.

A reporter struggled with that concept. He pointed out to Reagan that it wasn't necessary to smoke very much marijuana to get high. The reporter was probably trying to imagine a three-pack-a-day grass user. But clearly he had lost touch with the expertise of the candidate.

Nancy Reagan, who was with her husband, could see a possible slip-up coming. Reagan's deafness made whispering to him out of the question. So Nancy spoke right up, saying, "You wouldn't know."

"I wouldn't know," echoed Ronnie.

"...the supply of words...."

Lech Walesa, leader of Poland's Solidarity, visited the United States in the fall of 1989. His goal was to gain a pledge of economic assistance to help save the bankrupt Polish economy. Speaking before a joint session of Congress, Walesa thanked Americans for their expressions of support, but stressed that Poland needed action, not just admiration.

"I must tell you," he said, "that the supply of words on the world market is plentiful, but the demand is falling. Let deeds follow words...."

Quote/Unquote

Napoleon Bonaparte   (1769–1821)

In the eyes of those who found empires, men are not men but tools.

Heywood Broun   (1888–1939)

I have known people to stop and buy an apple on the corner and then walk away as if they had solved the whole unemployment problem.

Pearl Bailey   (1918–   )

We could use less foreign aid and more home aid.

· B ·

BREVITY

"You were brief," Canning said.

George Canning, British foreign secretary and briefly Prime Minister, could be caustic. Once, following a church service, the pastor asked him his opinion of the sermon.

"You were brief," Canning said.

"Yes," said the pastor, "so as to avoid being tedious."

"But you *were* tedious," said Canning.

"You, sir, speak for the present...."

Henry Clay of Kentucky was noted for his sharp wit.

Once when Alexander Smyth of Virginia was delivering a long, dull speech in Congress, he turned to Clay and said, "You, sir, speak for the present generation; but I speak for posterity."

Clay interrupted. "Yes, and you seem resolved to speak until the arrival of your audience."

"I'm not a speakin' man...."

In the age of television it's important to be able to speak in public. In earlier times it was also a great advantage—orators were widely admired—but it wasn't essential. Still, a man who couldn't speak in public was at a serious disadvantage.

Abe Lincoln used to tell the story of a man who was running for sheriff. He was a good man—honest, brave, and tough. His friends knew he would do a good

14

job, but the voters in the county didn't know much about him. His friends wished the candidate could appear on a platform and state his principles and beliefs. They felt that a man who didn't talk to the people wouldn't get many votes.

After much cajoling, the candidate for sheriff agreed to give a speech. He showed up for the occasion, looking grim and determined. A large crowd had assembled to hear him.

The candidate began quietly. "Feller citizens," he said, "I'm not a speakin' man, and I never stood up before a lot of people in my life before."

His voice rose as he reached the climax in his talk immediately. "I'm not goin' to make no speech," he thundered, "except to say that I can lick any man in the crowd!"

End of oration.

This taciturn English legislator....

Colonel Henry Lowther sat for 55 years in the House of Commons without ever opening his mouth. This taciturn English legislator made Calvin Coolidge sound like a motormouth.

It isn't that the Colonel never said anything at all in public. Once at an official banquet he opened up a little and observed, "Least said, soonest mended."

And on the day he beat Henry Brougham in a contested election, he said, "Gentlemen, I point to the poll."

"Then, sir, would you please yield...."

Senators are known for being long-winded, and this one was no exception. He had traveled many miles from Washington to be on hand for a hanging in his home state.

They asked the condemned man the usual question: "Do you have any last words." He said, "No."

At that the senator stood up and said, "Then, sir, would you please yield your time to me?"

The condemned man thought for a moment and said, "Sure—as long as they hang me first."

"I have been asked to give my address...."

Most speakers have had the bad luck to lose their scheduled time to a long-winded orator who preceded them. There may be no way in the world to make that speech in the fleeting few minutes that are left—but there is a good put-down. It comes from Lord Balfour, British Prime Minister in the early 1900s.

Balfour had lost his time to a garrulous toastmaster. The talkative host closed by saying, "Lord Balfour will now give his address."

Balfour arose and said, "I have been asked to give my address in the remaining five minutes. That I can do. Here it is: Ten Carlton Gardens, London, England."

"I do not choose to run."

President Calvin Coolidge had a well-deserved reputation for using no more words than were necessary.

When announcing he would not be a candidate for a second term, he said, "I do not choose to run."

When asked what a preacher had said in a sermon about sin, Coolidge replied, "He was against it."

When told by a woman that she had bet a friend she could get him to say more than three words to her, he answered, "You lose."

"Well, what's today? The 25th?"

For every word that Calvin Coolidge saved, Senator Everett Dirksen of Illinois wasted a dozen. Dirksen was often called a throwback to the great orators of the 19th century. But that was not really true. He had a mellifluous voice, but his words sounded more like those of Casey Stengel than of Daniel Webster.

When asked on September 25, 1963, the prospects for passage of a civil rights bill, this was Senator Dirksen's response:

"Well, what's today? The 25th? That's almost October. Which reminds me, I'd better start picking my apples. They're approaching a state of ripeness. So already you're into November. As you know so well, with November comes Thanksgiving, and that takes a big chunk out of a man's life. Before you know it, we're into December and then the Yuletide begins. It begins coursing through our veins. Downtown they'll be hanging wreaths and soon they'll be singing, 'Hark! The Herald Angels Sing' and after that, 'O Little Town of Bethlehem.' Where are we now? Who knows? Who is to say?"

"...if you talk 13 seconds...."

The Chicago Anti-Superstition Society met on October 13, 1962, with 13 U.S. Senators present. Everett Dirksen, the long-winded and polysyllabic Senator from Illinois, presented astronaut John Glenn with a wristwatch. It had the number 13 at each hour marking.

Dirksen said, "Now, Colonel, if you talk 13 seconds we'll love you. If you talk 13 minutes, we'll wonder how you ever got into orbit. And if you talk 13 hours, we'll all be in orbit."

Glenn responded, "I thought you were going to say that if I talked 13 hours I'd be in good company."

Hundreds of entries poured in.

Bureaucratic prose can be irritating. Many reformers have tried without success to improve it.

One such reformer was Senator Arthur V. Watkins of Utah. The senator had come across a mind-numbing 212-word sentence in the Internal Revenue Code. He read it, and read it again. He couldn't understand it. He showed it to his colleagues in the Senate. They couldn't understand it either.

Senator Watkins offered a prize, actually two prizes—a book on how to write clear prose and a copy of the Bible—to any American who could revise the IRS sentence into clear, understandable language. Watkins enlisted the aid of a committee from the School of Commerce of New York University to administer the contest.

Hundreds of entries poured in. A group of committee members poured over them. One by one, for various reasons, the entries were rejected. At last not a single entry remained. The committee concluded that the best statement possible was the 212-word sentence from the IRS.

The committee issued a formal statement. "Brevity," it concluded, "is not necessarily a virtue in official documents; precision is."

Quote/Unquote

Marcus Tullius Cicero   (106–43 B.C.)

Brevity is the best recommendation of speech, whether in a senator or an orator.

Calvin Coolidge   (1872–1933)

I have never been hurt by what I have not said.

Franklin D. Roosevelt   (1882–1945)

Be sincere; be brief; be seated.

Everett M. Dirksen (1896–1969)

I'll bet you don't know who Edward Everett was. He's the fellow who delivered the *other* speech at Gettysburg. It was a long speech, written out in great detail.

Hubert H. Humphrey (1911–1978)

I've never thought my speeches were too long—I've enjoyed all of them.

BUREAUCRACY

"They've extended bureaucracy...."

One day Dag Hammarskjöld, Secretary-General of the UN, was walking past the rose garden at UN headquarters. In the garden were four peacocks, sent as gifts from Switzerland.

As Hammarskjöld came closer, two of the peacocks strutted toward him on the pathway. As he reached them, one of the peacocks puffed out his chest and spread his feathers in a fan of gorgeous color.

Hammarskjöld stopped, smiled, and admired the display. Then he walked on. As soon as he left, the peacock closed his feathers and left the pathway.

"Good heavens!" said the man who accompanied the Secretary-General. "They've extended bureaucracy to the peacocks!"

"The longer the title...."

George McGovern disappeared from public view after his landslide loss to Nixon in the 1972 Presidential campaign. Still, by 1972 McGovern had observed government in action for a long time. He knew the ins and outs of bureaucracy, and one of his comments shows more common sense than he was later credited with having. "The longer the title," he said, "the less important the job."

A few weeks later, Dr. Ziegler....

The Government Printing Office used to put out a booklet called *Handbook for Emergencies*. Its number in the GPO catalog was 15700.

Dr. John Ziegler of Cincinnati ordered the booklet. He wrote down its catalog number as requested.

A few weeks later, Dr. Ziegler received 15,700 copies of the booklet.

"I've been here for 35 years...."

At a dinner party in Bethesda, Maryland, a British guest was fascinated by the twinkling fireflies on the lawn. He asked the host if it might be possible to establish some of them on his own estate in Surrey. No one knew, but the host suggested to the Britisher that he check the matter with the Department of Agriculture.

Next day the man set off for Washington. It took him a long search through the countless corridors to find the right office. But when he did, it was worth it. The department's expert on lightning bugs could hardly have been more cooperative. He held forth on the habits of lightning bugs for a full two hours. When the Britisher left, he thanked his instructor profusely.

No, the expert insisted. "Permit me to thank *you*. I've been here for 35 years studying lightning bugs, and this is the first time anybody has ever asked me anything about them."

"Is the government not helping *anybody*?"

A recent article in *The Wall Street Journal* may say more about bureaucracy than most bureaucrats would like to hear.

It seems that Matthew Lesko, a man who appreciates good government, offered a $5,000 first prize for the best "verifiable story of 250 words or less about how a government bureaucrat helped you." He offered two runner-up prizes of $500 each.

Lesko made every effort to publicize the contest. He sent out thousands of news releases. He appeared on Larry King's radio show and Pat Sajak's television show. He made his pitch on C-SPAN cable television.

He sat back and waited for the entries to pour in.

They didn't.

Lesko got just one entry—that from a bureaucrat in New York State who nominated her boss. She'd be eligible for the prize, according to Lesko... but did the lone entry in the contest deserve to win an award? He pondered the dismal response. A Lesko assistant asked sadly, "Is the government not helping *anybody*?"

It's true that many of Lesko's press releases weren't used. But still the results were eerie. Said Lesko, if he'd sponsored a contest on how a bureaucrat fouled something up, he'd have attracted 5,000 entries.

Quote/Unquote

Honoré de Balzac (1799–1850)

Bureaucracy is a giant mechanism operated by pygmies.

Sir Arthur Helps   (1813–1875)

An official man is always an official man, and he has a wild belief in the value of reports.

Alben W. Barkley   (1877–1956)

A bureaucrat is a Democrat who has a job some Republican wants.

I have never felt it is particularly fair of politicians to complain about "bureaucrats," when Congress itself creates the bureaus.

James F. Byrnes   (1879–1972)

The nearest approach to immortality on earth is a government bureau.

Eugene McCarthy   (1916–   )

The only thing that saves us from the bureaucracy is its inefficiency.

CHANGE

"No! I shave it clean...."

Peter the Great of Russia learned a great deal about the West from his year-and-a-half grand tour of Europe. But the first thing he did upon his return was symbolic. He called his boyars and ministers together and said, "Look at me. Do I hide my face behind a great bush of whiskers like a heathen Turk? No! I shave it clean like the civilized Christian rulers of Europe...."

At which he grabbed one of his ministers by the beard and clipped it off. The others stared in disbelief. But Peter was serious. He called on two barbers he had brought back from England. They set about shaving off the beards of nearly everyone present.

Peter's great reform of Westernization had begun.

"When the pie was opened...."

No sooner had the United States won its independence from Great Britain (or *their* independence as they would have said in those days), than pictures of King George began disappearing from textbooks. *The New England Primer* of 1794 replaced the word "whale" (for the letter *w*) with the word "Washington."

Even nursery rhymes were changed to reflect America's new independence. Remember these lines from "Four and Twenty Blackbirds"?

> When the pie was opened
> The birds began to sing;
> Was not that a pretty dish
> To set before a king?

Right after the Revolutionary War the word "king" (even when not followed by "George") was enough to raise hackles. Samuel Lathem Mitchell, a New York doctor—though definitely not a poet—revised the lines:

When the pie was opened
The birds they were songless;
Was not that a pretty dish
To set before Congress?

"What do you want, Mr. Randolph?"

"Take that away—change it," said John Randolph, the irascible Congressman from Virginia. He handed the waiter a cup and saucer.

"What do you want, Mr. Randolph?" asked the waiter.

"If that stuff is tea, bring me coffee," Randolph said. "If it's coffee, bring me tea."

"In that solemn moment...."

When Queen Victoria ascended the throne of England, she was 18 years old and unmarried. But she had already met Prince Albert of Saxe-Coburg-Gotha, whom she would marry two years later.

For the young German prince, this might seem to be a very desirable marriage, but he wasn't so sure. He didn't know what his status would be in the British royal hierarchy. In a letter to a friend he wrote, "My future lot is high and brilliant, but also plentifully strewn with thorns."

Victoria was a little doubtful too. At one point she told Lord Melbourne that she found the whole subject of marriage "odious."

So when the hour of the wedding approached, both were apprehensive. On the morning of the great day, Prince Albert wrote to his step-grandmother in Germany. He pictured himself standing before the altar with Victoria.

"In that solemn moment," he wrote, "I must once again ask your blessing, which shall be my protection...." And he added uneasily, "May God help me!"

"I have seen him often."

A few great men have composed their last words before the time came to speak them. One such man was Justice Oliver Wendell Holmes, Jr.

At the age of 94, Holmes wrote, "Why should I fear death? I have seen him often. When he comes, he'll seem like an old friend. If I were to die, my last words would be, 'Have faith and pursue the unknown end.'"

Despite that odd, contrary-to-fact clause—"If I were to die"—Holmes could hardly have expected to cheat death forever. When death did come, later that year, his words were less stirring.

Hospital attendants were putting up an oxygen tent around Holmes in the hospital. As he watched them, he breathed his actual last words: "Lot of damn foolery."

"If you want to make enemies...."

As President of Princeton University, Woodrow Wilson made a number of important policy changes. He kept on making them as Governor of New Jersey and President of the United States. He had no illusions about everyone liking these changes—or liking him.

"If you want to make enemies," he said, "try to change something."

Khrushchev phoned the cosmonauts....

Throughout the Cold War, people in the West used to marvel at the way leadership changed in the Soviet Union. One practice of Western Kremlinologists was to study Soviet photographs taken on state occasions. If a leader was missing or downgraded, or if a new face appeared in the photos, experts on Russia could draw conclusions on what had happened or might happen.

Richard Nixon tells this story about Nikita Khrushchev's sudden loss of power in late 1864.

Just before the launching of a Soviet space capsule, Khrushchev phoned the cosmonauts at the Baikonour space center. He was in an expansive mood, wished them a good flight, and said he was preparing a grand welcome for their return. He seemed firmly in control.

However, no sooner had he hung up than Leonid Brezhnev phoned the cosmonauts to add his best wishes for the flight. That sort of thing just didn't happen in the normal course of events.

Partway through the flight, Khrushchev talked to the cosmonauts by radiophone. He finished what he had to say, and then added these strange and fateful words: "Here is Comrade Mikoyan. He is literally pulling the telephone from my hands. I don't think I can stop him."

When the cosmonauts landed, a week after liftoff, Khrushchev was nowhere to be seen. During those seven days—on October 15, 1964, to be exact—he had been pensioned off to political oblivion. This man who had gained worldwide prominence as head of one of the two most powerful nations on earth remained under house arrest until his death in 1971.

"...this noble exercise in futility?"

It is a cliche of American history that much of the Populist Party platform of 1892, which was denounced as wildly radical at the time, became the law of the land in later years—voted in by good Democrats and Republicans.

Somewhat the same thing might be said of a number of conservative Republican proposals that began to surface in the mid-1960s. When William F. Buckley, Jr., announced he was running as the Conservative Party candidate for Mayor of New York in 1965 against John V. Lindsay and Abraham Beame, he made these six recommendations:

(1) A much larger police force to control rising crime

(2) Attention to civil rights with accompanying emphasis on civil responsibilities

(3) Improved public schools, with decentralized administration, in which education is the primary goal

(4) A reduction or elimination of the minimum wage rather than an increase in it

(5) A work requirement for all able-bodied welfare recipients

(6) Elimination of what Buckley called "the obsession with urban renewal" and its "big-think" public housing projects

With the exception of Buckley's fourth point, on the minimum wage, those proposals hardly sound revolutionary today. They certainly don't sound like the jabberings of a fool. Yet back in 1965 when they were made, the political climate was very different. In those days of high-flying liberalism, conservative ideas were dismissed as absurd.

An editorial in *The New York Times* asked, "What makes Mr. Buckley undertake this noble exercise in futility?" The *Herald Tribune* huffed that the mayoralty was "an office not thus to be trifled with." Dick Schaap and Murray Kempton took good-natured shots at Buckley's silly crusade.

Almost no one in the media considered Buckley's proposals on their merits. According to the conventional wisdom, the Conservative Party platform was irrelevant. And Buckley himself was no more than a meddlesome gadfly intent on checking the political ambitions of John V. Lindsay.

Some gadfly.

Quote/Unquote

Niccolò Machiavelli (1469–1527)

One change always leaves the way prepared for the introduction of another.

Napoleon Bonaparte (1769–1821)

There are very few kings who have not deserved to be dethroned.

Louis D. Brandeis (1856–1941)

Those who won our independence by revolution were not cowards. They did not fear political change. They did not exalt order at the cost of liberty.

W.L. Mackenzie King (1874–1950)

Over the grave of one who had unnecessarily sought change, there is written, "I was well, I wanted to be better, and here I am."

Elizabeth Janeway (1913–   )

If one is going to change things, one has to make a fuss and catch the eye of the world.

CHARACTER

"...there is a busy inquiry made...."

Times change, but human nature stays the same.

Plutarch lived almost two thousand years before the rise of today's politicians, journalists, and voters. But he had their number.

"Statesmen," Plutarch noted, "are not only liable to give an account of what they say or do in public, but there is a busy inquiry made into their very meals, beds, marriages, and every other serious or sportive action."

When the court jester was married....

Peter the Great became Tsar of Muscovy at the age of ten. He was too young to rule, and a faction led by his half sister Sophia seized power. At the age of 17 Peter defied Sophia and gained full power for his own faction.

Despite the coup, he had no interest in government. He left the day-to-day work to conservative aristocrats. Bored with the dull routine of the Kremlin, he embarked on a life of merrymaking that lasted almost five years.

Peter was physically a giant, standing nearly seven feet tall. He could straighten out a horseshoe with his bare hands. With his sword he could slash in two a handkerchief thrown in the air. He loved singing, dancing, boat racing, and war games.

He appointed a friend of his, Franz Lefort, a soldier-of-fortune, to serve as his official host. Peter built a banquet hall that would seat 1500 people. He gave Lefort plenty of money to buy food and drink, and their parties sometimes lasted for days.

When the court jester was married, Peter's celebration went on for three days. It ended with a parade into Moscow with the bride and groom mounted on a camel.

At another party Peter arrived accompanied by 24 dwarfs mounted on ponies. Lefort and Peter would occasionally ride off into the countryside to drill these court-sponsored dwarfs as a miniature cavalry.

It may seem strange that such an oddball as this could ever earn the title of "the Great." But Peter did. In 1695, when his prankster days were over, he turned first to war and then to reform. He westernized Russia. He built St. Petersburg (now Leningrad). He subordinated the church to the state.

Peter was a man of enormous ambition and spectacular accomplishments—a hardworking genius and a cruel tyrant, as well as a boisterous pleasure-seeker.

"He is a man of splendid abilities...."

Edward Livingston had a distinguished career in American politics. In the innocent days of the early 1800s, Livingston gave up all his property to pay back the debt of a subordinate who had embezzled government money. A famous statesman of the young nation, he served as U.S. Senator, as Secretary of State under Andrew Jackson, and as U.S. Minister to France. By all accounts he was an admirable and upright man.

Well, not by all accounts. John Randolph of Roanoke, a Senator from Virginia, had another view. Randolph, who was sometimes insane and always caustic, took an intense dislike to Livingston. In one of the more vivid similes in American politics, Randolph said of his fellow lawmaker: "He is a man of splendid abilities, but utterly corrupt. He shines and stinks like rotten mackerel by moonlight."

"So when a great man dies...."

From **Charles Sumner**
by Henry Wadsworth Longfellow

So when a great man dies,
For years beyond our ken,
The light he leaves behind him lies
Upon the paths of men.

"The Princess Victoria is sleeping...."

At five o'clock on the morning of June 20, 1837, a carriage arrived at the royal palace in Kensington, England. In it were the Archbishop of Canterbury and the Marquis of Conyngham. Their attendants pounded on the great door of the palace for admittance.

Finally, the two gentlemen were allowed in. They asked to see the 18-year-old Princess. "No," they were told. "The Princess Victoria is sleeping and cannot be disturbed."

But this was important state business. The young lady simply must be awakened, and she was. When she came into the room where the men were waiting, she wore a loose dressing gown. She paused for a moment at an open window.

Lord Conyngham dropped to his knees and announced the death of King William IV. Princess Victoria was now Queen Victoria.

She took the news calmly and said softly to the two men, "I will try to be good."

And so began the longest and one of the most popular reigns in British history. Seventy-five years later, as they were celebrating the Diamond Jubilee, her subjects generally agreed that she had indeed been good.

"We are not amused."

Alan Hardy, a British author, recently wrote a whole book to disprove the notion that Queen Victoria was a humorless old frump. The public's perception of the queen, Hardy felt, stemmed from one four-word sentence—"We are not amused"—that everyone has come to associate with her.

Hardy's first job was to find out when the sentence was spoken—and why. He came up with half a dozen stories, but the one he finally accepted was that of Alexander Yorke, the queen's groom-in-waiting for the final 16 years of her reign.

During a dinner party at Windsor Castle, Yorke was sitting next to a German guest. He told the German a slightly off-color story that brought on hoots of laughter. Queen Victoria had "a definite sense of fun," said Yorke, and she wanted to hear the story that had caused such loud guffaws.

Yorke knew better than to tell it, but the queen insisted. So he told the story to her and the rest of the guests. When he had finished, Queen Victoria drew herself up with much dignity and said, "We are not amused."

Rightly or wrongly, those four words have dogged her image and defined her character ever since.

"...Massachusetts has no foreign relations."

In an era when local politicians sometimes build their campaigns around national or international issues over which they have no jurisdiction, it's refreshing to look back at an earlier age and a more straightforward campaigner.

As Governor of Massachusetts, Calvin Coolidge was asked his opinion of President Wilson's proposed League of Nations. After thinking about the question for a bit he replied:

"I am the Governor of Massachusetts. The State of Massachusetts has no foreign relations. If ever I should hold an office calling for action or opinion on this subject, I shall put my mind on it and try to arrive at the soundest conclusions within my capacity."

Quote/Unquote

Ralph Waldo Emerson   (1803–1882)

Don't *say* things. What you *are* stands over you the while, and thunders so that I cannot hear what you say to the contrary.

Mark Twain   (1835–1910)

It could probably be shown by facts and figures that there is no distinctly native American criminal class except Congress.

There is no character, howsoever good and fine, but it can be destroyed by ridicule, howsoever poor and witless.

Charles de Gaulle   (1890–1970)

Faced with crisis, the man of character falls back on himself.... Difficulty attracts the man of character because it is in embracing it that he realizes himself.

Tip O'Neill   (1912–   )

Jack Kennedy... played the game of politics by his own rules.... During his early years in politics he hated shaking hands, which was highly unusual in a city where some politicians had been known to shake hands with fire hydrants and wave to telephone poles.

Jesse Jackson   (1941–   )

I am not a perfect servant. I am a public servant doing my best against the odds. As I develop and serve, be patient. God is not finished with me yet.

COMPARISON

"...I would have been glad to be a Washington...."

George Washington had just died at Mount Vernon when Napoleon Bonaparte became First Consul of France. Many people hoped that Bonaparte would become France's own George Washington. But it was not to be. There were basic differences between the two countries and between their revolutions.

Napoleon said later, "If I had been in America, I would have been glad to be a Washington...." He meant that he would willingly have governed under a democratic constitution. He added that had George Washington "been in France, under the dissolution within and the invasion from the outside, I [Napoleon] would have defied him to be himself. Or, if he had tried to be, he would merely have been a fool, and would only have perpetuated great misfortunes. As for me, I could only be a crowned Washington."

Crowned he was. Washington he wasn't.

"We have democracy on our lips...."

Simón Bolívar's war for liberation bore little resemblance to the American Revolution. Bolívar fought to overthrow the Spanish and to empower a native artistocracy in South America, not to establish democracy. The Liberator found it hard to recruit the lower classes for his army, since they saw no benefit to themselves. Many of them enlisted gladly in the royalist ranks.

During his "War to the Death," Bolívar declared, "We have democracy on our lips, aristocracy in our hearts."

...Webster said he felt like the deacon....

After his Seventh of March speech backing the Compromise of 1850, Daniel Webster was condemned throughout the North. He didn't respond immediately to the storm of criticism. When asked if he intended to reply to the abuse, Webster said he felt like the deacon who was faced with a similar problem. The deacon had said, "I make it a point never to shovel out the path until the snow is done falling."

"We will be branded as cowards...."

President Lincoln believed in not taking any more chances than were necessary. In the dark days of the Civil War, when it looked as if England or France or both might back the Confederacy, two of his cabinet members urged actions that would make such an event more likely.

Lincoln said no. The risk was too great.

"We must maintain our honor at any cost," Secretary of State Seward insisted.

And Secretary of War Stanton chimed in: "We will be branded as cowards before the entire world."

"But why run the greater risk when we can take the smaller one?" asked Lincoln. "The less risk we run, the better for us. That reminds me of a story...."

Lincoln recalled hearing about a soldier on the firing line. Bullets were zinging past his ears, and shells were exploding a few feet away. Finally, the young man's courage deserted him. He threw down his gun and took to his heels.

An officer just to the rear saw him coming. Drawing his revolver, the officer shouted, "Go back to your regiment at once, or I'll shoot you!"

The young soldier kept right on running. "Shoot and be hanged," he yelled. "What's one bullet to a whole hatful?"

"But after sitting next to Mr. Disraeli...."

William Gladstone and Benjamin Disraeli were outstanding Prime Ministers of England. But the similarity ended there. Gladstone was moralistic; Disraeli was wily.

One of the best-known stories about the two concerns a young lady who went to dinner with them on successive nights. When asked for her impressions of the two men, she said:

"When I left the dining room after sitting next to Mr. Gladstone, I thought he was the cleverest man in England. But after sitting next to Mr. Disraeli I thought I was the cleverest woman in England!"

"I always hate to compare Napoleon...."

After the Nazis had overrun most of Europe, people sometimes compared Hitler to that earlier conqueror, Napoleon Bonaparte. Winston Churchill, who called Hitler a "bloodthirsty guttersnipe" and "Corporal Schickelgruber," saw very little similarity. In a speech to the House of Commons in 1944, he said: I always hate to compare Napoleon with Hitler, as it seems an insult to the great emperor and warrior to compare him in any way with a squalid caucus boss and butcher."

"How different—how very different...."

Irvin S. Cobb, the journalist, used to tell the story of a friend of his who went abroad back when Queen Victoria was still on the British throne.

One night his friend saw Sarah Bernhardt play the role of Cleopatra in Shakespeare's *Antony and Cleopatra*. Bernhardt was at the top of her form as she acted the scene in which Cleopatra learns of Mark Antony's defeat at Actium.

The distraught Cleopatra stabbed the slave who brought her the news. She raged, frothing at the mouth, smashing scenery in her wild frenzy. As the curtain fell, she dropped to the stage in a shivering, despairing heap.

When the applause died down, Cobb's friend heard a middle-aged British woman remark to her neighbor, a bit smugly:

"How different—how very different—from the home life of our own dear Queen."

"I may be a pet coon...."

Back when Estes Kefauver was running for high office, his emblem was a coonskin cap. The tall, lanky senator from Tennessee wore a coonskin cap on the campaign trail. This emblem, plus his televised hearings on organized crime, gave Kefauver high voter recognition, although not high enough to gain him the Democratic Presidential nomination over Adlai Stevenson. Kefauver ran for Vice President in 1956.

Many people at the time knew the origin of the coonskin-cap emblem. Probably very few do today.

Eight years before his run for the Vice Presidency, Estes Kefauver had been making his first bid for a United States Senate seat. His opponent in the Democratic primary was the hand-picked choice of Ed Crump, a notorious political boss from Memphis. The Crump machine ran a full-page newspaper ad that compared Kefauver to a pet coon. It said:

"Kefauver reminds me of the pet coon that puts its foot in an open drawer in your room but invariably turns its head while its foot is feeling around in the drawer. The coon hopes, through its cunning by turning its head, he will deceive any onlookers as to where his foot is and what it is into."

Kefauver responded in two ways. First he said, "I may be a pet coon, but I'll never be Mr. Crump's pet coon." This remark was widely reported throughout Tennessee. Then Kefauver clapped a coonskin cap on his head and resumed campaigning. He buried Crump's candidate in the primaries, won in the general election, and went on to serve three terms in the U.S. Senate.

Henry Luce... never lacked for critics.

Henry Luce, the founder of *Time* magazine, never lacked for critics. One of them was Governor Earl Long of Louisiana.

Long said, "Mr. Luce is like a man that owns a shoestore and buys all the shoes to fit himself. Then he expects other people to buy them."

"Loyalty... when coupled with honesty...."

Sometimes it seems as if political advisers are shrewder than their candidates. Take the case of the media experts charged with making a television hero out of future Vice President Spiro T. Agnew.

Frank Shakespeare, Len Garment, and Harry Treleaven had just suffered through a TV documentary about Agnew. Although their staff had commissioned the film, the result was embarrassing. It was poor in a technical sense. And the Vice Presidential nominee did nothing to improve it. To a series of dull questions, Agnew gave a set of stupefying answers.

"Loyalty," said the next Vice President at one point, "is the most important principle—when coupled with honesty, that is."

Treleaven groaned, "I don't think the man has had an original observation in his life." Garment agreed that the candidate was an utter bore and declared, "I think Dexedrine is the answer."

The three downcast media men adjourned to Sardi's.

Treleaven suggested that at least the GOP Presidential nominee, Richard Nixon, looked good by comparison.

Len Garment could not be consoled, however. "God, that was awful," he said, shaking his head. "Both Agnew and the questions. Mush meets tapioca. A marriage of meringue."

"Your political life and mine...."

A sixth-grader was struck by the similarity of his experience and Richard Nixon's. He wrote to tell him:

Dear President Nixon:

"Your political life and mine are almost parallel. I lost my bid for the Presidency in 6th grade. I lost by a closer margin in a bid for a lesser position, and now I plan to make a big comeback."

"I got one sister who's a Holy Roller...."

No President ever suffered more at the hands of his brother than Jimmy Carter. Brother Billy was a self-proclaimed redneck. He even provided a definition of a redneck, drawing a contrast between that and a good old boy.

"A good old boy," said Billy, "is a guy who rides around in a pickup truck and drinks beer and puts the cans in a little bag. A redneck's a guy that rides around in a truck, drinks beer, and throws the cans out the window."

Billy, the redneck, also liked to compare himself favorably to his brothers and sisters. During the 1976 campaign, he said on a TV show, "I got one sister who's a Holy Roller preacher." For the record, that was Ruth (*The Gift of Inner Healing*) Carter.

"Another," Billy went on, "wears a helmet and rides a motorcycle." That was Gloria ("Go Go") Carter.

"And my brother," he said, "thinks he's going to be President." That was Jimmy ("national malaise") Carter.

Billy Carter, the man who later launched Billy Beer, drew the logical conclusion from his comparisons. "So," he said "that makes me the only sane one in the family."

"At your age George Washington...."

A teacher had assigned some math problems to his class. One student was having difficulty solving them. Finally, the teacher said in exasperation: "You ought to be ashamed of yourself. At your age George Washington was a surveyor."

The student looked the teacher straight in the eye and said: "Yes, and at your age he was President of the United States."

"In the picture business you're protected...."

Many news commentators thought that Ronald Reagan turned politics into a movie spectacular. But Nancy Reagan didn't feel that way at all, at least not at first. When her husband ran for Governor of California in 1966, Nancy was surprised to discover how starkly politics differed from show business.

"Politics is a completely different life," she said. "In the picture business you're protected somewhat—by the studio, by your producer, and so on." In politics, she said, it isn't like that. You're unprotected. People think they own you. They say and write whatever comes into their heads.

It was a startling revelation for Nancy. "On movie tours and junkets," she said, "studio staffs would surround us and create a little privacy. But you can't do this in politics."

Well, no matter. Whatever Ron and Nancy did in 1966, it turned out to be a good show. Reagan beat incumbent Governor Pat Brown by almost a million votes.

Quote/Unquote

Montaigne   (1533–1592)

The souls of emperors and cobblers are cast in the same mold.... The same reason that makes me wrangle with a neighbor causes a war between princes.

Elizabeth Cady Stanton   (1815–1902)

The queens in history compare favorably with the kings.

Sam Rayburn   (1882–1961)

A whore's vote is just as good as a debutante's.

Omar N. Bradley   (1893–1981)

The world has achieved brilliance without conscience. Ours is a world of nuclear giants and ethical infants.

Spiro T. Agnew   (1918–   )

If you've seen one slum, you've seen them all.

COMPETITION

Quote/Unquote

Henry Clay   (1777–1852)

Of all human powers operating on the affairs of mankind, none is greater than that of competition.

G.K. Chesterton   (1874–1936)

The more modern nations detest each other, the more meekly they follow each other; for competition is in its nature only a furious plagiarism.

Franklin D. Roosevelt   (1882–1945)

There is nothing I love as much as a good fight.

Dwight D. Eisenhower   (1890–1969)

I believe when you are in any contest you should work like there is—to the very last minute—a chance to lose it.

CONSISTENCY

"What name do you wish to write?"

In ancient Athens any free male adult could name the man he wished to see ostracized by scratching the man's name on a potsherd and putting it in an urn.

One day Aristides, a statesman known as "Aristides the Just," came upon an Athenian who wished to ostracize someone. The man was illiterate and asked Aristides to help him.

"What name do you wish to write?" Aristides asked.

The man replied, "Aristides."

Startled, the Athenian statesman asked, "Has Aristides injured you in some way? Is that why you wish to see him banished?"

"No," the man said. "I don't even know him. But I'm sick and tired of hearing him called 'the Just.'"

Aristides nodded, scratched his own name on the potsherd, and handed it back to the man.

"On the right side of temp'rance...."

Before it became a political crusade the temperance movement relied mostly on persuasion. And the persuasion was based mostly on close observation of the bad habits of tipplers. One vice led to another vice, it seemed. The "Temperance Hymn" went

We're coming, we're coming, our brave little band.
On the right side of temp'rance we now take our stand.
We don't use tobacco and also we think
That them what does use it
Is quite sure to drink.

"I want to stand by my country...."

Women throughout the United States did not have the right to vote in 1917, but Jeannette Rankin did. A Republican from Montana, Miss Rankin was the first woman elected to either house of Congress. She won election in 1916.

She has another distinction, too. Congresswoman Ranking was an unshakable pacifist. President Wilson may have thought it was a "fearful thing" to lead the United States into war. President Roosevelt may have hated war as much as he said. But it was Miss Rankin who voted against a declaration of war in 1917—and then voted against it again in 1941.

There was some opposition to President Wilson's call for a declaration of war. But the new Congresswoman from Montana felt she needed to explain her vote. "I want to stand by my country," she said, "but I cannot vote for war."

Twenty-four years later, when the Japanese bombed Pearl Harbor, Miss Rankin was still in Congress. This time there was almost no opposition to the President's war message. The United States had been attacked with heavy loss of life.

But Congresswoman Rankin was still a pacifist, and her principles still made war with Japan or any other nation unthinkable. On the declaration of war, she was the only member of the House to vote no.

Just before Clemenceau died....

Georges Clemenceau, the Premier of France in World War One, distrusted Germany intensely. He thought that even the harsh Treaty of Versailles was too lenient, that it left France vulnerable to future German invasion.

Just before Clemenceau died, on November 24, 1929, he expressed a last wish: to be "buried standing, facing Germany."

"That was the 'sewer' cartoon...."

Herblock, the political cartoonist, disliked Richard Nixon so much that people sometimes credited him with anti-Nixon cartoons he didn't draw.

It seemed to him that nearly everyone was amused by his cartoon with the caption under Nixon's face, "Would you buy a used car from this man?" But Herblock didn't originate the used-car line, and he didn't know who did.

Another cartoon supposedly from the acid pen of Herblock showed President Eisenhower and Vice President Nixon at the base of the Capitol steps. Ike had recently suffered a serious heart attack. The caption, as people remembered it, had Nixon saying, "Race you to the top of the stairs."

But, again, Herblock didn't draw it. In fact, he didn't recall ever having seen it, and doubted that any other nationally syndicated cartoonist had drawn it either.

Does this mean that Herblock was always nice to Nixon? Hardly. One of his most famous cartoons of all time appeared on October 29, 1954. Herblock said: "That was the 'sewer' cartoon—which is all that most people remember of it."

It's a classic, or a disgrace, depending on your viewpoint.

Nixon is shown on the campaign trail. A band led by a drummer is coming down the street. One spectator on the sidelines holds a "Welcome" sign. And there, front and center, is Nixon—not yet with the familiar stubble on his face—emerging from a manhole in the middle of the street. He's pushing a suitcase out ahead of him. The cheerful man with the "Welcome" sign is saying, "Here he comes now."

People often asked Herblock if he ever regretted drawing the sewer cartoon. His answer was no.

Quote/Unquote

Thomas Jefferson   (1743–1826)

The moment a person forms a theory, his imagination sees in every object only the traits which favor that theory.

John C. Calhoun   (1782–1850)

True consistency... is to act in conformity with circumstances—and not always to act the same way under a change of circumstances.

Ralph Waldo Emerson   (1803–1882)

A foolish consistency is the hobglobin of little minds, adored by little statesmen and philosophers and divines.

Winston Churchill   (1874–1965)

The only way a man can remain consistent amid changing circumstances is to change with them while preserving the same dominating purpose.

COOPERATION

"I'll pay for the lunch...."

Sometimes politicians can rise above the issues that divide them. An example in the 1970s was the Camp David agreement between Israel's Menachem Begin and Egypt's Anwar Sadat.

There have been others. In the 1920s France and Germany were at odds. Germans detested the harsh Treaty of Versailles, blaming it for their economic ills. The Germans were required to pay huge reparations, and they simply couldn't afford it. They were restless and angry. The French were worried, fearing a rebirth of German militarism. Nevertheless, on the twelfth anniversary of the Battle of the Marne, a French statesman and a German statesman were trying to find some common ground.

The Frenchman was Aristide Briand. The German was Gustave Stresemann. Each was his nation's foreign minister, and together they won the Nobel Peace Prize that year.

The two men, conferring at Geneva, wanted to keep their negotiations secret from prying journalists. To do so, they set up a meeting in a tiny village across the

French border. Stresemann was whisked by motorboat across Lake Geneva. A car was waiting for him there, and he drove off to the small hotel where he was to meet Briand.

Briand, meanwhile, approached from a different direction. He had given instructions to the border police to delay for at least twenty minutes all cars carrying journalists. He was sure the plan would work and that he and Stresemann could meet quietly.

There was one glitch. The French border police, as ordered, stopped all cars entering France. But one journalist was riding a motorcycle, and he breezed through. The order had been to delay cars, and the police took it literally.

As soon as the motorcyclist learned where the meeting was to be held, he did something remarkable. Rather than stay and enjoy his scoop, he raced back toward the border and let his fellow reporters in on the news. They all trooped to the small hotel to cover the secret meeting.

Much as the journalists were cooperating, so were the diplomats. The touchy question of reparations was discussed, and Briand and Stresemann reached an agreement. The payments would be lowered but not forgiven.

On that happy note, not long after the journalists arrived, the two men ended their luncheon. Stresemann insisted on paying the bill. Briand objected.

"No," he told Stresemann. "I'll pay for the lunch. You take care of the reparations."

"Do you teach that the world is round...?"

Lyndon B. Johnson, when he was a Senator from Texas, liked to tell this story about a schoolteacher in search of a job. It was during the early days of the depression, and jobs were hard to come by.

The schoolteacher gave a good account of himself before the hill country school board. He spoke well, and he seemed to know what he was talking about. so the school board said to him:

"Well, we think we would like to have you teach.... But tell us this: There is some difference of opinion in our community about geography, and we want to know which side you are on. Do you teach that the world is round, or do you teach that the world is flat?"

The applicant replied without hesitation, "I can teach it either way."

McCormack was an old man....

When John F. Kennedy was assassinated and Lyndon Johnson became President, the next man in line for the nation's highest office was Speaker of the House John McCormack.

McCormack was an old man, frail, feisty, and set in his ways. He knew what he wanted and what he didn't want. One of the things he didn't want was Secret Service protection.

The Secret Service bluntly insisted on its duty to the man who was one step away from the Presidency. McCormack refused to cooperate. He wanted nothing to do with "the shifty-eyed guardians of the Pooh-Bahs," he said.

Not long afterward, Speaker McCormack began noticing an assortment of priests hanging around the hallway outside his apartment. They seemed to be living in the flat next door, which was all right with him, except that they were constantly underfoot.

After a while it dawned on him that these ever-present priests looked a bit shifty-eyed themselves. And then he understood. The Speaker and possible President was being given Secret Service protection in spite of himself.

"Their coaches are running to meet them...!"

When President Jimmy Carter got the United States to boycott the 1980 Olympic Games in Moscow, many Americans were saddened by the decision. The boycott was for a worthy cause—to protest the Soviet invasion of Afghanistan—but the U.S. absence from the Games inspired few to celebrate.

In Japan they weren't too happy either. President Carter wanted to make the boycott as total as possible, so naturally he approached America's allies. Japanese athletes had been preparing diligently for the Olympics. A reporter for a Tokyo newspaper asked Katsuji Shibata, Japan's Olympic Committee chairman, to describe his greatest wish for the year.

Shibata described his vision—Japanese track stars "running out of the main stadium in Moscow to the marathon course along the river.... They were leading.... The Japanese athletes are now returning to the stadium as the top runners! They are running three abreast! Their coaches are running to meet them...! I am also beside myself with joy...."

It was not to be. By a vote of 29 to 13 the Japan Olympic Committee voted to back the U.S. position and boycott the Moscow Games.

They were not alone. In all, 66 countries refused to send their athletes to Moscow. It was an impressive display of cooperation with the United States—and it could hardly have been popular in many of those countries. Thousands of athletes throughout the world were bitterly disappointed.

It was especially unpopular in the Soviet Union. The Russians had made extravagant plans for the Olympic Games. They had installed a large electronic bulletin board to show the events and the results. Sometimes the mascot of the Games, a delightful little bear named Misha, appeared on the screen. On the final day of the Games, the illuminated Misha was shown shedding tears.

Quote/Unquote

Daniel Webster   (1782–1852)

There are many objects of great value to man which cannot be attained by unconnected individuals, but must be attained, if attained at all, by association.

Henry Wadsworth Longfellow   (1807–1882)

All your strength is in your union. All your danger is in discord.

Woodrow Wilson   (1856–1924)

The highest and best form of efficiency is the spontaneous cooperation of a free people.

Charles de Gaulle   (1890–1970)

The French will only be united under the threat of danger. Nobody can simply bring together a country that has 265 kinds of cheese.

COURAGE

Robespierre would not listen.

When the idealism of the French Revolution gave way to the excesses of the Reign of Terror, not every revolutionist went along. Late in 1793 the journalist Camille Desmoulins began to counsel moderation. His newspaper called for an end to the executions.

Robespierre would not listen. To show his anger at the defection of his old ally, Robespierre burned a copy of Desmoulin's newspaper at the Jacobin Club.

The journalist, who was present, rose to his feet. Recognizing the fate that now awaited him, he said calmly, "To burn is not to reply."

"I shall stand by the Union...."

Only one speech in American history is known by its date—Daniel Webster's famous "Seventh of March" oration. It was delivered on the floor of the Senate in 1850, and it was one of the most bitterly attacked speeches in American politics.

The three great Senators of the pre-Civil-War era—Daniel Webster of Massachusetts, Henry Clay of Kentucky, and John C. Calhoun of South Carolina—all played key roles in the events of that day.

First, Henry Clay, the "Great Compromiser": Clay was from a border state, and he often could and did find ways to keep peace between the antislavery North and the slaveholding South. His final peacemaking effort was the Compromise of 1850—the subject of Daniel Webster's speech on that memorable March day.

Webster detested slavery. He had promised the voters of Massachusetts always to fight against it. But with the South apparently prepared to secede over the issue, Webster reconsidered. Clay's compromise would permit the extension of slavery, something that Webster and most of the North opposed. However, in order to preserve the Union, Webster decided he was willing to accept the compromise. His speech would back Clay—and infuriate the abolitionists in his home state.

Webster was going to be condemned in the North after delivering his speech, and he knew it. But as he said to the Senate, "I will stand by the Union... with absolute disregard of personal consequences."

People came from all parts of the country to hear Webster's speech. They knew it would be an important statement in a time of peril. They also knew it would be one of the high points of the Senator's long and distinguished career. Webster may well have been the finest orator, then or ever, in the United States Senate.

Everyone assumed that John C. Calhoun would be absent for the speech. The Senator from South Carolina was dying. His brilliant arguments on behalf of the slaveholding South would never again echo in the Senate chamber. Indeed, all three Senators—Clay, Webster, and Calhoun—would be dead within three years. Calhoun would be dead within three weeks.

Webster's oration lasted for hours. His opening statement is often quoted: "I wish to speak today," he said, "not as a Massachusetts man, nor as a Northern man, but as an American.... I speak today for the preservation of the Union."

And so he did. During his speech, Webster voiced his regret that John C. Calhoun, his long-time Southern adversary, was unable to be there. But unnoticed by him, the dying South Carolinian had arrived and had been helped slowly into his seat on the Senate floor. Calhoun was wrapped in a black cloak, his body trembling. Finally, when Webster mentioned Calhoun's illness once again, the proud Southerner spoke up in a clear but hollow voice, almost literally from the grave. He said, "The Senator from South Carolina is in his seat."

Webster stopped speaking, visibly moved, and bowed toward the old man he had opposed for nearly four decades. Then he continued with his speech. It went on and on and ended without applause. The audience must have known that just as surely as Calhoun was dying physically, Webster was dying politically. Both were men of indomitable courage, but neither would survive that turbulent March.

It was all well and good for Webster to champion the cause of the Union, but to permit the extension of slavery—no. Abolitionist sentiment in the North was strong, and its spokesmen were poetic and articulate. Webster may have been right to accept the compromise, or may have been wrong. He himself had no second thoughts about his decision. But Northern opinion was fixed and unforgiving, and Webster's political career was over, his reputation in ruins.

What became increasingly clear as the years passed was that in March of 1850, Webster, Calhoun, and Clay all spoke and acted from deep personal conviction. They could not all have been right—they may all have been wrong—but they were all courageous.

"Shoot, if you must...."

In September 1862 Stonewall Jackson led his Confederate troops into Frederick, Maryland. According to legend, Barbara Frietchie, an old woman "of fourscore years and ten," defiantly waved the Stars and Stripes from her window. Historians doubt that she actually made this bold political statement, but it makes a rousing tale of courage and patriotism.

From **Barbara Frietchie**
by John Greenleaf Whittier

"Shoot, if you must, this old gray head,
But spare your country's flag," she said.

A shade of sadness, a blush of shame,
Over the face of the leader came;

• • •

"Who touches a hair on yon gray head
Dies like a dog! March on!" he said.

"How much does the damned scoundrel want?"

In his book *Profiles in Courage*, John F. Kennedy reintroduced Americans to Edmund G. Ross, a forgotten U.S. Senator from Kansas. It was Ross, along with six other Republican senators, who defied their leaders in Congress and voted to acquit President Andrew Johnson on impeachment charges in 1868.

You may recall the opening lines from Rudyard Kipling's poem "If":

> "If you can keep your head when all about you
> Are losing theirs and blaming it on you;
> If you can trust yourself when all men doubt you,
> But make allowance for their doubting too...."

Edmund G. Ross was surely Kipling's man. It would be hard to find a story that shows more clearly the kind of courage that Kipling's poem celebrates. Edmund G. Ross was a political nobody who stood rock solid against a tidal wave of pressure and sentiment that might have wrecked the American system of checks and balances.

The changes against President Johnson were trumped up. The overwhelmingly Republican Congress wanted to force Andrew Johnson out of office. A Tennessee Democrat, Vice President Johnson had become President upon the assassination of Abraham Lincoln. He was unpopular from the outset. He was stubborn and tactless. He had few friends in Congress. But he had committed no "high crimes and misdemeanors."

And that's what the trial was about. The House of Representatives had impeached Johnson on those charges. Now the Senate must try him. A two thirds vote would be necessary for conviction, which meant that at least 36 senators (out of 54) must vote for conviction. If it came down merely to party loyalty, Johnson was doomed. The Senate consisted of 42 Republicans and only 12 Democrats.

But to the chagrin of those bent on impeachment, six Republicans said almost at once that they saw no evidence which would lead to conviction. The Republican leadership was outraged—and worried—because the vote was now down to 36 to 18—exactly the margin needed to remove Johnson. No other Republican could defect, not a single one.

The only doubtful Senator was Edmund G. Ross of Kansas, who refused to say which way he was leaning. On the face of it, there should have been little doubt. Senator Ross disliked President Johnson and his policies. He had gained appointment to the Senate on the basis of a record that fit in well with the Congressional Republican majority.

The Republican leadership was a bit disturbed, therefore, when Senator Ross refused to commit himself. They were even more disturbed when he made the offhand remark that, despite his dislike of Johnson, he wanted to see a fair trial. Before long he was the object of threats, both political and physical. He had no constituency, the pros pointed out, and if he opposed the Republican leadership, he would have no future in the party.

Some guessed that what Ross really wanted was money. Chief prosecutor Ben Butler, an accomplished crook from way back, snorted, "There's a bushel of money. How much does the damned scoundrel want?"

The problem for the prosecution was that the Senator from Kansas didn't want any money, and he wasn't intimidated by threats. More than that, he wasn't swept up in the prevailing madness of the time. He saw, as few others in his party did, that making Congress dominant over the President in a purely political trial like this would be a bad mistake. It would change the nature of American democratic government.

When the trial was over and the roll was called on May 16, 1868, the 12 Democrats were joined by seven—not six—Republicans in voting for acquittal. Edmund Ross's dramatic "not guilty" vote kept his political enemy, Andrew Johnson, in the White House. The Chief Justice made the announcement: "35 Senators having voted guilty and 19 not guilty... the President is, therefore, acquitted...."

Not one of the seven independent Republicans ever won re-election to the Senate.

"I will make this speech or die."

In which Presidential election did a third-party candidate outpoll one of the major-party candidates?

The answer to that question is the election of 1912. Woodrow Wilson, a Democrat, won the election easily. William Howard Taft, a Republican running for reelection, ran a poor third. In second place was Theodore Roosevelt, two-term ex-President, running on the Progressive Party ticket.

The most notable event of the campaign occurred on October 14, 1912. Theodore Roosevelt was scheduled to give a speech in Milwaukee that night. As he was leaving his hotel to go to the hall, a fanatic shouting something about "no third term" shot Roosevelt in the right breast.

Roosevelt turned deathly pale. For all he or anyone else knew, the wound might have been fatal. Doctors on the scene tried to get him to go to a hospital, but he refused. He called for his driver to take him to the hall.

"I will make this speech or die," Roosevelt said firmly. "It is one thing or the other."

Roosevelt reached the hall and gave his speech. The audience sat fascinated but alarmed. His aides tried to get him to stop, but he plowed on, even though the speech was not very important and no one paid much attention to it. They were too worried about the health of the speaker.

Many people thought the incident symbolized Teddy Roosevelt's great fortitude. Historians might later call his actions "quixotic" or suggest they were "histrionic or childish." But few people at the time thought so. They saw Roosevelt as a courageous national leader undaunted even by a bullet in his chest.

"The world goes on because a few men...."

Henry Miller is best known for writing risque books that were once banned from Toledo to Timbuctoo. But just after World War Two he was in a reflective mood. He wrote: "The world goes on because a few men in every generation believe in it utterly, accept it unquestionably, underwrite it with their lives."

"Honey, I forgot to duck."

When John W. Hinckley, Jr., opened fire on President Reagan outside a Washington hotel, he failed to win the heart of Jodie Foster, as he had hoped. But if his crazed attack had no romantic results, it did have political results. For one thing, it helped ensure the passage of Ronald Reagan's economic legislation, with far-reaching and long-lasting effects.

Reagan's reaction to his sudden, serious injury would have done credit to one of his motion-picture heroes. When wife Nancy arrived worriedly at the hospital, Reagan quipped, "Honey, I forgot to duck."

Soon afterward, when the doctors were getting ready to operate, he said, "Please tell me you're Republicans."

And in the recovery room that night, he wrote on a notepad, "All in all, I'd rather be in Philadelphia."

The first quote was from Jack Dempsey, the last from W.C. Fields. Reagan's one-liners, which had been merely funny before, became inspiring under the circumstances. The President's wit, grace, and charm had always been valuable political assets. Now they were more than that.

As columnist David Broder wrote, "...he elevated those appealing human qualities to the level of legend."

Quote/Unquote

Andrew Jackson   (1767–1845)

One man with courage makes a majority.

Napoleon Bonaparte   (1769–1821)

Courage is like love: it must have hope to nourish it.

Elmer Davis   (1890–1958)

This will remain the land of the free only so long as it is the home of the brave.

John F. Kennedy   (1917–1963)

The courage of life is often a less dramatic spectacle than the courage of a final moment; but it is no less a magnificent mixture of triumph and tragedy.

Indira Gandhi   (1917–1984)

There exists no politician in India daring enough to explain to the masses that cows can be eaten.

· D ·

DECISION

He realized that crossing the river....

Julius Caesar and his Roman Legions were in winter quarters at Ravenna. Caesar had just returned in triumph from campaigns in Britain and Gaul. In Rome the Senate feared the ambition of this conquering hero. They passed a bill demanding that Caesar disband his army or be declared an enemy of the people.

Caesar knew he could rely on his soldiers to back him. He wasted no time. At the head of his troops he approached the Rubicon, a river dividing his province from Italy. He realized that crossing the river meant civil war.

Without hesitation he plunged into the current, shouting, "*Alea jacta est*," or "The die is cast."

Caesar's march to Rome became a triumphal procession. After proclaiming his dictatorship, he had himself elected consul 11 days later. That was his original goal—a goal he had hoped to attain peacefully.

"Too late! Sir Robert has a sister...."

Edward Bulwer-Lytton, the English writer, was thinking of writing a play about Sir Robert Walpole, a statesman that historians regard as the first British Prime Minister.

To check his facts, Bulwer-Lytton wrote a letter to a descendent of Sir Robert Walpole. He said: "I am thinking of writing a play about your great ancestor.... Had not he a sister, Lucy, and did she not marry a Jacobite?"

Walpole hastened to reply: "My dear Lytton: I care little for my family and still

47

less for Sir Robert, but I *do* know that he never had a sister Lucy, so she could not very well have married a Jacobite."

The denial was in vain. Bulwer-Lytton wrote back: "My dear Walpole: Too late! Too late! Sir Robert has a sister *now*; her name is Lucy, and she *did* marry a Jacobite! I've written the play!"

"There is no right to strike...."

President Reagan reportedly said that his favorite President was Calvin Coolidge. Although there would seem to be little in common between the gregarious Great Communicator and the tight-lipped Noncommunicator, there were some similarities. For example: strikebreaking. Reagan broke the air traffic controllers' strike. Coolidge broke the Boston police strike.

At first Governor Coolidge of Massachusetts refused to act. But when riots, robberies, and lootings broke out in unprotected Boston, Coolidge changed his mind. He called out the Boston units of the state militia, established order, broke the strike, and fired the absent officers. He then ordered the police commissioner to take over and to use the entire Massachusetts militia in their place.

When Samuel Gompers, president of the American Federation of Labor, tried to win back the strikers' jobs, Coolidge responded with the statement that more than anything else brought him the Republican nomination for Vice President in 1920:

"There is no right to strike against the public safety by anybody, anywhere, anytime."

"I regarded the bomb as a military weapon...."

Few people ever have to make as earth-shaking a decision as Harry Truman did in 1945. He had to decide how to use the first atomic bomb—in a demonstration over a deserted island, against a strictly military target, or against a Japanese city.

As FDR's vice president, Truman had been out of the loop. He knew nothing of the bomb. Only after Roosevelt died in April did he learn of its development. From the beginning he had no compunctions about its use. He believed the bomb could hasten the end of the war. In his memoirs he wrote, "I regarded the bomb as a military weapon and never had any doubt that it should be used."

He believed it should be "dropped on a military target." But in an era of total war the term military target could mean almost anything. It turned out to mean the Japanese industrial cities of Hiroshima (August 6) and Nagasaki (August 9).

A few days earlier, Allied leaders meeting in Potsdam had issued a surrender ultimatum to Japan. The ultimatum made no direct mention of the new weapon about to be unleashed, but it did promise the "prompt and utter destruction" of Japan.

This veiled threat did not end the war. Japan ignored the ultimatum, and its leaders vowed to fight on.

Truman had no second thoughts then or later. He had made his decision, and he stuck by it. He ordered the bombing plan to proceed.

"Tell him to go ahead...."

In 1955 Senator Lyndon Johnson ordered two suits from a Washington tailor. Before they were delivered, Johnson suffered a heart attack. The tailor phoned a Johnson aide at the hospital to see if he should complete the order.

Johnson thought about it for a moment and said, "Tell him to go ahead with the dark-blue suit. We can use that no matter what happens."

"I agree, Mr. President...."

Chester Cooper attended National Security Council meetings under President Lyndon Johnson. Like many others, Cooper soon learned that LBJ wanted yes-men, not critics, after he had made up his mind.

The President would announce his decision, then poll the room, asking each person, "Do you agree with the decision?"

Back came the answers. "Yes, Mr. President." "I agree, Mr. President." "Certainly, Mr. President."

Cooper says he often had a Walter Mitty dream while this was going on. He saw himself, when asked the question, stand up to his full height, allow his gaze to scan the room slowly, then fasten on the President.

Quietly but firmly he would say, "Mr. President, gentlemen, I most definitely do *not* agree."

But Lyndon Johnson was even tougher than Mr. Mitty. So when his turn actually came, Chester Cooper always heard himself saying, "Yes, Mr. President, I agree."

Quote/Unquote

Lord Mansfield (1705–1793)

Decide promptly, but never give any reasons. Your decision may be right, but your reasons are sure to be wrong.

William Ewart Gladstone   (1809–1898)

Decision by majorities is as much an expedient as lighting by gas.

George C. Marshall   (1880–1959)

Anybody who makes a real decision after four in the afternoon should have his head examined.

Walter Lippmann   (1889–1974)

Only the insider can make the decisions, not because he is inherently a better man, but because he is so placed that he can understand and can act.

Jimmy Carter   (1924–   )

Doubts are the stuff of great decisions, but so are dreams.

DEMOCRACY

"Nearly all the tyrants of old...."

Aristotle lived more than 2000 years ago, but many of his perceptions are timeless. He observed: "The insolence of demogogues is generally the cause of ruin in democracies. First, they malign the wealthy and arouse them against a common danger. Next, they produce the same result by stirring up the populace and creating a sense of insecurity. Nearly all the tyrants of old began by being demogogues."

"You never sink, but damn it...."

Fisher Ames was a Federalist in the new government of the United States, which means he was a conservative, a strong believer in law and order and in the rights of property.

In a speech delivered to the U.S. House of Representatives in 1795, he drew a memorable contrast between monarchy and democracy: "A monarchy," he said, "is like a merchantman. You get on board and ride the wind and tide in safety and elation but, by and by, you strike a reef and go down. But democracy is like a raft. You never sink, but, damn it, your feet are always in the water."

"...I was a picket and stood guard...."

Congressman John Mills Allen of Mississippi became forever known as "Private" John Allen as a result of a single brilliant campaign riposte. In the 1880 elections Allen was running to unseat Confederate General William Tucker who had served two terms in the state legislature.

One night during the campaign General Tucker recalled his days as commander of the District of Southern Mississippi and East Louisiana. "My fellow citizens," he said, "many years ago, after a hard-fought battle on yonder hill, I bivouacked under yonder clump of trees. Those of you who remember, as I do, those times that tried men's souls will not, I hope, forget their humble servant when the primaries are held."

Now, that was a speech with considerable appeal. General Tucker had served his state well as a military leader. But Allen knew the nature of democratic government, and he came back with a knockout punch:

"My fellow citizens," Allen said, "what General Tucker says to you about having bivouacked in yonder clump of trees on that night is true. It is also true, my fellow citizens, that I was a picket and stood guard over the general while he slept.

"Now then, fellow citizens, all of you who were generals and had privates stand guard over you while you slept, vote for General Tucker. And all of you who were privates and stood guard over the generals while they slept, vote for Private John Allen!"

The crowd loved it—and followed his advice. "Private" John Mills Allen was on his way to a distinguished career in politics.

"Hain't we got all the fools in town...?"

The duke and king are a pair of wily rascals in Mark Twain's *Huckleberry Finn*. The two of them are getting ready to make off with the townspeople's money. But the bogus duke is worried about the local doctor, who has spotted them as frauds.

"Cuss the doctor," says the king. "Hain't we got all the fools in town on our side? And ain't that a big enough majority in any town?"

"It's exactly the same with us."

When James F. Byrnes was Secretary of State, he tried to explain democracy to Soviet foreign minister Molotov. He used a simple example. "It's like this," he said. "I can go to Washington and enter the White House and no one will stop me. I can say to the President, 'Harry Truman, you're a damned fool,' and no one will shoot me. That's democracy."

Molotov looked at Byrnes, as stone-faced as ever. "It's exactly the same with us," he said. "I can go to Moscow and enter the Kremlin and no one will stop me. I can say to Comrade Stalin that Harry Truman is a damned fool, and no one will shoot me."

"It cannot be wiser than the people."

Adlai Stevenson ran for President twice against Dwight D. Eisenhower. He lost both times. But even his political opponents agreed he was among the most eloquent speakers of his day. One of his recurring themes was that democratic government is a mirror image of its people.

Democratic government, he said, "cannot be stronger or more tough-minded than its people. It cannot be more inflexibly committed to the task than they. It cannot be wiser than the people."

Stevenson always put the burden squarely on the people. "Government is like a pump," he said, "and what it pumps up is just what we are, a fair sample of the intellect, the ethics, and the morals of the people—no better, no worse."

Buckley had a grand time campaigning....

When William F. Buckley, Jr., entered the race for New York City mayor in 1965, no one gave him much chance. And they were right. The possibility of a conservative Republican winning the mayoralty of New York was remote, to say the least. Buckley had a grand time campaigning, though, and wrote a book about it afterwards called *The Unmaking of a Mayor*.

During the campaign, a reporter asked him what his first action would be if elected. His response, "I'd demand a recount."

Quote/Unquote

Alexander Hamilton   (1757–1804)

It is of great importance in a republic not only to guard against the oppression of its rulers, but to guard one part of society against the injustice of the other part.

Abraham Lincoln   (1809–1865)

Why should there not be a patient confidence in the ultimate justice of the people? Is there any better or equal hope in the world?

Woodrow Wilson (1856–1924)

The world must be made safe for democracy.

Charles Evans Hughes (1862–1948)

While democracy must have its organization and controls, its vital breath is individual liberty.

Alfred E. Smith (1873–1944)

All the ills of democracy can be cured by more democracy.

G.K. Chesterton (1874–1936)

Democracy means government by the uneducated, while aristocracy means government by the badly educated.

Reinhold Niebuhr (1892–1971)

Man's capacity for justice makes democracy possible, but man's inclination to injustice makes democracy necessary.

E.B. White (1899–1985)

Democracy is the recurrent suspicion that more than half of the people are right more than half of the time.

William F. Buckley, Jr. (1925–   )

We are so concerned to flatter the majority that we lose sight of how very often it is necessary, in order to preserve freedom for the minority, let alone the individual, to face that majority down.

DISCOVERY

When the sheriff ran for reelection....

Most of the 200 people in Lukens County lived in a tiny crossroads village, the county seat. When the sheriff ran for reelection, he learned that all those rumblings he'd been hearing weren't just his indigestion. He lost the election by a vote of 53 to 2.

Next morning the townspeople saw him ambling down Main Street with two six-shooters in his holsters. The local barber, standing on the curb, stopped him and said, "Hey, Fred, you got a measly two votes. You ain't sheriff no more. How come you're wearing them six-guns?"

"How come?" the sheriff echoed. "Listen, anybody as unpopular as me?—I gotta protect myself."

"Son, how much do you want for your cabbage?"

Governor Bob Taylor of Tennessee told of the farmer who drove his team of mules to town with a load of cabbage. He took along his son, a young man who registered somewhere on the scale between an imbecile and a moron.

In town the farmer had to go off to tend to some business. He told his son, "Don't say a word to anyone. If you do, they'll find out you're a fool."

No sooner had the farmer left than a prospective buyer came up and said, "Son, how much do you want for your cabbage?"

The young man remembered his father's warning and said nothing.

"Son," the merchant repeated, "how much do you want for your cabbage?" Still no answer.

The man repeated his question one more time, and was rewarded with the same blank stare. At that he exploded, "By God, you're a fool!" So saying, he walked away.

When the farmer returned, his son reported. "Hey, Pop," he announced, "I never said a word, but they found out anyway."

"If you don't come in...."

Like all American Vice Presidents, Thomas R. Marshall quickly discovered that the office doesn't amount to much. When visitors came to the Capitol during Woodrow Wilson's administration, some of them stopped and peered curiously into Marshall's office. Once in a while the Vice President was moved to shout back at them, "If you don't come in, throw me a peanut!"

One night the main dish was hash.

It's good to discover that your worst fears are unjustified. That happened to Calvin Coolidge when he was a student at Amherst College. Coolidge took his meals at a local boarding house for the reasonable sum of $3.50 a week. The owner of the house kept a large black cat.

One night the main dish was hash. Coolidge took a long look at it on his plate, called the person waiting on tables, and said, "Bring me the cat."

The waiter left and returned a few moments later with the struggling, lively feline.

Coolidge eyed it closely, took a bite of hash, and said, "Thank you."

"Now, I'm all for back-scratching...."

When James Tumulty of New Jersey went to Congress, he was surprised at how solemn the proceedings seemed. He said, "Somebody will get up and say, 'I thank the gentleman for his contributions,' when all the guy did was belch or gargle."

Tumulty hadn't expected a fun-house atmosphere in the House of Representatives, but he hadn't expected such sober deference either. "Now, I'm all for back-scratching," he said, "but I'd like to see a wink once in a while."

"Propaganda, only propaganda...."

As a failed artist living in Vienna, Adolph Hitler talked at great length with friends about the gullibility of people. He once made fun of a newspaper ad for a "secret pomade" promising beautiful hair.

"That is what I call advertising," Hitler said excitedly. "Propaganda, only propaganda is necessary." He was sure he could sell any ridiculous item to the public—for instance, a salve guaranteed to make glass windows unbreakable.

He said, "There is no end of stupid people."

Farley's first meeting with FDR....

Jim Farley, perhaps more than anyone else, helped to put Franklin D. Roosevelt in the White House. Many Americans at the time regarded Farley as the political genius of the Democratic Party. For years the association between Farley and Roosevelt paid big political dividends.

Farley's first meeting with FDR was hardly auspicious, though. It occurred during the 1920 Presidential campaign. The Democratic standard bearer was James M. Cox of Ohio. The Vice Presidential nominee was Roosevelt. At the time, Farley was Democratic county chairman of Rockland County, New York.

It was the first summer of Jim Farley's marriage, and he and his wife, along with a small army of the party faithful, put in a grueling day saying hello to Cox and Roosevelt and each other. That's all Farley really did that day—shook hands and said, "How do you do?" There was no psychic electricity between him and FDR.

In fact, about all Farley remembered later of the day was his exhausted young wife saying, "If I had ever realized that politicians spent their time going through such nonsensical performances, I would never have married you."

"Pan over to Lebanon!"

During the Suez and Hungarian crises of 1956, the members of the UN General Assembly put in long and grueling hours. Sometimes they fell asleep in their seats, to the annoyance of Emery Kelen, who was in charge of television at the UN. Kelen was not supposed to allow the camera to focus on a sleeping delegate.

One day the camera zoomed in on a Liberian who was sound asleep. It lingered there until Kelen shouted, "Pan over to Lebanon!"

The cameraman panned away from Liberia and moved over to focus on Lebanon. Unfortunately, the Lebanese delegate was also asleep.

"I should have had sufficient intelligence...."

One of Senator Sam Ervin's many stories involves Walter P. Stacy, a North Carolina judge. Stacy was the son of a circuit-riding Methodist minister. The old preacher had traveled the length and breadth of the state, making friends wherever he went.

When Stacy, the son, ran for a seat on the North Carolina Supreme Court, the candidate's supporters in each of dozens of counties claimed that their man had been born in that county. This gave Stacy junior a lot of birthplaces—and a lot of votes.

A defeated candidate, Benjamin F. Long, reported his discovery of the odds he faced. Said Long, "I should have had sufficient intelligence to comprehend I couldn't win over an adversary who was born in 50 of North Carolina's 100 counties."

...someone on the Carter staff asked the chef....

When Rosalynn Carter visited the White House before her husband was inaugurated, someone on the Carter staff asked the chef and cooks if they could prepare the kind of food the First Family had enjoyed in the South.

"Yes, ma'am," replied a cook. "We've been fixing that kind of food for the servants for a long time."

...smog lay heavily over southern California....

On the campaign trail in 1980, the Republican Presidential candidate, Ronald Reagan, faced tough questions about his views on environmental protection. This issue wasn't Reagan's strong suit, and he waffled on it.

Although Reagan had enlisted the Sons of the Pioneers to sing "...cool, clear water," the truth was that much American water wasn't all that clear. Besides which, smog lay heavily over southern California despite Reagan's assurances that air pollution was now substantially controlled.

At one point on the tour Reagan revealed his discovery that trees, since they give off nitrogen, are worse polluters of the air than factory smokestacks. This startling fact may not have convinced everybody, but it did set up a Mel Brooks-type sight gag.

When Reagan arrived on the campus of Claremont College near Los Angeles, he was met by a poster tacked to a tree. It read, "Chop me down before I kill again."

"Wasn't that Mr. Lightfoot?"

It can be revealing to see ourselves as others see us. Jim Lightfoot, a Congressman from Iowa's 5th District, discovered that anew, as he tells in this story:

"In 1987 I underwent a double bypass heart operation. A few days after leaving the hospital I was working on a small project at home when I discovered I needed a part that wasn't available in my home workshop.

"My son and I headed down to the local discount store to pick up the item. While I was glad to be up and around, this was the time period following the operation the doctors had warned me I probably would experience a feeling of depression. It's a normal reaction to major surgery.

"As we walked through the store in search of the needed items, we encountered a couple of ladies standing in the aisle we were going down. We all exchanged hellos, and then my son and I walked around the corner of a display.

"We were out of their line of vision, but not out of earshot, when we heard one lady ask the other, 'Wasn't that Mr. Lightfoot?'

"The other responded, 'I'm not sure, but whoever it was sure looked like death warmed over!'"

Congressman Lightfoot adds that if he wasn't depressed before the encounter, he surely was afterwards.

"That much I knew."

Senator Ralph Yarborough of Texas once called George Bush "the darling of the John Birch Society." But in fact that far-right group didn't like Bush very much. A John Birch pamphlet pointed out that Marvin Pierce, Bush's father-in-law, was President of the McCall Corporation.

"That much I knew," George Bush writes in his autobiography, *Looking Forward*.

McCall's, the pamphlet continued, publishes *Redbook Magazine*.
Bush knew that, too.
And *Redbook*, the Birchite publication proclaimed, was, as its name suggested, "an official publication of the Communist Party.
"That," admits Bush, "I hadn't known."

While taking a brief stroll....

Two weeks after President Reagan was inaugurated, journalists were discovering to their delight that the new chief executive had, as a *New York Times* reporter wrote, "a reliable sense of humor."
The *Times*man was especially amused by Reagan's reaction to his confinement in the White House. There were no open spaces as nearby as those available in Sacramento. While taking a brief stroll on the White House lawn, the new President said wistfully, "This is the outside, isn't it?"

Quote/Unquote

Henry Adams   (1838–1918)

Knowledge of human nature is the beginning and end of political education.

Clarence Darrow   (1857–1938)

When I was a boy I was told that anybody could become President; I'm beginning to believe it.

Gerald R. Ford   (1913–   )

I learned a long time ago in politics, never say never.

DOMINANCE

"'This little fellow,' said Themistocles...."

Themistocles had a son who was the darling of his mother. "This little fellow," said Themistocles, "is the sovereign of all Greece."
"How so?" asked a friend.
Themistocles replied, "Why, he governs his mother, his mother governs me, I govern the Athenians, and the Athenians govern all Greece."

One of the problems of a political system....

Most people would probably agree with the idea that a strong executive is always a good thing. But Frank Sullivan, who served as press secretary to Mayor Richard J. Daley of Chicago, held a different view.

Sullivan felt that Mayor Daley's one-man rule had a harmful effect on events surrounding the "police riot" at the 1968 Democratic National Convention. Reviewing it years later, he wrote, "One of the problems of a political system in which one man is so dominant is that his friends, allies, and employees seldom, if ever, speak out, partially because of concern that the leader does not want them to speak and partially because it's easier to leave it all to him."

With a publicity-shy and an administratively weak police superintendent, the Chicago cops had no real spokesman except Mayor Daley—and the national press had little use for Daley. According to Sullivan, the media trashed the Chicago police even before the demonstrators in the street did. The result was an angry and soon out-of-control police force.

A too-dominant mayor had overawed a too-withdrawn police superintendent, which contributed to the mayhem that occurred that August night at the corner of Balbo Drive and Michigan Avenue.

Quote/Unquote

Abraham Lincoln   (1809–1865)

Some single mind must be master, else there will be no agreement on anything.

Franklin D. Roosevelt   (1882–1945)

It is the duty of the President to propose and it is the privilege of the Congress to dispose.

Lyndon B. Johnson   (1908–1973)

Now there are many, many people who can recommend and advise, and a few of them consent, but there is only one who has been chosen by the American people to decide.

◆ E ◆

ECONOMY

Since Poor Richard preached frugality....

Since Poor Richard preached frugality in his *Almanack*, people thought that Benjamin Franklin was a penny-pincher. Everyone knew Franklin's line about the overpriced whistle: "He has paid dear, very dear, for his whistle." Surely the man who wrote that must be a bit tight-fisted.

The truth was just the opposite. Franklin was a free spender. He found it almost impossible to turn down requests for money. Only the thrift of his wife prevented him from squandering more money than he did.

Yet his reputation for stinginess persisted. When he decided to give a welcoming dinner to the members of the Constitutional Convention in May 1788, he planned a grand affair. However, many of the members were late in arriving in Philadelphia. Two weeks after the intended date of the dinner, only a few of them had reached the city.

Feeling he should wait no longer, Franklin gave the dinner. Naturally, there were not many guests present. The word spread quickly that Franklin had purposely held the affair early so as to keep expenses down.

"Now you must rent a house...."

Calvin Coolidge was one of the most frugal of men. When serving as Lieutenant Governor of Massachusetts he lived in one room at the Adams House, for which he paid a dollar a day.

After Coolidge was elected Governor, a friend of his said, "Now you must rent a house and bring Mrs. Coolidge down from Northampton." The friend thought the Governor needed more room so that he could entertain.

Coolidge said nothing, but he did stop living in his single room. He rented two rooms at the Adams House for two dollars a day.

He found a way to economize....

Senator Theodore Green, Democrat of Rhode Island, hated to spend his own money. He found a way to economize—and at the same time win votes for the Democrats. Just before an election he would stop tipping taxi drivers and waiters. He would then tell them earnestly, "Be sure to vote Republican."

"Wouldn't it be cheaper...?"

One youngster had an easy solution to the Vietnam war. He wrote President Nixon with the good news:

"Dear Mr. President:
I have been thinking about Viet Nam. Wouldn't it be cheaper to buy it?"

Quote/Unquote

Seneca   (4 B.C.–65 A.D.)

Economy is in itself a source of great revenue.

Benjamin Disraeli   (1804–1881)

There can be no economy where there is no efficiency.

Henry Ward Beecher   (1813–1887)

I do not say a dollar a day is enough to support... a man and five children if the man insists on smoking and drinking beer.

Calvin Coolidge   (1872–1933)

I am for economy—and then more economy.

Sir Anthony Eden   (1897–1977)

Everyone is always in favor of general economy and particular expenditure.

EDUCATION

"Nor yet any tales of warfare and intrigues...."

In *The Republic*, Plato (putting his words in the mouth of Socrates, as he does throughout the book) explains how the content of poetry should be censored for the use of schoolchildren. The poems he has in mind are those of Greek myths. "Even if such tales were true," he writes, "I should not have supposed they should be thoughtlessly told to young people."

Plato objects especially to stories involving the mistreatment of parents and the breaking of promises. He also disapproves of stories "like those of Hera being bound by her son, or of Hephaestus being flung from heaven by his father for taking his mother's part when she was beaten."

"A child," says Plato, "cannot distinguish the allegorical sense from the literal, and the ideas he takes in at that age are likely to become indelibly fixed." Therefore, according to Plato, the first stories a child hears should be those that will produce the best possible effect on his character.

Plato has no use for violence in these tales either. He writes, "Nor yet any tales of warfare and intrigues and battles of gods against gods." He believes such stories may cause children to take quarreling too lightly.

Just when his thoughts in *The Republic* begin to sound almost modern, Plato returns with a thump to ancient Athens. If such tales cannot be altogether suppressed, he says, "they should only be revealed in a mystery." This means that their telling will require a ceremony accompanied by a sacrifice. And, Plato adds darkly, not the sacrifice merely of a pig, but rather "of some victim such as very few could afford."

"If this boy passes the examinations...."

In 1848 Harvard University faced a crisis. A black student applied for admission, and it seemed likely he would be accepted. Faced with strong protests against the admission of a black, the president of Harvard, Edward Everett, responded with an equally strong resolve.

Everett said: "If this boy passes the examinations, he will be admitted. And if the white students choose to withdraw, all the income of the college will be devoted to his education."

"Does college pay?"

As college costs continue to soar, the question "Does college pay?" becomes increasingly hard to answer. The question isn't a new one.

Back in the 1920s, Will Rogers had an answer that makes a lot of sense. Rogers felt that, yes, college pays—"if you're a good open-field runner!"

"I didn't want them to go to jail...."

A month or so before John F. Kennedy was assassinated, Adlai Stevenson, a liberal Democrat, visited Dallas. He was met by a jeering crowd of right-wing demonstrators. The crowd got a bit out of hand. A woman hit Stevenson on the head with a placard, and a man struck him across the cheek.

The police were ready to arrest the two demonstrators on charges of assault, but Stevenson said no. He didn't want them punished. As he commented later, "I didn't want them to go to jail—I thought it would be better if they went to school."

"Nor would I adopt from the Belgian Constitution...."

Although President John F. Kennedy believed strongly in education, he once said, "I do not suggest that our political and public life should be turned over to college-trained experts." He added: "Nor would I adopt from the Belgian Constitution a provision giving three votes instead of one to college graduates—at least not until more Democrats go to college."

"Tell them you're under consideration...."

Ron Nessen, President Gerald Ford's press secretary, had a tough job. He was the successor to Ron Ziegler, Nixon's press secretary, who had spent months lying to the press.

And Nessen almost got off on the wrong foot. After accepting the position of Jerry Ford's press secretary, he met several reporters as he was leaving the White House.

"Are you going to be the new press secretary?"

Nessen replied, "Not that I know of."

No sooner had he arrived home than he got a phone call from John Hushen, Ford's deputy press secretary. Hushen told him it had been a mistake to lie to the reporters. Think about it, he said. That was what got Ron Ziegler in trouble. Hushen told Nessen it would be a good idea to phone the reporters who'd been present.

"Tell them you're under consideration for press secretary but any announcement will have to come from the White House."

Nessen began telephoning. He reached the last reporter just before midnight. He realized he'd learned a valuable lesson.

"The Red Sunshine Lighted Up...."

When George Bush was chief of the U.S. Liaison Office in the People's Republic of China, he got to observe first-hand the workings of the Communist regime.

One day he and Barbara visited a provincial school. The children sang songs with such titles as "I'm Longing to Grow a Pair of Industrial Hands" and "I Want to Hurry and Grow Up So I Can Fight for the Revolution."

Good grief.

One of the popular adult songs in Beijing at the time the Bushes were there was "The Red Sunshine Lighted Up the Platform Around the Steel Furnace."

Mao Tse-tung's wife headed up cultural affairs in China in those days. A few years afterwards she and other members of the so-called Gang of Four were convicted of committing crimes during the Cultural Revolution.

Crimes against music, certainly.

Quote/Unquote

James A. Garfield (1831–1881)

A pine bench, with Mark Hopkins at one end of it and me at the other, is a good enough college for me!

Friedrich Nietzsche (1844–1900)

Educators, educate!

Theodore Roosevelt (1858–1919)

A man who has never gone to school may steal from a freight car; but if he has a university education, he may steal the whole railroad.

H.G. Wells (1866–1946)

Human history becomes more and more a race between education and catastrophe.

G.M. Trevelyn (1876–1962)

Education... has produced a vast population able to read but unable to distinguish what is worth reading.

John F. Kennedy (1917–1963)

A child miseducated is a child lost.

EXAGGERATION

"Since we have four hundred thousand men...."

When President Lincoln was asked the size of the Confederate army, he answered, "About a million two hundred thousand men."

His questioner was surprised. He had never heard such a large estimate.

Lincoln explained: "Well, you see, all of our generals, whenever they get whipped, they say the enemy outnumbered them by three or four to one. I have to believe my generals. Since we have four hundred thousand men in the field, the enemy must have at least a million two hundred thousand."

"You're 125 years old...."

Arthur Talmadge Abernethy was a teller of tall tales. According to him, an old South Mountaineer residing a few miles south of Connelly Springs [North Carolina] had reached the age of 125 years. The Barnum and Bailey Circus learned of the event and sent an agent by train to Connelly Springs with a proposed written contract in his pocket providing that the circus would pay the old mountaineer a fancy salary to travel with it and be exhibited to its patrons as the oldest man on earth.

On arrival at Connelly Springs, the agent traveled by buggy over muddy roads to the old mountaineer's home and presented Barnum and Bailey's offer to him. The old mountaineer informed the agent that he was pleased with the offer and was inclined to accept it. Despite repeated entreaties of the agent, however, he refused to sign the proposed contract embodying the offer and told the agent he would not even consider doing so before the next day.

The agent told the mountaineer, "You surprise me. You tell me that you're pleased with the offer, but that you won't even consider accepting it before tomorrow. Why are you determined to postpone your decision until tomorrow?"

"That's an embarrassing question," the old mountaineer replied, "but I'll answer it. I want to consult my father. I've made it a practice all my life never to enter into any transaction without getting my father's advice."

The agent exclaimed, "You're 125 years old, and you tell me your father's living?" The old mountaineer said, "Yes." The agent inquired, "Where is he?" The old mountaineer responded, "He's gone up the creek to see Grandpa. Grandpa's been ailing lately."

The Speaker thought big....

No Speaker of the U.S. House of Representatives ever had more power than Uncle Joe Cannon. The Speaker thought big and often talked big.

One day he was telling Chauncey Depew about a fish that got away. Depew listened skeptically and said, "About the size of a whale, wasn't it?"

Uncle Joe replied, "I was baiting with whales."

...there's John P. Wintergreen....

Of Thee I Sing is the classic musical comedy about American politics. With a book by George S. Kaufman and Morrie Ryskind, lyrics by Ira Gershwin, and music by George Gershwin, it was the first musical to win a Pulitzer Prize.

On stage there's John P. Wintergreen running for President with no issue other than "Love Is Sweeping the Country." Even better known to most people is Alexander Throttlebottom, the incumbent Vice President whose name no one in the play can remember.

Throttlebottom is every Vice President's melancholy image of himself. One day Throttlebottom decides to join the D.C. Public Library. He doesn't make it, because the library requires two references, and he can't come up with them.

"Joe, you underestimate...."

Today Harry S Truman is viewed as one of our better Presidents. But he didn't have that reputation while he was in office.

A citizen of the small city of Dover, New Hampshire, offered the opinion that he knew 400 men in town who could run the government better than Harry Truman.

A friend of his replied, "Joe, you underestimate the men of Dover."

"I was born in a log cabin...."

Among the best self-parodying speeches ever was the one Barry Goldwater delivered to the Alfalfa Club in Washington, D.C., on January 20, 1962. At the time he made it, Goldwater, the idol of American conservatives, was on his way to the Republican Presidential nomination in 1964.

In his speech, he said, tongue-in-cheek, that he was prepared to lead the nation, as he put it, "back to the Old Frontier of McKinley's day." He went on: "The undertaking, naturally, overwhelms me. It takes my breath away, even though I feel the White House is ready for me since Jacqueline Kennedy remodeled it in an eighteenth-century decor."

Near the end of his speech, he invoked the log cabin. "I was born in a log cabin," he said with a smile, "which I had moved to Phoenix, and except for some air conditioning, a swimming pool, a bowling alley, a bar, a shooting range, and a golf course, it remains the simple log cabin it always was."

On integration he was straightforward: "When anyone askes me how I stand on integration, I've only got one answer—where are you from?"

And he concluded: "I have every confidence that with all of you behind me, I could be another Alf Landon...."

This bleak prophecy of Goldwater's came true in a sense. You may recall that Alf Landon received only eight electoral votes against Franklin D. Roosevelt in 1932. Barry Goldwater got more than six times that many in 1964—but even so he had only about one-tenth as many as his opponent, Lyndon Johnson.

On the national level, the conservative revolution began with Barry Goldwater, but it did not reach its full strength for a number of years. By then Ronald Reagan, another great self-parodist, was leading it.

The huge sports stadium....

Prince Rainier of Monaco was being given a guided tour of the Astrodome in Houston, Texas. The huge sports stadium covers about nine acres.

The Prince was asked, "How would you like to have the Astrodome in Monaco?"

"Marvelous," he said. "Then we could be the world's only indoor country."

"I'm taking a bath right now...."

In Ronald Reagan's first year in office, the Republican legislative program rolled through Congress like a Panzer division. By and large, the Democrats went along with what seemed to be the dismantling of their beloved New Deal.

House Speaker Tip O'Neill was one of the Democrats caught in the onrush. In his memoirs he said that he felt "like the guy in the old joke who gets hit by a steamroller. Somebody runs to tell his wife about the accident.

"'I'm taking a bath right now,' she says. 'Could you just slip him under the door.'"

Quote/Unquote

Mark Twain   (1835–1910)

Fleas can be taught nearly anything that a Congressman can.

H.L. Mencken   (1880–1956)

Consider, for example, a campaign for the Presidency. Would it be possible to imagine anything more uproariously idiotic—a deafening, nerve-wracking battle to the death between Tweedledum and Tweedledee...?

Adolf Hitler   (1889–1945)

In the size of the lie there is always contained a certain factor of credibility, since the great masses of the people... will more easily fall victim to a great lie than to a small one.

FAILURE

"I have offered that Pascagoula amendment...."

Not all pork-barrel legislation succeeds. Consider the sad ordeal of Congressman Albert Brown of Mississippi. At one point, back in the mid-1800s, Brown had asked for a $60,000 appropriation to make improvements on the Pascagoula River. He attached the request to another bill as an amendment, but it got nowhere. His colleagues voted down the amendment. He kept trying—and failing.

In 1852 Brown delivered a speech that has become a kind of pork-barrel classic. He began:

"I have offered that Pascagoula amendment for the last time. [At this his colleagues broke into laughter.] I stand here pretty much in the attitude of the man who visited General Jackson when he was President. He came on to Washington asking for the mission to England. It was refused him. He came down to a collectorship, and when that was refused him, he said he would put up with a clerkship. But that also was denied him. As a last dying hope he inquired of the old General if he could not give him a pair of old boots; and when they were refused he swore he would not be a Jackson man any longer. [The House laughed again.]

Brown made his final demand in the latest Pascagoula amendment—$2,000 for a survey. He warned, "If you do not give it to me, I shall surely vote against the bill." But his colleagues just laughed once more, and Congressman Brown ruefully admitted, "I do believe you think I mean to do it anyhow."

...no one voted for them.

Eight politicians in British history hold the ultimate record for futility—no one voted for them. The first was Lord Garvagh, who ran as the Liberal candidate for Reigate in 1832. He received not a single vote in the general election.

The last to fail so utterly was Mr. F. R. Lees in the Rippon special election of 1860. No one at all found Mr. Lees to be an acceptable candidate.

After the 1860 election the candidates were allowed to vote for themselves, thus assuring at least one vote for even the most unpopular politician.

"Mr. Speaker, I conceive...."

Mr. Addison, a member of the House of Commons, rose to speak on an important issue. He made no progress at all. Each time he tried to get going, he would say:

"Mr. Speaker, I conceive...."

Whether from nervousness or forgetfulness, Addison never got beyond those four words.

At last a member on the opposite side of the House interrupted, remarking that "the right honorable gentleman has conceived three times and brought forth nothing."

"Boy Bryan's defeat."

From **Bryan, Bryan, Bryan, Bryan**
"The Campaign of Eighteen Ninety-six,
as Viewed at the Time by a
Sixteen-Year-Old, etc."

by Vachel Lindsay

Election night at midnight:
Boy Bryan's defeat.
Defeat of western silver.
Defeat of the wheat.
Victory of letterfiles
And plutocrats in miles
With dollar signs upon their coats,
Diamond watchchains on their vests
And spats on their feet.
Victory of custodians,
Plymouth Rock,
And all that inbred landlord stock.
Victory of the neat.
Defeat of the aspen groves of Colorado valleys,
The blue bells of the Rockies,

And blue bonnets of old Texas,
By the Pittsburgh alleys.
Defeat of alfalfa and the Mariposa lily.
Defeat of the Pacific and the long Mississippi.
Defeat of the young by the old and silly.
Defeat of tornadoes by the poison vats supreme.
Defeat of my boyhood, defeat of my dream.

He spoke at every crossroads tavern...."

Long ago, when rural Georgia was solidly Democratic, a candidate for public office had to win that party's nomination. If he did, the rest was easy. Nomination meant election.

Now, there was a man in Jeff Davis County who kept turning up in the primaries, always seeking one job or another. The voters got to know him, but somehow the poor fellow never got the nod on his party's ticket.

At last he decided he couldn't win as a Democrat. He said the Democrats just didn't appreciate him. He was a good man and he deserved to win, but he'd have to try a new tactic.

His new tactic was to enter himself as the Republican nominee for sheriff. He made the most of his nomination. He campaigned up and down the county. He spoke at every crossroads tavern, every rural schoolhouse. He pulled out all the stops.

When election day came, he had high hopes.

Alas—he received just two votes. Worse yet, he was arrested that same evening for voting twice.

"I believe it is peace for our time."

One of the most stunning political failures of the 20th century occurred at Munich in 1938. In those dark days Neville Chamberlain, Britain's prime minister, thought he had succeeded in maintaining world peace. He was elated when Adolf Hitler promised to stop German aggression—but not until the Nazis had taken Czechoslovakia's Sudetenland.

Prime Minister Chamberlain's foolish remark of September 30th, "I believe it is peace for our time," has gone down in history as the classic declaration of appeasement.

Not many people are aware of French premier Edouard Daladier's feelings about the tragic decision at Munich. Daladier was weak, but he was no Chamberlain. He knew all too well that a temporary peace had been bought at a terrible price. On his way back to Paris, he was deeply depressed. He felt guilty. He expected the French people to condemn him for what he had agreed to. France, he knew, had gone back on its long-standing pledges to the Czechs. There was no cause for celebration.

To his amazement, the crowds at the airport and along his route to Paris greeted him with enthusiasm. Like Chamberlain, the people of Paris seemed to think they had been granted peace in a dangerous hour.

Daladier knew better. As the crowds waved and shouted, he found no reason whatever to smile or even respond. "Imbeciles," he thought. "They are cheering me. For what?"

"We were hungry for danger, glory...."

On Monday, July 23, 1945, Marshal Henri Pétain of France went on trial for treason. He was in his late 80s, a legendary figure from the past. He was the military commander who in 1916 had uttered the famous words, "They shall not pass." The German army did *not* pass—although the defense of Verdun in World War One cost the Allies a million lives—and Marshal Pétain became one of the great heroes of France.

Now he faced a French court, accused of treason. World War One had made Pétain a hero; World War Two made him an accused traitor. As the head of Vichy France, Pétain collaborated with the Nazis. His supporters—and there were many—argued that he did it for the good of France. But the Allies won the war, and those who backed Charles de Gaulle and Free France were unforgiving.

Jules Roy, for many years an officer in the French army and air force, joined the RAF midway through World War Two. Before that he had sided with Pétain. Long after Pétain's trial and conviction, Roy wrote a book about the court proceedings of July and August, 1945. He concluded, as others have, that Pétain, through a failure of political judgment, had sacrificed not only his own honor but that of young French soldiers such as himself.

Roy, unlike the court, did not see Pétain as a traitor. Instead he saw him as a well-meaning but misguided old man, already in his mid-80s when he took the reins of government. Roy acquitted Pétain of the worst accusation. But he made an accusation of his own: "We were hungry for danger, glory, and love," he wrote. "You gave us gall and wormwood."

"'Our spirit of enjoyment....'"

President Kennedy was an avid student of history and often used quotations from other times and circumstances to illustrate his points. He once said: "When France fell to the Nazis, one of its most illustrious leaders declared: 'Our spirit of enjoyment was greater than our spirit of sacrifice. We wanted to have, more than we wanted to give. We spared effort, and met disaster.'"

"I will say candidly and clearly...."

In the 20th century the king of American political cartoonists was probably Herblock, the scourge of Richard Nixon. Herblock chronicled the triumph and downfall of America's 37th President.

Herblock became almost obsessed with the enigma of Nixon. His hundreds of cartoons about the unindicted co-conspirator were all hostile, except for the one after Nixon's Presidential victory in 1968. In that cartoon he showed a barber's sign saying, "This shop gives to every new President of the United States a free shave."

But Herblock was only human. When the Nixon Presidency fell apart, his cartoonist-critic crowed triumphantly in print as well as in pictures. He suggested that Nixon might like a rewrite of the Parson Weems cherry-tree story in which George Washington had said, "I cannot tell a lie."

Herblock's revision, á la Nixon, went like this: "I cannot tell a lie. I will say candidly and clearly that this orchard is infested with beavers."

"...the Inspector Clouseau...."

The Central Intelligence Agency has had its ups and downs in the public mind. Just how capable its agents are has been a matter of debate. The anecdotal evidence is not always reassuring.

Take the case of Edwin Gibbons Moore.

Mr. Moore, a CIA employee, left the agency in 1973. Three years later he decided the time had come to make a fast buck. He packaged up a set of classified documents he had pilfered from the files while working there. He tossed the package, unannounced, over the fence of the Soviet embassy's residential complex in northwest Washington.

Thus began his own personal Bay of Pigs disaster.

The Soviet guards were frightened by the sudden descent of the package. They thought it was a bomb. They called in the U.S. Secret Service to have a look-see.

This was not the way Gibbons had planned it at all. The Secret Service took possession of the package, along with a note from Gibbons promising more classified material for a payment of $200,000.

The ex-CIA man, being in a hurry, specified a place for the exchange of cash and documents for the very next night.

George Bush, heading the CIA at the time, called Gibbons "the Inspector Clouseau of volunteer spying." Indeed he was. The place he specified for the exchange was in his own neighborhood.

At the appointed time, FBI agents drove by the site and dropped a package, presumably containing $200,000.

A child who happened to be playing in the neighborhood spotted the drop, and cheerily ran over to pick up the package. But fledgling spy Edwin Gibbons Moore, who had been raking his lawn a short distance away, ran over, chased the child away, and copped the package.

He found no $200,000.

Instead, there was an arrest, followed by an indictment on charges of espionage, and eventually a 25-year prison term.

And it had seemed like such a good idea at the time.

Quote/Unquote

Abraham Lincoln   (1809–1865)

...I have a congenital aversion to failure....

Georges Clemençeau   (1841–1929)

A man's life is interesting primarily when he has failed—I well know. For it is a sign that he tried to surpass himself.

Theodore Roosevelt   (1858–1919)

It is hard to fail, but it is worse never to have tried to succeed.

Lyndon B. Johnson   (1908–1973)

The guns and the bombs, the rockets and the warships, are all symbols of human failure. They are necessary symbols. They protect what we cherish. But they are witnesses to human folly.

John W. Gardner   (1912–   )

One of the reasons mature people stop learning is that they become less and less willing to risk failure.

FAME

"I would rather have people ask...."

A friend of Cato the Elder felt that Rome should have a statue honoring the great soldier, statesman, and writer.

"No," Cato said. "I would rather have people ask why there is no statue to Cato than to ask why there is one."

"Adieu my darling, darling wife...."

No one has ever questioned the fame of Alexander Hamilton. A coauthor with James Madison of the *Federalist* papers, Hamilton helped bring about the ratification of the U.S. Constitution. As Washington's Secretary of the Treasury, he established the new government on a firm financial footing. His portrait is on our ten-dollar bill.

Like any famous statesman, Hamilton had enemies. One of them was Aaron Burr. And no wonder. Hamilton had denied Burr the presidency in 1800 by throwing his support to Jefferson, a man he disliked but regarded as less "dangerous" than Burr. Four years later Hamilton contrived to keep Burr from becoming governor of New York. Burr, furious, forced a duel.

Hamilton had no wish to die, but he knew that Burr was renowned for his marksmanship. Indeed, Hamilton had little hope of surviving, especially since he intended to aim his own first shot high. On the night before the duel he wrote in his farewell letter, "Adieu my darling, darling wife."

Burr, meanwhile, had been spending hours in his garden taking pistol practice. His mind was on killing the man who had thwarted his highest ambitions. He had no intention of aiming high.

They met on a shelf of level ground above the Hudson River in Weehawken, New Jersey. Hemmed in by rocks and overarched by trees, it was a secluded area and a favorite dueling spot.

The rules were explained, the two men paced off the distance; they turned, and fired. Burr heard a whizzing sound overhead, and a branch from a tree fell beside him. When the smoke cleared, he saw Hamilton lying on the ground.

A doctor raced up to the fallen figure. "This is a mortal wound," Hamilton cried. And it was. He died the next day.

His opponent was well satisfied. His only regret was that Hamilton might now be viewed as a martyr.

"He may thank me," Burr said coldly. "I made him a great man."

"My glory! Why do they wrench it from me?"

Today Simón Bolívar is recognized as the greatest Latin-American hero. But when he died in 1830, his reputation was not so high. Ill and embittered in the last years of his life, he wailed to a friend, "My glory! My glory! Why do they wrench it from me? Why do they slander me?"

Bolívar himself sometimes thought he had failed in his life's work. His ambition was so great, and his later failures so galling, that he underestimated his actual accomplishments. So did most of the people of the world—in 1830.

In time his old enemies passed away. Some of them, like José Antonio Páez, came to see Bolívar in a clearer light. Páez, in his autobiography, praised the Liberator extravagantly.

Eventually, monuments were built. In 1883 Venezuela held lavish Bolívar birthday centennial celebrations. Biographies were written, many of them in worshipful tones.

Bolívar, who died almost in disgrace, gradually became an international hero. Today there is hardly a town in Spanish South America without a statue honoring him.

"The more I see of people...."

This story comes from Lowell L. Blaisdell, Professor of History at Texas Tech:

In 1848 there was a revolution in France, and the immediate outcome was a very shaky republic. During the early, strife-torn months of this interim government, Alphonse de Lamartine, a famous poet, served as Foreign Minister. Given the ticklish internal situation, Lamartine did a pretty good job.

After the interim period came a constitution, followed by preparations to elect a President for the new republic under the new constitution. One of the candidates was Lamartine. Probably he, as well as many others, figured he had a good chance of being elected, given his recent showing as Foreign Minister.

However, another candidate was in the race: Louis Napoleon Bonaparte, the nephew of Napoleon I. During the strain and strife of the interim period in the spring and summer of 1848, Louis Napoleon had held no important job and had exercised no responsibility at all. For part of the time he was not even in France, but in England.

But he had a *name*!—something like the Kennedy name in the United States. Indeed, a Napoleon in France had an even more impressive cachet than a Kennedy in Boston.

When the election took place, Louis Napoleon buried Lamartine in the returns, winning by a landslide and becoming President of France.

When Lamartine heard the news, he was thoroughly disgusted. "The more I see of people," he said, "the better I like my dog."

One John Francis Kennedy, no relation....

By the early 1950s the Kennedys of Boston and Hyannisport were so popular in Massachusetts that other Kennedys began to cash in on their fame.

One John Francis Kennedy, no relation to the "real" Kennedys, ran three times for state treasurer against the person endorsed by the Democratic Party. So potent was the Kennedy name that this bogus JFK knocked off the Party's choice each time.

In 1960 he decided to put his magic name to use again by running for Governor against John Ward, the man designated as the candidate by the Democratic convention.

A reporter asked Ward what he thought the upstart Kennedy's chances were. Ward, no fool, replied, "He has a magic name, and believe me, a name in politics is like Ivory soap in business, or like Coca-Cola."

But the brand name failed John F. (for Francis) Kennedy in 1960. John Volpe, a Republican, won the race for Governor.

Representative Ronald Coleman of Texas....

You always knew there were some famous comedians in Congress, right? Well, it's true. The 100th Congress featured Representative Jerry Lewis from—where else?—California. And out of Oklahoma came a wisecracking Senator by the name of Don Nickles. Oh, wait. That should be Rickles, shouldn't it?

Never mind. There were plenty of other celebrities whose names studded the roster of the 100th Congress. One was New Jersey Senator Bill Bradley, the real thing, late of the Princeton Tigers and the New York Knicks. Another was Kentucky Representative Jim Bunning, also the real thing, late of the Detroit Tigers and the Philadelphia Phillies.

And then there was Florida Senator Connie Mack, late of the... No, wait. That should be "the late Connie Mack," shouldn't it? The Florida Senator, narrowly defeated for reelection in 1988, never managed the Philadelphia A's.

The 100th Congress also featured a smiling assortment of Hollywood types: Representative Ronald Coleman of Texas was one. A famous actor—wasn't he?—the guy who picked up an Oscar for his role in the 1947 movie *A Double Life*. The title of that film seems fitting and proper. A double life indeed.

And if you happened to want to get your fence whitewashed, how about Representative Tom Sawyer of Ohio? Surely, he could have gotten the job done.

Now, superachievers with high name-recognition come and go, even in Congress. The 100th Congress briefly had a great golfer, a matinee idol, and a storybook character to rival any of Mark Twain's. I'm not talking about three people here, but about one. And according to some people, that one legislator was a brilliant stand-up comic as well. I'm thinking, of course, of Indiana's Senator Dan Quayle, who quickly moved on to another and loftier position.

Quote/Unquote

Montaigne   (1533–1592)

Fame and tranquillity can never be bedfellows.

Sir Walter Raleigh (1552–1618)

Fame's but a hollow echo.

Benjamin Disraeli (1804–1881)

He was one of those few men who awake one morning and find themselves famous.

Thomas B. Reed (1839–1902)

A statesman is a successful politician who is dead.

George Santayana (1863–1952)

The highest form of vanity is love of fame.

Henry Kissinger (1923–   )

Now when I bore people at a cocktail party they think it's their fault.

FREEDOM

Quote/Unquote

Warren G. Harding (1865–1923)

Now, a woman has a perfect right to talk temperance... but her right to wear pants and make the night hideous on the street is questioned.

W. Somerset Maugham (1874–1965)

If a nation values anything more than freedom, it will lose its freedom; and the irony of it is that if it is comfort or money that it values more, it will lose that too.

Gerald W. Johnson (1890–1980)

Freedom is always purchased at a great price, and even those who are willing to pay it have to admit that the price is great.

Dwight D. Eisenhower (1890–1969)

The history of free men is never really written by chance but by choice—their choice.

John Foster Dulles   (1888–1959)

Freedom and duty always go hand in hand, and if the free do not accept the duty of social responsibility, they will not long remain free.

Sam Ervin, Jr.   (1896–1985)

The foes of freedom never tire. Consequently, freedom is always in jeopardy.

Adlai E. Stevenson   (1900–1965)

The sound of tireless voices is the price we pay for the right to hear the music of our own opinions.

Lillian Hellman   (1905–1984)

For every man who lives without freedom, the rest of us must face the guilt.

FRIENDSHIP

...Desbrough had hunted in India....

When people talk about personal diplomacy today, they usually mean stiff, formal meetings between heads of state, punctuated by photo opportunities. Things were different in Theodore Roosevelt's day. As President, Teddy Roosevelt was a close personal friend of a number of ambassadors to the United States. Most of them, like him, favored the strenuous life.

At Oyster Bay, Teddy taught Hermann Speck von Sternberg, the German ambassador, how to play polo. He swam naked in the Potomac with Jean Jules Jusserand, the French ambassador. When the British were casting about for a new ambassador, they put Lord Desbrough high on their list. The reason was that Desbrough had hunted in India, Africa, and the Rockies. He had rowed across the English Channel, swum the Niagara River, and mastered the art of fly fishing.

Teddy invited new ambassadors for a walk in Rock Creek Park. This was more of an endurance test than a walk, and Britain's Mortimer Durand failed it. Even though Sir Mortimer rode well and played a fine game of cricket, he failed to measure up to Roosevelt's rigorous standards.

Did Roosevelt's friendships have any affect on Roosevelt's foreign policy? Indeed they did. Teddy's personal diplomacy was one factor that led to the uneasy neutrality preceding World War One. His best-known foreign relations triumph, though, came at Portsmouth, New Hampshire, in 1905, where he acted as a personal peacemaker between the Russians and the Japanese. In relations with the

Far East, as with Europe, Roosevelt tried and on the whole succeeded in maintaining the United States as what he called an "honest broker."

"No, No! Jimmy Stewart for *Governor*...."

As an actor, Ronald Reagan often played the role of best friend—the nice guy who didn't get the girl. Thus when movie producer Jack Warner learned that Reagan was running for Governor of California, he reportedly quipped: "No, no! Jimmy Stewart for *Governor*; Reagan for *best friend!*"

Quote/Unquote

Benjamin Franklin (1706–1790)

There are three faithful friends—an old wife, an old dog, and ready money.

George Washington (1732–1799)

True friendship is a plant of slow growth, and must undergrow and withstand the shocks of adversity before it is entitled to that appellation.

Thomas Jefferson (1743–1826)

...friendship is precious, not only in the shade, but in the sunshine of life.

Talleyrand (1754–1838)

Never speak ill of yourself; your friends will always say enough on that subject.

Abraham Lincoln (1809–1865)

The better part of one's life consists of his friendships.

Ambrose Bierce (1842–1914)

Friendship: *n.* A ship big enough to carry two in fair weather, but only one in foul.

Woodrow Wilson (1856–1924)

You cannot be friends upon any other terms than upon the terms of equality.

Eleanor Roosevelt (1884–1962)

Friendship with oneself is all-important, because without it one cannot be friends with anyone else in the world.

· G ·

GOVERNMENT

"The government is mainly an expensive organization...."

You may never have heard of Edgar Watson Howe, the "Sage of Potato Hill." But around the turn of the century he was a well-known homespun newspaper editor in Atchison, Kansas, and a champion of the common people. Howe put his faith in the governed rather than in the system.

He wrote: "The government is mainly an expensive organization to regulate evildoers and tax those who behave; government does little for fairly respectable people except annoy them."

"Lord Northcliffe sees no advantage...."

Lord Northcliffe, the British press lord, was noted for his egomania. In 1916 he toyed with the idea of exercising power by holding a government office rather than through his newspaper.

When Lloyd George became Prime Minister in 1916, he invited Lord Northcliffe to an interview at 10 Downing Street. With World War One at its midpoint, the Prime Minister was prepared to name Northcliffe Director of the British Air Ministry.

The press lord had already received this offer in private and had been thinking about it. Now the time had come to decide. Northcliffe, never the most tactful of men, sent Lloyd George this lofty reply:

"Lord Northcliffe sees no advantage in any interview between himself and the Prime Minister at this juncture."

It was probably just as well. Northcliffe was something of a zany and might have done real harm to the British war effort. However, when Lloyd George countered with an offer to make him Director of Propaganda in Enemy Countries, the press lord accepted.

In his book *Eminent Edwardians*, Piers Brendon remarks acidly that "Northcliffe was thus induced to devote his energies to undermining the German rather than the British government."

"Alexander Hamilton started the U.S. Treasury...."

Federal budget deficits are hardly new. As Will Rogers said, "Alexander Hamilton started the U.S. Treasury with nothing—and that was the closest our country ever was to being even."

"This compassionate gentleman's dedication...."

Representative Tom Moore, Jr., of Waco, Texas, wanted to prove a point. In 1971 he introduced a special bill in the Texas House of Representatives. It commended a certain Albert DeSalvo for meritorious service to his country, his state, and his community.

The citation read in part: "This compassionate gentleman's dedication and devotion to his work has enabled the weak and lonely throughout the nation to achieve a new degree of concern for their future. He has been officially recognized by the state of Massachusetts for his noted activities and unconventional techniques involving population control and applied psychology."

The bill passed unanimously. All such special bills passed with ease, Representative Moore pointed out. And they shouldn't.

Moore then explained that Albert DeSalvo—in fact and more or less as described in the bill—was the man convicted of 13 murders in the Boston area. He was better known as "the Boston Strangler."

"Government is like a baby...."

Long before he became President, Ronald Reagan had developed the philosophy that guided his later actions. Concerning government he was quoted as saying, "Government is like a baby. An alimentary canal with a big appetite at one end and no sense of responsibility at the other."

Quote/Unquote

Confucius (551–479 B.C.)

An oppressive government is more to be feared than a tiger.

Thomas Paine (1737–1809)

Government, like dress, is the badge of lost innocence; the palaces of kings are built upon the ruins of the bowers of paradise.

James Madison (1751–1836)

If men were angels, no government would be necessary.

Alexander Hamilton (1757–1804)

Why has government been instituted at all? Because the passions of men will not conform to the dictates of reason and justice, without constraint.

Johann Wolfgang von Goethe (1749–1832)

It is a maxim of wise government to deal with men not as they ought to be but as they are.

John C. Calhoun (1782–1850)

The very essence of a free government consists in considering offices as public trusts, bestowed for the good of the country, and not for the benefit of an individual or a party.

Thomas Carlyle (1795–1881)

In the long run every government is the exact symbol of its people, with their wisdom and unwisdom.

George Bernard Shaw (1856–1950)

A government which robs Peter to pay Paul can always depend on the support of Paul.

Will Rogers (1879–1935)

I don't make jokes. I just watch the government and report the facts.

Hubert H. Humphrey (1911–1978)

The moral test of government is how it treats those who are in the dawn of life, the children; those who are in the twilight of life, the aged; and those who are in the shadows of life, the sick, the needy, and the handicapped.

William F. Buckley, Jr. (1925–   )

The protection of the individual against the criminal is the first and highest function of government.

GREED

"I'm now minister of foreign affairs!"

Modern politicians, as a group, are probably no more corrupt than earlier politicians. Even some of the world's great statesmen have been in it for the cash.

Take Talleyrand. He was the French minister of foreign affairs under Napoleon and a brilliant negotiator at the Congress of Vienna. You might think his motives would be noble and his chances for profiteering limited.

Actually, when he received the news that he was to be named minister of foreign affairs, he went into transports of joy. In his coach he crowed repeatedly to a friend: "I'm now minister of foreign affairs! Minister of foreign affairs! I'll make an immense fortune out of it! A truly immense fortune!"

"You seem to have a great appetite...."

Anthony Trollope, an English novelist of the Victorian era, often wrote on politics. His reputation, though, rests on the close observation of ordinary people. He understood human drives and emotions.

He also exemplified them. Once at a dinner party a lady observed Trollope putting away serious quantities of every dish in sight.

She commented on his performance, saying, "You seem to have a great appetite, Mr. Trollope."

"Not at all, madam," he replied, "but thank God, I am greedy."

Hundreds of speculators were ruined.

Whenever an Ivan Boesky or a Michael Milken appears, we tend to think of it as a unique occurrence. But such wheeler-dealers have always operated on Wall

Street, most successfully when government regulation was at a low ebb and the President wasn't minding the store.

"Black Friday"—September 24, 1869—came about because President Ulysses S. Grant was literally out of touch. He was playing croquet at Newport, Rhode Island. Grant, a capable general but a babe in the woods in financial matters, had been conned by Jay Gould and Jim Fisk.

Their scheme required that Grant be talked into demanding that he personally approve of the U.S. government's selling of gold. Once that order was obtained—and, incredibly, it was—the President would be isolated in some nice, quiet place (Newport would do fine), while Gould and Fisk proceeded to corner the New York gold market.

The plan came within an ace of working. The price of gold rose steadily throughout September. Gould and Fisk continued to buy, and the price rose to 142, then 144. The magic figure was 200. At that price, Gould and Fisk intended to unload.

Next day, Black Friday, gold opened at 145. The press had been demanding that the government sell gold. But President Grant's order stood. Gould, however, upon receiving word that the President might decide to sell, began quietly to sell on his own. Fisk and his cohorts continued to buy wildly. The price soared to 162. At that price no one offered to sell.

The Secretary of the Treasury, George Boutwell, could do nothing, or so he thought, even though a flood of telegrams demanded action. Boutwell wired Grant for instructions. Finally, the old soldier said okay, start selling gold at once. Continue selling until the near corner is broken.

The effect was spectacular. A reporter for the *New York Herald* noted that as the bells of Trinity Church started to peal the hour of noon, gold stood at 160. When the echo of the bells died away, it had dropped to 138.

Hundreds of speculators were ruined. But not the shrewd Jay Gould, who used his inside sources of information to bail out. The gregarious Fisk was also fortunate. His buying had been done at the sole responsibility of his brokers, who failed.

At a Congressional hearing Fisk hinted darkly at complicity in Congress and in the White House. As the Congressmen fidgeted, Jim Fisk tossed off one of the revealing remarks of the Gilded Age:

"Let everyone carry out his own corpse!"

Quote/Unquote

Abraham Lincoln   (1809–1865)

The Bible says somewhere that we are desperately selfish. I think we would have discovered that fact without the Bible.

Horace Greeley (1811–1872)

The darkest day in a man's career is that wherein he fancies there is some easier way of getting a dollar than by squarely earning it.

Ambrose Bierce (1842–1914)

Mammon: *n*. The god of the world's leading religion. His chief temple is in the holy city of New York.

Franklin D. Roosevelt (1882–1945)

We have always known that heedless self-interest was bad morals; we now know that it is bad economics.

Dwight D. Eisenhower (1890–1969)

I find myself in enthusiastic agreement with your rebellion against the reduction of every value, every incentive to the materialistic. If man is only an educated mule, we should eliminate him and turn the earth back to the birds and the fishes and the monkeys.

HONESTY

"It is no, no—not a sixpence."

Mark Twain said, "Always do right. This will gratify some people and astonish the rest."

In the early days of the United States, a good many men in government tried to put that principle into practice. Three such men were Charles C. Pinckney of South Carolina, Elbridge Gerry of Massachusetts, and John Marshall of Virginia. The American president, John Adams, sent them on a mission to France. Their goal was to get France to stop having its warships prey on American merchant ships on the high seas.

The French foreign minister was the brilliant but corrupt Talleyrand. He sent three of his assistants to make what he thought would be a tempting offer. French attacks on American shipping would cease immediately if the U.S. would pay the French government—that is, Talleyrand and his friends—$240,000. Talleyrand figured it was a small price for America to pay for a major diplomatic victory.

Pinckney, Gerry, and Marshall were aghast. Here was one of the great powers of Europe asking them for a payoff. The three Americans returned home and published an indignant report of the incident. In it they called Talleyrand's three assistants X, Y, and Z—thus the name "X, Y, Z affair." When asked for their answer on the matter of a bribe, the Americans said they had replied, "No... It is no, no—not a sixpence."

America gained prestige for its honesty. It also gained something else. Lacking a diplomatic agreement with France, the U.S. moved to arm three hundred of its merchant ships. These ships were the start of the United States Navy.

87

"An honest politician...."

Simon Cameron served briefly as Secretary of War in the Lincoln administration. Corruption ran rampant. After that, no one ever accused the notorious wheeler-dealer from Pennsylvania of being an honest politician.

But Cameron framed the classic definition of one. "An honest politician," he said, "is one who, when bought, will stay bought."

"I don't care what people write."

Boss Tweed of New York was not the first politician to assume that every man has his price. In more than twenty years of looting the city, he had seen no evidence to the contrary. His power was bought and paid for. He had bought the Republican swing vote on the Board of Supervisors. He had bought out six top Republican leaders at the state level for $40,000 each. He knew a man's price might be high, but he couldn't imagine the possibility of coming across a man who refused to be bought.

In 1871, to his sorrow, he came across two of them. One was George Jones, the crusading editor of *The New York Times*. Tweed knew that buying out the *Times* would cost him plenty. He sent his city controller to Jones with an offer of five million dollars to stop the *Times'* exposé of the Tweed Ring. Jones turned it down.

The second man was Thomas Nast, whose savage cartoons in *Harper's* magazine served the same purpose as Jones' verbal attacks. If anying, the cartoons made Tweed even angrier. "I don't care what people write," Tweed once said. "My people can't read. But they have eyes, and they can see as well as other folks."

The Tweed Ring offered Nast half a million dollars to stop drawing his pictures and take a trip. Nast turned it down.

Now The Boss was up against the wall. Money had always worked before. All it took was a big enough offer. But Jones and Nast weren't looking for the right offer. They weren't looking for an offer at all. They were honest men, period. They weren't going to sell out at any price.

The *Times* kept publishing its exposés. Nast kept drawing his cartoons. Finally, the public demanded action. At the end of 1871, Boss Tweed was indicted on 120 counts of forgery, grand larceny, and conspiracy to defraud. He fled the country, but was traced to a Spanish sailing ship—and identified from a Thomas Nast cartoon. In 1878 the once invincible Boss Tweed died in Manhattan's Ludlow Street jail.

"Ma, Ma, where's my Pa?"

The only President to admit to fathering an illegitimate child was Grover Cleveland. The ensuing scandal became a big issue in the Presidential campaign of 1884. Cleveland's stubborn insistence on telling the truth may actually have won him the election that year.

The mother was Maria Halprin, and the child was ten years old by the time the story broke. It broke, as such stories often do, at a critical time—at the height of the Presidential campaign.

Cleveland flatly refused to deny the truth of the story. Yes, he admitted, he and Maria, a widow in Buffalo, had had an affair. A child, a son, was born. Cleveland had supported his son from the beginning, and indeed had taken legal action later to protect the boy from his mother, who had become an alcoholic.

The mitigating details meant nothing to the gleeful Republicans. Their happy chant became one of the best-known campaign slogans or ditties of all time. It went:

"Ma, Ma, where's my Pa?
Gone to the White House, ha, ha, ha."

The United States was a lot more puritanical in 1884 than it is today, and that chant should have done in the erring candidate. Cleveland's opponent was James G. Blaine, the "armed warrior," the "plumed knight," but also the "continental liar from the state of Maine." Blaine was a model of personal rectitude, as far as anyone knew. No sex scandal there, although his public life was not so spotless. He had some chinks in his armor.

It was a close election, but enough people voted for Grover Cleveland to make him President of the United States. After their victory the Democrats sang a little ditty of their own:

"Hurrah for Maria! Hurrah for the kid!
I voted for Cleveland,
And I'm damned glad I did!"

"They couldn't make the park complete...."

George Washington Plunkitt of Tammany Hall was a machine politician all the way. He was proud of what he did, and what he did mainly was to make himself rich. Honest graft, he called it, and he was more than willing to define it.

"I'll tell you of one case," he said. "They were goin' to fix up a big park, no matter where. I got onto it, and went about lookin' for land in that neighborhood.

"I could get nothin' at a bargain but a big piece of swamp, but I took it fast enough and held on to it. What turned out was just what I counted on. They couldn't make the park complete without Plunkitt's swamp, and they had to pay a good price for it. Anything dishonest in that?"

"Honesty isn't an issue...."

John W. Davis, who was running for President against Calvin Coolidge, announced that his policy would be "Honesty."

When Will Rogers heard that, he quipped, "Honesty isn't an issue in politics—it's a miracle."

"We can divide it into two parts."

Senator Sam Ervin used to tell the story about two party workers who visited a graveyard in the dead of night to take voters' names off tombstones.

One was reading the names, and the other was writing them down. The reader said, "Okay, here we have 'Sacred to the memory of Israel Sherinstein.'"

"Wait a minute," said the writer. "That's a long name. We can divide it into two parts. That'll give us two votes instead of one."

"'No, sir,'" the other said indignantly. "If I'm going to have anything to do with this, it's got to be honest."

"When I'm lying in bed...."

As Prime Minister of Canada, Pierre Elliott Trudeau was one of the more free-spirited politicians in high office. His answers to questions from interviewers were often refreshingly honest. Not for him the weasel words of the average hack.

A student once asked him, "But tell me, what does Pierre Trudeau really think about the problems of the Canadian economy when he's lying in bed at night."

Trudeau replied, "When I'm lying in bed at night, I really don't think about the problems of the Canadian economy."

"A pat on the back for being honest?"

When Mayor Ed Koch of New York met with city inspectors in Brooklyn, a woman in the audience told him that honest workers should get a pat on the back.

Hizzoner bristled. "A pat on the back for being honest?" he answered. "That's ridiculous. We demand that."

Quote/Unquote

Cardinal Richelieu (1585–1642)

Give me six lines of an honest man's biography and I will destroy him.

Thomas Jefferson (1743–1826)

Men are disposed to live honestly if the means of doing so are open to them.

Finley Peter Dunne (1867–1936)

I pretind ivry man is honest, and I believe none iv them ar-re. In that way I keep me friends an' save me money.

Herbert Hoover (1874–1964)

No public man can be just a little crooked.

HUMILITY

"To think that I attempted...."

Charles V served as Holy Roman Emperor for most of his adult life. After the Peace of Augsburg in 1555, which acknowledged the success of the Reformation, Charles abdicated and retired to a monastery. For several weeks he spent his leisure time trying to synchronize two clocks. He found it all but impossible. After repeated failures, Charles said to his assistant:

"To think that I attempted to force the reason and conscience of thousands of men into one mold, and I cannot make two clocks agree!"

"Hey, Carpenter Pieter...."

When Peter the Great, Tsar of Russia, began his European tour on March 19, 1697, no Russian ruler had visited Western Europe in six centuries. Peter planned to travel incognito as Peter Mikhailov, a bombardier, or artilleryman.

In Holland he worked for a few months as a common laborer on the East India Wharf in Zaandam. Once when an English visitor asked to see the Tsar of

Muscovy, the master shipwright shouted, "Hey Carpenter Pieter, why don't you give your comrades a hand?" The sweating tsar obediently put down his saw and hurried to help some men who were trying to lift a large timber.

"No man... should... accept a degree...."

Millard Fillmore, the 13th President of the United States, had plenty to be modest about—as Winston Churchill once said of Clement Atlee, the British Labor Party leader.

Fillmore accomplished little in the Presidency, and he knew it. He was neither brilliant nor well educated. When Oxford University offered him an honorary degree, he turned it down. He felt that people might joke about it. "Who's Fillmore?" they would ask.

The Oxford degree, he knew, would be in Latin, and that in itself was a reason to refuse it. "No man," said Fillmore," should... accept a degree he cannot read."

"If elected, I shall be thankful...."

When Lincoln first ran for the Illinois state legislature, his opening speech was brief. Here it is:

"Gentlemen, fellow citizens: I presume you all know who I am. I am humble Abe Lincoln. I have been solicited by many friends to become a candidate for the legislature. My politics are short and sweet, like an old woman's dance. I am in favor of a National Bank. I am in favor of the internal improvement system, and a high protective tariff. These are my sentiments and political principles. If elected, I shall be thankful; if not, it will be all the same."

"I began to see what the great teachers...."

Most Americans knew that Franklin D. Roosevelt had been struck by polio. They knew he couldn't walk without assistance. When Roosevelt was out of public view, he was often carried from place to place.

The American people knew this—and yet in a way they didn't know it. FDR's campaign workers, assistants, and friends made every effort to keep his disability as inconspicuous as possible.

Louis Howe, one of the men closest to him, insisted that Roosevelt never be carried in public. But what if an unusual situation arose—one in which he simply had to be carried?

That situation arose during his campaign for Governor of New York. FDR was to speak in a small hall in the Yorkville section of Manhattan. The hall was so crowded that the only way Roosevelt could get to the stage was by means of a fire escape.

He either had to be hoisted into the building by his assistants or else pass up the speaking engagement. He elected to speak. Two men carried him up the fire escape, into the building, and to the platform. Once there, he balanced himself on his braces, took his son Jimmy's arm, and walked slowly to the podium.

Frances Perkins, who would later become his Secretary of Labor, saw the incident. She wrote, "I began to see what the great teachers of religion meant when they said that humility is the greatest of virtues, and that if you can't learn it, God will teach it to you by humiliation."

FDR's press secretary, Steve Early, went even further. He claimed that polio and paralysis in effect changed Roosevelt from a playboy into a President.

"...the taller the bamboo grows...."

Carlos Romulo of the Philippines, while president of the UN General Assembly, used to tell this story about a youthful experience of his.

He had just won a high school oratorical contest in Manila. Pleased with his victory, he shook the hands of many parents. But he ignored the congratulations of one of the other contestants.

His father asked, "Why didn't you shake hands with Julio?"

Romulo said that he had no use for Julio, who had been ridiculing him before the contest.

Romulo's father put his arm around his son's shoulder and said, "Your grandfather used to tell me that the taller the bamboo grows, the lower it bends. Remember that always, my boy."

And he did remember it. He tried to use that lesson in humility as a guiding principle in his life.

"There is an epitaph in Boothill...."

President Harry S Truman has become something of a folk hero in recent years. He is rated highly by some historians, although while in office he was generally unpraised and unpopular.

In a letter to his daughter Margaret, Harry Truman gave his own modest assessment of his Presidency:

"Your dad will never be reckoned among the great. But you can be sure he did his level best and gave all he had to his country. There is an epitaph in Boothill Cemetery in Tombstone, Arizona, which reads: 'Here lies Jack Williams; he done his damndest.' What more can a person do?"

Quote/Unquote

William Penn   (1644–1718)

No more lessen... thy merit than overrate it; for though humility be a virtue, an affected one is not.

Jefferson Davis   (1808–1889)

Never be haughty to the humble; never be humble to the haughty.

Abraham Lincoln   (1809–1865)

I fear that the great confidence placed in my ability is unfounded. Indeed, I am sure it is.

Golda Meir   (1898–1978)

Don't be humble. You're not that great.

INCONSISTENCY

"Effective suffrage—no reelection."

When Porfirio Díaz was elected President of Mexico in 1876, his campaign slogan was this: "Effective suffrage—no reelection." He then proceeded to rule his nation as a dictator for the next 35 years.

There is a postscript to the story. When Francisco Madero tried to run for President in 1910, more than three decades later, he adopted Díaz's old slogan: "Effective suffrage—no reelection."

The aging Díaz clapped him in jail.

"Don't let the guy bluff you, O'Rourke."

The municipal election in New York was close and hard-fought. It looked as if the Tammany ticket might lose. That couldn't be allowed to happen, of course, so a small army of repeaters—illegal voters—descended on a downtown voting place.

"Your name?" asked the election clerk of the first of these voters. The young man, who had freckles, red hair, a pug nose, and a black eye, glanced down at a slip of paper in his hand.

"Isadore Mendelbaum," he said carefully.

A challenger from the reform ticket looked the young man over and said, "That's not your name, now is it?"

"It is," insisted the repeater. "And I'm going to cast me vote."

A cigar-smoking Tammany Hall wheelhorse was standing nearby. He said in a loud voice: "Don't let the guy bluff you, O'Rourke. Soitin'ly your name is Mendelbaum."

"Was I a protectionist or a free trader...?"

If Arthur Balfour is remembered at all today, it is because of the Balfour Declaration, which gave official British approval to Zionism. Balfour, who was Prime Minister of Great Britain from 1902 to 1905, shouldn't be given too much credit for his pro-Zionism, though. Basically, he was an anti-Semite.

Balfour was born inconsistent and never changed. His motives in pushing the Balfour Declaration were mixed. The declaration itself was ambiguous. No one knew exactly what it meant. But that was Arthur Balfour for you.

Fourteen years earlier, as Prime Minister, Balfour had been embroiled in a knock-down tariff fight between protectionists and free traders. As usual he tried to walk a tightrope. He expressed contradictory views. When pressed to clarify his position, he produced what one opponent called "a hedge within a hedge." He refused to be pinned down. In fact, his arguments became so confusing that even he was puzzled by them.

Later, long after the fight was over, he asked his niece, "Was I a protectionist or a free trader in 1903?"

She replied, "That is what all the country wanted to find out."

"I have never said an unfriendly word...."

An Irish Catholic named Tim McGuire arose to give a speech at a gathering in Belfast. His goal was to help cool inflamed tempers in Northern Ireland.

He began: "I have never said an unfriendly word against Orangemen—misguided, bigoted, and besotted though they be."

"The South is dry...."

Prohibition seemed like a good idea at the time. But it didn't work, not even on the TV screen with Eliot Ness as a one-man strike force. Too many Americans wanted a drop or two of hooch. Bootlegging and speakeasies flourished from coast to coast. The nation went on a binge. The mob got rich.

Even as Prohibition was failing, there remained a surprising amount of local support for it, especially in the South.

"The South is dry and will stay dry," said Will Rogers in 1926. "That is, everybody sober enough to stagger to the polls will."

"If you don't shut up your claptrap...."

The Longs of Louisiana knew how to garner votes. They had mastered the art of saying one thing while meaning something else. Sometimes their inconsistency served a good purpose, as when they pushed various reform measures.

Other times, the inconsistency was just there. Take the 1960 Louisiana primary in which Huey's younger brother Earl tried to win a third term as governor. He was speaking in Alexandria, Louisiana, where a sign above the speaker's platform read, "GOVERNOR LONG SPEAKS." At the bottom of the sign was a curious notice that read, "Nothing will be said to offend or hurt anyone."

A.J. Liebling, the journalist, was writing a piece that year for *The New Yorker* magazine on the redoubtable Earl of Louisiana. Liebling arrived late in Alexandria, and the first words he heard were from an obviously irate governor. Long was shouting, "If you don't shut up your claptrap, I'm going to have you forcibly removed. You just nothing but a common hoodlum and a heckler."

Maybe Long hoped that would quiet the man without offending or hurting him. But it didn't. The man, a local lawyer, kept right on needling the governor.

Long thundered again: "Mr. Gravel, I got nothing against you personally. Now you keep quiet and I won't mention your name. If you don't, I'll have you removed as a common damn nuisance."

Later, Long confided to the crowd that, "He used to be a nice fellow, but now he just a goddamned hoodlum."

And so it went. The sign over Earl Long's platform was almost correct. The governor said nothing to offend or hurt anyone—anyone, that is, except Mr. Camille Gravel, and that sapsucker may have been asking for it.

"Maybe I was wrong then...."

Politicians often give tortured explanations of why they took one position a couple of years ago and now take exactly the opposite position. They sense that this kind of inconsistency gives their enemies aid, comfort, and ammunition.

Maybe they should think again. Joseph Spainhour, a political leader Sam Ervin knew from his early days in Morganton, North Carolina, had a better way. Instead of trying to tiptoe around an inconsistency, Spainhour would say, "Maybe I was wrong then, but I'm right now."

"Nixon is the kind of politician...."

It was said of Adlai Stevenson that he was too witty to be elected President. His toughest problem, though, was probably that he ran twice "against Ivory soap"—which is to say, against Dwight D. Eisenhower.

Stevenson aimed a lot of barbs at General Ike and later at Barry Goldwater, but his favorite target was always Richard M. Nixon. He accused Nixon of a variety of sins, among them the sin of inconsistency. He said, "Nixon is the kind of politician who would cut down a redwood tree, then mount the stump for a speech on conservation."

...they were going to vote for Reagan anyway.

After the overwhelming defeat of the Ferraro-Mondale ticket in 1984, Geraldine Ferraro sat down to write a book about the lopsided race. She remained as frustrated after the election as she had been during it. She couldn't understand her party's inability to get its message across to the American people.

"Every poll we took," she wrote, "showed that many of the voters were with us on the major issues"—but they were going to vote for Reagan anyway. The President's personal popularity made him hard to attack, and his theme of optimism played well nationally.

When Ferraro pointed out the huge disparity between Reagan's 1980 balanced-budget promises and the mushrooming deficit, she would joke, "Well, folks, he's only a quarter of a trillion dollars off."

No one seemed to care—or else, with some justification, they blamed Congress. Ferraro concluded sadly, "It was hard for people to sense a risk to their future when the present seemed so rosy."

Quote/Unquote

Seneca   (4 B.C.–65 A.D.)

We are mad, not only individually but nationally. We check manslaughter and isolated murders; but what of war and the much vaunted crime of slaughtering whole peoples?

James Russell Lowell   (1819–1891)

This imputation of inconsistency is one to which every sound politician and every honest thinker must sooner or later subject himself. The foolish and the dead alone never change their opinions.

Artemus Ward   (1834–1867)

Let us all be happy, and live within our means, even if we have to borrer money to do it with.

Winston Churchill   (1874–1965)

Few people practice what they preach, and no one less so than Mr. [George] Bernard Shaw.

Morris K. Udall   (1922–   )

If you're looking for world-class examples of fickleness, politicians are the ones to study.

Ron Ziegler (1939–   )

> If my answers sound confusing, I think they are confusing because the questions are confusing, and the situation is confusing, and I'm not in a position to clarify it.

INNOVATION

"We might as well require a man...."

America's Founding Fathers are so revered today that we tend to forget their true natures. They were revolutionaries, and they often talked that way. Thomas Jefferson for instance, was a student of history, but he wasn't awed by the wisdom of those who had gone before.

Jefferson said: "Some men look at constitutions with sanctimonious reverence, and deem them like the ark of the covenant, too sacred to be touched. They ascribe to the men of the preceding age of wisdom more than human, and suppose what they did to be beyond amendment. We might as well require a man to wear the coat that fitted him as a boy, as civilized society to remain ever under the regime of their ancestors."

One cat romped home within five hours.

Homing pigeons were used as letter-carriers during World War One. But how about enlisting cats for the same job?

Back in 1877 someone in Belgium dreamed up the idea of using cats to make mail deliveries. The theory was that since cats have a superb homing instinct, they could be used to carry important letters.

A society was formed to promote the idea. As a test, the group put 37 cats from Liege in a gunnysack, took the cats 20 miles outside of town, and released them. One cat romped home within five hours. All 37 of them made it back within 24 hours.

It was an impressive showing, but the idea never caught on.

"What good is this?"

British Prime Minister Benjamin Disraeli was shown a dynamo by its inventor, Michael Faraday.

Disraeli, a brilliant politician but no scientist, was puzzled by the prototype of all later generators.

"What good is this?" he asked.
Replied Faraday, "What good is a baby."

Smith and Roosevelt did shake hands....

Alfred E. Smith and Franklin D. Roosevelt were powerful New York State politicos who had a falling out in the early 1930s. Al Smith was disgruntled at having lost the Presidential election of 1928 at the same time Roosevelt was winning the governorship of New York. Smith personally opposed FDR's nomination for President four years later.

When Roosevelt won the nomination in 1932 despite Smith's opposition, a reconciliation seemed in order. Both men were expected to attend the New York State Democratic convention at Madison Square Garden, New York City. It would be an ideal occasion to patch up their differences, the party stalwarts thought.

Smith and Roosevelt did shake hands on the platform at Madison Square Garden, and Smith supposedly said to his victorious rival, "Hello, you old potato." At least that's what the press reported.

The public took the greeting to their hearts. Why, it seemed just like plain old Al Smith, that gutsy, folksy Happy Warrior from the Lower East Side. "Hello, you old potato." Perfect! Maybe it didn't mean much, but it seemed to symbolize the happy days that the Democrats hoped were here again.

There was one problem, though. Some time after this friendly greeting was reported, Fred Storm of the United Press admitted he had made it up. Al Smith did say *something* on the platform all right, but no one could hear what it was. So reporter Storm took the liberty of inventing an appropriate remark.

"The first is freedom of speech and expression...."

Franklin D. Roosevelt and his aides were working on the fourth draft of the President's annual message to Congress. As they were completing their work, FDR announced that he had an idea for a peroration. He leaned back in his swivel chair and stared for a long time at the ceiling.

Then he dictated to his secretary a memorized text that began: "We must look forward to a world based on four essential human freedoms.

"The first is freedom of speech and expression—everywhere in the world.

The second is freedom of every person to worship God in his own way—everywhere in the world."

The last two freedoms—freedom from want and freedom from fear—were explained in somewhat greater detail.

Roosevelt asked his advisers for their thoughts on the peroration. Harry Hopkins wondered about "everywhere in the world." Did Americans really care about Java, for example? But he didn't argue strenuously, and the phrase stayed. No one seemed too excited about it, or about the "Four Freedoms" generally.

The part of the speech they really liked, according to Sam Rosenman, who was there, dealt with American executives who wanted to do business with Hitler at the expense of national security. Writer Robert Sherwood contributed the following sentence to the annual message of January 6, 1941:

"We must especially beware of that small group of selfish men who would clip the wings of the American eagle in order to feather their own nests."

Rosenman thought this sentence would become an immediate, widely quoted hit. But no one seemed to notice it—while the Four Freedoms statement became one of the classic expressions of American ideals and aims.

"...permit me to tax your memories...."

A Republican member of a Congressional bipartisan committee was trying to make a point. "Gentlemen," he said, "permit me to tax your memories for a moment."

"Ah!" murmured one Democratic member to another. "Why didn't we think of that?"

Quote/Unquote

Niccolò Machiavelli (1469–1527)

There is nothing more difficult to take in hand, more perilous to conduct, or more uncertain in its success, than to take the lead in the introduction of a new order of things.

John Locke (1632–1704)

New opinions are always suspected, and usually opposed, without any other reason but because they are not already common.

Joseph Addison (1672–1719)

When men are easy in their circumstances, they are naturally enemies to innovations.

Thomas Jefferson   (1743–1826)

Great innovations should not be forced on slender majorities.

Thomas Carlyle   (1795–1881)

Every new opinion, at its starting, is precisely in a minority of one.

Calvin Coolidge   (1872–1933)

Promises and good intentions are not enough. We cannot afford rash experiments.

INTELLIGENCE

"If the tariff is too high...."

H.L. Mencken, the caustic journalist of the 1920s, once said, "No one ever went broke underestimating the intelligence of the American people."

It's good for a politician to keep that in mind, too. In an election for Governor of Tennessee, one of the candidates was James K. Polk, later to become the 12th President of the United States. Polk made a long, well-researched, and boring speech on the subject of the tariff.

His opponent was James C. Jones, better known as "Lean Jimmy Jones." Lean Jimmy was no orator and no intellectual either. But he knew that the Tennessee voters' interest in the tariff was a lot less ardent than Polk's.

He said, "My friends, this tariff question is really not the intricate matter it has been represented; in fact, it is as simple as the alphabet. Now, what would I do in regard to the tariff? Why simply this: If the tariff is too high, I'd lower it; but if it was too low I'd hist it."

Mencken would hardly be surprised to learn that Lean Jimmy Jones carried the day and won the election.

"Intelligence is not all that important...."

Henry Kissinger, a highly intelligent man, doubted the need for exceptional intelligence in either leadership or diplomacy. He said, "Intelligence is not all that important in the exercise of power and is often, in point of fact, useless. Just as a leader doesn't need intelligence, a man in my job doesn't need too much of it either."

Although Kissinger later became Secretary of State, at the time he made this statement he was President Nixon's adviser for national security affairs.

Quote/Unquote

Marcus Tullius Cicero (106–43 B.C.)

Intelligence and reflection and judgment reside in old men, and if there had been none of them, no states could exist at all.

Robert G. Ingersoll (1833–1899)

There is no slavery but ignorance. Liberty is the child of intelligence.

Harry S Truman (1884–1972)

The "C" students run the world.

Joseph Goebbels (1897–1945)

I can reckon with the wickedness of men, but their stupidity is often incomprehensible.

Pierre Elliott Trudeau (1919–)

Let us overthrow the totems, break the taboos. Or better, let us consider them cancelled. Coldly, let us be intelligent.

INTENSITY

"I never quarrel, sir."

One of the great Senators in the era of Clay, Calhoun, and Webster was Thomas Hart Benton of Missouri. Benton was a foe and later a friend of Andrew Jackson. He was a man about whom Theodore Roosevelt would one day write a book.

Benton, whose hard-money stand earned him the nickname of "Old Bullion," had a well-earned reputation for toughness. He was no stranger to duelling, having killed a man in St. Louis in 1817.

"Mr. President," he once said on the floor of the Senate, "I never quarrel, sir. But sometimes I fight, sir, and whenever I fight, sir, a funeral follows."

That vote was unacceptable to Asa T. Soule....

Political arguments often get overheated, but usually they stop short of armed conflict. A hundred years ago, during the wild land boom beyond the Mississippi, things were not so civilized. Bloody clashes occurred in what are known as the County Seat Wars.

County Seat Wars? Does that sound a bit silly? Well, it wasn't in the 1880s, not to the people involved. It was dead serious—with the accent on dead.

The most famous of the County Seat Wars occurred in Gray County, Kansas, in 1889. The good citizens of Gray County had peaceably voted to make Cimarron the county seat. That vote was unacceptable to Asa T. Soule, whose home (and sizable real-estate investments) were in the little town of Ingalls, Kansas. Soule saw that he had backed the wrong boom town—and he decided to reverse the decision.

According to the law of the day, possession of the county court records determined the location of the county seat. All a mover and shaker like Asa T. Soule had to do to change the county seat was to steal the records from one town and move them to another.

No problem. Soule put up $1000 and asked Sheriff Bill Tilghman to deputize some hired guns to make off with the records housed in Cimarron. Neal Brown and a couple of the Masterson boys were among those who signed on.

They almost got away with it, but a Cimarron resident spotted them late in the game and aroused his neighbors. Before you could say "Bill Tilghman," four of the hired invaders from Ingalls bit the dust. Their corpses, along with the court records, were tossed in a wagon and hurried back to Ingalls.

But the Mastersons and Neal Brown were trapped in the courthouse. A gun battle consumed the whole next day. During it, the news of the standoff reached Denver, where big Bat Masterson hung out. Bat let it be known that if the trio, including two Mastersons, weren't released pronto, a whole new gang of gunmen would descend on Cimarron. At that, the trapped three were allowed to leave under a flag of truce.

Note well: Asa T. Soule won the battle. Ingalls, not Cimarron, became the county seat of Gray County, Kansas. A later election changed it back again—today's county seat is Cimarron, with about 900 people—but back then tiny Ingalls won. The law on the frontier truly came out of the barrel of a gun.

"The audience acted like a trained choir...."

The high drama of the Democratic national convention of 1896 has seldom been equaled. William Jennings Bryan, a young, out-of-office politician from

Nebraska, delivered a speech that nearly carried him to the White House. It was the famous "Cross of Gold" speech, thrilling and irresistible, delivered in a magnificent voice that sent many delegates into near hysteria.

Later the myth grew that Bryan's speech was fresh and unrehearsed. Far from it. He had given almost the same speech, with the same stirring phrases, in Congress in 1894 and then up and down the Mississippi Valley for almost two years. It had been effective in the West. It was dynamite to the assembled delegates in Chicago. Bryan himself was stunned by the effect of the speech. "The audience acted like a trained choir," he wrote later. "I noted how instantaneously and in unison they responded to each point made."

Bryan's pitch was for free silver and against the gold standard. Few voters, and probably few delegates, really knew what Bryan was proposing. He may not have known it very well himself. But as historian Dixon Wecter pointed out, the phrase "free silver" had "a real selling potency. It seemed to promise something for nothing." Who could resist that? Certainly not the delegates at the Democratic national convention.

Bryan's final sentence has echoed down the years as one of the most memorable statements in American politics. Wecter called the whole speech "full of mixed platitudes and bad logic," possibly even "blasphemous." True enough, but it roused the delegates to a fever pitch.

Bryan concluded: "You shall not press down upon the brow of labor this crown of thorns, you shall not crucify mankind upon a cross of gold."

The crowd went crazy. The demonstration that followed could well be the model for all the fake-spontaneous demonstrations in all the conventions that followed. It lasted nearly an hour. And it was genuinely spontaneous.

Bryan went on to win the Presidential nomination but lose the election. From the moment of his defeat he entered into a decline in promise, prestige, and popularity that is unparalleled in American history. When Bryan delivered his "Cross of Gold" speech in 1896, he was a shining hero to working class Americans. When he died in 1925—after Clarence Darrow had humiliated him in the Scopes' "Monkey Trial"—his promise, his prestige, and his popularity had all fled.

"Give 'em hell, Carter!"

Senator Carter Glass of Virginia usually spoke in a slow and rather cold manner. But one day the subject of his talk aroused his emotions. He began to sound excited and angry.

"Give 'em hell, Carter!" shouted one of his supporters.

"Hell?" said Glass in a milder tone. "Why use dynamite when insect powder will do?"

"...I still find myself wedded to the marigold...."

Even political opponents of Illinois Senator Everett Dirksen found themselves charmed, or at least amused, by the Senator's never-ending, never-successful fight to make the marigold the national flower.

A great many words and a good deal of passion went into Dirksen's perennial plea for the marigold. Here is an excerpt from one of his speeches:

"Two or three years ago, I introduced a joint resolution to make the marigold the national flower. That stirred quite a controversy; and, as a result, the corn tassel and the rose and other flowers were advanced as candidates for our national floral emblem. But I still find myself wedded to the marigold—robust, rugged, bright, stately, single-colored and multicolored, somehow able to resist the onslaught of insects; it takes in its stride extreme changes in temperature, and fights back the scorching sun of summer and the chill of early spring evenings. What a flower the marigold is!...

"So once again I find myself impelled to introduce a joint resolution to make the American marigold... the national flower of our country."

Clare Boothe Luce had two careers....

Clare Boothe Luce had two careers—one as a playwright, one as a diplomat. Or really three, if you want to consider her marriage to Time, Inc. founder Henry Luce an occupation in itself. In any case, she was a remarkable woman, with a remarkably sharp tongue. About a heated political campaign she said, "The politicians were talking themselves red, white and blue in the face."

"When Cicero finished an oration...."

John F. Kennedy and Adlai Stevenson were both excellent speakers, although their speaking styles were different. Stevenson compared his style to that of the classical orator Cicero—Kennedy's to that of Demosthenes.

"When Cicero finished an oration," said Stevenson, "the people would say, 'How well he spoke.' Ah, but when Demosthenes finished speaking, the people would say, 'Let us march!'"

"The nation cries out...."

Not long before Ronald Reagan announced his candidacy for President, he made a speech in New York City.

He was introduced by Barry Gray, a New York radio personality, who proclaimed, "The nation cries out for desperate leadership."

Quote/Unquote

Karl von Clausewitz (1780–1831)

War is the continuation of politics by other means.

George Bernard Shaw (1856–1950)

Nothing is ever done in this world until men are prepared to kill one another if it is not done.

George Santayana (1863–1952)

Fanaticism consists in redoubling your efforts when you have forgotten your aim.

Mahatma Gandhi (1869–1948)

There is more to life than increasing its speed.

Winston Churchill (1874–1965)

A fanatic is one who can't change his mind and won't change the subject.

Harry S Truman (1884–1972)

If you can't stand the heat, stay out of the kitchen.

Dwight D. Eisenhower (1890–1969)

What counts is not necessarily the size of the dog in the fight—it is the size of the fight in the dog.

Russell Baker (1925–   )

There are no liberals behind steering wheels.

· J ·

JOURNALISM

The critics of Lincoln's own day....

Lincoln's *Gettysburg Address* appears in all the high school literature anthologies. Most Americans consider it to be one of the best speeches ever written. Short as it is, teachers find a great many stylistic virtues in it.

The critics of Lincoln's own day were not so kind. In *The Book of Insults, Ancient and Modern*, Nancy McPhee quotes a review from the *Chicago Times*:

"...We did not conceive it possible that even Mr. Lincoln would produce a paper so slipshod, so loose-jointed, so puerile, not alone in literary construction, but in its ideas, its sentiments, its grasp. He has outdone himself. He has literally come out of the little end of his own horn. By the side of it, mediocrity is superb."

Well, that was then and this is now. But the comparison is striking. Did journalists like this one actually read the *Gettysburg Address* before jumping into print with comments on it? Or did they just follow their political leanings and assume it was terrible?

"...thank God! the/British journalist."

From Over the Fire
by Humbert Wolfe

You cannot hope
   to bribe or twist,
thank God! the
   British journalist.

But, seeing what
  the man will do
unbribed, there's
  no occasion to.

"I wonder how many such 'well researched' facts...?"

In his autobiography, Emery Kelen, a political cartoonist, tells this story of a bogus headline by a bogus journalist:

It seems that a Budapest newspaper, *Az Est*, had hired a law student to cover the news from Geneva, Switzerland. When Count Apponyi, the Hungarian delegate to the League of Nations died in Geneva, the law student decided to embellish the event. The count, he felt, should have uttered some inspiring last words.

So he made some up. The next day *Az Est*, Hungary's leading newspaper, carried in enormous headlines the ringing exit line of Count Apponyi:

"Hungarians! Hold the Line! Victory Is in Sight!"

The law student was quickly fired for the hoax. He died in an insane asylum. But the headline in Hungary's newspaper of record is there for future researchers to find and use.

Kelen concludes sadly: "I wonder how many such 'well researched' facts have wiggled their way into history books?"

"You don't need to muzzle...."

Aneurin Bevan, the British Labour Party's most brilliant orator, opposed censorship of the press even during World War Two. It wasn't that he admired British journalism. Quite the contrary. He had little use for what he called the 'kept' press. But he saw no reason to fear or censor it. "You don't need to muzzle sheep," he said.

"And these, gentlemen, are the conclusions...."

Most politicians come to dislike the press. Even Adlai Stevenson, who had a highly favorable press, expressed some reservations about journalists and commentators. He thought many of them wrote from a personal viewpoint. They chose or slanted facts to fit that viewpoint, rather than trying to discover the whole truth.

Stevenson told the story of an old lawyer who followed the same practice. In his summation to the jury, the lawyer said, "And these, gentlemen, are the conclusions on which I base my facts."

"...their reporters file the Bible...."

When Ben Bradlee was Washington bureau chief for *Newsweek*, he had a close relationship with President John F. Kennedy. In his book, *Conversations with Kennedy*, Bradlee provides some insight into how the President viewed the press.

JFK related to Bradlee the comment that Romulo Betancourt, the President of Venezuela, had made about rival newsmagazine *Time*. Betancourt had great respect for *Time*'s correspondents in Latin America. But he was disappointed in the stories that appeared in the magazine.

According to Kennedy, Betancourt said, "The trouble is, their reporters file the Bible to New York, and the magazine prints the Koran."

...politicians and journalists are natural adversaries....

No President ever enjoyed better relations with the press than John F. Kennedy. Nevertheless, politicians and journalists are natural adversaries, and not everything that appeared in print pleased the 35th President.

At an Inter-American Press Association meeting in Miami Beach, Kennedy remarked that two of the guests were "former Prime Ministers of Peru and are now publishers of newspapers."

He concluded: "It does suggest to those who hold office that when the time comes... as they say in the United States, if you can't beat them, join them."

"...NBC has a peculiar form of editorializing."

By 1968 television flackery was a well-developed art form. Joe McGinniss's book, *The Selling of the President 1968*, is by now ancient history. But some of the lessons it teaches about television reporting (as well as advertising) are timeless.

In making a TV commercial Richard Nixon's men used clips from the CBS tape of the acceptance speech. "Better camera angles," one of them explained. "And besides," he added, "NBC has a peculiar form of editorializing. For instance, they'll cut to some young colored guy who's not applauding while Nixon talks of bridges to human dignity."

"There will be no West Coast interest...."

Ah, Watergate!

The press, especially the Washington *Post*, earned many plaudits for its investigative reporting of the strange affair that brought down President Nixon. A book was written. A movie was made.

But the story was very slow to break. Nixon managed to coast to an easy second-term victory between the time of the actual break-in and the time of reckoning.

Top journalists didn't recognize the potential of the story. The owner of the San Francisco *Chronicle* turned down syndication rights. It seemed like a trivial incident at the Democratic national headquarters in Washington. Who needed it?

"There will be no West Coast interest in the story," the owner of the *Chronicle* declared.

Quote/Unquote

Charles A. Dana   (1819–1897)

Journalism consists in buying white paper at 2 cents a pound and selling it at 10 cents a pound.

Henry Adams   (1838–1918)

The newspapers discussed little else than the alleged moral laxity of Grant, Garfield, and Blaine.... In spite of all such criticism, the public nominated Grant, Garfield, and Blaine, and voted for them afterwards....

George Bernard Shaw   (1856–1950)

Newspapers are unable, seemingly, to discriminate between a bicycle accident and the collapse of civilization.

Walter Lippmann   (1889–1974)

As the free press develops, the paramount point is whether the journalist, like the scientist or scholar, puts truth in the first place or in the second.

Harold J. Laski   (1893–1950)

A people without reliable news is, sooner or later, a people without the basis of freedom.

Richard J. Daley   (1902–1976)

There is nothing more immoral than a newspaperman.

Richard M. Nixon   (1913–   )

The media are far more powerful than the President in creating public awareness and shaping public opinion, for the simple reason that the media always have the last word.

Hodding Carter III   (1935–   )

The mass media in America have an overwhelming tendency to jump up and down and bark in concert whenever the White House—any White House—snaps its fingers.

JUSTICE

These two local champions....

In colonial times the Connecticut towns of Lyme and New London both claimed the same small piece of land. The matter seemed too trivial to take before the colonial legislature, so the two towns reached a rough-and-ready solution. Each town would choose two bareknuckle sluggers to fight it out. These two local champions met on the appointed day at the appointed place. The result was that Griswold and Ely of Lyme administered a sound thrashing to Ricket and Latimer of New London. As previously agreed, Lyme took possession of the parcel of land.

"...advised large classes to commit murder."

In theory everyone wants justice, but in practice the scales often tip too far one way or the other. Today the common complaint is that courts are too lenient, that judges favor the defendant over the victim. It was not always so.

More than a hundred years ago the Haymarket bombing outraged the citizens of Chicago. A small crowd had been listening to some rather mild anarchist talk when a platoon of police moved in. One of the leaders of the demonstration shouted, "We are peaceable!" But almost immediately someone threw a bomb—to this day no one knows who. Seven policemen were killed or fatally wounded. More than 40 others were injured.

A wave of fear and rage swept over Chicago. Ten anarchists were quickly indicted. Two were released for lack of evidence. The other eight went on trial for murder. Jury members were chosen who admitted having read about the affair and having formed strong opinions. The judge showed little regard for the rights of the accused.

No one could identify the bomb thrower. The judge said it didn't matter. The anarchists had "generally by both speech and print advised large classes to commit murder." That was enough. All eight were convicted.

Four were hanged. One committed suicide. The remaining three languished in jail until 1893. In June of that year John P. Altgeld, Governor of Illinois, pardoned the three men, calling their trial a farce. The press condemned Governor Altgeld.

But one person who praised the Governor for his courage was Vachel Lindsay, the poet. Lindsay called Altgeld the "eagle forgotten." An extreme liberal for his time, Altgeld is regarded today as a champion of individual liberty. Lindsay wrote:

The others that mourned you in silence and terror and truth,
The widow bereft of her crust, and the boy without youth,
The mocked and the scorned and the wounded, the lame and the poor
That should have remembered forever,... remember no more.

"A legislature trembling before five men...."

Few Americans have had more distinguished careers in public life than Charles Evans Hughes. Elected Governor of New York just after the turn of the century, Hughes went on to become Secretary of State and Chief Justice of the U.S. Supreme Court. In 1916 he ran for President against the highly regarded incumbent, Woodrow Wilson, and nearly won. The final electoral vote was 277 for Wilson, 254 for Hughes.

Yet nothing in Hughes's long and illustrious life showed more clearly his passion for justice than something he did as a concerned private citizen—as a volunteer. The year was 1920, and the so-called Red Scare was at its peak. After the First World War, a surprising wave of intolerance struck the nation. Radicals, or people suspected of being radicals, were arrested without cause and held incommunicado. Homes were searched without warrants; property was seized.

Even the New York State legislature got into the act. There were, and had been for some time, five Socialist Party members in the Assembly. At the beginning of the 1920 session, the five Socialists were summoned to the legislature, denied their seats by the Speaker pending an investigation, and escorted from the chamber by the sergeant-at-arms.

When Hughes, a lawyer and a private citizen, heard of this, he could hardly believe it. These five men had been elected by their districts and had served prior terms in the Assembly. Hughes sat down and wrote a scathing letter to the Assembly Speaker. He could not imagine, he said, how the elected representatives of a legal political party could be tossed out of the legislature in such a fashion. He fumed, "This is not, in my judgment, American government."

Next he went to Albany to appear before the Assembly Judiciary Committee, where the Socialists were "on trial." In his testimony he said, "It reminds me of the English State trials in the sixteenth and seventeenth centuries.... We have passed beyond the stage in political development when heresy-hunting is a permitted sport."

In fact, Hughes was wrong. The legislature promptly expelled the Socialists and outlawed the Socialist Party. But Hughes had made his point, and if the legislature didn't listen, the nation as a whole did.

A Harvard professor of law at the time wrote, "A legislature trembling before five men—the long-lost American sense of humor revived and the people began to laugh. That broke the spell." Hughes had lost the battle but won the war. His voice played a major part in ending the excesses of the Red Scare.

"He has given the crane a long, slim neck. ..."

Many years ago a Democratic Congressman from Arkansas, Samuel W. Peel, gave a speech in which he attacked a bill that he felt would benefit bankers and brokers but hurt the working class.

Peel compared bankers and brokers to long-legged cranes in his tongue-in-cheek conclusion. He said: "Mr. Chairman, it reminds me of the boy's answer to his father after he had given him a graphic description of the goodness of God in the formation of the crane.

"'See how good and wise the Lord is,' the father said. 'He has given the crane a long, slim neck, a long, sharp bill, long legs, and a broad web foot. With his long legs he can wade in the water, with his broad web foot he can hold down the fish until he reaches down with his long neck and sharp bill and takes him in for food.'"

Although the boy was much impressed, he had a nagging feeling that there were two sides to the matter.

"'Yes, Dad,' he said, 'it's mighty nice for the crane, but it's hell on the fish.'"

"We can't see him back here!"

Near the end of World War Two, Benito Mussolini and his mistress, Clara Petacci, died before a firing squad of Italian partisans. The dictator who "made Italy's trains run on time" had little success in World War Two. By 1945 not much sympathy remained for him in his devastated country.

After the execution, Mussolini's body and Clara's were trucked to Milan and dumped on top of the corpses of 17 other Fascists. The people of Milan crowded the square to see their fallen leader. An eager partisan tried holding Mussolini's body aloft for viewing, but voices cried, "Higher! We can't see him back here."

Finally, some partisans tied ropes around the ankles of both bodies and hoisted them from lampposts. They were later cut down and tossed in the gutter to be spat upon. On May first Il Duce and his mistress were buried in a pauper's plot in Milan.

Mussolini had pronounced his own epitaph 13 years earlier when he said, "Everyone dies the death befitting his character."

"Son, I hate to do this...."

Vice President Alben W. Barkley was a strong believer in justice for witnesses hailed before Congressional investigating committees. Writing just after the Joe McCarthy era, he still had vivid memories of witnesses being subjected to the browbeating of Tail-gunner Joe.

Such a witness is almost helpless, the Vice President said. He is like the boy who is being brutally whipped by his father. Between blows his father grunts, "Son, I hate to do this to you. I'm only doing it because I love you."

The son replies, "I sure wish I was big enough to return your affection!"

"(Expletive deleted), get it."

Watergate made the phrase "expletive deleted" famous. In most of the taped conversations the deletions were just that: expletives—obscene or profane expressions. But one of the "expletive deleted"s went to the very heart of the case.

President Nixon, Bob Haldeman, and John Dean were discussing how to guarantee the silence of Howard Hunt, a deeply involved White House "plumber." Hunt, a cagey character with none of the loyalty of G. Gordon Liddy and others, was demanding $120,000 plus an assurance of clemency to keep him from talking to prosecutors about the plumbers' activities.

The White House gave the special prosecutor the following transcript version of Nixon's words:

"(Expletive deleted), get it. In a way that—who is going to talk to Colson? He is the one who is supposed to know him?"

Nixon's lawyers argued that this edited statement proved nothing. The President was merely exploring his options. Although cynics thought that even the doctored statement was fairly damning, most people continued to withhold judgment. It *was* hard to figure out just what Nixon meant.

And then the House Judiciary Committee got the actual tapes. What Nixon said between those parentheses left very little room for doubt. He said:

"Well, for Christ's sakes, get it."

When Leon Jaworski, the special prosecutor, heard Nixon's direct order on tape, he said, "I'm afraid the President engaged in criminal conduct."

Jaworski was right, and within a few days Richard Nixon, facing almost certain impeachment and conviction, resigned the Presidency.

"Americans would memorialize this historic event...."

When G. Gordon Liddy, one of the Watergate conspirators, appeared before Senator Sam Ervin's committee in 1973, he was asked the routine question, "Do you solemnly swear to tell the truth, the whole truth, and nothing but the truth, so help you God?"

Liddy answered, "No."

It was the perfect capstone for this whole improbable affair, a comic extravaganza that had begun on June 17, 1972, with the bungled break-in at the headquarters of the Democratic National Committee in the Watergate apartment complex in Washington, D.C.

Before it was over, President Richard M. Nixon had been forced to resign from office, and most of the President's men were on their way to jail.

Art Buchwald suggested commemorating the date of the break-in and the arrest of five Watergate conspirators as a national holiday. In his words, "Americans would memorialize this historic event by taping other people's doors, tapping telephones, spying on their neighbors, wearing red wigs, and making inoperative statements."

Quote/Unquote

Benjamin Disraeli   (1804–1881)

Justice is truth in action.

Abraham Lincoln   (1809–1865)

A jury too frequently has at least one member more ready to hang the panel than to hang the traitor.

Clarence Darrow   (1857–1938)

There is no such thing as justice in or out of court.

H.L. Mencken   (1880–1956)

Injustice is relatively easy to bear; what stings is justice.

Eleanor Roosevelt   (1884–1962)

Justice cannot be for one side alone, but must be for both.

Lyndon B. Johnson   (1908–1973)

Until justice is blind to color, until education is unaware of race, until opportunity is unconcerned with the color of men's skins, emancipation will be a proclamation but not a fact.

Martin Luther King, Jr.   (1929–1968)

Injustice anywhere is a threat to justice everywhere.

· L ·

LANGUAGE

"The learned fool writes...."

In his later years Benjamin Franklin was a consummate diplomat, as much admired in France and England as he was in the United States. He was viewed as both a down-home philosopher and a master politician.

Franklin retained the skepticism and pithy good sense of "Poor Richard" all his life. He once said, "The learned fool writes his nonsense in better language than the unlearned, but it is still nonsense."

"You replace Monsieur Franklin?"

In 1785 Thomas Jefferson arrived in Paris to represent the U.S. government. He presented himself to the French minister of foreign affairs.

"You replace Monsieur Franklin?" the foreign minister said.

"I *succeed* him," Jefferson replied. "No one can replace him."

"...if Mr. Gladstone were to fall into the Thames...."

Somebody once asked Benjamin Disraeli to define the difference between a misfortune and a calamity. Disraeli, one of the sharpest wits in British politics, invoked the name of his great rival, William Gladstone, in his explanation.

"Well," Disraeli said, "if Mr. Gladstone were to fall into the Thames, that would be a misfortune. But if anyone were to pull him out, that would be a calamity."

117

"We'll shout for our man...."

Campaign rhymesters sometimes like to work the name of the Vice Presidential candidate into their verses. It can be tough when the nominee has a name like Ferraro or Agnew, and in such cases the rhymester usually turns to other possibilities.

But in 1884 when the Democrats nominated Grover Cleveland and Thomas A. Hendricks, the Chicago *Herald* reported the appearance of a campaign rhyme—well, almost a rhyme. It went like this:

"We'll shout for our man and his important appendix!
We'll whoop 'er up lively for Cleveland and Hendricks!"

...the Kaiser took time out....

When the German Kaiser learned that King George V of Great Britain was changing the name of the British royal family from the German-sounding Saxe-Coburg-Gotha to the English-sounding Windsor, he was amused.

World War One raged in France, but the Kaiser took time out for a joke. He said that he would be delighted to attend a performance of that well-known opera, *The Merry Wives of Saxe-Coburg-Gotha*."

Shantytown "Hoovervilles" were springing up....

In the depths of the Great Depression, Congress changed the name of Hoover Dam to Boulder Dam. Shantytown "Hoovervilles" were springing up across the country, and the Democrats in Congress didn't want Hoover's name attached to the magnificent new dam on the Colorado River.

Will Rogers wrote at the time, "Lord, if they feel that way about it, I don't see why they don't just switch the two words."

"Are you aware that Claude Pepper...."

When Claude Pepper was running for Senator in Florida in 1950, his opponent was George Smathers. Someone on the Smathers team dreamed up the following statement. It was produced as a campaign leaflet and distributed throughout rural Florida. Sad to say, it played a part in Pepper's defeat in the election.

"Are you aware that Claude Pepper is known all over Washington as a shameless extrovert? Not only that, but the man is reliably reported to practice nepotism with his sister-in-law, and he has a sister who was once a thespian in Greenwich Village. He has a brother who was a practicing homo sapiens. And he went to college where he matriculated. Worst of all, it is an established fact that Mr. Pepper, before his marriage, practiced celibacy."

"I am running as a favorite son."

A well-known governor gave a speech announcing that his name would be put in nomination for President at the party's national convention. He said, "I am running as a favorite son."

Someone in the crowd shouted, "That's the greatest unfinished sentence in American politics!"

Some called him the Wizard of Ooze.

Everett Dirksen, the Republican Senator from Illinois, had a deep, mellifluous voice and a love of long words. Some called him the Wizard of Ooze. One of Dirksen's favorite pastimes was criticizing the Democrats for their profligate ways. Once when faced with an array of overly-optimistic budget projections, he called the figures "...hallucinatory estimates for masquerade and mirage in an extravaganza of political chicanery...."

"How old was your father...?"

Senator Everett McKinley Dirksen of Illinois had a million stories. One of them dealt with a man who was filling in an application form for an insurance policy. There was a question that bothered him. It read: "How old was your father when he died and of what did he die?"

Now, in actual fact, his father had been hanged, but he hated to put that on the application. He thought about it for quite a while.

Then he wrote: "My father was 65 when he died. He came to his end while participating in a public function when the platform gave way."

"...as if a gazelle had entered...."

Translations can easily go awry.

Andrei Vyshinsky, the Soviet foreign minister, had just listened to an impassioned speech by a Latin American delegate to the U.N. General Assembly. He remarked that he felt as if Hazel had gotten into the room. That seems like an odd statement unless one realizes that hurricane Hazel was on everyone's mind at the time.

Well, not on everyone's. It wasn't on the mind of the translator, who couldn't figure out what Vyshinsky was talking about. The translation announced that Vyshinsky felt "as if a gazelle had entered the room."

"You need to watch out...."

William F. Buckley, Jr., brought a powerful vocabulary and a respect for the English language to bear on his 1965 race for the mayoralty of New York. After his defeat he ruminated on the language of politics, particularly the "royal 'we.'"

Buckley points out that you and I refer to ourselves as "I" or "me." You would say, "I will do everything I can to help the Red Cross."

Not so the politician. As soon as one becomes a candidate, there seems to be an irresistible urge to switch to the royal "we" and say, "We will do everything we can to help the Red Cross."

Buckley is careful not to condemn this practice across the board. After all, he says, the politician often does include a number of people in his pledge—"his administrative assistants, his uncles and aunts, friends and votaries."

But, Buckley concludes, "You need to watch out when the politician has got so given to thinking of himself as a collectivity that he is capable of writing in his diary, 'At 8 a.m. we got up and took a shower.' When that happens, he has elided from modesty to something else."

Idi Amin was a true tyrant....

One of the most murderously repressive governments since World War Two was that of Uganda's Idi Amin. The horror stories out of Uganda boggled the mind.

Idi Amin was a true tyrant of the 20th century. And like most other tyrants he could dream up euphemisms with ease. He called his gruesomely effective 2,000-man secret police force the "State Research Bureau."

Alliteration in American politics....

Alliteration in American politics didn't begin with Spiro Agnew, although Agnew's tongue-twisting description of the mass media as "nattering nabobs of negativism" is a well-known example.

Actually, the pattern was set some years earlier by Richard Nixon. While running for Vice President in 1952, Nixon referred to Adlai Stevenson, the Democratic candidate for President, as "a Ph.D. from Dean Acheson's cowardly college of Communist containment."

A translator who shall be nameless....

When President Jimmy Carter visited Poland, he created a few misunderstandings. A translator who shall be nameless had difficulty getting Carter's words into the proper idiom. At the Warsaw airport the President spoke of his "desires for the future." It came out as "lusts for the future."

Carter made an innocuous comment about the airplane flight from Washington. His translator startled the Polish audience by telling them that Carter had, quote, "left America never to return."

Quote/Unquote

Niccolò Machiavelli (1469–1527)

You cannot govern states with words.

Abraham Lincoln (1809–1865)

He can compress the most words into the smallest ideas of any man I ever met.

Warren G. Harding (1865–1923)

I don't know much about Americanism, but it's a damned good word with which to carry an election.

Eugene McCarthy (1916–   )

In American politics... one can say rather extreme, even radical things, if one says them in such a way that people don't remember.... Clear language... in politics is dangerous.

LAW

When Solon was finished....

The Athenians, who had suffered under the harsh laws of Draco, asked Solon to prepare a code of laws for them. When Solon was finished, they asked him, "Have you prepared for us the best laws you could?"

Solon replied, "No, I have not, but I have prepared the best laws that the Athenians are able to bear."

"Then, gentlemen of the jury, it is to you...."

No one knows for sure how the term "Philadelphia lawyer" arose. It may have referred first to Andrew Hamilton, the lawyer who defended John Peter Zenger against libel charges. Zenger, you may recll, was a colonial printer. His *New-York Weekly Journal* had called Governor William Cosby a "rogue governor," a man who "did a thousand things for which a small rogue would have deserved a halter."

Hamilton was quite a lawyer; Cosby was quite a rogue; and the Zenger trial was an absolute sensation—high drama as well as a landmark case in the fight for freedom of the press.

The trial took place a long time ago, 40 years before the American Revolution. William Cosby, New York's royal governor, was a despot and a fool. Writers in Zenger's paper attacked him mercilessly. Cosby asked a grand jury to indict Zenger for libel, but the grand jury refused. The attacks went on, and Cosby tried again. The second grand jury also refused to indict. At last Cosby simply had Zenger arrested, thrown in jail, and tried on the libel charges.

Zenger's defense lawyer, appointed by the crown, was young and inexperienced. Few people expected an acquittal, although the lawyer did succeed in getting a jury of ordinary workmen rather than the upper-class jurors the crown wanted.

No sooner had the trial begun than an elderly and distinguished man stood up in the back of the courtroom. He came forward and announced that he wished to participate in Zenger's defense. The man was Andrew Hamilton, former attorney general of Philadelphia and at one time speaker of the Pennsylvania assembly. He was perhaps the best trial lawyer in the colonies.

Had Chief Justice DeLancey been older and more experienced he probably would have thrown Hamilton out of court. He could have done so, but he didn't—and he soon came to regret it.

Although Hamilton was frustrated at every turn, and Zenger's supporters feared of the verdict, the old Philadelphia lawyer intended to win. Seeing that the chief justice would, in effect, direct the jury to bring a verdict of guilty, Hamilton turned his back on the justices and spoke to the men in the jury box:

"Then, gentlemen of the jury," he said, "it is to you we must now appeal."

In bypassing the justices, Hamilton risked immediate dismissal, disbarment, and possibly prison. But once again Chief Justice DeLancey failed to see the threat, and failed to act. He let Hamilton continue. He let him point out that the jury was free to decide as it wished—that DeLancey had no power to punish the jurors for reaching a decision he happened to dislike.

Only after Hamilton's stirring finale did Chief Justice DeLancey speak in angry tones. He explained the law to the jruors. He told them they were not free to make new law. The case was open and shut. Zenger had printed the statements in his paper as charged. That was all that was required for a libel conviction. There was no possible verdict but guilty.

The jurors retired. They returned in only ten minutes. DeLancey must have been pleased when he saw them. It was inconceivable that the jury had considered Hamilton's revolutionary arguments seriously in that length of time.

The clerk asked the jury foreman whether the defendant, John Peter Zenger, had published the statements as charged. (Again, this was an accurate statement of the law, because the justices, not the jury, were to decide if the statements were libelous.)

The jury foreman, a sailor named John Hunt, replied, "Not guilty."

DeLancey was stunned. Shouts and cheers rocked the courtroom as he and the other justices gathered up their robes and stalked out.

Now, it's true that Hamilton's defense of Zenger was bad law. The jury's verdict made no legal sense. Nevertheless, a precedent for freedom of the press had been set that remains one of the glories of the nation today.

As a British barrister wrote less than three years after the verdict: "If it is not law, it is better than law; it ought to be law; and will always be law wherever justice prevails."

From the man's glum expression....

When Lincoln was practicing law in Illinois, the attorney on the other side was young and ambitious. The case was unimportant, but the youthful lawyer was determined to win it. He worked hard and long, and argued the case far into the night. It finally went to the jury.

Next morning Lincoln met the young lawyer at the courthouse. From the man's glum expression, Lincoln figured the jury had already brought in a verdict.

"Good morning," Lincoln said. "What has become of the case?"

The young lawyer shook his head sadly and said in a mournful tone, "It's gone to hell."

"Oh, well," said Lincoln cheerfully, "then you'll see it again."

"He couldn't fool me...."

Roscoe Pound, the great jurist, taught for many years at Harvard Law School. He liked to tell a tale from his younger days as a lawyer in Omaha, when he was working for a firm that represented a number of big railroads.

Then as now, there were populist judges who seldom if ever found merit in the arguments of corporation counsel. Such judges ruled regularly in favor of the down-home plaintiffs.

On one occasion Roscoe Pound was sent into the backcountry to try to win a judgment for a big railroad client against a small merchant. The merchant had cost the railroad money through a delay in shipping.

The elderly justice of the peace who was trying the case had a long history of anti-railroad judgments. Even so, he was a good friend of one of the senior members of Pound's law firm.

Pound argued his case well, and, to his amazement, the JP ruled in favor of the railroad. Pound was ecstatic. He returned to Omaha, boasting that he had won an impossible judgment against a populist judge.

But his jubilation was short-lived. The justice of the peace wrote a letter to his senior-partner friend at Pound's law firm. In it he pointed out that the firm had recently sent a clever young lawyer to his town to plead a case. This fledgling lawyer, too cute by half for the judge's taste, had tried to convince the old JP that the railroad, not the merchant, was the plaintiff.

The JP knew better. The railroad was *never* the plaintiff. The plaintiff was always a small-time operator—a merchant or a farmer—not a giant corporation.

"He couldn't fool me," crowed the old JP. "I knew the railroad couldn't be a plaintiff—so I gave judgment for the plaintiff as usual."

"I know the law."

George E. Allen, not to be confused with the football coach, served in the Presidential administrations of FDR and Harry Truman. Around the White House he was always good for a laugh, and his autobiography, *Presidents Who Have Known Me*, is good for a bushel of laughs.

Allen tells the story of his father, a lawyer, who lost a case concerning the recovery of a cow. It was tried in Booneville, Mississippi, before a judge who had little liking for Allen.

When the judgment went against Allen's client, Allen was outraged. He started toward the bench, waving a volume of Blackstone angrily at the judge.

The judge shouted, "Sit down, Mr. Allen. I know the law."

"Of course you do, Your Honor," the lawyer shot back. "I just wanted to read this to you to show you what a damned fool Blackstone was."

"...the Law of Gravity...."

In Art Linkletter's book, *A Child's Garden of Misinformation*, kids speak out on the mysteries of American politics.

When asked to name an early law passed by Congress, one child responded: "One of the first laws passed by Congress was the Law of Gravity, which was a reminder to not go flying around without an airplane."

Quote/Unquote

Plato (427–347 B.C.)

When there is an income tax, the just man will pay more and the unjust man less on the same amount of income.

Aristotle (384–322 B.C.)

The law is reason free from passion.

Marcus Tullius Cicero (106–43 B.C.)

The good of the people is the chief law.

Edmund Burke (1729–1797)

Bad laws are the worst sort of tyranny.

Benjamin Disraeli (1804–1881)

When men are pure, laws are useless; when men are corrupt, laws are broken.

Herbert Spencer (1820–1903)

What a cage is to the wild beast, law is to the selfish man.

Oliver Wendell Holmes, Jr. (1841–1935)

The life of the law has not been logic; it has been experience.

Roscoe Pound (1870–1964)

The law must be stable, but it must not stand still.

Finley Peter Dunne (1867–1936)

No matter whether th' constitution follows th' flag or not, the supreme court follows th' iliction returns.

Charles Evans Hughes (1862–1948)

We are under a Constitution, but the Constitution is what the judges say it is.

Herbert Hoover (1874–1964)

If the law is upheld only by government officials, then all law is at an end.

Sam Ervin, Jr.   (1896–1985)

I test the wisdom of the law not upon what a good man can do with it, but what a bad man can do with it....

Martin Luther King, Jr.   (1929–1968)

It may be true that the law cannot make a man love me, but it can keep him from lynching me, and I think that's pretty important....

LEADERSHIP

Get Parson Weems on the phone.

If there's one thing a leader can count on, it's that a lot of people won't like him or her.

Which American President is most revered by the public today? Probably George Washington. Even though Lincoln is usually rated by historians as the greatest, Washington has been put on a higher pedestal. George Washington—the man who led his army to victory over the British and his nation to independence. George Washington—the first President, the one who set the pattern for all succeeding Presidents.

He was even admired in his own time, wasn't he? Yes, he was, by many people. But not by everybody.

General Charles Lee, a Revolutionary army officer, referred to Washington as that "dark, designing, sordid, ambitious, vain, proud, arrogant, and vindictive knave."

Thomas Paine, the author of *Common Sense,* called Washington "treacherous in private friendship" and "a hypocrite in public life."

William Duane, a Jeffersonian journalist, regarded Washington as the man "who is the source of all the misfortunes of our country." Duane saw, or thought he saw, the wreck of Washington's character "crumbling to pieces."

Quick. Get Parson Weems on the phone. Or maybe Lee Atwater. This George Washington guy has a serious image problem.

"...an incurable consumption of Central Imbecility."

It's common knowledge that a leader has to endure criticism, even outrageous criticism. No leader escapes it, certainly not the President of the United States.

The Reverend Henry Ward Beecher, pastor of the Plymouth Church, Brooklyn, received the princely sum (for those days) of $20,000 a year and liked to carry uncut gems in his pockets. He had a devoted following at the church, and after becoming editor of a religious newspaper, *The Independent*, he had a much larger audience.

Beecher was an abolitionist. He had no use for President Abraham Lincoln's cautious approach to emancipation. Beecher undercut the President at every opportunity.

In *The Independent* he wrote: "...Never was a time when men's prayers so fervently asked God for a leader! He has refused our petition!... Not a spark of genius has he [meaning Lincoln]; not an element for leadership. Not one particle of heroic enthusiasm...."

Beecher even blamed Northern military defeats on Lincoln. After the Second Battle of Bull Run he wrote: "It is a supreme and extraordinary want of executive... talent... that is bringing us to humiliation. Let it be known that the Nation wasted away by an incurable consumption of Central Imbecility."

Although Beecher's prestige was enormous, the American people—like nearly all later historians—sided with Lincoln.

"No leaders, no principles...."

When Woodrow Wilson was 22 and a senior at Princeton University, he wrote an essay that was bitterly critical of Congress. He called for a cabinet government patterned on the British system. In his essay he bemoaned the decline of leadership in American political life. "No leaders, no principles," he wrote; "no principles, no parties." He called for a revival of national leadership.

Young Wilson's essay is not highly regarded by historians today—although Wilson himself is. The Virginia-born Democrat's lifelong fascination with political leadership led him all the way to the White House. He is generally regarded as one of America's great Presidents.

Curiously, the person who chose young Wilson's essay for publication was a 29-year-old blue-blooded Boston Republican named Henry Cabot Lodge. Lodge at the time was a tutor at Harvard and an editor of the *International Review*. He found Wilson's analysis impressive.

Forty years down the road Henry Cabot Lodge had risen to become known as one of the powerful leaders of the Republican Party. By then he was a United States Senator, a grim isolationist violently opposed to the League of Nations. The leader of the Democratic Party was none other than President Woodrow Wilson.

By that time the essay may have been forgotten by both men. But the call for leadership had been heeded. Unfortunately for Wilson and the League of Nations,

Senator Lodge's Congressional leadership proved more than equal to the leadership from the ailing and disillusioned President.

"I thought it would be by far the best plan."

In May 1940 Winston Churchill was serving as First Lord of the Admiralty. Neville Chamberlain, despite his repeated failures, was still Prime Minister. But Chamberlain's days were numbered. Speaker after speaker arose in Parliament to denounce him and his policies.

Churchill was aware that he might be the one called upon to form a new government. He took that possibility in stride. As he said, "The prospect neither excited nor alarmed me. I thought it would be by far the best plan. I was content to let events unfold...."

On the morning of May 10th German troops invaded Belgium and the Netherlands. Within hours Neville Chamberlain submitted his resignation to the king. At six in the evening Winston Churchill was summoned to the royal palace.

"I want you to form a government," the king said.

Churchill agreed to do so—almost with relief. "At last," he wrote, "I had the authority to give directions over the whole scene. I felt as if I were walking with Destiny, and that all my past life had been but a preparation for this hour.... I was sure I should not fail."

His success over the next five years and three months is legendary.

"The mediocrity of his thinking...."

We are so used to regarding Sir Winston Churchill as one of the great statesmen of the 20th century that we tend to forget (as we do with Washington and Lincoln) that Churchill faced bitter political opposition in his own time.

One British leader who opposed Sir Winston was Aneurin Bevan, known as "Nye." Nye Bevan was definitely no slouch when it came to insults. He called Churchill "a man suffering from petrified adolescence." And Nye was just warming up to his subject with that one.

"The mediocrity of his thinking," said Bevan, "is concealed by the majesty of his language."

The Laborite leader had still more to say about Britain's great wartime leader. For example: "He mistakes verbal felicities for mental inspirations." And still more: "He refers to a defeat... as though it came from God, but to a victory as though it came from himself."

It was Eugene O'Neill, I think, who wrote, "Even being God ain't no bed of roses."

"Management is one thing. Leadership...."

In his book *Leaders*, Richard Nixon makes a distinction between management and leadership. He comments on the widespread belief in the United States "that what the country really needs is a top-flight businessman to run the government, someone who has proven that he can manage a large-scale enterprise efficiently and effectively." But, says Nixon, "This misses the mark. Management is one thing. Leadership is another."

He quotes Warren G. Bennis of the University of California's business school: "Managers have as their goal to do things right. Leaders have as their goal to do the right thing."

It's an interesting distinction, one that American voters seem to have taken to heart. The nation has had many lawyer-Presidents, a number of farmer-Presidents, some soldier-Presidents, even a notable actor-President. A few Presidents, like Warren G. Harding and Jimmy Carter, have run small businesses. But so far not a single CEO of a major corporation has made it to the Oval Office.

It still may happen, but Nixon seems to doubt it. "The leader," he writes, "represents a direction of history." A manager merely "represents a process."

Quote/Unquote

Plutarch   (46–120)

An army of stags led by a lion is more formidable than an army of lions led by a stag.

Abraham Lincoln   (1809–1865)

[General George B.] McClellan... comprehends and can arrange military combinations better than any of our generals, and there his usefulness ends. He can't go ahead—he can't strike a blow.

Oscar Wilde   (1854–1900)

Those who try to lead the people can only do so by following the mob.

Sam Rayburn   (1882–1961)

You cannot be a leader, and ask other people to follow you, unless you know how to follow, too.

Winston Churchill   (1874–1965)

The leadership of the privileged has passed away; but it has not been succeeded by that of the eminent. We have entered the region of mass effects.

Harry S Truman   (1884–1972)

Men make history and not the other way 'round. In periods where there is no leadership, society stands still.

Walter Lippmann   (1889–1974)

The genius of a good leader is to leave behind him a situation which common sense, without the grace of genius, can deal with successfully.

Charles de Gaulle   (1890–1970)

Adversity attracts the man of character. He seeks out the bitter joy of responsibility.

André Malraux   (1901–1977)

To command is to serve, nothing more and nothing less.

LIBERTY

"The next gale that sweeps from the north...."

Patrick Henry is known for two speeches that were delivered ten years apart. The theme was the same for both—liberty.

The first took place in the House of Burgesses in colonial Williamsburg, Virginia. Speaking against the British-imposed Stamp Act in 1765, Henry worked himself into quite a dudgeon.

He said: "Caesar had his Brutus; Charles the First his Cromwell; and George III—"

At which point the Speaker of the House cried, "Treason!"

But Patrick Henry continued forcefully, "—*may profit by their example. If this* be treason, make the most of it."

Ten years later Henry spoke before the second Virginia convention in Richmond, Virginia. War with England was imminent, he told his audience.

"Gentleman may cry, Peace, peace!' he thundered, "but there is no peace. The war has actually begun. The next gale that sweeps from the north will bring to our ears the clash of resounding arms!"

He was right. Lexington and Concord were less than a month away. Patrick Henry chided his fellow Virginians for their lack of activity.

"What is it that the gentlemen wish?" he asked. "Is life so dear or peace so sweet as to be purchased at the price of chains and slavery? Forbid it, Almighty God."

And he concluded with the words that have echoed down the years: "I know not what course others may take, but as for me, give me liberty or give me death!"

"...a word that shall echo forevermore!"

The following lines appear in the poem "Paul Revere's Ride" by Henry Wadsworth Longfellow:

And so through the night went his cry of alarm
To every Middlesex village and farm—
A cry of defiance, and not of fear,
A voice in the darkness, a knock at the door,
And a word that shall echo forevermore!

One hundred and eighty years later, President Sukarno of Indonesia opened the Bandung Conference in the Far East. He reminded the African and Asian delegations that the date marked the anniversary of "the first successful anti-colonial war in history."

Sukarno quoted Longfellow's lines, and concluded, "Yes, it *shall* echo forevermore!"

"A mighty woman with a torch...."

The New Colossus
by Emma Lazarus

Not like the brazen giant of Greek fame,
With conquering limbs astride from land to land:
Here at our sea-washed, sunset gates shall stand
A mighty woman with a torch, whose flame
Is the imprisoned lightning, and her name
Mother of Exiles. From her beacon-hand
Glows world-wide welcome; her mild eyes command
The air-bridged harbor that twin cities frame.
"Keep, ancient lands, your storied pomp!" cries she
With silent lips. "Give me your tired, your poor,
Your huddled masses yearning to breathe free,
The wretched refuse of your teeming shore.
Send these, the homeless, tempest-tost to me,
I lift my lamp beside the golden door!"

Quote/Unquote

Benjamin Franklin   (1706–1790)

Those who would give up essential liberty to purchase a little temporary safety deserve neither liberty nor safety.

Edmund Burke   (1729–1797)

Abstract liberty, like other mere abstractions, is not to be found.

John C. Calhoun   (1782–1850)

It is harder to preserve than to obtain liberty.

George Bernard Shaw   (1856–1950)

Liberty means responsibility. That is why most men dread it.

Woodrow Wilson   (1856–1924)

America was established not to create wealth but to realize a vision, to realize an ideal—to discover and maintain liberty among men.

Dorothy Thompson   (1894–1961)

It is not the fact of liberty but the way in which liberty is exercised that ultimately determines whether liberty itself survives.

LOGIC

"A king who is threatened...."

King Charles X of France was both ignorant and pompous. The King's 75-year-old Prime Minister, Talleyrand, decided that Charles had to go. Working deviously as always, he began to stir up trouble.

Before long, King Charles saw the threat. He said to Talleyrand, "A king who is threatened with revolution has no choice. It is either the throne or the scaffold."

The Prime Minister suggested another option. "Sire," he said coldly, "Your Majesty forgets the post chaise."

[*A post chaise is a closed, four-wheeled, horse-drawn carriage.*]

"And do you forgive your enemies?"

In the 19th century there was a Spanish general named Leopoldo O'Donnell who decided to enter the political arena. The politics of the day involved ruthless infighting, and in this no-holds-barred atmosphere General O'Donnell more than held his own. He served as War Minister, then put in several terms as Premier of Spain.

The story goes that on his deathbed O'Donnell called in a priest to confess his sins in preparation for leaving this world. Once the confession was finished, the priest asked, "And do you forgive your enemies?"

O'Donnell answered, "Oh, I have no enemies, Father."

The priest asked, "How could you, a general and a politician, have no enemies?"

Said O'Donnell, "Well, Father, I had them all shot."

"An epigram abolished slavery...."

Ben Butler of Massachusetts was one of the prominent political generals of the Civil War. A month after the war began, Major General Butler, with no military experience, commanded twelve Union regiments at Fortress Monroe, Virginia.

Butler faced an immediate problem—runaway slaves. Abraham Lincoln had called for troops to suppress the rebellion, not to free slaves. Under the circumstances, what was a military commander to do with slaves who escaped to the Union lines? Butler certainly wasn't going to send them back to their owners.

A happy thought struck him. The slaves were someone's property, weren't they? No slave owner would argue with that. And didn't Butler have the power to seize rebel property and use it in the best interests of the United States. Of course he did.

So when Colonel Mallory brought Butler three escaped slaves, Old Cock-eye, as Butler was called because of his crossed eye, knew just what to do. He took up his pen and wrote out a receipt for them. He gave the receipt to Mallory and then turned the runaways over to his quartermaster.

Later that day a Confederate major arrived at Fortress Monroe under a flag of truce. He asked Butler a number of questions. One of them was what Butler intended to do about fugitive slaves. Old Cock-eye replied that the Union and the Confederacy were at war. Therefore, the slaves were to be considered "contraband of war." They would remain behind Union lines. They would not be returned to their owners.

The phrase "contraband of war" created a sensation. It spread rapidly. If fugitive slaves were contraband of war, then for all practical purposes they were free. Butler had said so. Lincoln's Emancipation Proclamation wouldn't come for another year and a half, but Ben Butler had struck upon an imaginative way to deal with runaway slaves.

Theodore Winthrop, an officer on Butler's staff, exaggerated only a little when he said, "An epigram abolished slavery in the United States."

"The heated mind resents...."

One of the great Prime Ministers of England, William Gladstone, often became embroiled in arguments. Like most other politicians, he had little doubt that his own position was the correct one. And he could argue his position with great eloquence.

He was especially scornful of opponents who let their passions run away with their reason. "The heated mind," said Gladstone, "resents the chill touch and relentless scrutiny of logic."

"Do you think it will stop?"

Senators J.C. Spooner of Wisconsin and W.B. Allison of Iowa were leaving the Capitol one evening. Suddenly, it began to pour.

"Do you think the rain will stop? Spooner asked.

"Always has," said Allison.

"Mind your own business...."

Senator Jacob H. Gallinger of New Hampshire used to tell about a character in his district known as Sailor Stevens. One day after having tossed down a few too many pints of ale, the old Sailor tried to saddle a horse. Senator Gallinger noticed that he had put the pommel toward the horse's tail.

"Mr. Stevens," the senator said, "you seem to have that saddle on backwards."

The sozzled gent looked at Gallinger in disgust. His voice full of indignation, he said, "Mind your own business, sir. How do you know which way I'm going to travel?"

"...I voted Republican the first time...."

Franklin D. Roosevelt's decision to run for a third term as president aroused some controversy. When FDR was talking to a neighbor during his third term campaign, he asked the man, "How are you voting this year."

"Republican," the man said.

"I see," said Roosevelt. "Does the third term bother you?"

The man shook his head. "Not at all. But look here, I voted Republican the first time you ran. Then I voted Republican the second time. Now I'm going to vote Republican again, because I never had it so good."

"Stay with it, Pat!"

A favorite story, told by Senator Everett Dirksen and others—often in connection with the economy—has to do with the man who fell from the 30th floor of a skyscraper.

A friend of his was standing at a sixth floor window and saw him sailing downward. As the man, arms flailing, dropped past the sixth floor, his friend shouted:

"Stay with it, Pat! You're okay so far!"

...first, that they would build a new jail....

A county board of freeholders passed a resolution to this effect: first, that they would build a new jail; second, that they would build the new jail out of materials composing the old one; and third, that the old one should stand until the new one was built.

"What makes you so sure?"

This story has probably been told at ten-year intervals ever since the beginning of the U.S. census.

It seems that the government enumerator was visiting a small home where she found the head of the household deeply engrossed in a large book. The book, it turned out, was a volume of the *Encyclopedia Britannica*, which a traveling salesman had managed to sell him. The good citizen had been reading it faithfully, volume by volume, since then.

The census-taker asked the man his name, age, marital status, and then his wife's name and age.

"How many children do you have?" she asked.

"Three," he replied. "They're seven, four, and two. And that's all we're going to have. You can take my word for it."

"What makes you so sure?" the enumerator asked.

"I know it for a fact," the citizen said in a positive tone. "It says here in the book that every fourth child born in the world is Chinese."

"Say, Dan, I'm the one...."

President Kennedy used to tell the story of a very close election in Fall River, Massachusetts. The man running for mayor won by only one vote. Afterwards he had to endure the same comment from everyone he met: "Say, Dan, I'm the one who put you in office."

"Is it news that some fellow...."

President Reagan didn't admit that unemployment in the 1981–82 recession—the worst since the Great Depression—had anything to do with lack of opportunity.

He found the whole subject a bit annoying. He once asked, "Is it news that some fellow out in South Succotash someplace has just been laid off?"

Since it *was* news, he occasionally had to address the issue. One technique he used was to hold up the help wanted pages of the Washington *Post*. The first time he did it, the paper contained 24 pages of classified ads of employers looking for workers. Another time it had 33½ pages of such ads.

The implication was clear. There were plenty of jobs available. It was just that the people of Washington were too lazy or too fond of welfare to apply for them.

There was a logical fallacy at work here. The American Vocation Association did an analysis of the jobs being offered. Approximately 85% percent of them required a high level of training. They were jobs for professionals and skilled technicians. But the unemployed in Washington, by and large, were the less educated.

So the truth about unemployment wasn't that laziness ruled the District of Columbia. Instead there was a gaping mismatch between job requirements and job skills. A high school graduate, no matter how ambitious, couldn't get that investment analyst's position.

Quote/Unquote

Calvin Coolidge   (1873–1933)

When more and more people are thrown out of work, unemployment results.

Clare Boothe Luce   (1903–1987)

Anyone who isn't thoroughly confused isn't thinking clearly.

Gerald R. Ford   (1913–   )

If Lincoln were alive today, he'd be turning over in his grave.

Alan Cranston (1914–   )

Inflation is not all bad. After all, it has allowed every American to live in a more expensive neighborhood without moving.

Pierre Elliott Trudeau (1919–   )

Some commentators have suggested that I do not really exist, that I am the figment of the imagination of certain newspaper columnists and television producers. Personally, I reject this extreme view.

Frank Rizzo (1920–   )

The streets are safe in Philadelphia; it's only the people who make them unsafe.

LONGEVITY

"I have always been a prudent man...."

Justice Oliver Wendell Holmes, Jr., known as the "Great Dissenter," was still serving on the bench at the age of 90. The year was 1931, and Congress, faced with the Great Depression, found it necessary to reduce the pay of Supreme Court justices.

When Holmes heard of it, he chuckled and said: "I have always been a prudent man, so this cut in pay will not hurt me, but I am distressed that I cannot continue to lay aside as much as usual for my old age."

"If I had anticipated I would live so long...."

Wilson Warlick, a North Carolina judge, was speaking on the same platform as Senator Sam Ervin. Both men were well past the age of 80, and the master of ceremonies felt obliged to comment on this fact.

Judge Warlick responded: "That's true. If I had anticipated I would live so long, I would have taken better care of myself when I was young."

"Oh, you're thinking about that 15 years...."

Many of Abe Lincoln's stories came from his days as a circuit-riding lawyer. Once when he and Thurlow Weed were discussing a politician from Maryland, Lincoln said he was reminded of the story of a witness in a neighboring county.

The judge asked the witness for his age.

"Sixty," the old man replied.

The witness looked much older, and the judge repeated his question.

"Sixty," the man said again.

At that the judge gently suggested that the witness must be mistaken.

A light came to the old man's eyes. He said, "Oh, you're thinking about that 15 years that I lived down on the Eastern Shore of Maryland. That was so much lost time and don't count."

"...when I'm around 99 years old...."

The President of the United States gets plenty of mail, some of it from children. President Nixon received the following letter from an unusually patient youngster:

"Dear Mr. Nixon and the secretary who is reading this,

"Thought you could fool me, huh? I know how secretaries always read people's mail and answer: Signed, Richard M. Nixon.

"My hobby is collecting President pictures straight from the White House. So far I have pictures from Kennedy and Johnson. This hobby of mine is kind of slow—every four or eight years. But when I'm around 99 years old I'll have lots of President pictures.

"Will you please send me some pictures of President Nixon? Thank you!"

Quote/Unquote

Lord Palmerston   (1784–1865)

Die, my dear Doctor? That's the last thing I shall do.

Oliver Wendell Holmes, Jr.   (1841–1935)

What I wouldn't give to be 70 again!

Theodore Green   (1867–1966)

Most people say that as you get old, you have to give things up. I think you get old *because* you give things up.

Martin Luther King, Jr.   (1929–1968)

Like anybody, I would like to live a long life. Longevity has its place. But I'm not concerned about that now. I just want to do God's will.

LOYALTY

"I had rather live, but...."

Benjamin Disraeli, First Earl of Beaconsfield and Prime Minister of England, retained his wit and spirit to the end. His last words—although observers never seem to be quite sure of these things—were probably, "I had rather live, but I am not afraid to die."

It was not bad as an exit line, although less clever than something he had said earlier. Suspecting he was on his deathbed, Disraeli had sent a note to Queen Victoria, implying the graveness of his condition. She responded with flowers and warm letters wishing him a complete recovery.

When it was suggested to Disraeli that the Queen might also visit him, he shook his head. He remembered all too well Victoria's obsessive devotion to her beloved husband, Prince Albert, now dead for some 20 years.

"No," said Disraeli, "it is better not. She would only ask me to take a message to Albert."

"...whenever I think you are right."

The dictionary definition of *loyal* is "unswerving in allegiance."

Sir John A. Macdonald, Canada's first Prime Minister, had that in mind when he responded to a remark by Senator A.R. Dickey of Amherst, Ontario.

Dickey had promised Macdonald, "I will support you whenever I think you are right."

Sir John's answer was, "That is no satisfaction. Anybody may support me when I am right. What I want is a man that will support me when I am wrong."

"Please don't overlook me...."

In the early days of the Cold War, the U.S. government was looking for Communists under every bed and behind every closet door. Loyalty oaths and loyalty checks were common.

One confused lady was prompted to write the following letter to Senator Harley Kilgore of West Virginia:

Dear Senator:

"I understand the government is giving loyalty checks to its employees.

"I worked for the War Department two years during the war and I had an excellent efficiency rating during that period, so I think I deserve mine.

"Please don't overlook me when the government starts to hand out those checks."

"I pledge allegiance to the flag...."

The Pledge of Allegiance became a big issue in the Presidential campaign of 1988 for reasons that were never quite clear. Most people knew, or learned, that the Pledge hadn't even existed prior to 1892. The Founding Fathers said nothing about a pledge. They required no loyalty oath of any kind.

The story of the Pledge is hardly as stirring as that of "The Star-Spangled Banner." The much-ballyhooed Pledge began as nothing more than a promotional campaign for a weekly magazine called *The Youth's Companion.* The original Pledge of Allegiance appeared in that magazine under the heading "The Youth Companion's Flag Pledge." It was similar to the Pledge we recite today. Here it is:

"I pledge allegiance to my flag and to the Republic for which it stands: one nation, indivisible, with liberty and justice for all."

No one knows for sure who wrote it—there are two main claimants. But the man who took up the cause of the Pledge most earnestly was one Gridley Adams, who wanted the words changed, particulary the words "my flag."

"I didn't like a pledge," he said later, "that any Hottentot could subscribe to."

The words "under God" were added in 1954 as a result of a voter's letter to a Michigan Congressman.

It's hard to say how effective the Pledge is as a device to instill loyalty. There are many stories about children misinterpreting the words. The word "allegiance" can become "a legion." "Indivisible" can become "invisible."

A citizenship education teacher in upstate New York once began each day with the Pledge of Allegiance in her homeroom. One day in class she asked her students to name the kind of government under which the United States functions. The class agreed that the correct answer is "democracy." She then asked, "Could we call the country a republic?" The students expressed serious doubts. Some of them said flatly, "No." Picking out the most vociferously negative student, she said quietly, "Please recite the Pledge of Allegiance."

The student began, "I pledge allegiance to the flag of the United States of America and to the republic...."

"That's far enough," said the teacher.

Curley, like Robin Hood....

Loyalty is more common among voters than it probably ought to be. Take the case of James M. Curley, the colorful Mayor of Boston, U.S. Congressman, and Governor of Massachusetts.

In Boston they called him "the Mayor of the Poor," and they reelected him even when he was headed for prison. Curley, like Robin Hood, stole from the rich—actually he stole from the city of Boston. He also dispensed countless favors to the poor, not all of whom stayed poor for long.

When Curley was ordered to repay $30,000 he had stolen from the city, his loyal fans flocked around his house to contribute money. They donated quite a bit more than the $30,000 he needed to repay the theft.

Curley had no qualms at all about his freebooting while in office. With his usual flair, he called his autobiography, *I'd Do It Again.*

Quote/Unquote

King George III (England)   (1738–1820)

I desire what is good; therefore, everyone who does not agree with me is a traitor.

Theodore Roosevelt   (1858–1919)

It is better to be faithful than famous.

Edward R. Murrow   (1908–1965)

We must not confuse dissent with disloyalty.

LUCK

The law wasted no time....

In the annals of British politics, only one Prime Minister has ever been assassinated. And yet the event is hardly more than a footnote to history, because the victim, Prime Minister Spencer Perceval, was of little importance, and the killer, John Bellingham, had no real motive for his act.

The facts are clear enough. On the afternoon of May 11, 1812, John Bellingham, a bankrupt and apparently crazed merchant, stepped forward in the lobby of the Houses of Parliament and shot Spencer Perceval in the chest. The Prime Minister cried, "I am murdered, murdered," or something such, and quickly proved it.

Why did Bellingham do away with the inoffensive Perceval? It seems that he harbored a vague grudge against the British government for not acting on a complaint he had against the Russian authorities in St. Petersburg. But Bellingham had no specific target in mind on that fateful day in May. He wanted to shoot someone in the government, and Prime Minister Perceval happened on the scene.

The law wasted no time in the case of John Bellingham. He was tried and hanged within a week.

"Henry Heitfeld, having received...."

In their amusing book, *One-Night Stands with American History*, Richard Shenkman and Kurt Reiger tell the remarkable story of Henry Heitfeld of Idaho.

The year was 1896, the high-watermark of the Populist movement in the United States. Heitfeld, a member of the Idaho legislature, was a Populist.

In those days United States Senators were elected not directly by the people but by the state legislatures. Idaho was in the process of choosing a man to send to the U.S. Senate.

Heitfeld was not an active candidate, but he was a man in the middle. Many Democrats were vying for the Senate seat, and none of them could build enough support to go over the top. Vote after vote was taken. Each time differing groups of legislators, playing a numbers game, would vote for Heitfeld. Amused, Heitfeld always voted for someone else. But he did keep a running tally of the votes.

Time wore on. The voting continued. On the umpteenth ballot Heitfeld routinely voted for another candidate. Then he noticed something strange. He was piling up an unusually large number of votes. Whatever his opponents' strategy, they were putting him very close to victory.

When the roll call ended, Heitfeld stood up and declared: "Mr. President, I desire to change my vote. I wish to vote for Heitfeld."

The chamber found his switch amusing and burst out in a roar of laughter. His fellow legislators continued to joke with him as the clerks added up the official totals.

Finally, the presiding officer announced the result: "Henry Heitfeld, having received a majority of all the votes, is hereby declared elected United States Senator for the term of six years."

Heitfeld's tally had been correct. Having observed to his astonishment that he was just one vote from winning, Heitfeld withdrew his vote from one of the Democratic hopefuls and instead voted for himself.

The Populists were unintentionally handed a seat in the United States Senate.

...the luck of Calvin Coolidge.

Everyone talked about the luck of Calvin Coolidge. One reporter said he wouldn't dare to take the Presidential nomination if Coolidge were to be his Vice President. When asked why, he said, "Because I would die in a little while. Everything comes to Calvin Coolidge in a most uncanny and mysterious manner."

President Harding *did* die, of course, and Vice President Coolidge took over. Even the timing was lucky. Silent Cal was up in Plymouth, Massachusetts, in his father's house, when the news of Harding's death came through. Coolidge's father, being a notary public, could legally administer the Presidential oath of office.

And he did—at 2:47 A.M. by the light of a kerosene lamp. An artist did a painting of the scene, and soon reproductions of it hung in homes throughout America.

Here's the lucky part. If Harding had died a day earlier, the artist's picture would have been quite different. Silent Cal had spent the previous night at the baronial mansion of a wealthy friend of his, Guy Currier of Peterborough, New Hampshire.

"I claim to be a mere mortal."

Mahatma Gandhi gained such immense prestige throughout India that many regarded him as the incarnation of God. This "meaningless deification," as he called it, bothered him, but there was little he could do about it. "I claim to be a mere mortal," he insisted, but his denials were lost on the faithful.

Generally, those who deified him were uneducated, but not always. One day the train Gandhi was on came to a sudden stop. A passenger had pulled the emergency cord when he saw a lawyer fall headfirst from the train.

The lawyer stumbled to his feet, unhurt. It appeared to be an obvious case of good luck, but the lawyer said no, it wasn't luck. He told Gandhi he had escaped injury because he was riding on the same train as the great Mahatma.

Gandhi laughed and said, "Then you shouldn't have fallen out at all."

"It was the nation...."

Winston Churchill received much praise for inspiring the British people during the dark hours of World War Two. He claimed that others deserved the praise. "It was the nation," he said, "... that had the lion's heart. I had the luck to be called upon to give the roar!"

"To be a man of destiny...."

Quentin Crisp, author of *The Naked Civil Servant*, made this comment on the random nature of greatness: "To be a man of destiny," he said "is to arrive at a point in history when the only gift you have to offer has suddenly become relevant."

Quote/Unquote

Lord Halifax   (1633–1695)

He that leaveth nothing to chance will do few things ill, but he will do very few things.

Ralph Waldo Emerson   (1803–1882)

Shallow men believe in luck.... Strong men believe in cause and effect.

Abraham Lincoln   (1809–1865)

I claim not to have controlled events, but confess plainly that events have controlled me.

Adolf Hitler   (1889–1945)

A fellow has got to be lucky.

MATURITY

"The state will set up monuments...."

According to Article II of the U.S. Constitution, a person has to be at least 35 years old to be eligible for the Presidency. Plato would consider that far too young.

And Plato would be amused by American parents who begin to doubt that their 30-year-old children in graduate school will ever find paying jobs.

These young Presidents and old graduate students are mere kids. Plato's educational program for his philosopher rulers spans 50 years.

During the first 18 years, the children chosen as future leaders in Plato's republic study literature, music, and elementary mathematics. They aren't put under much pressure at the beginning. Their field trips involve going to watch battles.

For the next two or three years, those who have done well spend their whole time in rigorous military and physical training. No academic study is required.

At about the age of 20, an important selection is made. The best prospects continue their education; the others, so it seems (Plato is not clear about this), remain as "auxiliaries," or soldiers. Those who continue their education face a grueling ten years of mathematics.

Then they're 30, but still vulnerable. More students are washed out at this point, to do... what?—Plato doesn't say. The ones who hang in there have to study "dialectic" for approximately five years. That's formal logic, and Plato makes it clear that future rulers are to take the subject seriously, not just learn how to score debating points.

At the age of 35 they're philosophers. But of course they have no practical experience. They're like those Harvard MBAs who want to begin their careers by making corporate policy decisions. Happily, Plato, like Lee Iacocca, knows better. His philosopher-students need to put in some working time.

In fact, they need to put in 15 years of working time. Into the trenches they go—which is to say into junior military or political jobs. They're watched carefully during these 15 years; they're being groomed—although the truth is, they're still going to spend most of the rest of their lives in study. But along the way they'll be required to take a few years out for "the troublesome duties of public life."

After that, they "will depart to dwell in the Islands of the Blest," says Plato. The state will set up monuments for them and sacrifices, honoring them as divinities, if the Pythian Oracle approves...."

"It is a grand thing...."

Archduke Francis Joseph of Austria, 18 years old, was busily at work on his studies when he learned what had happened. His uncle, the Emperor Ferdinand I, had suddenly abdicated.

Ferdinand was a well-meaning man who suffered from fits of insanity. Faced with an uprising in Vienna in 1848 and the failure of his policy, he was persuaded to resign. In doing so, he named his nephew, Francis Joseph, as his successor.

It was quite a surprise to the young Archduke. One day he was a schoolboy, the next day Emperor of Austria. The change was popular with the people. One army officer wrote, "It is a grand thing to be able to be enthusiastic about one's Emperor."

But Francis Joseph himself could foresee the radical changes in his life that had been thrust upon him. When one of his friends greeted him as "Your Majesty," Francis Ferdinand murmured, "Farewell to my youth."

Ted Williams of the Boston Red Sox....

When John F. Kennedy was running for President in 1960, a persistent Republican charge was that he was too young—that he lacked experience.

On one occasion Kennedy answered by mentioning a new story coming out of his home city of Boston. Ted Williams of the Boston Red Sox had just retired from baseball.

Said Kennedy, "It seems that at 42 he was too old. It shows that perhaps experience isn't enough."

"...it will be easier for us to soothe...."

Masaru "Massy" Ikei, a professor at Keio University in Tokyo points out that nations as well as individuals sometimes have to make decisions based on the maturity of the other party or parties.

For many years Germany and the Netherlands shared the island of New Guinea—the Germans controlled the eastern half, the Dutch the western half. At the end of World War Two, the eastern part (Papua New Guinea) became independent, but the western part (West Irian) remained under the control of the Netherlands.

Newly independent Indonesia resented the presence of the colonial Dutch. Although Japan had no direct part in the squabble, the Japanese got dragged in over a matter of protocol. The Dutch, it seemed, wanted their ships to stop at one or more Japanese ports after delivering soldiers and supplies to West Irian.

This angered Indonesia, and President Sukarno asked Japan to refuse permission to land. The Japanese replied that international protocol allowed the visit. The Dutch ships were welcome. At first Sukarno reluctantly agreed, but when protests in Indonesia broke out, he changed his mind. He asked once again that Japan refuse to open its ports to the Dutch ships.

This left the Japanese Foreign Ministry in a quandary. Should Japan anger the Netherlands or Indonesia? One side or the other was sure to be upset by whatever decision was reached.

The Foreign Vice Minister of Japan, Hisanari Yamada, announced the decision. Japan would ask the Netherlands not to land its ships there after the voyage to West Irian. The Netherlands complied.

There were those in Japan who criticized this decision, arguing that it showed weak and wavering diplomacy. Yamada disagreed. His point was that Indonesia, as a young and restless country, could not easily accept a decision that went against it. The Netherlands, on the other hand, was a mature and diplomatically experienced nation. The Dutch would feel slighted, but, according to Yamada, "If we have to make a choice to annoy Indonesia or the Netherlands, it will be easier for us to soothe the more mature country, the Netherlands."

He was almost certainly right.

MISTAKE

Incredibly, the letter was mailed collect.

Most of the stories about Zachary Taylor have to do with his appearance. Taylor was a general and a military hero. He fought in the War of 1812, the Black Hawk War, the Seminole War, and the Mexican War. "Old Rough and Ready," they called him. He seldom wore a uniform, and many people, including many young military officers, mistook him for a farmer.

But the most serious mistake anyone ever made in regard to the heavyset, unassuming general was made by the Whig Party in 1848. The Whig's national convention in Philadelphia bypassed Senator Henry Clay and General Winfield

Scott and gave their party's Presidential nomination to Old Rough and Ready. Since Taylor was in Baton Rouge at the time, the party informed him by letter of his nomination. Incredibly, the letter was mailed collect. At the time General Taylor wouldn't pick up any unpaid-for mail, so the official word of his nomination didn't reach him, only newspaper accounts.

Many weeks later the chairman of the convention sent him a duplicate of the official letter—this time paying for it—and Zachary Taylor accepted the Whigs' nomination. He went on to win the Presidency, serving without much distinction until iced milk and cherries led to a fatal illness two years into his term.

"It isn't the '23' club."

The matter before the Senate Finance Committee was a tax on nightclubs. During the hearing, Senator Eugene D. Millikin of Colorado repeatedly referred to New York City's "23" Club.

Reporters cornered him after the hearing. "It isn't the "23" Club," one of them told him. "It's "21."

"I know, I know," said the Senator. "But in politics you've got to appear ignorant of things like that."

When Winston Churchill was accused....

When Winston Churchill was accused of making a political mistake, he answered the charge in the House of Commons by quoting the French statesman Georges Clemenceau: "Perhaps I have made a number of other mistakes of which you have not heard."

The builders needed 20 million tons of cement....

Government planners sometimes go astray. Consider the case of Nigeria. In 1974 that country's planners decided on a massive building program. New roads, new government buildings, new airfields. The builders needed 20 million tons of cement, they figured.

So they ordered it—all at once. The cement began arriving by freighter from all over the world.

There was one small problem. The Nigerian port of Lagos could handle only two thousand tons a day. At that rate it was going to take 27 years to unload the cement that was already on its way.

Fully one third of the world's cement was headed for Lagos when the awful reality of the arithmetic hit the government planners. Nigeria scaled down its building plans.

The press release gave the gist...."

Senator Joseph Montoya of New Mexico arrived late for a dinner meeting in Albuquerque. He was to give a speech, and there was no time to do anything except rush for the podium. As he raced by, an assistant thrust a copy of a press release into his hands. The press release gave the gist of the speech Montoya was to give.

The Senator began to speak. "Ladies and gentlemen," he said, "it is a great pleasure to be with you today." Then he glanced down at the paper in his hand. Without thinking, he plunged on. He said, "For immediate release...."

...and called the city "Cedar Rapids"....

President Jimmy Carter, a Democrat, visited Grand Rapids, Michigan, during his campaign for reelection in 1980. At a speech there he misspoke and called the city "Cedar Rapids."

Now, ex-President Gerald Ford, a Republican, lived in Grand Rapids, and he jumped on the Carter misstatement. He blurted to the TV cameras that Jimmy Carter apparently didn't realize that Michigan is one of the 48 states.

Ford, thinking he saw Carter on the ropes, had blundered again. He had to spend the next few days explaining that, yes, he knew there were 50 states, not 48.

"There is no Soviet domination...."

"My friends," said Gerald Ford as he took over the Presidency from Richard Nixon, "our long national nightmare is over."

Two years later when he debated Jimmy Carter he seemed to think that Poland's long national nightmare was over, too. On the night of October 6, 1976, as radio and TV viewers listened in astonishment, President Ford said, "There is no Soviet domination of Eastern Europe, and there never will be under a Ford administration."

Max Frankel of *The New York Times* followed up on Ford's amazing assertion. He suggested the reality of Soviet domination there. This gave Ford a chance at clarification, a way out.

But Ford persisted, saying: "I don't believe that the Yugoslavians consider themselves dominated by the Soviet Union ... [or] the Romanians ... [or] the Poles. Each of those countries is independent, autonomous...."

Jimmy Carter now jumped in and blistered him. After all, this was 1976. The Cold War was still on. There were Russian army divisions in Poland. *Glasnost* and *perestroika* were more than 20 years away.

Ford's statements haunted him for the rest of the campaign and may have cost him the election.

"You just pointed your finger...."

In 1989 Jack Raines was running for governor of Texas. He wanted to become the education governor, so he issued a 10-point education reform plan.

A sharp-eyed reporter noted that Raines' 10-point plan for upgrading education contained only 9 points.

The candidate had a ready answer to cover his mistake. "You just pointed your finger," Raines said "and emphasized the problem we're trying to resolve."

Quote/Unquote

Cato   (234–149 B.C.)

I can pardon everybody's mistake except my own.

Lord Morley   (1843–1905)

I am always very glad when Lord Salisbury makes a great speech.... It is sure to contain at least one blazing indiscretion....

Winston Churchill   (1874–1965)

If we look back on our past life we shall see that one of its most usual experiences is that we have been helped by our mistakes and injured by our most sagacious decisions.

Pearl S. Buck   (1892–1973)

Every great mistake has a halfway moment, a split second when it can be recalled and perhaps remedied.

Claude Pepper   (1900–1989)

The mistake a lot of politicians make is in forgetting they've been appointed and thinking they've been anointed.

MISUNDERSTANDING

The Tsar fled to an inn....

Peter the Great, Tsar of Muscovy, made his famous grand tour of Europe in 1697 and 1698. This was the trip that convinced him of the need to Westernize his country.

Many people think of Peter's journey as a solitary trek across Europe. Nothing could be further from the truth. Peter called his trip a "Great Embassy" to emphasize its diplomatic and fact-finding mission. The embassy consisted of 150 people—diplomats, interpreters, priests, singers, dwarfs, and servants.

With a retinue like that, it's no wonder that Peter's desire to travel incognito was often thwarted. In Zaandam, Holland, a crowd of boys stopped the easily recognized Peter on the street—he was nearly seven feet tall—and asked him for the plums he was carrying. He willingly gave away all he had, but the boys who got no plums complained. When Peter laughed at them, they began throwing mud and stones at him.

The Tsar fled to an inn and sent for the burgomaster. That worthy gentleman issued a proclamation to the citizens of Zaandam. It prohibited "insults to personages who wish to be unknown."

There were *two*....

Mark Twain, who was still very much alive, cabled from London: "The reports of my death are greatly exaggerated."

Thomas Jefferson might have done the same thing in 1800—if there had been a telegraph. In that year reports began circulating that the writer of the Declaration of Independence (and a Presidential hopeful) had passed away on his Virginia estate after a brief illness.

His political opponents probably wished it were true, at least secretly. His friends and supporters were in a tizzy.

In that era of slow communications it took more than a week to track down the truth. There were *two* Thomas Jeffersons of Monticello, Virginia. The one who had written the Declaration of Independence was still alive, and would soon be President.

The other one was a very old slave on the Founding Father's estate, and he indeed had died.

"....a Chinese mandarin came forward...."

All London had been waiting for this day. For almost a year they had watched as the magnificent Crystal Palace took shape. This huge, glittering building in Hyde Park housed the Great Exhibition of 1851. Flags from many countries fluttered from its iron columns. Its glass walls sparkled in the sunlight. The theme of the Exhibition was "Progress."

During the *Hallellujah Chorus*, Queen Victoria noticed that "a Chinese mandarin came forward and made his obeisance." His appearance posed a problem. Immediately following the music, the Queen and her entourage would be leading a procession of statesmen through the length of the hall. According to protocol, these statesmen had to walk in order of rank.

Now, what exactly was the rank of this unknown Chinaman? The Lord Chamberlain discreetly talked it over with the Queen and Prince Albert. It would be unthinkable to underrank him. The Chinese were sticklers for decorum. There must be no embarrassing mistake.

So the Chinese mandarin took his place between the Archbishop of Canterbury and the Duke of Wellington. In that exalted position he made his way through the Crystal Palace. Spectators were delighted to see this honored representative from the far-off Celestial Empire.

But wait. Someone recognized the Chinaman, and next day the story came out. He was not a mandarin at all. He was the keeper of a Chinese junk, recently transported to England and docked on the river Thames. The man charged people a shilling each to visit his boat.

The Chinaman had not been trying to put anything over on the Queen or Prince Albert. He had simply come to Hyde Park with the rest of the curious to catch a glimpse of the Crystal Palace.

"Why in the world didn't they *stop*...?"

A person in Newport, New Hampshire, was reading aloud an account of Lincoln's assassination. He reached the part where John Wilkes Booth leaped to the stage.

One of his listeners jumped up and asked excitedly, "Why in the world didn't they *stop* the stage? Why didn't they shoot the driver?"

"You're a Seymour man, aren't you...?"

The 1868 Presidential election matched Ulysses S. Grant, a Republican, against Horatio Seymour, a Democrat. At the height of the campaign, a crowd of men were sitting on the porch of a hotel in northern New Hampshire.

An old man ambled up. A stranger to the crowd, he was ragged, dirty, and unshaven. The men on the porch began to ply him with questions. One of them asked, "You're a Seymour man, aren't you, old fellow?"

The man drew himself up and replied, "From my present appearance you would probably take me for a Democrat, but I ain't. I learned my politics before I took to drink."

"Ah, 'twas a fine occasion."

William Howard Taft, our most portly American President, enjoyed telling stories at his own expense. One of them concerned a wedding party he attended in New England early in his Presidency.

Taft's aide, Major Archie Butts, was there in full dress uniform. A handsome man, Butts attracted a great deal of attention.

After the ceremony, the hostess was talking about it with her Irish gardener. Taft put in the Irish brogue whenever he told the story.

"Ah, 'twas a fine occasion," said the gardener.

"Yes," the hostess answered, "and it was pleasant to have the President of the United States."

"Yes, madam, yes it was. He's a fine-looking man. And what a beautiful uniform he had! But who the devil was the fat old man that was following him around?"

"The first two days were all right...."

When Hungary became a republic during World War One, most Hungarians didn't know what a republic was. Soldiers at the front shot their officers and deserted. The peasants thought a republic meant "Down with landowners," so they took to looting the castles of the wealthy.

A journalist asked one of the peasants how he liked the republic. The peasant scowled. "The first two days were all right," he said, "but then the sheriff came and took everything back."

They were worried about their table manners.

President Calvin Coolidge once invited some friends to dine at the White House. They were worried about their table manners, so they decided to do everything that Coolidge did.

The meal passed smoothly until coffee was served and Coolidge poured his coffee into a saucer. Since the guests wanted to do the right thing, they poured their coffee into their saucers. Then Coolidge added sugar and cream. The visitors did the same.

Then Coolidge leaned over and gave his saucer of coffee to the cat.

"...I'd like you to meet Red Grange...."

The great football player Red Grange recalls the time that Senator William Brown McKinley of Illinois introduced him to President Calvin Coolidge.

The Senator said, "Mr. President, I'd like you to meet Red Grange, who plays with the Bears."

Coolidge shook the hand of the famous running back and said, "Nice to meet you, young man. I've always liked animal acts."

One scheme was to buy a hundred gondolas....

New York City never had a more flamboyant mayor than Jimmy Walker. Hizzoner, handsome and debonair, was full of wild schemes and crooked deals. One scheme was to buy a hundred gondolas for the lake in Central Park.

The price tag for the gondolas was going to be high, and a Brooklyn alderman objected. The alderman said, "Look, a hundred of 'em is out of the question. Let's buy one male gondola and one female gondola, and let nature take its course."

"Daniel didn't write...."

The political speaker liked to invoke great names from the past.

He began a speech by saying, "As Daniel Webster defined the word in his early dictionary...."

"Wait!" someone in the audience shouted. "Daniel didn't write the dictionary. It was Noah."

"You are mistaken, sir," the speaker said patiently. "Noah built the ark."

"What did he say?"

Senator Reed Smoot of Utah was speaking before a large audience of Swedes. They were polite enough, but there was hardly any applause.

The speaker who followed Smoot addressed the crowd in Swedish. Loud and prolonged applause greeted his words. Not wanting to seem grumpy, Smoot joined enthusiastically in the clapping and cheering.

As the speech ended, he turned to the chairman of the meeting and asked, "What did he say?"

The chairman replied, "Why, he was interpreting your speech to them."

"He's a son of a bishop."

One of Franklin D. Roosevelt's favorite stories concerned a new deacon at the church. A young man was introducing the deacon to his slightly deaf and very conservative father.

"Dad," the young man said, "this is our new deacon."

"New *Dealer*?" replied the old man with obvious distaste.

"No, no. Our new *deacon*, Dad. He's a son of a bishop."

The father smiled knowingly. "They all are," he said.

"Let him which is on the house*top*...."

Most Americans remember Senator Sam Ervin of North Carolina for the part he played in the Watergate investigation. The year was 1973, and by then Ervin had been around for a long time. Twenty years earlier, he had served on the Senate committee that recommended censure of Senator Joe McCarthy, the man who gave the word "McCarthyism" to the English language. McCarthyism meant, and means, personal attacks and unfounded charges against supposed Communists.

Sam Ervin always told a good story. When he noticed Senator McCarthy lifting statements out of context—one of Tail-gunner Joe's favorite techniques—Ervin was ready with an anecdote.

It involved a 19th-century fire-and-brimstone preacher down in North Carolina. In those days it was common for women to wear their hair in topknots. For some reason the preacher found this practice sinful. He searched the Good Book for an appropriate text—and he found it. That Sunday he preached a baleful sermon called "Topknot Come Down."

No sooner had he finished than a woman came up to him. She wore a distinct topknot and an equally distinct look of anger. "No such text exists in the Bible," she snapped.

The preacher thumbed his Bible open to the Book of Matthew, Chapter 24, Verse 17, and read it to her with an air of finality, emphasizing the key words: "Let him which is on the house*top not come down* to take everything out of his house."

As an out-of-context quote, it was classic and outrageous. If the woman had known her New Testament well, she might have recited for the preacher's benefit the very end of Chapter 24. It goes: "The lord of that servant... shall cut him asunder, and appoint him his portion with the hypocrites: there shall be weeping and gnashing of teeth."

When asked why daughter-in-law Joan Kennedy....

Rose Kennedy was the mother of one President and two Presidential hopefuls, not counting her oldest son Joe, who was killed in World War Two. She knew her boys well.

When asked why daughter-in-law Joan Kennedy was living in Boston while son Ted stayed in Virginia, she replied:

"Who's Virginia?"

"Vote for any candidate...."

It's hardly news when a recently deceased candidate is elected to office. But it's something out of the ordinary when a foot powder is elected Mayor.

According to the Reuters news service, it happened in the coastal town of Picoaza, Ecuador. The town's 4,100 people were electing a mayor in a campaign that had aroused little interest.

During the campaign, a manufacturer of foot powder launched an advertising campaign. "Vote for any candidate," the ad said, "but if you want well-being and hygiene, vote for Pulvapies."

On the day before the election, another ad appeared—a widely distributed leaflet that read: "For Mayor: Honorable Pulvapies."

Call it the power of advertising. The foot powder Pulvapies defeated the other candidates easily.

"It reminds them of hippies."

When Richard Nixon ran for President in 1968, the Vietnam War was at its height. One of Nixon's TV commercials showed a photo of an American soldier in Vietnam with the word "Love" written on his helmet.

The image bothered Harry Treleaven, one of Nixon's media men. "It reminds them of hippies," he said. "They don't think it's the sort of thing soldiers should be writing on their helmets."

So Len Garment, another Nixon media guru, had the photo taken out of the ad. The "Love" soldier was replaced with a soldier wearing a plain helmet.

The producers of the commercial were unhappy about losing the photo. "It was such a beautiful touch," one of them said. He thought it was a very interesting young man "who would write 'Love' on his helmet even as he went into combat."

About a week later a letter arrived from the mother of the soldier. She said how thrilled she was to see the photo of her son in Nixon's TV commercial. She wondered if she could obtain a copy of the photo.

The letter was signed "Mrs. William Love."

"Almighty God—"

Jimmy Carter liked to call on God for support in times of crisis. During the gasoline shortage of 1979, Carter invited 40 Senators and Representatives to Camp David to discuss the situation. One of them was Senator Mark Hatfield of Oregon, noted for his prayer-meeting breakfasts in Washington.

Before the session started, while everyone was milling around, President Carter said quietly to Senator Hatfield, "Mark, why don't you start with the prayer?"

Hatfield needed no further urging. He shouted above the other Congressmen's idle chatter; "Almighty God—"

Senator Bennett Johnston of Louisiana, who was standing near his shoulder, looked at Hatfield in surprise. "Say, Mark," he said, "aren't you taking this gas thing a bit seriously?"

"He thinks manual labor...."

Not long ago, Clifford Goldman, the former state treasurer of New Jersey, was making a speech at Princeton University. He said that being on campus and seeing the students there reminded him of his own son, also a student.

Said Goldman: "He thinks manual labor is the Spanish ambassador."

"...this is a local problem."

Congressman Dean Gallo of New Jersey tells this story, crediting a version of it to Representative Bill Hughes:

A newly elected New Jersey Congressman held his first town meeting. During the question and answer session, a voter complained bitterly about the lack of snow removal on her street during a recent storm.

The Congressman responded, "With all due respect, ma'am, this is a local problem. Have you told the Mayor about your concern?"

The woman replied, "No. I didn't want to start that high up."

MONEY

"Pitt has no share in the business...."

One of William Pitt's policies as prime minister of England was to increase taxes to reduce the national debt. Pitt was generally popular, but his new taxes were not.

Richard Brinsley Sheridan told a story about Pitt and his taxes—or rather about a tradesman named Patterson. This Patterson, who owned a shop in Manchester, painted a sign on his cart that read "Pitt and Patterson."

Now, everyone knew that Patterson had no partner in his business. Someone asked him why he had put the name Pitt before his own on the sign. The questioner said, "Pitt has no share in the business, has he?"

"Ah," said Patterson, "he has indeed no share in the business, but a very large share in the profits of it."

"Is that your wood?"

When it became clear that the North was likely to win the Civil War, the value of Confederate currency dropped to almost nothing. Various names were applied to the neatly printed but almost worthless bills. One name was wildcat currency.

Lincoln told a story about going down the Mississippi on a riverboat. The wood for fuel was getting low, and the captain told the pilot to steer toward the nearest woodpile.

As they approached shore, the captain shouted to a man standing there, "Is that your wood?"

"Sure is," the man said.

"Do you want to sell it?"

"I sure do."

"Good. Will you take wildcat currency?"

There was a slight pause. Then the owner said, "Yes."

"And how will you take it?" the captain asked.

The man replied, "Why, cord for cord."

"I do not wish to hold in my hands...."

James A. Garfield is not one of our better known Presidents. He died too soon of an assassin's bullet. But Garfield was a man of some substance—a Civil War general, a college president, and a Congressman from Ohio—before being elected President.

As a Congressman, Garfield knew the value of a dollar. He said, "I am an advocate of paper money, but that paper money must represent what it professes on its face. I do not wish to hold in my hands the printed lies of the government."

"'If you will give me Aristotle's system....'"

In 1899 Congressman John S. Little of Arkansas made these observations on political debate:

"Mr. Speaker, I recollect reading once in an old book a comment on logic. One of the old philosophers said, 'If you will give me Aristotle's system of logic, I will force my enemy to a conclusion: give me the syllogism, that is all I ask.'

"Another philosopher replied, 'If you will give me the Socratic system of interrogatory, I will run my adversary into a corner.'

"Another old philosopher standing by said, 'My brethren, if you will give me a little ready cash, I will always gain my point. I will always drive my adversary to a conclusion, because a little ready cash is a wonderful clearer of the intellect.'"

...Coolidge received dozens of invitations....

After he became Vice President, Calvin Coolidge received dozens of invitations to become an honorary member, or even the honorary president, of this or that organization.

One day the president of a small bank in Washington asked Coolidge if he would be willing to make a deposit—however small—in his bank. He assured the Vice President that the institution was solid and well run. He told him how great an honor it would be for the bank to have an account in the name of the Vice President.

Tongue-in-cheek, Coolidge replied, "Why don't you make me an honorary depositor?"

When Ms. Priest came to write....

You've probably noticed that the Treasurer of the United States is most often a woman. Some years ago that woman was Ivy Baker Priest. When Ms. Priest came to write her autobiography, the title just had to be *Green Grows Ivy*.

The ex-Treasurer makes some good points in the book. One of them is this: "We women ought to put first things first," she writes. "Why should we mind if men have their faces on the money, as long as we get our hands on it?"

"...what did he write?"

When Willy Brandt was mayor of West Berlin, he visited Israel. In Tel Aviv his host invited him to see the magnificent new Mann auditorium.

Brandt expressed surprise and appreciation that Israel had named the auditorium after the German writer Thomas Mann. His host corrected him. The hall was actually named for one Frederic Mann of Philadelphia.

"Oh," said Brandt, "what did he write?"

"A check," his host replied.

"'I hope I break even this year.'"

Farmers in the United States have traditionally voted Republican. President John F. Kennedy expressed surprise at this, since times had been hard in the farm states during the Eisenhower years.

In the campaign of 1960, Kennedy said to a group of farmers, "I understand nearby there was a farmer who planted some corn. He said to his neighbor, 'I hope I break even this year. I really need the money.'"

Quote/Unquote

Marcus Tullius Cicero   (106–43 B.C.)

The sinews of war, unlimited money.

George Washington   (1732–1799)

Few men have virtue to withstand the highest bidder.

Thomas Jefferson   (1743–1826)

Money, and not morality, is the principle of commerce and commercial nations.

Thomas Babington Macauley   (1800–1859)

Even the law of gravitation would be brought into dispute were there a pecuniary interest involved.

Benjamin Disraeli   (1804–1881)

As a general rule, nobody has money who ought to have it.

Abraham Lincoln   (1809–1865)

There cannot justly be any objection to having railroads and canals... provided they cost nothing. The only objection is paying for them....

Henry George   (1839–1897)

Great wealth always supports the party in power, no matter how corrupt it may be.

Boies Penrose   (1860–1921)

I believe in a division of labor. You send us to Congress; we pass laws... under which you make money... and out of your profits you further contribute to our campaign funds to send us back again to pass more laws to enable you to make more money.

Calvin Coolidge   (1872–1933)

No great question has ever been decided by the people of this nation on the sole basis of dollars and cents.

Will Rogers   (1879–1935)

Politics has got so expensive that it takes lots of money to even get beat with.

MOTIVATION

"The Widow Beauharnais"

When he first met his wife Josephine, Napoleon was engaged to a charming young girl, Desiree Clary. With Desiree, the future Emperor felt comfortable and a little superior. With Josephine, he felt at first a kind of awe.

This is odd, because Josephine, who signed her notes "The Widow Beauharnais," was the mistress of another man and a lady of decidedly easy virtue. But she did have political connections, an elegant little town house, and a great deal of money—or so he thought.

Desiree had none of those.

So even though Napoleon felt like a petty provincial beside his "viscountess" (a title Josephine had bestowed on herself), he had the temerity to propose marriage. She accepted.

Josephine's former lover, a high-ranking general, promptly made Bonaparte commanding general of the Army of Italy. It may have been a wedding gift.

In later years Napoleon would say frankly of his marriage to Josephine, "For me it was a good piece of business."

"... he is a sturdy rogue...."

H. L. Mencken, the caustic columnist of the 1920s, had no use for politicians. The politician's business, he wrote, "is never what it pretends to be." Far from being altruistic and devoted to the service of the people, the politician is up to something else entirely.

"Actually," wrote Mencken, "he is a sturdy rogue whose principal and often only aim in life is to butter his parsnips."

"No Irish Need Apply."

Speaker of the House John McCormack was a tireless champion of the less fortunate, of people who struggled within the free-enterprise system but couldn't

make it. A brilliant Irish politician from Massachusetts, he had made it himself...
had made it to the very pinnacle of national politics. But he never forgot his roots.

When someone asked him, "Why are you always fighting for minorities?"
McCormack replied:

"No Irish Need Apply."

It was a heartfelt answer. To the Speaker of the House, discrimination against
the Irish was a recent memory. Just a few years before, a shopkeeper didn't even
have to spell out his prejudices. He could advertise a job in his store window and
simply add an acronym: NINA, which, as everyone knew, meant "No Irish Need
Apply."

The McCormacks, the O'Neills, and even the Kennedys had once been a
discriminated-against minority. No more. But others were, and the frail but tough
Irish Congressman from Massachusetts was determined to help them succeed...
just as he had succeeded.

Did the Congressman have a vision...?

After the death of President John F. Kennedy, many people, including politicians, were scouting around for a "new" Kennedy—that is, a Presidential possibility with youth, good looks, and charisma.

In New York City some Republicans thought they had found their man in
John V. Lindsay, a Congressman who had recently swamped his Democratic
opposition in a district that on the books belonged to the Democrats.

To broaden his base, Lindsay decided to become Mayor of New York. The
Liberal Party endorsed him right away, and with Liberal as well as Republican
support lined up against a lackluster Democratic opponent, Lindsay appeared to
stand a good chance of winning.

This situation enraged conservative Republicans in the city, who regarded
the Congressman as a donkey in elephant's clothing—and an ultraliberal donkey at
that.

William F. Buckley, Jr., a staunch and verbal conservative, wrote an acid
newspaper column in which he questioned Lindsay's motive for running. Did the
Congressman have a vision for the City of New York? Or was it only a vision for his
own political future? What were his ideas? Buckley found them wanting.

He also found the New York media wanting, as always. The press loved
Lindsay. "One metropolitan newspaper," Buckley wrote, "has carefully and enthusiastically recorded his attributes, the most significant of which, some observers
have noted, is the brilliance of his teeth."

And it was true. One paper *had* given that as a factor in Lindsay's favor.
Shades—or pearls—of JFK!

"I'd like that translated, if I may."

People around the world were astonished on October 12, 1960, when Nikita Khrushchev, Premier of the Soviet Union, took off his shoe at the United Nations in New York City, waved it in the air, and proceeded to pound it on the table. The photographs and motion pictures of the incident are still etched in many people's memories.

No one is quite sure what Khrushchev hoped to accomplish. The immediate cause of his outrage was a statement by a member of the Philippine delegation. The delegate had said, truthfully enough, that the peoples of Eastern Europe were being deprived of political and civil rights.

Premier Khrushchev, always a volatile character, had been acting up at the UN for two weeks prior to the shoe-pounding—ever since his arrival in New York. On September 29, Prime Minister Harold Macmillan of Great Britain was speaking. Suddenly, for no apparent reason, Khrushchev interrupted him with angry shouts in Russian.

Macmillan calmly sipped a glass of water and looked over his shoulder at the Assembly President, Frederick H. Boland. He murmured, "I'd like that translated, if I may." Instead, Boland gaveled the Russian Premier to order and told Macmillan to continue.

There was no immediate response to Khrushchev's table pounding. The diplomats were apparently left speechless by the Premier's display of anger. From that day to this, there has been no real explanation of what it all meant.

Quote/Unquote

Niccolò Machiavelli (1469–1527)

For the great majority of mankind are satisfied with appearance, as though they were realities, and are more often influenced by the things that seem than by those that are.

Miguel de Cervantes (1547–1616)

Do away with the motive, and you do away with the sin.

Oliver Wendell Holmes, Jr. (1841–1935)

Consciously or unconsciously we all strive to make the kind of a world we like.

Henry Kissinger (1923–   )

The public life of every political figure is to rescue an element of choice from the pressure of circumstance.

OBJECTIVE

Who cares about Button Gwinnett?

On May 19, 1777, Button Gwinnett went to his reward. As you may know, Button Gwinnett was one of the 56 signers of the Declaration of Independence. As you may not know, he was killed in a duel with Lachlan McIntosh, who lived on to become a brigadier general in the Continental army.

Who cares about Button Gwinnett? Autograph hunters, that's who. Gwinnett, a Georgia merchant and planter, spent little of his life in the public eye. He seems to have signed his name very few times. So if your goal is to collect the autographs of all 56 signers of the Declaration of Independence—and a number of people have that goal—you're likely to come a cropper on Button Gwinnett.

The *Guinness Book of World Records* tells the story. Under "Most Expensive Autographs" there he is. The highest price ever paid for a single letter, $110,000, went for a tiny receipt signed by this little-known Georgia politician who died in his early 40s at the hands of Lachlan McIntosh.

"What did he run for?"

"Breathitt County, Kentucky, was a rough and ready place in those days," the old-timer said. "I had an uncle in politics there."

"What did he run for?" asked his friend.

The old-timer smiled. "The county line," he said.

" 'If we left off fighting....' "

In the dark days before the fall of France, British Prime Minister Winston Churchill had no use for pacifists.

Broadcasting to the nation in March, 1940, he said: "Thoughtless, dilettante, or purblind worldlings sometimes ask us: 'What is it that Britain and France are fighting for?' To this I answer: 'If we left off fighting, you would soon find out.'"

"Why not?" asked the startled priest.

Chicago Mayor Richard J. Daley, when facing major surgery, told the story of the man on his deathbed who was asked by a priest if he renounced Satan.

"No," the man said.

"Why not?" asked the startled priest.

"Because in my condition," the man replied, "I can't afford to make any enemies."

Quote/Unquote

Juvenal (60–140)

Two things only the people anxiously desire—bread and circuses.

Lord Palmerston (1784–1865)

We have no eternal allies, and we have no perpetual enemies. Our interests are eternal and perpetual, and those interests it is our duty to follow.

Ralph Waldo Emerson (1803–1882)

A man plunges into politics to make his fortune, and only cares that the world should last his days.

Susan B. Anthony (1820–1906)

The true Republic: men, their rights and nothing more; women, their rights and nothing less.

Mahatma Gandhi (1869–1948)

Men say I am a saint losing myself in politics. The fact is that I am a politician trying my hardest to be a saint.

Barry Goldwater (1909–   )

Nations do not arm for war. They arm to keep themselves from war.

Eric Sevareid (1912–   )

The difference between the men and the boys in politics is, and always has been, that the boys want to *be* something, while the men want to *do* something.

Martin Luther King, Jr. (1929–1968)

I want to be the white man's brother, not his brother-in-law.

OUTCOME

"And if he does come back?"

King Philip of Spain had a jester who entered in a notebook the names of those who committed foolish acts.

One day the King gave one of his Moors a large sum of money to take to Arabia to buy horses. The jester, surprised at the King's naivete, wrote the King's name in his notebook.

Some time later the King was looking at the notebook and noticed his name. He asked for an explanation.

"Sire," the jester replied, "it was foolish to give so much money to the Moor. You will never see it again."

"And if he does come back?"

The jester smiled. "I will cross out your name and replace it with his."

Joseph Wright was doing a life mask....

In some of the busts made of George Washington, his lips seem tightly compressed. Washington explained why.

Joseph Wright was doing a life mask of the first President. First he oiled Washington's face. Then he began applying plaster. While this was going on, Martha came into the room. Apparently surprised to see her husband looking the way he did, she let out a sudden cry.

Washington began to smile, which, he said, "gave a slight twist of compression to the lips that is now observable in the busts which Mr. Wright afterwards made."

"Never before did I see the fable realized...."

Edmund Burke rose in the House of Commons with a large bundle of papers in his hand.

A rough-hewn man from the country watched him with a look of despair. The man exclaimed, "I hope the honorable gentleman does not mean to read that large bundle of papers, and bore us with a long speech into the bargain."

For some reason this mildly insulting remark so enraged Burke that, without a word, he swept out of the chamber.

George Selwyn, bishop of Litchfield, repeated this story often. He always ended it by saying, "Never before did I see the fable realized, a lion put to flight by the braying of an ass."

"If my name ever goes into history...."

Four days after the Union victory at the Battle of Antietam, President Lincoln called his cabinet to the White House. He had been waiting for this moment. He had an announcement to make.

Tens of thousands of Union soldiers considered the Civil War to be an antislavery crusade. Yet through most of 1861 and 1862 the stated purpose of the war had been to save the Union, nothing more. Now, with a military victory to bolster his statement, Lincoln was prepared to announce the freeing of all slaves in areas that were "in rebellion against the United States."

He read his proposed message—the Emancipation Proclamation—to the members of his cabinet. It was late September. He told them he would sign the historic document on January 1, 1863.

And he did.

All that morning he had been shaking hands with well-wishers, and his right arm was stiff and tired.

To his Secretary of State, William Seward, he said: "If my name ever goes into history, it will be for this act, and my whole soul is in it. If my hand trembles when I sign the Proclamation, all who examine the document hereafter will say, 'He hesitated.'"

Lincoln then picked up his pen and wrote in a strong and steady hand, "Abraham Lincoln."

With that stroke of a pen, Lincoln changed the purpose of the Civil War. Even though the Proclamation was geographically limited, and even though its immediate effects were slight, no one doubted the eventual outcome. If the Union won the war, slavery in the United States was finished.

Two and a half years later, in the very month of Lincoln's assassination, the Union won the war.

As her first official act....

Wyoming was the first state to give full voting rights to women. The state is proud of that distinction, as well it might be, but the story behind the voting law is a bit curious.

There were fewer than a thousand women of voting age in the Wyoming Territory in 1869. The territorial legislature, all Democrats, evidently thought it would be great fun to grant women the right to vote, and, by doing so, force the appointed Republican governor to veto the bill. Amid what the *Wyoming Tribune* called "the greatest hilarity" and "the presentation of various funny amendments," the legislature gave women the right to vote and hold public office. It was all a good laugh.

But Wyoming's governor was no patsy. He crossed up the legislature by signing the bill into law.

One big mistake apparently wasn't enough for the Democrats of Wyoming, because on Valentine's Day, 1870, a justice of the peace resigned so that a woman could be appointed to fill the vacancy. This justice seems to have thought that no woman would apply for the position, or, if one did, that she would prove to be too weak and flighty to handle it.

Wrong again. Esther Morris, a formidable, lantern-jawed woman from South Pass City, Wyoming, filed the necessary papers and received the post of justice of the peace—not to replace the man who had resigned, but a different one. This second male JP indignantly refused to turn over his docket to the new female justice.

Esther Morris was not going to put up with such nonsense as that, then or later. As her first official act, she had him arrested and seized his docket. In office Mrs. Morris proved to be firm but fair, sometimes telling obstreperous lawyers, "Boys, behave yourselves."

It was now clear that what had started as a joke would have major consequences. Women's suffrage gained new life as a national movement. And Wyoming took its place in history as the pioneer state that had given women the right to vote.

"Every time I fill a vacant office...."

James A. Garfield, the twentieth President of the United States, was shot and killed by a disappointed office-seeker. Most heads of state fare better than Garfield, but all are familiar with his problem.

Louis XIV of France, the Sun King, said, "Every time I fill a vacant office, I make a hundred malcontents and one ingrate."

Finally the steamboat stopped....

"Uncle Joe" Cannon, Speaker of the House of Representatives, liked to tell a story about his father's experience while coming up the Mississippi River on a stern-wheel steamboat. Along the way the elder Cannon saw two boys in a skiff rowing out from the bank. They were pulling with all their might and shouting at the top of their lungs.

Finally the steamboat stopped, and a mate hollered down to them, "What's the matter?"

At that the two boys turned their skiff around and rowed furiously back toward the bank. Uncle Joe's father heard one of them yelling, "We stopped a steamboat, by golly!"

"This is a bit of a musical comedy...."

When publisher Cass Canfield, the head of Harper and Brothers, visited Leon Trostky in a suburb of Mexico City early in 1940, he was amused by the armed guards and strict security precautions he saw.

"This is a bit of a musical comedy," Canfield said to his wife. "I can't imagine that Trotsky's life would be in any particular danger in Mexico City."

Trotsky could. He had been around Joseph Stalin long enough to know that he was in mortal danger, no matter how far away from the Kremlin he might be. Although Trotsky had been a hero of the Bolshevik revolution, that was ancient history. Stalin had marked him for death.

Leon Trotsky's small fortress had walls twelve feet high, a watchtower, heavy iron doors, trip wires to set off alarms—not to mention six private guards plus the local police.

Nevertheless, early in the morning of May 25, 1940, Trotsky was awakened by what he thought at first were fireworks. His wife whispered, "They're shooting—they're shooting into the room—" The two of them rolled off the bed and onto the floor, shielded from the door by the bed.

The firing continued. A shadowy figure appeared in the doorway and raked the bedroom and bed with submachine-gun fire. The smell of gunpowder filled the room. A hand grenade exploded somewhere in the house.

Incredibly, Leon Trotsky and his wife survived.

This May attempt on Trotsky's life must have convinced Cass Canfield that Stalin's reach extended to Mexico City. If not, the finale a few months later surely did. In August the assassination attempt was made by one man with an ice pick—and it succeeded. Trotsky died of a stab wound to the head on August 20, 1940.

"Why is your chief so violent...?"

In his book *The Gathering Storm* Winston Churchill tells about the time he almost met Adolf Hitler. Churchill was visiting Munich when an associate of the Führer approached him in his hotel. The man said that Churchill ought to meet Hitler. It would be easy to do, because the Führer came to the hotel every day at five o'clock.

During the conversation, Churchill happened to ask, "Why is your chief so violent about the Jews? How can any man help how he is born?"

The questions must have been transmitted to the Führer—at least that was Churchill's suspicion—because the next day the associate returned. He said that Hitler would not be coming to the hotel that afternoon.

"Thus," writes Churchill, "Hitler lost his only chance of meeting me."

"Well, I have three criticisms."

Vice President Alben W. Barkley graduated from Marvin College, a school that no longer exists. He once read a prepared speech to the alumni association of that college.

He was satisfied with his talk, but the chairman of the association wasn't. The chairman said, "Well, I have three criticisms. In the first place, you read it. In the second place, you read it poorly. And in the third place, it was not worth reading."

That made quite an impression on Barkley, who often told the story on himself in later life.

Once it backfired.

After Barkley had related his three-criticisms anecdote in some extemporaneous remarks, the other speaker of the day arose to give his talk. He was Senator Theodore Green of Rhode Island.

Senator Green leaned toward Barkley and growled, "You blankety-blank, you've ruined me!"

Green then reached into his jacket pocket and came out with the typewritten copy for a long prepared speech.

"I have here in my hand...."

The word "McCarthyism" appears in all the standard dictionaries. Senator Joe McCarthy died not long after being censured by his colleagues in the U.S. Senate. His star had fallen. Yet despite strong evidence to the contrary, there are those who think that "Tail-gunner Joe" was on to a vast and dangerous Communist conspiracy back in the 1950s.

A remarkable aspect of McCarthyism is how unplanned it was. When Senator McCarthy gave his kickoff communists-in-government speech in Wheeling, West Virginia, on February 9, 1950, it was little more than a throwaway talk. In January he had been casting around for a suitable campaign issue. That night in Wheeling he was speaking to a small group of women—party workers at the county level.

The text of the speech—if one existed—got thrown away. A tape recording of the talk was almost immediately erased as being of no consequence. But a Wheeling reporter, Frank Desmond, did jot down some notes that became a story in the local newspaper the next day.

Desmond quoted McCarthy as saying, "I have here in my hand a list of two hundred and five [members of the Communist Party and members of a spy ring] that were known to the Secretary of State . . . and who nevertheless are still working and shaping the policy of the State Department."

When this story was picked up by the national media, McCarthy changed the number to 57, then upped it to 81, then dropped it to 10, and finally, when the questioning got specific, said he would stand or fall on a single case, that of Owen Lattimore.

The Senator would have fallen on his single case, because Owen Lattimore was cleared of all charges. But long before that happened, Senator Joe McCarthy had become a hero to a lot of Americans. He was seen by many as a bold warrior in the fight against domestic Communism.

This isn't the place to go into the complexities, or simplicities, of the Senator's crusade. That isn't the point.

The point is that a national political figure could deliver a silly, unsupported speech on a touchy subject to a small, partisan audience—and have it mushroom into a movement that could, and did, wreck careers, frighten office-holders at the highest levels, and menace the political stability of the country.

The paper that McCarthy held in his hand, by the way, was an outdated letter from Secretary of State James Byrnes that proved nothing at all of what McCarthy was charging.

Tail-gunner Joe himself must have been stunned by the reaction to his Wheeling speech. But he was shrewd enough and devious enough to make hay while the sun shone. A vast Communist conspiracy took shape out of that unthinking speech—all of it without a shred of real evidence or a single proven charge.

"What you make is your income...."

Art Linkletter used to collect the funny sayings of kids. One youngster offered this definition: "What you make is your income, and what the government takes is the outcome."

"Doesn't all that coffee keep you awake?"

The masquerade party of a famous Washington host and hostess began to wind down at about four in the morning. At their invitation, a Brazilian diplomat was staying overnight. Before the diplomat went to bed, he asked if he could have a couple of cups of coffee. The hostess said yes, and the diplomat proceeded to have three full cups without sugar or cream.

This surprised the hostess, who asked him, "How many cups of coffee do you generally take in the course of a day?"

"Oh, 25 to 30," the diplomat replied.

The hostess looked concerned. "Doesn't all that coffee keep you awake?" After a moment's thought, the diplomat said, "Not always—but it helps."

Quote/Unquote

Edmund Burke (1729–1797)

The only thing necessary for the triumph of evil is for good men to do nothing.

Dwight W. Morrow (1873–1931)

Any party which takes credit for the rain must not be surprised if its opponents blame it for the drought.

H.M. Tomlinson (1873–1958)

How many grave speeches, which have surprised, shocked, and directed the nation, have been made by great men too soon after a noble dinner, words winged by the press without an accompanying and explanatory wine list.

W.L. Mackenzie King (1874–1950)

The promises of yesterday are the taxes of today.

Robert A. Taft (1889–1953)

War, undertaken even for justifiable purposes... has often had the principal results of wrecking the country intended to be saved....

Henry Kissinger (1923–   )

This job has done wonders for my paranoia. Now I *really* have enemies.

PATRIOTISM

"This is my own, my native land...."

From **The Lay of the Last Minstrel**
by Sir Walter Scott

Breathes there a man with soul so dead
Who never to himself hath said:
   "This is my own, my native land"?
Whose heart hath ne'er within him burned
As home his footsteps he hath turned,
   From wandering on a foreign strand?
If such there breathe, go mark him well;
For him no minstrel raptures swell;
High though his titles, proud his name,
Boundless his wealth as wish can claim,
Despite those titles, power and pelf,
The wretch concentred all in self,
Living, shall forfeit fair renown,
And, doubly dying, shall go down
To the vile dust from whence he sprung,
Unwept, unhonored, and unsung.

On the same day in Quincy, Massachusetts....

In 1826 there were people who believed that Providence had guided the United States from the beginning. They were further convinced of it on July 4th of that year. For on the Fourth of July 1826—50 years to the day after the signing of the Declaration of Independence—Thomas Jefferson died at Monticello, Virginia.

On the same day in Quincy, Massachusetts, 91-year-old John Adams—the President who had preceded Jefferson in office—also died. He lived just a few hours longer than his great contemporary. Adams's last words, "Thomas Jefferson survives," were touching but untrue.

People were amazed, even awestruck to learn of these two almost simultaneous deaths on the 50th anniversary of American independence. It was one of the most striking coincidences in our history. Adams and Jefferson, two of the prominent Founding Fathers, had often disagreed politically, but after July 4, 1826, they were linked forever in the popular mind.

The miracle didn't end there. Five years later, on the Fourth of July 1831, James Monroe—the fifth American President—died in New York City. By then, even the skeptical were beginning to wonder about signs and symbolism. The second, third, and fifth presidents had all died on Independence Day.

James Madison—the fourth President—was still alive in 1831. And, sure enough, the frail Madison held on for another five years.

Did he die on July 4th, 1836—the 60th anniversary of the Declaration of Independence? Not quite—but almost. Eighty-six years old and in poor health, Madison clung to life until late June. Patriots wanted him to take stimulants to keep himself alive until the fateful day. He refused.

On June 28, 1836, James Madison died, missing the magic date by just six days.

"Thou, too, sail on...."

From The Building of the Ship
by Henry Wadsworth Longfellow

Thou, too, sail on, O ship of State!
Sail on, O Union, strong and great!
Humanity with all its fears,
With all the hopes of future years,
Is hanging breathless on thy fate!
We know what Master laid thy keel,
What workman wrought thy ribs of steel,

Who made each mast, and sail, and rope,
What anvils rang, what hammers beat,
In what a forge and what a heat,
Were shaped the anchors of thy hope!
Fear not each sudden sound and shock,
'Tis of the wave and not the rock;
'Tis but the flapping of the sail,
And not a rent made by the gale.
In spite of rock and tempest's roar,
In spite of false lights on the shore,
Sail on, nor fear to breast the sea!
Our hearts, our hopes, are all with thee,
Our hearts, our hopes, our prayers, our tears,
Our faith triumphant o'er our fears,
Are all with thee—are all with thee!

"Tell them to obey the laws...."

Stephen A. Douglas, who is best known for his debates with Abraham Lincoln, spent a lifetime in politics. On June 3, 1861, as he lay dying, he was asked if there were any instructions he wished to leave his sons.

Many men would have said something about the disposition of property, but not Stephen A. Douglas. He said: "Tell them to obey the laws and support the Constitution of the United States."

"They'll nail anyone who ever scratched...."

While observing the hearings of the House Committee on Un-American Activities in 1947, actor Humphrey Bogart said, "They'll nail anyone who ever scratched his ass during the National Anthem."

"A patriot goes to work...."

In a 1989 Middlebury College Commencement Address, Senator Bill Bradley of New Jersey gave an extended definition of patriotism:

"Patriotism—it's like strength. If you've got it you don't need to wear it on your sleeve.

"The patriot isn't the loudest one in praise of his country... or the one who never admits we could do anything better.

"...Patriotism doesn't need a war for its highest expression. Patriotism is often unpretentious greatness. A patriot goes to work every day to make America a better place."

[Bradley's grandfather] said "America was great because it was free and because people seem to care about each other. Those two, freedom and caring, are the two inseparable halves of American patriotism."

Quote/Unquote

Voltaire   (1694–1778)

It is lamentable that to be a good patriot we must become the enemy of the rest of mankind.

Samuel Johnson   (1709–1784)

Patriotism is the last refuge of a scoundrel.

G.K. Chesterton   (1874–1936)

"My country, right or wrong," is a thing that no patriot would think of saying except in a desperate case. It is like saying, "My mother, drunk or sober."

Theodore Roosevelt   (1858–1919)

The man who loves other countries as much as his own stands on a level with the man who loves other women as much as he loves his own wife.

William Randolph Hearst   (1863–1951)

A politician will do anything to keep his job—even become a patriot.

Everett M. Dirksen   (1896–1969)

Men died here and men are sleeping here [at Gettysburg] who fought under a July sun that the nation might endure, united, free, tolerant, and devoted to equality. The task was unfinished. It is never quite finished.

Al Capone   (1899–1947)

My rackets are run on strictly American lines and they're going to stay that way.

Adlai Stevenson   (1900–1965)

I venture to suggest that patriotism is not a short and frenzied outburst of emotion but the tranquil and steady dedication of a lifetime.

PERFECTION

"They have heard plenty of eloquence...."

Plato put forward the idea of a philosopher king—an almost godlike ruler, an artist who would "take society and human character as his canvas, and begin by scraping it clean."

He admits that this is an ideal vision. He has Socrates say, "...it is no wonder that most people have no faith in our proposals, for they have never seen our words come true in fact. They have heard plenty of eloquence... and artfully matched antitheses; but a man with a character so finely balanced as to be a match for the ideal of virtue in word and deed, ruling in a society as perfect as himself—that they have never yet seen in a single instance."

"Now, sir, you must let me forget...."

Gilbert Stuart was one of the great portrait painters of his day. George Washington sat for him three times, and Stuart expanded those sittings into hundreds of portraits. They were good likenesses—perhaps too perfect. They emphasized the distortions of Washington's mouth, distortions produced by ill-fitting false teeth.

Those false teeth of the first President are now legendary. They weren't made of wood. They were made of substances such as hippopotamus ivory. They were hinged at the back, and opened and closed with the aid of springs. Although the President's false teeth were state-of-the art items back in the late 1790s, they looked terrible.

Why did Stuart insist on painting Washington's deformed mouth? After all, other portrait painters tried to idealize the great President. Not Stuart. He had the skill to create perfect likenesses, and he did. He said that historical accuracy demanded it.

Maybe he was telling the truth, and maybe he wasn't. Stuart had taken a dislike to Washington early on. Trying to get the great man to relax for his portrait, Stuart had said, "Now sir, you must let me forget that you are General Washington and I am Stuart the painter."

To which Washington replied stiffly: "Mr. Stuart need never feel the need for forgetting who he is and who General Washington is." Apparently, he meant that to be polite, but it came across to the painter as snobbish.

So it's possible that Stuart was being a bit vindictive in his Presidential portraits. We know he took offense at things. As Washington biographer James Thomas Flexner points out, Stuart used a portrait of General Henry Knox as the door of his pigsty.

Quote/Unquote

Stephen Leacock   (1869–1944)

With perfect citizens any government is good. In a population of angels a socialistic commonwealth would work to perfection. But until we have the angels we must keep the commonwealth waiting.

Franklin D. Roosevelt   (1882–1945)

Perfectionism, no less than isolationism or imperialism or power politics, may obstruct the paths to international peace.

PERSEVERANCE

"As he had never before gained a victory...."

Robert the Bruce's struggle to gain control of Scotland was long and difficult. Before and after being crowned Robert I, King of Scots, he met with a series of disasters. Defeated by the English at Methven, Robert is said to have taken refuge on the island of Rathlin off the Irish coast.

He spent a bitter winter there in a fisherman's hut on the beach. It was in this forlorn abode, according to Sir Walter Scott, that Robert noticed a spider spinning its web on a beam above him. Six times the spider tried to swing across to the next beam, and six times it failed.

As Robert watched, fascinated, he reflected that he himself had made six futile attempts against the English. His situation looked desperate. But he decided that if the persistent spider could make it to the beam on the seventh try, he, too, would try again.

The spider did make it on the seventh try. And Robert the Bruce went on to reconquer most of Scotland, winning independence and changing the course of Scottish history. Of Robert and the spider incident, Sir Walter Scott wrote, "As he had never before gained a victory, so he never afterwards sustained any considerable or decisive... defeat."

"I shall be very *dry*...."

The wheelbarrow plays a big part in the story of election betting. It may not be as common as a peanut being pushed down the street with one's nose, but it isn't far behind.

Major Benjamin Perley Poore was the man who started it all. He was convinced that Millard Fillmore would beat John C. Frémont in the Massachusetts primaries. His friend, Robert I. Burbank, a lawyer, disagreed. They made a bet: The loser would have to wheel a barrel of apples from his home to the home of the winner.

This was an easier bet to make than it was to deliver on. The two men's homes were more than 36 miles apart, and a barrel of apples weighed 185 pounds.

On election day Major Poore's candidate went down to a lopsided defeat. The Major readied the wheelbarrow and bought the apples. But Robert I. Burbank, who lived at the Tremont House in Boston, was a compassionate man. He wired his friend to forget the bet.

Major Poore said no. He had made the bet, he had lost, and he would live by the result. He wired back that he was on his way. He added, "I shall be very *dry* when I get to the Tremont House." So saying, he harnessed himself to the wheelbarrow with a strap and headed for the city.

It took him two days of pushing. At the Charlestown bridge he was greeted by a cheering crowed of Fillmore supporters. By then Poore's hands were badly blistered. His back was black and blue. He had lost twelve pounds.

But he was almost there. And naturally he had attracted a lot of notice. A band joined him; a group of marchers surrounded him. A banner bore the legend: "Major Poore—may the next administration prove as faithful to their pledges as he was to his." A small platform was thrown up in front of the Tremont House, and Burbank stood on it, beaming. He made a brief speech.

Then Burbank and the exhausted Major went inside, where it's safe to assume the winner asked the loser what he would like as a cure for his dryness.

Congress had decided 101 years earlier....

On a wooden platform more than 550 feet above Washington, D.C., a group of six men braced themselves against a high wind. It was December 6, 1884, and they were assembled to do something which many people had despaired of ever seeing. They were placing a 100-ounce aluminum tip on the Washington Monument. The world's tallest structure (at the time) was finally finished.

Far below them, a crowd cheered as a flag was unfurled and a salute was fired. You may wonder about the significance of the date. Why December 6, 1884? The answer is that the date had no significance. The job was done, the monument completed—that was all.

And what a job it had been! Congress had decided 101 years earlier, in 1783, to build a monument to George Washington. He liked the idea. But nothing much happened for the next 50 years. Then a group of private citizens tried to get the project moving. Still, things moved slowly. Not until 1848 was the cornerstone laid.

After that, construction went swimmingly for six years. The monument rose 152 feet—and stopped cold for many more years. A group of Know-Nothing Party members had seized control of the monument commission. The Know-Nothings were also do-nothings. The unfinished monument stood idle until Congress took charge two decades later and appropriated some money to finish it.

The completion date was set for July 4, 1876... then for October 19, 1881—the centennial of Washington's victory over Cornwallis at Yorktown... then for... whenever. It turned out to be December 6, 1884.

The formal dedication was held on Washington's birthday the next year. Three years after that the monument was opened to the public. It had been a long, long wait, but visitors today probably agree it was worth it.

"Felix, Felix, I'll tell the Tsarina."

It took a lot of persistence to murder Grigori Rasputin, the mad monk of imperial Russia. The events surrounding his death are bizarre almost to the point of fantasy. Rasputin, like the villain of all those *Friday the 13th* movies, just wouldn't die.

He has been called an evil genius. In many ways he resembled the modern cult killer and madman Charles Manson. Imagine Charley Manson as a trusted adviser to the President of the United States, and you'll have some idea of how bad things were under Tsar Nicholas II.

Rasputin, a dissolute "holy man" with fiery eyes and an unkempt black beard, won over Tsarina Alexandra completely because of his amazing ability—never explained—to stop the bleeding of her hemophiliac son. The Tsarina controlled the weak and inept Tsar, while Rasputin controlled the Tsarina. His political influence during the last years of the tsarist government grew to be enormous—and disastrous.

Enter Prince Felix Yusupov, a wealthy young nobleman, with a plot to kill the mad monk. Yusupov and four co-conspirators would dine with Rasputin at Yusupov's place in St. Petersburg. During the meal they would poison him with potassium cyanide.

No problem. Rasputin arrived, dined, ate the poisoned cake, drank the poisoned wine—and showed almost no ill effects. He seemed a little sleepy, nothing more. Impatiently, Yusupov pulled a gun and shot the mad monk in the chest. Rasputin appeared to be dead. But a few minutes later, as Yusupov bent over him, the mad monk opened those piercing eyes of his, leapt to his feet, and flailed away at Yusupov, who fled upstairs to join his co-conspirators.

One of them came downstairs and began to chase Rasputin across the courtyard. The monk was screaming, "Felix, Felix, I'll tell the Tsarina." No, he wouldn't. The conspirator fired four times with his revolver, and Rasputin fell to the ground, hit by two of the bullets. He was apparently dead, but the conspirator kicked him savagely anyway. Later Yusupov bashed Rasputin's head with a blackjack for good measure.

At 5:30 in the morning the conspirators dumped the body of the mad monk in the River Neva. The police found it the next day. An autopsy reportedly showed traces of water in Rasputin's lungs, suggesting that he had died of drowning—that is, he was still alive when thrown into the river.

Upon his release, De Valera returned....

Eamon De Valera, like many Irish political leaders, spent some of his life in British prisons. He was once arrested for an inflammatory speech he made at Ennis in County Clare. His prison sentence was one year.

Upon his release, De Valera returned to Ennis. He began his speech with these words:

"As I was saying when I was interrupted...."

Quote/Unquote

Henry Wadsworth Longfellow (1807–1882)

> The heights by great men reached and kept
> Were not attained by sudden flight,
> But they, while their companions slept,
> Were toiling upward in the night.

Abraham Lincoln (1809–1865)

> The fight must go on. The cause of civil liberty must not be surrendered at the end of one or even one hundred defeats.

> I do the very best I know how—the very best I can; and I mean to keep doing so until the end.

Josh Billings (1818–1885)

> Consider the postage stamp: its usefulness consists in the ability to stick to one thing till it gets there.

Winston Churchill (1874–1965)

> We have not journeyed all this way across the centuries, across the oceans, across the mountains, across the prairies, because we are made of sugar candy.

POLITICS

Quote/Unquote

Aristotle   (384–322 B.C.)

Man is a political animal.

Cato   (234–149 B.C.)

The politician creates his little laws,
And sits attentive to his own applause.

John Arbuthnot   (1667–1735)

All political parties ultimately die from swallowing their own lies.

Thomas Jefferson   (1743–1826)

If I could not go to heaven except with a political party, I would rather not go there at all.

Benjamin Disraeli   (1804–1881)

Politics is nothing but organized opinion.

William McKinley   (1843–1901)

Our differences are politics, our agreements are principles.

Rutherford B. Hayes   (1862–1948)

All free governments are party governments.

Will Rogers   (1879–1935)

All politics is applesauce.

POWER

"...everything will be cured with my recipe...."

His full name was Simón José Antonio de la Trinidad Bolívar y Palacios, but he was better known as the Liberator. The title fit the man. Five countries in South America—Venezuela, Colombia, Ecuador, Peru, and Bolivia—owe their freedom to him.

Bolívar was a brilliant military leader. He once said, "...all begin to fear me very much; they... say that everything will be cured with my recipe: an ounce of lead and four drams of powder."

"Watch the morgue. They'll show up there."

Nowhere did the Roaring Twenties roar louder than in Cicero, Illinois. The western Chicago suburb was controlled by the Capone gang, from its mayor, Joseph Z. Klenha, on down. Al Capone's private guard of about 800 gun-toters made the 50-man police force look puny by comparison.

The municipal election of 1924 featured gangsters in black limousines patrolling the streets. Opponents of Klenha were beaten up, their ballots were snatched and marked "Klenha," and honest poll watchers were kidnapped. Klenha won easily.

The decent citizens of Cicero were cowed. Al Capone held the city in his hands, operating from behind bulletproof steel shutters and armed guards at the Hawthorne Inn on 22nd Street. Mayor Klenha was simply a puppet. Once when hizzoner angered Capone, the mobster knocked the mayor down on the steps of the town hall and kicked him in the groin for good measure.

Clearly, the mayor and the police were no match for Al Capone. But another mobster arose who might be able to unseat him. The newcomer's name was Hymie Weiss. Unfortunately, Hymie Weiss had no more subtlety or civic spirit than Capone.

On September 20, 1926, eleven automobiles rolled slowly by the Hawthorne Inn. The cars were loaded with gangsters, and the gangsters were loaded with artillery. They pumped more than 1,000 bullets into the two-story brown brick building, using mainly Thompson submachine guns. The marksmen perforated at least 35 automobiles at the curb, along with a citizen or two, but they failed to perforate Al Capone.

When it was all over and the innocent bystanders were hauled away, Capone made it clear that he was irritated. He refused to speculate on who had done the shooting, but he did say, "Watch the morgue. They'll show up there."

No doubt many of them did. One who did for sure was Hymie Weiss, who was wheeled in cold 20 days later.

A Secret Service man casually remarked....

Thunderclouds outside the window suggested that a storm was brewing. A Secret Service man casually remarked on this fact to President Calvin Coolidge.

"Well," asked Coolidge, "what are you going to do about it?"

The man replied: "Mr. President, I'm only a Secret Service man. But you are President of the United States. What are *you* going to do about it?"

Mussolini's men used revolvers, clubs....

No one ever accused Benito Mussolini of being subtle. Early in his career, when his Fascists were struggling for power, Mussolini's men used revolvers, clubs, and daggers to make their political points.

The Archbishop of Milan didn't like what was going on, and he spoke out against the activities of the Fascists. Mussolini saw no point in arguing about it. Instead, he stopped a man on the street and paid him ten lire to deliver a package to the Archbishop.

Fortunately for the cleric, the time bomb in the package failed to go off. The Archbishop went on to become Pope Pius XI. Mussolini went on to become dictator of Italy.

"I like to see independent thinking."

In the movie *No Way Out*, and before that in the novel *The Big Clock*, there's a powerful man who gets himself into a lot of trouble. In the movie he's with the government. In the novel he's a magazine publisher.

This character is modeled on Henry R. Luce, the founder of *Time* magazine. Kenneth Fearing, the author of *The Big Clock*, had worked at *Time* and had observed Luce in action. He had seen Luce's power up close and wouldn't have been surprised to hear Luce express his philosophy like this:

"I want good editors with independent minds. I like to see independent thinking. If it's going the wrong way, I'll straighten them out fast enough."

Quote/Unquote

Samuel Johnson   (1709–1784)

Power is always gradually stealing away from the many to the few, because the few are more vigilant and consistent.

John Adams   (1735–1826)

Power must never be trusted without a check.

Napoleon Bonaparte   (1769–1821)

Great men are meteors destined to burn up the earth.

Leo Tolstoy   (1828–1910)

In order to obtain and hold power a man must love it. Thus the effort to get it is not likely to be coupled with goodness, but with the opposite qualities of pride, craft, and cruelty.

Lord Acton   (1834–1902)

Power tends to corrupt, and absolute power corrupts absolutely.

James F. Byrnes   (1879–1972)

Power intoxicates men. It is never voluntarily surrendered. It must be taken from them.

Mao Tse-tung   (1893–1976)

Every Communist must grasp the truth: "Political power grows out of the barrel of a gun."

Milton Friedman   (1912–   )

Concentrated power is not rendered harmless by the good intentions of those who create it.

Henry Kissinger   (1923–   )

Power is the great aphrodisiac.

PREDICTION

"The Athenians will kill you one day...."

Demosthenes, the greatest of the Greek orators, had many enemies. One of them was Phocion, an Athenian general.

One day Demosthenes shouted at Phocion, "The Athenians will kill you one day when they are in a rage!"

Phocion replied, "And they will kill you one day when they are in their senses."

"The Ides of March have come...."

One of the most famous predictions in history occurred back in 44 B.C. Spurinna, the Roman augur, or fortune-teller, warned Julius Caesar that a great danger to him would exist on March 15, the Ides of March.

On that day Caesar set off for the Senate house as usual. He met Spurinna on the way and smiled. "The Ides of March have come," he said.

Spurinna did not smile. "True," she replied. "They have come—but not yet gone."

"Three days before Your Majesty."

Back when political leaders had court astrologers—or do they still?—signs and auguries were taken seriously. When the court astrologer to Louis XI of France correctly predicted the exact day on which the King's mistress would die, Louis was badly shaken.

He thought the prediction had somehow caused the death of his beloved. He decided to have the astrologer killed.

He sent for the man. Fearing the worst, the astrologer went to see the King.

"Tell me," said Louis cunningly, "when *you* are to die."

The astrologer saw his chance for salvation. "Three days before Your Majesty," he said.

The King immediately changed his mind about murdering the astrologer and instead took great pains to guard the man's life.

...he underestimated Napoleon's destiny.

As a young man Napoleon Bonaparte impressed his commanding officers. One of them, General Jean-Pierre du Teil, predicted a bright future for the young lieutenant—but even so he underestimated Napoleon's destiny.

Du Teil said, "No question about it—this officer will reach one of the highest posts in the royal artillery corps."

"...the present question is a mere preamble...."

For decades the question of extending or not extending slavery into new states and territories dominated domestic policy. The first important law to deal with the issue was the Missouri Compromise of 1820. By its terms Missouri was to be admitted to the Union as a slaveholding state, but henceforth slavery would be prohibited in any new states north of the latitude of Missouri's southern boundary.

John Quincy Adams, who was Secretary of State at the time, noted in his diary: "I take it for granted that the present question is a mere preamble—a title page to a great, tragic volume."

He was right.

"Who would have prophesied...?"

When Simón Bolívar was 17, he was in Madrid playing battledore and shuttlecock with the future King Ferdinand VII of Spain. Bolívar, a Creole, came from Caracas, Venezuela. His family was wealthy and aristocratic, but since he had not been born in Spain, he was looked down on by the Spanish court.

During the game, Bolívar accidentally knocked the future King Ferdinand's hat off. The young heir to the Spanish crown expected an apology, but 17-year-old Simón offered none.

Many years later, Bolívar said, "Who would have prophesied to Ferdinand VII that this was a sign that one day I might tear the costliest jewel from his crown?"

"All our livestock must be slaughtered...."

Prophecy is a tricky business. When it involves the raising of the dead, it's best to question the prophet. A South African tribe, the Gealeke Xhosa, learned this the hard way.

Back in 1857 a 14-year-old prophetess arose in their midst. She reported a vision she had seen in a local river. Deep down in the water, shimmering up at her, were the faces of the dead elders of the tribe.

Her understanding of the vision was that those dead leaders could be brought back to life. Yes, but how?

She answered confidently: "All our livestock must be slaughtered," she said, "on or before February 18, 1857."

That was pretty specific. The tribe decided to go along with her. They slaughtered their livestock by the required date.

No elders appeared—but the action did have its consequences. The entire tribe starved to death.

"Ay, sir, and though I sit down now...."

Benjamin Disraeli expected his maiden speech in the House of Commons to be a triumph. He knew all the forms of address. He had composed his speech carefully. At the age of 33, he was renowned as a dashing personage and brilliant orator. He was eager to speak.

His chance came as a response to Daniel O'Connell, a House member he despised. Supporters of O'Connell were not inclined to be polite toward him. As soon as Dizzy used a few of the long words he loved so well, laughter broke out. He went on, but more laughter greeted him, along with hisses, catcalls, and the scraping of feet. Things weren't going well at all.

"Now why smile?" he asked the hecklers. At that, they didn't just smile, they roared with laughter. "Why envy me?" More loud laughter.

Disraeli kept his composure, even though it was clear the speech would be a disaster. They wouldn't let him speak more than two or three sentences before interrupting with shouts of "Oh, oh!" and "Question, question!"

After one rumble of laughter, he said, "Nothing is so easy as to laugh." That was followed by great roars of laughter. It kept up, so that Dizzy could barely deliver single sentences over the din.

Finally, he stopped and stared in cold fury at his audience. He said nothing for a few moments, then raised his hands and thundered out his conclusion. The clamor in the chamber had subsided only a bit, but Disraeli's words rang out across the bedlam—words of frustration and prophecy:

"Ay, sir, and though I sit down now, the time will come when you will hear me."

Alf Landon carried just two states....

Public opinion polls were popular but not completely reliable in 1936, the year Franklin D. Roosevelt ran for a second term. The *Literary Digest* opinion poll predicted a clear-cut victory for Alf Landon of Kansas, Roosevelt's opponent in the Presidential election. Although *Literary Digest* polls had been accurate in the past, they had a built-in flaw that would soon be apparent.

Jim Farley, FDR's good friend and campaign manager that year, had a more accurate picture of the coming election. He was in daily touch with state and national committee chairmen, newspaper reporters, and other grass-roots sources. When asked to predict on the outcome of the election, he did. He said that Republican Alf Landon would carry two states—Maine and Vermont, for a total of eight electoral votes. Roosevelt would carry the rest, for a total of 523.

Many people, even Democrats, considered Farley's prediction so far-fetched as to be embarrassing. But when the votes were counted, Farley had the last laugh. Alf Landon carried just two states—Maine and Vermont. Roosevelt carried all the rest, winning in the Electoral College by a vote of 523 to 8.

Why was Farley so right and the *Literary Digest* so wrong? Well, Farley drew his information from every possible source. He used his eyes, his ears, his campaign workers, and his native shrewdness. The *Literary Digest*, on the other hand, based its prediction entirely on telephone polling. In the dark days of 1936, in the midst of the Great Depression, the people who had telephones were mostly people with money. And that generally meant Republicans, who were likely to be Alf Landon voters.

So Landon won the telephone poll easily. But the November election was quite another matter.

"...you're going to carry Illinois."

Mayor Richard Daley of Chicago knew how to deliver votes. When John F. Kennedy was running for President in 1960, he asked Daley how the situation looked in Illinois.

Daley is reported to have promised, "Mr. President, with a little bit of luck and a few close friends, you're going to carry Illinois."

He was right. JFK carried Illinois by a razor-thin margin—fewer than 9,000 votes out of more than four and a half million cast. (At least that's what the official tally said.)

"Unless man can match his strides...."

Because of the Bay of Pigs fiasco and the Cuban missile crisis, John F. Kennedy gained a reputation for being bellicose. But he always recognized the steep risks of war in the modern world.

He said: "Unless man can match his strides in weaponry and technology with equal strides in social and political development, our great strength, like that of the dinosaur, will become incapable of proper control and, like the dinosaur, vanish from the earth."

"He will have his bar mitzvah...."

In 1965 Allen Schwartz became the law partner of Edward I. Koch. At that point Koch was nearly 40 years old and had made only a slight ripple in the sea of New York City politics.

Nevertheless, as Schwartz and Koch sat in their law office at 53 Wall Street early in 1966, Koch made a startling prediction. Schwartz's wife had just given birth to a son, David, and the two men were talking about it.

"He will have his bar mitzvah in Gracie Mansion," Koch said, sounding as if he meant it.

Schwartz looked at him, amazed. His modestly successful law partner was promising to be Mayor of New York City by the time of David's bar mitzvah. He thought Koch had lost his mind.

Thirteen years later, Ed Koch was Mayor of New York, and David Schwartz had his bar mitzvah at Gracie Mansion.

...Congresswoman Ferraro was having dinner....

On July 19, 1984, Geraldine Ferraro became the first woman nominated by a major party for Vice President of the United States. The mood in San Francisco that night was euphoric. Democrats, and especially Democratic women, looked forward to a Mondale-Ferraro victory in November.

As everyone knows, the Mondale-Ferraro ticket went down to a shattering defeat, receiving only 13 electoral votes to President Reagan's 525.

It shouldn't have happened that way, according to a Chinese fortune cookie. Late in 1983 Congresswoman Ferraro was having dinner with a group of politically active women in Washington. After the order-in Chinese meal at an apartment on Connecticut Avenue, the women opened their fortune cookies.

Ferraro's read, "You will win big in '84."

Quote/Unquote

Mark Twain   (1835–1910)

He could foretell wars and famines, though that was not so hard, for there was always a war and generally a famine somewhere.

Winston Churchill   (1874–1965)

It is a mistake to look too far ahead. Only one link in the chain of destiny can be handled at a time.

PREPARATION

"My end is my beginning."

Mary, Queen of Scots, is one of the romantic figures in world history. A woman of intelligence, beauty, and charm, she made the mistake of contending for power with Elizabeth I of England. A series of plots designed to help Mary gain the English throne led finally to her imprisonment at Fotheringhay Castle.

Mary was tried and convicted of treason. Only after much soul searching did Elizabeth sign the death warrant. But preparations were already underway at Fotheringhay. The great hall was cleared of its usual furniture. Near the upper end of the hall workmen erected a small platform. On it the focus of attention was an ordinary wooden chopping block.

While the stage was being set for Mary's execution, Mary made careful plans of her own. She had no chance of escape... only a chance to embarrass those who opposed her.

Her motto had been, "My end is my beginning." Perhaps it would be true. Certainly she was about to become a martyr.

On the platform Mary spoke of forgiveness. She seemed perfectly composed.

Then her serving ladies removed the black gown she was wearing. Underneath she was dressed all in bright red, the color of martyrdom. She knelt over the chopping block.

Two chunks of the ax marked the end of Elizabeth's rival.

One more task remained. The masked executioner must exhibit Mary's head and cry, "Long live the queen!"

When he tried to do so, he got a shock. He found himself holding nothing but a kerchief pinned to an auburn wig. Mary's head, with a fine silver stubble, rolled toward the edge of the platform.

Even in death, Mary had confounded her enemies.

"Young Sheridan wasn't too clear...."

Thomas Sheridan, the son of playwright Richard Brinsley Sheridan, became the candidate to represent a Cornish borough in Parliament.

Young Sheridan wasn't too clear about his political leanings. He told his father, jokingly, that if he was elected he would put a label reading "To Let" on his forehead. Then he would side with the party that made the best offer.

"Right, Tom," said his father, "but don't forget to add the word "Unfurnished.""

If there was an all-night session....

Historians rank Wisconsin's Robert M. LaFollette, the leader of the Progressive movement, as one of the great United States Senators. He championed the little people, as Leona Helmsley would later call them, against the powerful political and economic bosses of his day.

When LaFollette was first elected to Congress, he was the youngest member of the House. He had never been east of Chicago, he felt ill-prepared to tackle far-reaching issues, and he decided to take a crash course in national politics.

He had been elected to the 49th Congress, which was to meet in December 1885. LaFollette went to Washington in January of that year in order to sit in on the closing session of the 48th Congress. He was resolved to learn all he could about how Congress functioned and about the pressing national questions with which he would have to deal.

He attended all the sessions of the House. He studied the rules. He followed every debate. He read the *Congressional Record* every day. If there was an all-night session, he stayed all night.

In addition, he made friends with some of the members. All this at the age of 29 and before he had officially joined the House. No one in Congress could doubt that this young politician from the Badger State was serious about the office he had won.

"What was his first name?"

During the 1960 Presidential campaign, a reporter reminded Senator John F. Kennedy that he had been promised a military intelligence briefing from the White House. The reporter asked him if he had received such a briefing.

"Yes," Kennedy replied. "I talked on Thursday morning to General Wheeler from the Defense Department."

The reporter asked, "What was his first name."

Kennedy smiled and admitted, "He didn't brief me on that."

Quote/Unquote

George Washington Plunkitt   (1842–1924)

Some young men think that the best way to prepare for the political game is to practice speakin' and becomin' orators. That's all wrong. We've got some orators in Tammany Hall, but they're chiefly ornamental.

Benito Mussolini   (1883–1945)

As the Russians say, to become a complete man it takes four years in a public school, two in a university, and two more in jail.

Earl Long   (1895–1960)

I have the experience to be Governor. I know how to play craps. I know how to play poker. I know how to get in and out of the Baptist church and ride horses. I know the oil and gas business. I know both sides of the streets.

Everett M. Dirksen   (1896–1969)

I've scribbled a few notes on this [laundry ticket] and out of it will come thousands of words. I wonder what they will be?

PRESSURE

"I was shouted at from every editorial sanctum...."

Public pressure for action can result in foolish decisions. The public and media clamor for freeing hostages in the Mideast, for example, led straight to President Reagan's arms-for-hostages deal. Although it's hard for a leader to hold out against aroused public opinion, he or she may have to. One aspect of leadership is the ability to do just that—to ignore an insistent public demand for the wrong kind of action.

Woodrow Wilson's attorney general, A. Mitchell Palmer, failed his leadership test in a way worse than most. It seems too bad. By all accounts Palmer was a man of liberal opinions, a careful and conscientious lawyer. But a series of terrorist bombings, many of them apparently the work of anarchists, convinced Palmer that he had to do something. But what?

Palmer wasn't sure. He began a sensible and systematic plan to find out who the bombers were. Unfortunately, the country was in a panic. It wasn't interested in sensible and systematic plans. It wanted to see some heads roll—and fast. When the Communist Party and the Communist Labor Party held separate conventions in Chicago, many people took it as a sign that Bolshevism had arrived full-blown in the United States.

The press cried out for action. Palmer said later, "I was shouted at from every editorial sanctum in America from sea to sea." President Wilson had suffered a life-threatening stroke, and Palmer was free to act on his own. The pressure built. His colleagues were convinced that the Red menace was real. And of course they knew its source—Russia.

On the night of November 7, 1919, federal agents and New York City policemen surrounded a four-story brownstone on East 15th Street, Manhattan. The building was called the Russian People's House. It was a meeting place and recreation center for Russian aliens. Evening school was in session when the agents and cops rushed in, arresting everyone in sight, and aiming blackjacks at the frightened aliens as they were herded to the paddy wagons. Thirty-three of the two hundred or so "suspects" required medical attention.

A search of the building turned up no weapons, no incriminating documents, nothing at all on which to pin a case. But that was overlooked in the general euphoria. That night there had been raids on Russian centers in nine other cities, with equally inconclusive results.

Yet by the morning of November 20th, A. Mitchell Palmer was a hero from coast to coast. To his amazement, the Red Scare began to look like his ticket to the White House. The once careful and liberal lawyer became an anti-Red activist almost literally overnight. He conducted an even bigger—and even less defensible—series of raids on January 2nd.

The American public loved it. Palmer's crusade enjoyed widespread popular support.

But then some investigations of his actions began. Public officials voiced their qualms. The press reported serious miscarriages of justice. An investigating committee found clear misuses of federal power. Predicted Red uprisings failed to occur. The public lost interest.

A. Mitchell Palmer, who had at first reacted against his will to public pressure, now fell victim to public indifference. Nevertheless, he remained a leading Presidential contender at the Democratic national convention of 1920. However, his strength by then was mainly among federal officeholders. He had little public support. The Red Scare was yesterday's news. The eventual Democratic nominee was James Cox of Ohio, who lost by a landslide to Warren G. Harding.

"Thank God, Henry, you have seen the light."

Henry Ashurst, a Senator from Arizona, made a long and persuasive speech in favor of a cause that he and his constituents favored. He sprinkled it with allusions from Shakespeare, Dante, and the Bible.

But when the roll call came, Senator Ashurst voted against the bill he had just praised so eloquently.

A Senator who had opposed him in the debate congratulated him on his switch. The colleague said, "Thank God, Henry, you've seen the light."

"Oh, no," Ashurst corrected him. "I didn't see the light. I felt the heat."

Quote/Unquote

Winston Churchill (1874–1965)

Dictators ride to and fro upon tigers which they dare not dismount. And the tigers are getting hungry.

Christabel Pankhurst (1880–1958)

Never [to] lose your temper with the press or the public is a major rule of political life.

Lester B. Pearson (1897–1972)

The strongest pressure in the world can be friendly pressure.

Edward R. Murrow (1908–1965)

Difficulty is the one excuse that history never accepts.

Henry Kissinger (1923–   )

There can't be a crisis next week. My schedule is already full.

PRIDE

"The difference between us...."

A descendent of Harmodius, a Greek hero for his struggle against tyranny, was taunting Iphicrates for being of low birth. Iphicrates had recently come to fame through his brilliant organization of an army group that won success in the Corinthian War.

Young Iphicrates was not about to take any guff from this effete, self-important critic. His reply has been quoted for more than two millennia.

"The difference between us," he said, "is that my family begins with me while yours ends with you."

He carried on his imperial duties....

Vespasian is not one of the better-known Roman emperors, but he was a man of considerable ability and immense pride. He carried on his imperial duties even while on his deathbed. As he was dying, he tried to arise, saying to his attendants, "An emperor ought to die standing."

"I always got the girl."

It irritated Ronald Reagan when people made fun of his films. Acting was Reagan's career—a career in which he took considerable pride.

And he resented it when people said "he never got the girl" in his movies. In an interview with journalist Lou Cannon in 1968 Reagan rattled off the movie heroines he had "gotten"—Ann Sheridan in *King's Row* and *Juke Girl,* Priscilla Lane in *Million Dollar Baby,* Shirley Temple in *That Hagen Girl,* Eleanor Parker in *The Voice of the Turtle,* Doris Day in *The Winning Team,* Virginia Mayo in *The Girl from Jones Beach,* Barbara Stanwyck in *Cattle Queen of Montana,* and Patricia Neal in *John Loves Mary.*

Reagan added that he was married to Nancy (then Nancy Davis) in *Hellcats of the Navy.* In other words, he suggested, "I always got the girl."

PRIORITIES

"You will listen to me, all ears...."

Even the Greek orator Demosthenes couldn't always get his audience to pay attention. Once he was speaking on a matter of great public importance, but the crowd had tuned out.

When serious words failed to make an impression, he told the audience a tale. It seems, he said, that a man was going from Athens to Piraeus. Another man overtook him and offered to buy his donkey. After a bit of bargaining, they concluded the sale.

It was a hot day, so the ex-owner sat down to rest. He chose the shadow of the donkey as the coolest place he could find. The new owner objected, saying he had bought the donkey, and with his purchase went full rights to the donkey's shadow.

The discussion grew hotter than the afternoon sun. The ex-owner claimed he had just as much right to the shadow as the new owner. He hadn't sold the shadow, he bellowed.

Demosthenes paused at this point. He asked his audience, "And how do you think this quarrel ended?"

The crowd yelled, "Go on! Go on! Tell us what happened!"

The orator then made the observation he was leading up to. "You will listen to me, all ears," Demosthenes said, "when I tell you a silly story about a donkey. But when I speak about important matters of state you will not listen."

He then traded in the coonskin....

Davy Crockett, Tennessee frontiersman and Congressman, found that his campaign audiences had one main requirement—whiskey. As Crockett put it, "They could not listen to me on such a dry subject as the welfare of the nation until they had something to drink." And of course they expected the campaigner to supply that something.

Crockett was broke at the time, but he used his frontier skills to shoot a coon. He then traded in the coonskin for some of "Job Snelling's extract of cornstalk and molasses." After a bit of boisterous drinking, said Crockett, "I want out and mounted the stump without opposition, and a clear majority of the voters followed me to hear what I had to say about the good of the nation."

But before he was halfway through his speech, a listener interrupted to say he would like to wash down the words already spoken with a shot or two more of Job Snelling's product. The rest of the audience loudly agreed, and everyone adjourned to the shanty where the whiskey was stored.

By now Davy Crockett understood the true extent of the thirst his speaking could raise. "I began to reckon," he said, "that the fate of the nation pretty much depended upon my shooting another coon."

"Must you fall asleep...?"

The session of the House of Commons had dragged on and on. Now one of Winston Churchill's opponents was delivering a long and boring speech. Churchill listened for a while, then slid down in his seat and closed his eyes.

The speaker noticed him dozing off and said in a loud voice, "*Must* you fall asleep when I am speaking?"

Churchill didn't move or open his eyes. But he did speak. "No," he said, "It's purely voluntary."

"If Hitler invaded Hell...."

No one hated Soviet Communism more than Winston Churchill. But when Hitler invaded Russia in 1941, Churchill found himself unexpectedly on the same side as the Soviet Union. He had no choice but to advocate support for Stalin and the Russians.

When someone asked him how he could abandon his long-standing hatred for Stalin, he replied: "If Hitler invaded Hell, I would make at least a favorable reference to the Devil in the House of Commons."

"I can't find Doug Dillon or Foster...."

Presidents don't spend all their time thinking Presidential thoughts. That's obvious enough, but it can still come as a shock to the uninitiated.

Take Louis Jefferson. He was John Foster Dulles's bodyguard back in the Eisenhower days. At first he had an awed regard for great men. But one day at the American Embassy residence in Paris he gained a new insight into the minds of the high and mighty.

Jefferson walked into the embassy residence expecting to find his boss there. Instead he found Eisenhower. The President was in a bathrobe and in a state of considerable agitation.

"Where in *hell* is Foster?" he demanded.

Jefferson couldn't find his voice.

"Goddammit!" Ike shouted. "Speak up! Where's Foster? I can't find Doug Dillon or Foster or anybody when I really *need* them." (Dillon at the time was U.S. Ambassador to France.)

Jefferson stammered that Dulles was probably still at the French foreign office. He saw that Ike was extremely tense, very wrought up. He wondered what important affair of state was being delayed by the absence of John Foster Dulles and Douglas Dillon.

He watched in amazement as Ike, who seemed near hysteria, danced from place to place around the Dillons' drawing room. Finally, the President stopped. He seemed to have what Jefferson called the "frozen shakes" as he blurted out the matter that was troubling him.

"Where in the *hell*," he demanded, "does Doug Dillon keep the Chivas Regal?"

"How do you define the greatest good?"

A young reporter was questioning a five-term state Senator about his philosophy of government. "Tell me Senator," the reporter asked, "what do you consider to be the object of legislation?"

"Well," the old politician replied, "it's to achieve the greatest good for the greatest number."

The reported continued. "How do you define the greatest good?" he asked.

The Senator thought for a moment. Then he said, "I suppose you'd have to say it's economic. Money. People want money and security."

The reporter nodded. "That makes sense," he said. "But can you define the greatest number?"

"Oh, yes," said the Senator promptly. "The greatest number, that's easy—it's number one."

Ervin didn't argue....

Death threats against national political figures are an unfortunate hazard of the game. There isn't much funny about them, but sometimes humor can spring from the most unlikely sources.

After Senator Sam Ervin had given a speech at the University of Cincinnati, he returned to find two grim-faced police officers guarding his motel suite. An anonymous telephone caller had threatened Ervin's life, and the Cincinnati police department had responded.

Ervin didn't argue about the need for protection, but he did discuss the threat with the police officers.

During this conversation, one of the men in blue observed dryly: "I don't know how much the chief is concerned with your assassination. But I'm absolutely convinced he doesn't want it to happen in Cincinnati."

They were all at the Egyptian Embassy....

In her amusing book about scandal, rumor, and gossip in the nation's capital, Diana McLellan of the Washington *Post* has nothing good to say about the cheapjack aspects of the Jimmy Carter administration. She was especially annoyed by the parties that featured peanuts, popcorn, pretzels, and corn chips.

She tells about the time when finance ministers from 140 countries assembled in Washington for a World Bank conference. The chairman of the Federal Reserve Board and the Secretary of the Treasury invited all 140 finance ministers to a party at the Corcoran Gallery of Art.

The word spread quickly that the food at this gathering would be basic Jimmy Carter fare—rubber chicken on sticks, sliced ham and cheese in concentric rings on plates, and very little else.

Only two ministers showed up. One was from mainland China. He was pleased to have been invited at all. The other was from Grenada, a tiny nation Ronald Reagan would later make famous for fifteen minutes or so.

Now, where were the other 138 finance ministers?

They were all at the Egyptian Embassy, where a more typical Washington reception, sponsored from far-off Cairo, offered them caviar, pita, grape-leaf delights, and whole roast lamb.

Actress Jane Wyman might have been....

Actress Jane Wyman might have been the First Lady of the land, but she had other ambitions. When her husband, Ronald Reagan, took up politics, the first Mrs. Reagan began to lose interest in their marriage.

As she told a friend, it was irritating "to have someone at the breakfast table, newspaper in hand, expounding on the far right, far left, conservative right, the conservative left, the middle of the road."

And so she divorced him.

Quote/Unquote

Julius Caesar   (100–44 B.C.)

For my part, I had rather be the first [in this town] than second in Rome.

John Maynard Keynes   (1883–1946)

In the United States it is almost inconceivable what rubbish a public man has to utter today if he is to keep respectable.

Claude Pepper   (1900–1989)

If more politicians in this country were thinking about the next generation instead of the next election, it might be better for the United States and the world.

J. William Fulbright   (1905–   )

A nation's budget is full of moral implications; it tells what a society cares about and what it does not care about; it tells what its priorities are.

PROBLEMS

For a birthday gift....

Catherine the Great of Russia had problems with her underlings, just as most leaders do. She never hesitated to criticize, but she did it in a positive way—sometimes in a symbolic way.

When she learned that one of her provincial governor-generals had been accepting large bribes, she waited before reprimanding him. For a birthday gift she sent him an empty purse.

The case of the ransomed trousers....

Everyone has problems, but not many people have the kind of problem that faced the distinguished British diplomat, Lord Curzon, at a peace conference in Lausanne in the 1920s. The stuffy statesman lost his trousers.

Here's how it happened, as told by Emery Kelen in his book *Peace in Their Time:*

Lord Curzon had recently hired a new valet. The valet proved to be very bad news—a boozer and a womanizer. When his lordship received an early morning telephone call from a young woman with amour on her mind, he realized at once that the call was not for him, but for his valet.

He fired the valet on the spot. He then left for his own day's activities.

That night Lord Curzon was to attend an official banquet. He was reduced to having to dress himself, since his valet had vacated the premises. His lordship donned a winged collar and went to the wardrobe to get his dress trousers.

Surprise. The dress trousers were gone. So were all the rest of Curzon's trousers. Not a pair remained.

Furious, Lord Curzon put his battalion of secretaries to work. Find those trousers. Lausanne had only a limited number of hotels, and, sure enough, the valet was soon tracked down. But he refused to return the trousers. Or rather he demanded a rather large payment for their return.

Lord Curzon huffily said no. However, his secretary who was conducting the negotiations asked him to think about it. The valet, after all, was threatening to go public, to wave Lord Curzon's trousers aloft for the benefit of the otherwise bored journalists of the conference.

And besides, how would his lordship go to this evening's official function? In borrowed trousers?

The case of the ransomed trousers had reached its climax. The antagonists stood eyeball to eyeball. Who would blink?

Curzon, that's who. His lordship finally saw the need of making an arrangement with his former valet. The distasteful deed was done. A secretary appeared on the streets of Lausanne carrying many pairs of trousers back to their rightful owner.

"I am in love with a streetwalker...."

This one stretches belief to the limit, but never mind....

Back in the late 1940s Juliet Lowell asked members of Congress to send her the funniest letters they had received from their constituents. She assembled the best of them into a book called *Dear Mr. Congressman*.

Naturally, many of the letters dealt with problems. Here's the classic problem-letter from her book, a letter addressed to Congressman L. Mendel Rivers of South Carolina.

"Dear Mr. Rivers:

"I am a sailor in the United States Navy and have a cousin who is a Democrat.

"My father has epilepsy and my mother has syphilis, so neither can work. They are totally dependent on my two sisters, who are prostitutes in Louisville, Kentucky, because my only brother is serving a life term in prison for murder.

"I am in love with a streetwalker who operates near our house and she knows nothing about my background, and insists that she loves me dearly. We intend to get married as soon as she settles her bigamy case which is now in court. When I get out of the Navy, we intend to move to Detroit, Michigan, and open a small house.

"Now, Mr. Rivers, my problem is this; in view of the fact that I intend to make the girl my wife and bring her into the family, should I or should I not tell her about my cousin who is a Democrat?"

His constituents didn't like the way....

If you're feeling unwanted, consider the case of Senor José Ramón Del Cuet. Del Cuet was the mayor of a small city in Mexico. He was forced to think seriously about new job options when 4,000 angry townspeople stormed his office, waving aloft an unsigned letter of resignation. His constituents didn't like the way he was running things. They didn't like him. First they forced him to eat 12 pounds of bananas. Then they forced him to sign the letter of resignation.

Del Cuet could see right away that his chances of reelection were slim.

"And is he a good husband?"

A woman went to the Governor of Tennessee with a problem. "Governor," she said, "my husband is in the penitentiary and I'd like you to get him out."

"What is he in for?" asked the Governor.

"For stealing a ham."

"I see," said the Governor. "And is he a good husband?"

"No, he isn't. He drinks too much, and he beats me and the children."

The Governor didn't understand. "Then why do you want him out of prison?" he asked.

"Well, sir," the woman explained, "we're out of ham again."

"He is forever poised...."

Harold Macmillan held the office of foreign secretary before he became Prime Minister. In speaking of the problems that beset a foreign minister, Macmillan said, "He is forever poised between a cliché and an indiscretion."

"It won't go over with the WASPs."

In 1962, when Ted Kennedy turned 30 and was getting set to run for the U.S. Senate, reporters broke the story about his cheating at Harvard. Young Ted had persuaded someone else to take a language exam for him. Kennedy was expelled, but he was allowed to return after two years.

Ben Bradlee, then the Washington bureau chief of *Newsweek*, asked President John F. Kennedy what effect he thought this scandal would have on kid brother Ted's chances for the Senate nomination.

JFK's response had a frosty tinge: "It won't go over with the WASPs," he said. "They take a very dim view of looking over your shoulder at someone else's exam paper. They go in more for stealing from stockholders and banks."

...if you want a friend in Washington....

During Congressman Jim Lightfoot's first campaign, he tried to travel as inexpensively as possible. He didn't have a lot of money, and he refused to borrow more for the campaign. One of the ways he conserved money was to stay overnight in private homes rather than in motels or hotels.

In one Iowa town a pleasant couple offered to provide a night's lodging. It was the end of a long day, and the bed in an upstairs room was more than welcome.

However, along about two in the morning Lightfoot had the sudden, panicky feeling that someone was watching him. Worse yet, warm breath on his cheek suggested that someone was actually in bed with him.

A big, wet tongue gave the candidate a friendly lick. Here was Lightfoot's first clue that he might be in the bed normally occupied by the family dog. Sizewise, this dog was a regular Hooch, something along the lines of a St. Bernard or a Newfoundland. And the dog made it clear that this bed was *his,* not some strange guest's.

The Congressional candidate spent a long night after that, contending for bed space with the huge canine.

Lightfoot concludes by noting that Harry Truman said if you want a friend in Washington, get a dog. Well, says the Congressman, "I started recruiting them even before I got here."

...he can pick up his new car....

During a Presidential trip in 1985, Ronald Reagan told this story to officials traveling with him:

In Moscow a Soviet citizen was called by the Ministry of Transportation and was told that he could pick up his new car exactly ten years from that day.

The Moscow resident immediately asked, "Morning or afternoon?"

The Ministry official replied, "I've just told you that you must wait another ten years for a new car, and you ask morning or afternoon?"

Apologetically, the Soviet citizen said: "I'm sorry to ask, but I have the plumber coming that day."

Quote/Unquote

Marcus Tullius Cicero (106–43 B.C.)

The greater the difficulty, the greater the glory.

John Foster Dulles (1888–1959)

The measure of success is not whether you have a tough problem to deal with, but whether it's the same problem you had last year.

A.J. Liebling (1904–1963)

When a political side becomes all-inclusive, there isn't enough gravy to go around.

Russell Baker (1925–   )

Eventually America will run smack into the problem problem. The essence of the problem problem can be summarized in the question, What are we going to do when the problems run out?

Geraldine A. Ferraro (1935–   )

My problem as a woman was how to look Vice Presidential.

PROGRESS

"He will be good...."

When Abraham Lincoln was a very young man he wrote this verse:

Abraham Lincoln
His hand and pen
He will be good but
God knows when.

For Christmas, each poor adult in Windsor....

During the 1988 Presidential campaign, George Bush talked about "a thousand points of light." No one was quite sure what he meant, but it definitely had to do with private charity and not the public dole. Bush didn't believe in government handouts.

What would the President have thought of Queen Victoria and Prince Albert? When their second son was born—the boy who would become King Edward VII, or "Bertie"—it was nearly Christmas. The Queen's good will and generosity knew no bounds.

For Christmas, each poor adult in Windsor town received four pounds of beef, two pounds of bread, one pound of plum pudding, a peck of potatoes, and two pints of ale. Each child received half that allowance, and every family got a sack of coal.

That was in 1841. The safety net was in place.

"It is outrageously selfish to destroy...."

No one ever accused P.T. Barnum of being a starry-eyed liberal. Barnum believed in material progress. The great showman of the nineteenth century advocated the right of Americans to make a buck. He himself was one of the great masters of advertising and publicity. He exhibited freaks and oddities. He had his prize attraction, Jumbo, a six-and-a-half ton African elephant, stuffed and mounted after the huge beast died.

But P.T. Barnum was more than a circus promoter. He was also the mayor of Bridgeport and for a time served in the Connecticut legislature. He held strong opinions on many issues. One of them was outdoor advertising. Although Barnum made great use of advertising, he drew the line at despoiling scenes of natural beauty. In his book *The Humbugs of the World,* published in 1866, he sounds almost like a modern crusader. He says:

"No man ought to advertise in the midst of landscapes or scenery in such a way as to destroy or injure their beauty by introducing totally incongruous and relatively vulgar associations. Too many transactions of the sort have been perpetrated in our own country. [Remember that Barnum was writing in the 1860s.] The principle on which the thing is done is to seek out the most attractive spot possible—the wildest, the most lovely, and there in the most staring and brazen manner to paint up advertisements of quack medicines [and] rum... in letters of monstrous size, in the most obtrusive colors, in such a prominent place, and in such a lasting way as to destroy the beauty of the scene both thoroughly and permanently.

"Any man with a beautiful wife or daughter would probably feel disagreeably if he should find branded indelibly across her smooth white forehead or on her snowy shoulder in blue and red letters such a phrase as this: 'Try the Jigamaree Bitters!' Very much like this is the sort of advertising I am speaking of....

"It is outrageously selfish to destroy the pleasure of thousands for the sake of a chance of additional gain. And it is an atrocious piece of vulgarity to flaunt the names of quack nostrums and of the coarse stimulants of sots among the beautiful scenes of nature... it is about as nauseous to find "Bitters" or "Worm Syrup" daubed upon the landscape as it would be upon the lady's brow."

P.T. Barnum wrote those words more than 120 years ago, long before automobiles appeared on the scene, a hundred years before Lady Bird Johnson launched her anti-billboard campaign.

Ah, progress.

"....I would write the word 'insure'...."

When Americans think about Winston Churchill, they tend to focus on World War Two. But Churchill had been in and out of Parliament for almost 40 years before he took over as Prime Minister from Neville Chamberlain.

In his early years Churchill was a Liberal and a strong advocate of social reform. On May 23, 1909, he gave a speech in Manchester on national insurance that sounds as up-to-date as tomorrow's headlines—and as liberal as Senator Ted Kennedy.

"If I had my way," Churchill said, "I would write the word 'insure' over the door of every cottage, and upon the blotting book of every public man, because I am convinced that by sacrifices which are inconceivably small, which are all within the power of the very poorest man in regular work, families can be secured against catastrophes which otherwise would smash them up forever."

"The Child Labor Law...."

Americans believe in progress—in the passing of good laws and the repeal of bad laws.

As one slightly befuddled child told Art Linkletter: "The Child Labor Law abolished children. Of course it has since been repealed."

"...today was a very good and very useful meeting."

Even today you will sometimes hear of the "Spirit of Glassboro." The phrase came from the 1967 summit meeting in Glassboro, New Jersey, between President Lyndon B. Johnson and Soviet Premier Alexei Kosygin.

The phrase means absolutely nothing.

When the Glassboro summit adjourned, the press asked Johnson about what progress had been made. None had been made, but Johnson couldn't say that. Instead he said that "this meeting today was a very good and very useful meeting."

Vice President Hubert Humphrey chimed in later with his praise for the "Spirit of Glassboro." It struck a responsive chord. A phrase was born. The media picked it up. It sounded good. It made it seem that LBJ was making headway with the hard-nosed Communists of the day.

What few in the media pointed out was that Hubert Humphrey was forever seeing a bright day dawning. Prior to the Spirit of Glassboro, the upbeat Vice President had hailed with equal enthusiasm the "Spirit of Honolulu," the "Spirit of Manila," and the "Spirit of Guam."

Quote/Unquote

George Santayana (1863–1952)

Progress, far from consisting in change, depends on retentiveness.... Those who cannot remember the past are condemned to repeat it.

H.G. Wells (1866–1946)

Without the idea of progress, life is a corrupting marsh.

William Allen White (1868–1944)

I am not afraid of tomorrow, for I have seen yesterday and I love today.

G.K. Chesterton (1874–1936)

Progress is the mother of problems.

Winston Churchill (1874–1965)

Reciprocal extermination was impossible in the Stone Age.

Adlai E. Stevenson (1900–1965)

All progress has resulted from people who took unpopular positions.

John F. Kennedy (1917–1963)

According to the ancient Chinese proverb, "A journey of a thousand miles must begin with a single step."

Russell Baker (1925–   )

There is actually far less progress than most people suspect. In the year 1894 there was absolutely no progress whatsoever anyplace on earth, in spite of what a lot of people thought at the time.

Robert F. Kennedy (1925–1968)

Few will have the greatness to bend history itself; but each of us can work to change a small portion of events, and in the total of all those acts will be written the history of this generation.

PUBLICITY

A little girl in New Hampshire....

It's an axiom of show business that any publicity is good publicity. Obviously that isn't always true in politics. Gary Hart's publicity in the 1988 Presidential race—the "Monkey Business" business—deep-sixed him, even though at the time the story broke he was the Democratic front-runner.

Hart invited the disaster, of course. He told reporters to check up on him, and they did.

In the 1952 Presidential primaries, Robert A. Taft didn't invite trouble, but he got it anyway. A little girl in New Hampshire asked Taft for an autograph. He refused, saying that he would shake hands, but that if he agreed to all autograph requests he'd never get his campaigning done.

Well, he should have agreed to that one, because the incident was caught on television. It appeared over and over on TV in the days before the critical New Hampshire vote. Taft got a lot of publicity he could have done without, and Dwight D. Eisenhower rolled to an easy victory.

"....to dwell upon McCarthy's choice of words...."

The media are unable to resist a rip-roaring story. Terrorists make effective television use of bloodshed. An urban demagogue provides more photo ops than a visiting princess. Convicted felons sign lucrative book contracts.

No one ever worked the press more effectively than the late Senator Joe McCarthy. In President Eisenhower's view, McCarthy was a pure creation of publicity. Without screaming headlines, the junior Senator from Wisconsin would have had no large following. Therefore, when the press clamored for President Eisenhower to take a public stand against the Senator's anti-Communist demagoguery, Ike refused.

He wrote his brother Milton that "only a shortsighted or completely inexperienced individual would urge the use of the office of the Presidency to give an opponent the publicity he so avidly desires."

It infuriated Ike that the creators of McCarthyism, as he saw it, wanted to raise the publicity stakes even higher—straight to the Oval Office. He wrote, "No one has been more insistent and vociferous in urging me to challenge McCarthy than the people who built him up, namely writers, editors, and publishers."

He complained that important matters were being "dismissed to the sixth page of our daily papers in order to dwell upon McCarthy's choice of words in broadcasting his completely unwarranted and despicable insinuations...."

It's a problem that won't go away. Whether Eisenhower was right or wrong in ignoring McCarthy as he did, the fundamental question remains: How does a responsible leader react to the publicity that a skilled agitator attracts?

Does he say, as Ike did, "I will not get in the gutter with that guy"?

Or is there a better way?

...assassins become celebrities....

It's an unfortunate fact that assassins become celebrities. John Wilkes Booth and Lee Harvey Oswald are household names. Even failed assassins—Squeaky Fromme and John Hinckley—are widely recognized. The man who tried to kill

Presidential hopeful George Wallace in 1972 was thinking book contract all the way.

Two spaced-out characters who didn't become celebrities rate a single paragraph in *The Flying White House,* a book about Air Force One, the President's jet. These two klutzes, a man and a woman, had a suicide pact.

Here was their plan:

As Air Force One, carrying President Eisenhower, began to taxi toward the runway, the man would rush forward brandishing a pistol—a water pistol. Air Force security guards would take no chances... of that the pseudo-assassins were sure. Shots would be fired. The couple would die.

The next day's newspapers would carry heavy-black-headline accounts of the incident. The two conspirators would be dead, but famous for a day. History would give them a footnote.

It didn't work out that way. Air Force police and Secret Service agents picked up the suspicious-looking couple as they loitered at Andrews Air Force Base. The government never released a word about the incident. The names of the pair are unknown to this day. Said an Air Force official, "We didn't want to give other people any ideas."

Langhorne Bond was not a household name....

Self-promotion is a part of life in official Washington. Sometimes the press will help out, but many times the public servant simply has to go out and do it on his own.

Langhorne Bond was not a household name in the nation's capital. He was Federal Aviation Administrator, a responsible position, but no one seemed to care very much. He was just another faceless bureaucrat.

What could he do about it? How could he get his name in the public eye?

He came up with a happy answer. He had a custom bumper sticker made up. Thereafter, people in and around Washington sometimes caught sight of a car—his car—whose bumper-sticker message read "IMPEACH LANGHORNE BOND."

So modest was Tommy Hamilton....

When George E. Allen was a Commissioner in the District of Columbia, he received some publicity, but not a lot. His wife used to kid him that his old friend, Tommy Hamilton, then head football coach at Navy, got far more publicity than he did. She twisted the knife by saying that this was true even though Hamilton tried to avoid publicity while her husband sought it.

One day, to support her case, she pointed to a newspaper article about Navy's big win over Army. Since it was the first time in years that Navy had beaten the

Cadets, the Naval Academy was planning a big homecoming bash for the coach and his team. So modest was Tommy Hamilton that he left the train at Baltimore in order to let the team, not him, get all the cheers.

Allen wasn't impressed. He argued that any reasonably modest person would have done the same thing.

"George," scoffed his wife, "you know very well you would have put the team off at Baltimore."

"...if Barney Frank can come out of the closet...."

Former House Speaker Tip O'Neill never pretended to be a statesman. He was an old-fashioned Massachusetts pol, and it shouldn't have surprised anyone when, after retirement, he started cashing in on his celebrity by doing TV commercials.

One of these commercials showed Tip arising like a jet-set Neptune from the inside of a suitcase. It was a gas. But Andy Rooney and many others took him to task for it, saying he was demeaning himself and the high office he had held.

At the time Tip O'Neill was being bombarded with criticism for these ads, Barney Frank, another Congressman from Massachusetts and an admitted homosexual, was having public-relations problems of his own. O'Neill proposed a parallel.

"Hey," said the good-natured Tip, "if Barney Frank can come out of the closet, I can come out of the suitcase."

QUICK-THINKING

"The fever has just left me."

Antigonus, learning that his son Demetrius was ill, went to see him. At the door he passed a beautiful young woman who was just departing.

Inside the room Antigonus sat down and took his son's pulse.

Demetrius said, "The fever has just left me."

"Yes," his father replied, "I met it going out the door."

"...by the splendor of God...."

A prince, wrote Machiavelli, must imitate both the lion and the fox. A lion is able to frighten wolves, and a fox can recognize traps. Machiavelli thought that too many rulers want only to be lions. Thus, they fall into traps.

To convert this observation from metaphor to reality, take the case of William of Normandy. The good Duke wanted to rule England. With that object in mind, he set sail with a sturdy army of Normans and landed at Hastings.

The Duke's knights and archers came treading off the ships first. Finally, William himself disembarked. As he leapt to the shore, he somehow stumbled and fell. A groan went up from his assembled army. To the superstitious Normans it seemed like a bad omen.

But William was as much a fox as a lion. From his prone position, he quickly filled his hands with sand. He stood up and showed the sand to his followers.

"See, my friends, " he cried, "by the splendor of God I have seized England with my two hands!"

The Normans were reassured.

A few days later, at the Battle of Hastings, they soundly defeated the Saxons. Not long afterwards the Archbishop of York crowned William of Normandy King of England.

"True, for my words are my own...."

The Earl of Rochester, who composed the following lines, didn't care much for King Charles II of England.

Here lies our mutton-loving king
Whose word no man relies on.
Who never said a foolish thing,
And never did a wise one.

The story goes that when King Charles saw these lines, he remarked, "True, for my words are my own, but my deeds are my ministers'."

"Wilkes," said Sandwich, "you will die...."

Lord Sandwich, who gave his name to Dagwood Bumstead's favorite snack (not to mention a group of islands in the South Pacific) accosted John Wilkes.

"Wilkes," said Sandwich, "you will die either on the gallows or of the pox."

To which Wilkes replied quickly, "That must depend on whether I embrace your lordship's principles or your mistress."

North stirred from a deep sleep....

Many statesmen have been observed sleeping in Parliament, none of them more often than Lord North. Once when a speaker noted for his long-windedness arose to speak on a topic requiring a great deal of historical background, Lord North asked a colleague to wake him when the speaker began to approach the present day. He then dozed off.

When his colleague thought the time was right, he leaned over and tapped North on the shoulder.

North stirred from a deep sleep, and asked, "Where are we?"

His colleague answered, "At the Battle of La Hogue, my lord."

Lord North groaned. "Oh, my dear friend," he complained, "you have woke me a century too soon."

"Dr. Lucky of Pittsburgh...."

A group of teachers attended a White House reception during Grover Cleveland's first term as President. An introducer spoke each teacher's name as he or she approached the President.

"Dr. Lucky of Pittsburgh," the introducer said as a handsome gentleman stepped forward to shake Cleveland's hand.

The group was supposed to be introduced all together, but somehow a tramp had gotten in with the teachers. This dilapidated fellow was the next person to step forward. The introducer, taken aback, said nothing.

But Cleveland extended his hand cordially and said in a cheerful tone, "How are you, my friend? Your name must be Dr. Unlucky, I suppose."

Even the tramp joined in the laughter.

"Not in the House, my dear."

Senator Barkley of Kentucky was one of the well-known raconteurs of American politics. He used to tell this story about President Grover Cleveland. It seems that Cleveland had just let a tax bill become law without his signature.

That night Mrs. Cleveland woke him up in the wee hours. She said she thought she heard burglars in the house.

Without a moment's hesitation the President said, "Not in the House, my dear. In the Senate."

"If there is a goldbug here...."

When we hear the word *goldbug,* most of us think of the Edgar Allan Poe story of that title. But *goldbug* had a political meaning in the days of William Jennings Bryan. It meant a person who supported the gold standard—as against Bryan, who was for "free silver."

One night in 1896 a blustering defender of free silver was addressing a crowd in backwoods Pennsylvania. The audience was so strongly with him that he figured there were no gold men in the house.

With great gusto he bellowed out: "If there is a goldbug here, I should like to ask him his name, and where he lives, and how he feels."

Ah, there's always one in the crowd. A lanky fellow stood up in the rear of the hall and shouted back at him: "Well, stranger, I am a goldbug. My name is Elmer Sweet, I live down here by the crossroads, and I feel like a thoroughbred horse in a field of jackasses."

"Friends, tonight my little wife...."

When Williams Jennings Bryan was campaigning against William McKinley for the Presidency in 1900, he told a crowd: "Friends, tonight my little wife will be going to sleep in a cramped hotel room on the other side of town. But come next March she'll be sleeping in the White House."

A voice in the crowd roared back, "Well, if she does, she'll be sleeping with McKinley, because he's going to win."

In fact, he was so close-mouthed....

Charles F. Murphy was Tammany Hall's most enlightened leader. True, he got rich on the job, but he wasn't a greedy, rapacious type like other Tammany bosses. He was quiet and efficient. In fact, he was so close-mouthed that people seldom knew what he was thinking.

At a Fourth of July celebration, a journalist noticed that Murphy didn't join in with the rest in singing "The Star-Spangled Banner." He was just standing there mute. The journalist asked one of Murphy's aides why the grand sachem wasn't singing.

The aide shrugged and said, "Maybe he doesn't want to commit himself."

Taft glanced over at the cabbage....

President William Howard Taft weighed well over 300 pounds, but he was anything but a jovial fat man. Once, though, he managed to get off a good one-liner. He was campaigning in a rural district when a local yokel tossed a cabbage on the platform. Taft glanced over at the cabbage and said, "It appears that one of my opponents has lost his head."

"Well, you may quote me as saying...."

When Woodrow Wilson was Governor of New Jersey, he received a telephone call telling him that a good friend of his, a United States Senator from New Jersey, had died. Wilson was stunned by the news.

As he sat at his desk in shocked silence, the phone rang a second time. On the other end was a New Jersey politician that Wilson knew. The man wasted no words. "Governor," he said, "I would like to take the Senator's place."

Wilson stared grimly into the receiver. After a long pause, he replied: "Well, you may quote me as saying that's perfectly agreeable to me if it's agreeable to the undertaker."

They feared that such a trip....

Woodrow Wilson was more noted for his eloquence than his wit, but he did get off a good line now and then.

After World War One, President Wilson had pushed hard for America's entry into the League of Nations. When the Senate opposed him, Wilson decided to take his case directly to the people. He scheduled an arduous speech-making tour across the United States.

His advisers warned against it. They had already seen the President's health broken by the fight for the League. They feared that such a trip would kill him.

One adviser argued, "But Mr. President, you'll ruin your constitution."

Wilson replied. "Then I'll live on my bylaws."

...the reporters found Jimmy Walker....

Jimmy Walker, New York's Mayor in the days of Prohibition, made no secret of his fondness for speakeasies. His city boasted 20,000 of them.

One afternoon a rumor circulated that the Mayor had been shot. Hurrying to his office, the reporters found Jimmy Walker alive and well.

"Gentlemen," he told them, "at this time of day I am not even half shot."

"Tell them all you know, Al."

Al Smith, campaigning for the Presidency in 1928, was taunted by a heckler: "Tell them all you know, Al. It won't take long."

Quick as a whip, Al shot back: "I'll tell them all we both know, and it won't take any longer."

"It takes strong brains...."

Louisiana's Huey Long never hesitated to insult his opponents.

"How could you have had brain fever?" he once snarled at a Republican Senator. "It takes strong brains to have brain fever."

The Senator snapped back: "How did you find that out?"

"Winston, if you were my husband...."

The first woman in the British House of Commons was also one of its finest wits. She was Lady Astor, American-born and an advocate of women's rights and temperence.

After one particularly nasty skirmish with Winston Churchill, she reportedly said, "Winston, if you were my husband, I'd poison you."

And Churchill, quite a wit himself, shot back, "If you were my wife, I'd take it."

"Nye is his own worst enemy."

Aneurin Bevan, leader of the British Labor Party, had a reputation for rudeness to friends and foes alike. Winston Churchill called him the Minister of Discourtesy. When someone remarked to a fellow Laborite, "Nye is his own worst enemy," the man replied: "Not while I live."

"The lady of the house...."

Edward R. Murrow was probably the best known Director of the United States Information Agency, although the man who replaced him was notable too. He was Carl Rowan, a black journalist, who wrote a syndicated column before and after his government service.

Rowan, his wife, and three children moved to Washington in 1961. They lived in a large house with a big front lawn in a recently integrated neighborhood. The story goes that one Saturday morning Rowan was out mowing his lawn in Bermuda shorts and a T-shirt. A white man driving by the house stopped at the curb and yelled, "Hey, boy, how much you get for cutting the grass?"

Switching off his power mower, Rowan grinned, walked over to the car, and said, "The lady of the house lets me live with her."

When Walter Mondale accused Ronald Reagan....

When Walter Mondale accused Ronald Reagan of "government by amnesia," the President came back with the perfect self-effacing reply.

He said, "I thought that remark accusing me of having amnesia was uncalled for. I just wish I could remember who said it."

REALISM

"I am what you call an optimist...."

Despite the partisan nature of politics, President Grover Cleveland tried to maintain a positive outlook on life. He saw little point in letting rancor take over from reason. Once when he was praised for looking on the bright side of things, he said, "I am what you call an optimist, but I hope never to be an 'ifist.'"

What did he mean by an "ifist"? Cleveland explained: "An ifist is a slave to the little word 'if,' whereas an optimist hopes for the best in a sane manner. There was once an ifist who was lost in the woods with some companions. When night came, they were all quite hungry but had nothing to eat. With a perfectly serious face one of the group turned to the rest and said, 'If we only had some onions, we'd have onions and eggs—if we only had some eggs.'"

"I think it would do more good...."

Will Rogers, the great American humorist, made a number of shrewd comments about American politics and politicians. When Al Smith, governor of New York, was running for President against Herbert Hoover, many people thought Smith's Roman Catholicism would cost him the election.

Will Rogers said, "Some have suggested that he would be elected if he changed his religion and turned Protestant. I think it would do more good if he kept his religion and turned Republican."

"We have all heard how Dr. Guillotin...."

Speaking in Parliament in 1931, Winston Churchill said, "We have all heard how Dr. Guillotin was executed by the instrument he invented.

A member of the House, Mr. Samuel, knew better, and shouted, "He was not!" .

Churchill turned to the dissenter and said, "Well, he ought to have been."

Winston Churchill believed in learning....

Winston Churchill believed in learning the lessons of history. In a speech to the House of Commons in 1938 he said, "We cannot say 'the past is the past' without surrendering the future."

"We shall fight on the beaches...."

Winston Churchill's speech of June 4, 1940, has become perhaps the most quoted one of the 20th century. At the time he gave it, the British had just evacuated Dunkirk, the Nazis seemed invincible, and the future of Shakespeare's "sceptred isle" was gravely in doubt.

Churchill's speech is a rhetorical masterpiece. And his delivery of it was every bit as inspiring as his words.

"We shall fight on the beaches," Churchill intoned; "we shall fight on the landing grounds, we shall fight in the fields and in the streets, we shall fight in the hills."

The Dean of Canterbury, who was sitting next to Churchill, recalled the prime minister putting his hand over the microphone and adding, "And we'll beat them over the head with beer bottles. That's all we've really got."

"You were one of Stalin's colleagues...."

Nikita Khrushchev was the first Soviet Premier to denounce Stalin. Once when he was giving an anti-Stalin speech at a public meeting, a voice from the audience interrupted him. "You were one of Stalin's colleagues," the man shouted. "Why didn't you stop him?"

Khrushchev looked in the direction of the voice. "Who said that?" he demanded loudly. There was absolute silence. Everyone stared straight ahead.

Lowering his voice, the Soviet Premier said, "Now you know why."

Gore-Booth couldn't resist the opening.

Paul Henry Gore-Booth held a number of positions in the British Foreign Office. One day he received a telegram from the Middle East that read: "Ruler has died suddenly. Please advise."

Gore-Booth couldn't resist the opportunity. He wired back: "Hesitate to dogmatize, but suggest burial."

"...give the paper an acid test...."

Politicians soon learn to be wary of oral promises. If the promise isn't in writing, it isn't worth much.

Vice President Alben W. Barkley, a kindly gentleman in most respects, advised politicians to "get it in writing"... and then, as he said, "to read not only between the lines, but on the other side of the paper, and, finally, to give the paper an acid test to determine if there are any 'whereases,' 'and/ors,' or 'maybe, ifs' written on it in invisible ink."

"You don't change the course of history...."

Jawaharlal Nehru, the first prime minister of independent India, favored a policy of nonalignment in foreign affairs. As time went by, though, he found himself leaning more and more toward the West.

One day in a conversation with Nikita Khrushchev, he told the Soviet premier gently, "You don't change the course of history by turning the faces of portraits to the wall."

Ervin, a foe of government spending....

One of Senator Sam Ervin's stories predates both inflation and the women's movement. Ervin, a foe of government spending, told this tale when big appropriation bills were up for a vote:

A couple of men were talking about their wives. One said, "My wife is the most extravagant woman. She's always wanting fifty cents for this, fifty cents for that, and fifty cents for the other thing."

His friend said, "What does she do with all that money?"

Not to worry, his friend replied. "She doesn't get it."

Quote/Unquote

Niccolò Machiavelli (1469–1527)

He who establishes a dictatorship and does not kill Brutus, or he who establishes a republic and does not kill the sons of Brutus, will reign only a short time.

Thomas G. Masaryk (1850–1937)

Dictators always look good until the last minutes.

Will Durant (1885–1981)

A statesman cannot afford to be a moralist.

David Ben-Gurion (1886–1973)

In Israel, in order to be a realist you must believe in miracles.

Dwight D. Eisenhower (1890–1969)

We have to play the cards we've been dealt.

So far as the economic potential of our nation is concerned, the believers in the future of America have always been the realists.

Margaret Chase Smith (1897–   )

Before you can become a statesman you first have to get elected, and to get elected you have to be a politician pledging support for what the voters want.

RESOURCEFULNESS

"How many towns are there in Russia?"

When Catherine became Empress of All the Russias, she decided the time had come to learn certain basic facts about her country. She went to the Senate, a group of thirty distinguished men that included the heads of the ministries.

Catherine asked, "How many towns are there in Russia?"

The men looked at one another, mystified. No one knew. Catherine suggested that they look at a map. The Senate had no map, she was told.

Catherine took five rubles from her purse and told a clerk to go to the

Academy of Sciences and buy one. He crossed the Neva and returned with an up-to-date map of Russia, which Catherine presented to the Senate.

Then they counted the towns.

"Sir, I have been interrupted...."

Lord North was speaking to the House of Commons on a serious matter of the day. In the middle of his speech, a dog suddenly dashed out from under a table and ran across the floor of the House.

The members exploded in a burst of laughter. This might have disturbed a less able speaker, but Lord North took it in stride. He waited gravely until the roar had subsided. Then he turned to the speaker and said:

"Sir, I have been interrupted by a new member, not yet acquainted with the forms of the House. I therefore yielded to him. But as he has concluded his argument, I shall resume mine."

A messenger told Dolley Madison....

Dolley Madison waited patiently in the White House. Dinner stood ready on the table. Her husband, the President, was off in Maryland with the American troops.

The United States was at war with Great Britain—"the second war for independence"—and British forces were advancing toward Washington. A messenger told Dolley Madison she should leave at once.

With remarkable presence of mind, Mrs. Madison had her servants pack four boxes of her husband's papers. She then had the gardener take the famous Gilbert Stuart portrait of George Washington off the wall. With these valuable items out of harm's way, she made her escape, first to the house of an acquaintance, later to Wiley's Tavern in Virginia, where her husband finally found her.

Dolley Madison's escape—and her saving of the Presidential papers and the Gilbert Stuart painting—came none too soon. The next day, August 24, 1814, British troops burned the Capitol and the White House.

"Stop the express at Somerville...."

William Howard Taft was the heaviest U.S. President, tipping the scales at something over 300 pounds. He was a bulky figure even in his younger days when he worked as a lawyer in Cincinnati.

One day while doing research on a case in the tiny village of Somerville, he missed the last local train back to Cincinnati. An express would still be coming through, but the express wouldn't stop for a single passenger.

"Would it stop for a number of people?" asked Taft.

"Yep," said the telegraph operator.

So Taft wired the railroad, saying, "Stop the express at Somerville for a large party."

Later that day the express train to Cincinnati ground to a stop in Somerville. William Howard Taft, all alone, began to climb aboard.

The conductor came over to him, "Say, where's the large party I was to take on?"

Taft replied, "I'm it."

LaGuardia challenged the man to a debate....

Once when Fiorello H. LaGuardia was running for Congress, his opponent accused him of being anti-Semitic. LaGuardia challenged the man to a debate—one in which both candidates would have to speak Yiddish.

His opponent failed to show up, and LaGuardia proceeded to deliver a campaign speech entirely in Yiddish. The Little Flower, as he was called, had been an interpreter at Ellis Island and spoke many languages.

"How do you stand on the cotton issue?"

A politician has to be shrewd when it comes to expressing an opinion on a controversial issue. Any straightforward answer will anger some voters, so it pays to be imprecise.

Senator Tom Connolly of Texas had the technique down to a science. Once when he was running for reelection, he came to the end of a vague speech, and someone in the audience shouted, "How do you stand on the cotton question?"

Connolly reached into his bag of tricks and said, "I'm okay on that one. Any other questions?"

Since all of Heidelberg's records....

In his book *Man of the House,* former Speaker Tip O'Neill spins dozens of yarns about life in Washington. One of them has to do with Mike Kirwan, a veteran Congressman from Ohio.

Kirwan wanted very much to join Washington's exclusive University Club. He couldn't get in, though, because University Club members had to be college graduates, and Kirwan's background was in coal mining.

Things looked bleak until one of his friends suggested a way out—or rather in. He told Kirwan to say on his application that he was a graduate of the University of Heidelberg, Germany. Since all of Heidelberg's records had been destroyed in the war, there would be no way to disprove the claim.

According to Speaker Tip, that's what Kirwan did—after checking to make sure Heidelberg's records were really gone. They were. And the University Club checked his background no further. They accepted his credentials and made him a member.

The fib wasn't completely untrue either. Far back in time, back when he was an eight-year-old breaker boy, little Mike Kirwan had sorted coal at a mine in Heidelberg, Pennsylvania.

"I didn't want to lose the audience."

Ronald Reagan used to tell this story about his days as a play-by-play radio announcer of baseball games. In those days it was common for announcers to work in the studio from wire-service bulletins, creating the illusion that they were actually at the ball game. Reagan became a master at this verbal sleight-of-hand.

One day he was broadcasting a Cubs' game for radio station WHO in Des Moines. The person receiving the teletype messages in the studio would hand Reagan the slips of paper with their brief messages.

With Bill Jurges at the plate, Reagan got a slip that read, "The wire's gone dead." Since the opposing pitcher had already delivered the ball, Reagan had to think fast. As he admitted when telling the story later, "I didn't want to lose the audience."

Reagan had done his semifictional play-by-play enough to know that foul balls were a good solution. Foul balls don't get in the scorebook, and their number is theoretically unlimited. So Reagan had Jurges foul the pitch into the third base stands. There he created two kids who fought over possession of the ball. When one of them finally held it aloft in triumph, Reagan hoped the teletype machine would be fixed.

It wasn't.

Another foul ball was needed. This one was drilled deep down the left-field line. Eighteen inches to the right and it would have been a home run. Reagan nursed the drama of that foul for a while, too.

Still the machine wasn't fixed. No one in the studio, least of all Reagan, knew what Bill Jurges had actually done.

The audience at home was better informed. As time passed, they knew that the Cubs' shortstop was fouling off enough pitches to give him a shot at the *Guinness Book of World Records*.

Then at last the teletype was fixed.

Reagan breathed a sigh of relief. But he could hardly keep from laughing when the operator handed him the first slip. It said, "Jurges popped out on the first pitch."

You or I might have been chastened....

The art of padding one's expense account isn't restricted to Washington, but it's sometimes more open there than elsewhere.

Take the case of a prominent lobbyist for a trade association. He submitted his usual enormous monthly expense account. On it was a fifty-dollar lunch with a local official. The catch was that this official had died unexpectedly, a week before the supposed lunch.

The lobbyist's boss riffled grimly through old newspapers. He found the obituary, cut it out, clipped it to the expense account, and sent it back to the lobbyist.

You or I might have been chastened by this. But not the lobbyist. He crossed out "Lunch," wrote in "Flowers," and resubmitted the expense account.

Quote/Unquote

Napoleon Bonaparte   (1769–1821)

After making a mistake or suffering a misfortune, the man of genius always gets back on his feet.

George Washington Plunkitt   (1842–1924)

The politician who steals is worse than a thief. He is a fool. With the grand opportunities all around for the man with a political pull, there's no excuse for stealin' a cent.

Franklin D. Roosevelt   (1882–1945)

When you see a rattlesnake poised to strike, you do not wait until he has struck before you crush him.

RETIREMENT

"Are you going to stop...?"

In August 1902 Oliver Wendell Holmes, Jr., was Chief Justice of the Massachusetts Supreme Court. On the 11th of that month he was nominated to the United States Supreme Court.

Holmes wasn't sure he wanted to go from being the Chief Justice in Massachusetts to being the newest Associate Justice in Washington. He was 60 years old, and the prospect of a new job was less appealing than it once was. But his wife Fanny had no doubts:

"Are you going to *stop*," she asked, "just because the calendar says '60'?"

Holmes still wasn't sure. He told Fanny how much their lives would change. They would have to dine with the President. "In tails," he added, "and white satin." They would sit next to ambassadors and ministers of state.

Fanny turned and tapped the cage of a chirping Japanese robin that they kept. "The Judge is frightened, Koko," she said.

Of course, he really wasn't. He took the position and served on the U.S. Supreme Court for the next 30 years, until his retirement at the age of 90.

A reporter asked Sir Winston Churchill....

A reporter asked Sir Winston Churchill if he had any plans to retire. Churchill replied, "Not until I am a great deal worse and the Empire a great deal better."

"....too old to begin a new career...."

The youth of President Kennedy—like the age of President Reagan—served as a topic for some self-deprecating humor. Early in his brief term of office, Kennedy said:

"It has recently been suggested that whether I serve one or two terms in the Presidency, I will find myself at the end of that period at what might be called the awkward age—too old to begin a new career and too young to write my memoirs."

Golda Meir, a proud and capable woman....

Golda Meir, born in Russia and educated in the United States, emigrated to Palestine as a young woman. By the time of Israeli independence, she was a shrewd and experienced politician. She held many posts in the Israeli government before becoming prime minister in 1969.

As prime minister, Meir had her problems. In 1971 she defeated a "no-confidence" vote in Parliament. Two years later she received bitter criticism for unpreparedness after a Syrian-Egyptian attack. A year after that she failed twice to put together a coalition government.

Golda Meir, a proud and capable woman, was well into her 70s by then. She was tired of the endless struggle. On April 11, 1974, she resigned, and her four-word statement said it all:

"I have had enough."

Quote/Unquote

Winston Churchill   (1874–1965)

One does not leave a convivial party before closing time.

Claude Pepper   (1900–1989)

Mandatory retirement arbitrarily severs productive persons from their liveli-
hood....

SARCASM

"Age cannot wither...."

President Andrew Jackson's cabinet was in an uproar over the morals of Peggy Eaton. The daughter of a tavernkeeper and the wife of Jackson's Secretary of War, Mrs. Eaton had been John H. Eaton's lover while she was still married to another man. And all Washington knew it.

Wives of other cabinet members shunned her. The men of Washington took the affair far less seriously, however. Jackson defended her in the strongest terms. And Henry Clay of Kentucky, paraphrasing Shakespeare, quipped, "Age cannot wither nor time stale her infinite virginity."

"Tell Foote that I will write...."

Personal feuds in Congress are not uncommon. One of the more famous was that between Senator Henry S. Foote of Mississippi and Senator Thomas Hart Benton of Missouri.

Senator Foote once made the comment that he would write a little book in which Mr. Benton would figure very largely.

When Benton heard this, he replied, "Tell Foote that I will write a very large book in which he shall not figure at all."

One who proved especially useless....

Abraham Lincoln had trouble with all of his top generals prior to the promotion of U.S. Grant. One who proved especially useless was John Pope.

Pope was the only Union general that Robert E. Lee personally disliked. Lee wasn't alone. Most of the Union soldiers in Pope's command disliked him, too. When Pope first took command of his small Army of Virginia, he issued a blustery proclamation about how he intended to make winners out of losers.

The soldiers laughed. They laughed even louder when he announced that his headquarters would be in the saddle. A wit remarked that he was putting his headquarters where his hindquarters should be.

"Do you pray for the Senators...?"

Edward Everett Hale is best known as the author of *The Man Without a Country*. Hale was a Unitarian clergyman who spent the last years of his life as chaplain of the U.S. Senate.

He was once asked, "Do you pray for the Senators, Mr. Hale?"

The clergyman replied, "No, I look at the Senators and pray for the country."

...a friend of his went to Conkling....

Roscoe Conkling of New York and James G. Blaine of Maine were leading Republican politicians after the Civil War. Conkling was a lawyer. Blaine, the so-called "Plumed Knight," was a newspaper editor. They were bitter personal and political enemies.

When Blaine won the Republican Presidential nomination in 1884, a friend of his went to Conkling to see if the New York lawyer would campaign for Blaine.

"I can't," said Conkling. "I've retired from criminal practice."

"Yes, I am a Jew...."

Daniel O'Connell, the great Irish political leader, was a long-time foe of the Conservative Party's Benjamin Disraeli. In a speech at a trade union meeting in Dublin, O'Connell blasted Disraeli: "It would not be supposed...that when I speak of Disraeli as the descendent of a Jew, that I mean to tarnish him on that account. They were once the chosen people of God. There were miscreants among them, however, also, and it must certainly have been from one of these that Disraeli descended."

If O'Connell was a master of sarcasm, so was his acid-tongued opponent. Disraeli's response has become a classic in the art of turning away such slurs. He said, "Yes, I am a Jew, and when the ancestors of the right honorable gentleman were brutal savages in an unknown island, mine were priests in the temple of Solomon."

"I know 'em already."

Will Rogers said that one day, while at the White House, he asked the President if he wanted to hear the latest political jokes.

The President replied, "You don't have to, Will. I know 'em already. I appointed most of 'em."

"...a one-cylinder intellect."

During the Jazz Age most Americans regarded President Calvin Coolidge as a wise and thoughtful man. Some members of the press disagreed. One journalist called him "a colorless personality" with "a one-cylinder intellect."

H.L. Mencken, the sardonic sage of Baltimore, wrote, "He will be ranked among the vacuums."

...at the expense of the late Calvin Coolidge.

Dorothy Parker sometimes directed her sharp wit at politicians. Her best quip came at the expense of the late Calvin Coolidge—although too late for him to enjoy it.

When told that the laconic Coolidge had died, she said, "How could they tell?"

"There but for the grace of God...."

Long ago, Sir Sidney Clift was standing with his friend Winston Churchill near the House of Commons. Sir Stafford Cripps, a politician Churchill despised, walked briskly past them. Frowning, the future Prime Minister of England said of Cripps: "There but for the grace of God goes God."

"He can best be described...."

When roused to anger, Winston Churchill could be bitingly sarcastic. Back in 1914, as First Lord of the Admiralty, Churchill endured the criticism of Lord Charles Beresford for quite some time.

Finally, he said this about Beresford: "He can best be described as one of those orators who, before they get up, do not know what they are going to say; when they are speaking, do not know what they are saying; and, when they have sat down, do not know what they have said."

"What do you expect...?"

During the negotiations leading to the Treaty of Versailles, Georges Clemenceau of France was viewed by most Americans as a hard-bitten old man. Still, "the Tiger" found his work at Versailles trying. Lloyd George of Great Britain was a tough, canny negotiator whose sole aim was to further his country's interests. Woodrow Wilson of the United States was, from Clemenceau's standpoint, an insufferable moralist.

One day someone remarked to Clemenceau that he seemed not to be obtaining enough for France. The tired old Tiger is reputed to have replied, "What do you expect, with Napoleon on one side of me and Jesus Christ on the other?"

"Have you read Beard's last book?"

Charles A. Beard was a progressive historian whose economic interpretation of U.S. history upset many conservatives of his day. One of those his views riled was Nicholas Murray Butler, President of Columbia University.

An associate once asked Butler, "Have you read Beard's last book?"
Butler minced no words. "I hope so, " he said.

"If it isn't dear Mr. Ickes."

The talkative society matron met Harold Ickes on a street in Washington. Ickes was Secretary of the Interior at the time and was on his way to an important conference.

The matron smiled brightly. "If it isn't dear Mr. Ickes," she said. "And how do you find yourself these brisk winter mornings?"

Ickes, who was known for his curt manner, barked, "I just throw back the comforter, madam, and there I am."

"I see that Dewey...."

Harold Ickes, FDR's Secretary of the Interior, came up with the perfect squelch of a youthful candidate. When New York racket-buster Thomas E. Dewey announced his candidacy for the presidency in 1940, the press noted his age— under forty.

Hard-bitten old Harold Ickes commented, "I see that Dewey has thrown his diaper into the ring."

Bricker was a handsome, conservative....

The Republican Vice Presidential nominee in 1944 was Senator John Bricker of Ohio. Bricker was a handsome, conservative member of the Old Guard. The journalist William Allen White called him "an honest Harding." He credited the phrase to Alice Longworth Roosevelt.

But the most devastating comment on Bricker came from John Gunther, the author of *Inside U.S.A.* Gunther said of Bricker, "Intellectually he is like interstellar space—a vast vacuum occasionally crossed by homeless, wandering clichés."

"Is it not true that you...."

A politician was giving a speech before the French Chamber of Deputies. Before becoming a politician the man had been a doctor of veterinary medicine. A deputy hostile to his position interrupted him:

"Is it not true that you are actually a veterinary, my good man?"

The politician glared at him. "It is sir," he said. "Are you ill?"

Mrs. Dulles learned about Eden's joke....

British statesmen didn't care much for John Foster Dulles, the American Secretary of State. Winston Churchill called him "the only bull I know who carries his china closet with him." And Anthony Eden, Churchill's successor, liked to tell the joke about "dull, duller, Dulles."

Mrs. Dulles learned about Eden's joke from a Scotland Yard inspector. The man from the Yard didn't think she should take it too seriously, though, because Eden was such a "fopwash." Secretary Dulles wanted a French translation of that word "fopwash" so he could pass it on to General de Gaulle, who had once described Churchill as being like aging brandy—"fine if taken in small doses."

On balance, in this Cold War battle of words, John Foster Dulles, the author of brinkmanship, probably got the worst of it.

"Can't believe you're 45...."

For the Jimmy Carter White House, 1979 was a year to forget. Inflation was out of control. Lines at the gas pumps lengthened. A nuclear accident at Three Mile Island frightened the nation. Iran was holding hostages from the American embassy.

Among the messengers carrying all this bad news was ABC correspondent Sam Donaldson. A bundle of aggression, Sam Donaldson had never been the sweetheart of official Washington. He asked tough questions, and he insisted on honest answers, which he seldom got.

On the occasion of Donaldson's birthday, the Carter White House sent him this caustic greeting: "Can't believe you're 45. You don't act a day over 14."

Quote/Unquote

Richard Brinsley Sheridan   (1751–1816)

The right honorable gentleman is indebted to his memory for his jests and to his imagination for his facts.

Sam Houston   (1793–1863)

He has all the characteristics of a dog—except loyalty.

Thomas Carlyle   (1795–1881)

Sarcasm, I now see to be, in general, the language of the devil.

Gerald R. Ford   (1913–   )

Ronald Reagan doesn't dye his hair—he's just prematurely orange.

SELF-IMAGE

"He sometimes forgets that he is Caesar...."

Augustus Caesar, the first Roman emperor, was a remarkable leader. He built new roads and a new forum. He beautified the streets of Rome. He made taxes more equitable. He supported the arts. He established the Pax Romana, or Roman peace. All in all, he was quite an imperial presence.

But he had a problem—his daughter Julia. She was... well, in the old days they called it licentious. She lived high and loose. And it grieved her moralistic father, who, despite his many achievements, considered himself not so much an autocratic ruler as "the first citizen of Rome." Julia was an embarrassment to him.

When a friend suggested to her that she try to mend her ways—that she try to live more as her father wanted her to—Julia replied: "He sometimes forgets that he is Caesar, but I always remember that I am Caesar's daughter."

"Qualis artifex pereo."

The Roman emperor Nero has come down to us as one of history's villains. He fiddled while Rome burned. According to Christian tradition, he was responsible for the murders of Saint Peter and Saint Paul, who died in the persecutions that followed the great fire in Rome. He killed many other people too, including his mother and his wife.

Yet Nero always had artistic ambitions. He rebuilt Rome in spectacular fashion after the fire. By that time, however, he was cordially hated. When the Praetorian Guard, his own private soldiers, revolted, Nero committed suicide. Among his last words were these: *"Qualis artifex pereo"*—"What an artist the world is losing in me."

"...the prince cherished by all of France."

After the Emperor Napoleon's smashing victory over an army led by the emperors of Russia and Austria, the people of France were eager to welcome him like a conquering Roman. Two hundred and fifty pieces of captured artillery were to be melted down and made into a monument "in accordance with the proportions of Trajan's Column."

A statue of Charlemagne that the revolutionary armies had taken from Aachen was to be placed atop the column. However, the captured statue looked too crude and "Gothic," and a fawning French minister suggested that its place be taken by a statue of "the prince cherished by all of France." The prince himself considered this a capital idea. When the statue was finished, Napoleon would stand 148 feet high and be clothed like a Roman emperor.

His only reservation was the toga. He would prefer to be shown in battle dress, he said. And so he was.

"...the greatest Senator...."

Most politicians have towering egos, but few have ever topped that of Missouri's five-term Senator Thomas Hart Benton. One journalist of the day thought Benton's egotism was so ingrained in the man that it was not really offensive at all. Instead, he said, it was "a sort of national institution in which every patriotic American could take pride."

One tale of Benton's egotism became a part of Missouri folklore. It concerns a political gathering in Washington, where the praise for Benton escalated as the drinking proceeded. One guest called Benton "the greatest Senator in the United States." Another raised the ante: "...not only the greatest Senator in the United

States; he is the greatest man in the United States." And so it went: "... the greatest man not only in the United States but in the world: ... "not only the greatest man in the world, but he is the greatest man who ever lived" ... not only the greatest man who ever lived, but he is the greatest man who ever will live."

Finally, Benton got up, bowed to his admirers, and said: "My friends, you do me but simple justice."

Stevens wore an ill-fitting wig....

Some men are embarrassed to admit to wearing a wig. Not grim old Thaddeus Stevens, the antislavery leader of the House of Representatives during the Civil War.

Stevens wore an ill-fitting wig and made no secret of the fact. When a female admirer asked him for a lock of his hair, he yanked off his whole wig and offered it to her.

"....I will retire to the cloakroom...."

"Private" John Allen, an ex-Confederate soldier from Tupelo, Mississippi, served eight terms in the House of Representatives. He had a sharp wit combined with a strong ego.

Once when the Speaker of the House warned him that his time was up, Allen ended his speech by saying, "This is a pity, for I had many other things of great interest to say, but as my time has expired, and not wishing to further interrupt the proceedings, I will retire to the cloakroom to receive congratulations."

Gladstone made it a point to say his prayers....

People often convince themselves they are doing God's will. In his biography of Disraeli, Andre Maurois pictures British Prime Minister William Gladstone as such a person. Gladstone made it a point to say his prayers twice a day. He led a "Sunday school life," according to Maurois, and had a deep interest in religion.

Maurois noted Gladstone's tendency "to believe that his desires were those of the Almighty. He was reproached, not so much for always having the ace of trumps up his sleeve as for claiming that God had put it there."

...on hearing himself compared to Robespierre....

No one ever accused French President Charles DeGaulle of lacking an ego. Once on hearing himself compared to Robespierre, DeGaulle responded: "I always thought I was Joan of Arc and Bonaparte. How little one knows oneself."

"Eggheads, unite! You have nothing to lose...."

American voters tend to favor just-folks candidates over more intellectual ones. A man like Pappy "Pass the Biscuits" Daniel is more likely to win public office than a scholarly professor of political science at the University of Texas.

There are exceptions, of course, but Adlai Stevenson of Illinois wasn't one of them, at least not in his Presidential bids. Stevenson was well aware of the liability of being an egghead. His best-known line was probably, "Eggheads, unite! You have nothing to lose but your yolks."

Stevenson once made the following remark to a convention of textile workers: "I think one of the greatest compliments that ever befell me," he said, "was by the man who introduced me as a 'practical idealist'—sort of a hard-boiled egghead...."

"Don't worry, you'll be...."

Bill Adler, New York author, editor, and agent, has collected hundreds of quips and quotes of famous politicians. He started in 1964 with *The Kennedy Wit,* a book that became an instant best-seller. Adler's second collection of Kennedy stories came out the next year. It led off with an anecdote that is a variation on an old theme—the politico who sees himself as the Almighty. Here it is.

In 1958 a number of Democrats were in the race for the Presidential nomination two years later. One was John F. Kennedy. Two others were Lyndon Johnson of Texas and Stuart Symington of Missouri.

Kennedy would tell how he'd dreamed that the Lord touched him on the shoulder and said, "Don't worry, you'll be the Democratic Presidential nominee in 1960. What's more, you'll be elected."

When Kennedy told this story to Stuart Symington, the Missouri senator said, "Funny thing, I had exactly the same dream about myself."

They both told their dreams to Lyndon Johnson, who looked thoughtful and replied, "That's funny. For the life of me, I can't remember tapping either of you two boys for the job."

"What's the *I.* stand for?"

Three New York City journalists collaborated on a book called *I. Koch.* It's a "Decidedly Unauthorized Biography"—as the subtitle says—of Gotham's 105th Mayor, Edward I. Koch.

The authors include a note to explain their title.

It seems that a reporter who had never covered Mayor Koch raised a question about the usual opening line of one of hizzoner's press releases; to wit: "Mayor Edward I. Koch today...."

"What's the *I.* stand for?" the new guy asked a veteran journalist on the Koch beat.

The old-timer, a cynic like all old-timers, replied, "His favorite personal pronoun."

Note: The *I.* stands for *Irving*.

Quote/Unquote

Catherine the Great   (1729–1796)

I shall be an autocrat: that's my trade. And the good Lord will forgive me: that's His.

Napoleon Bonaparte   (1769–1821)

I either give orders or I remain silent.

Margaret Fuller   (1810–1850)

I now know all the people worth knowing in America, and I find no intellect comparable to my own.

Henry Adams   (1838–1918)

The Senate is much given to admiring in its members a superiority less obvious or quite invisible to outsiders.

Eugene Talmadge   (1884–1946)

I swear, sometimes I think the po' folks of this state have only three friends left in the world—Gawd Almighty, Sears Roebuck, and Eugene Talmadge.

Eleanor Roosevelt   (1884–1962)

No one can make you feel inferior without your consent.

Henry Kissinger   (1923–   )

The longer I am out of office, the more infallible I appear to myself.

William F. Buckley, Jr.   (1925–   )

Self-appreciation is a cardinal necessity for successful politics.

STRATEGY

This fiction is the "Myth of the Metals,"....

In Plato's *Republic* it soon becomes apparent that his "republic" is what might be called "an ideal state." It is not a form of government resembling that of the United States. Far from it. Plato's republic is a kind of enlightened monarchy.

There are three groups of citizens—rulers, auxiliaries, and craftsmen. The first two groups are drawn from the so-called "guardian" class. The craftsmen are people who are not involved in running the state.

Once Plato has explained his plan for the ideal state, he makes a curious suggestion (at least to modern readers). He proposes to ground the whole setup on a myth, a "bold flight of invention." This fiction is the "Myth of the Metals," which he hopes every citizen, including the rulers, will eventually believe.

According to the myth, all citizens are brothers. But the gods have seen fit to put gold in the blood of the rulers, silver in that of the auxiliaries, and iron and bronze in the craftsmen. In other words, Plato's ideal state contains a fairly rigid class structure.

It *is* possible to move up or down, though. The rulers are supposed to keep a close watch on "the mixture of metals in the souls of the children." If a child of silver is born to parents of bronze, the child steps up to the auxiliary class. This is a high honor, no doubt, but the parents lose custody of their child. Moving down a class is also possible.

Plato (putting his words in Socrates' mouth, as he does throughout *The Republic*) says, "Such is the story; can you think of any device to make them—[the people of his ideal state]—believe it?" He obviously doubts that his Myth of the Metals is going to go over with most people on the first telling.

His older brother replies, "Not in the first generation; but their sons and descendents might believe it, and finally the rest of mankind."

It didn't happen. Or did it?

He decided he should be crowned....

Ivan IV, Grand Duke of Muscovy, was only 14 years old, but he was a youngster of furious drive and ambition. He decided he should be crowned Tsar—which is to say "Caesar"—of all the scattered Russian states.

Now, Muscovy was the premier state among them. However, it was unlikely that the princes and boyars of the lesser states would cater to Ivan's whim.

Ivan therefore adopted a bold strategy. In these more enlightened days it would be called a cruel, or even a horrific strategy. But Ivan at 14 was no shy schoolboy.

He summoned the princes and boyars to a meeting. Sullenly they came. The leader of the group was one Prince Shuiski. They hadn't been assembled long when Ivan ordered his huntsman to seize the Prince. His huntsmen did so and immediately threw the startled nobleman to a hungry pack of hounds. In a few moments there was literally nothing left of him.

The princes and boyars looked somber but impressed. They decided that maybe Ivan should be Tsar of All the Russias after all. Not long afterwards, in a ceremony at Moscow, he accepted both the crown and the title.

No wonder they called him Ivan the Terrible.

"Respect, that is all I ask for France."

One of the most amazing diplomatic triumphs in the history of the world occurred at the Congress of Vienna in 1815. The master strategist who accomplished it was Talleyrand, the French minister of foreign affairs.

France came to the bargaining table as a defeated nation. Napoleon had been exiled to Elba, and the four great powers—Russia, Austria, England, and Prussia—were deciding how to carve up Europe among themselves.

Enter Talleyrand. As shrewd a statesman as ever lived, Talleyrand did not confront the great powers right away. First, he went about ingratiating himself with representatives of all the smaller states of Europe. Once he could speak for a good-sized bloc of smaller nations, he reasoned, he would be able to gain a seat at the bargaining table.

The strategy worked. The four great powers became five, with defeated France joining the four victorious nations in determining the new map of Europe.

In fact, Talleyrand's success was even more spectacular than that. For he knew that a good deal of hatred existed among the four great powers. He figured that any time there was a two-to-two split—which would be often—he, Talleyrand, would have the decisive voice.

Once again, he was right. Talleyrand, the representative of defeated France, wielded more power than the diplomats from Russia, Austria, England, and Prussia. "Respect, that is all I ask for France," he said. And over and over he repeated, "France wants nothing."

Maybe not, but with Talleyrand dominating the Congress of Vienna, France, although defeated, remained one of the great powers of Europe.

"Rumpsey, dumpsey, rumpsey, dumpsey...."

A good campaign slogan has been an important part of election strategy for a long time. One of the best-known slogans is "Tippecanoe and Tyler too," which helped William Henry Harrison, the Whig Party candidate, with the Presidency in 1840.

Four years earlier a slogan based on another Indian battle didn't help the Democratic Vice Presidential candidate at all. This candidate was Richard M. Johnson—Martin Van Buren's running mate. Van Buren won the election, but Johnson didn't. In those days voters chose the President and Vice President separately.

Maybe the problem was Johnson's campaign slogan, a verse based on his claim that he had personally killed the Shawnee Indian chief Tecumseh at the Battle of Tippecanoe. The ditty went like this:

"Rumpsey, dumpsey, rumpsey dumpsey
Colonel Johnson killed Tecumseh."

Not great poetry, you'll admit. Not much of an argument for competence, either. And considering that Tecumseh was one of the outstanding figures in American Indian history, not a very worthy claim.

In any case it didn't work. Despite Van Buren's convincing win, Johnson failed to win enough electoral votes to give him the Vice Presidency. The election was thrown into the Senate for the first and only time in American history. The Senate chose Johnson to serve for four years in the pint-sized shadow of Van Buren.

That "rumpsey dumpsey" bit just didn't impress enough voters to put Johnson in office on his own.

"Why did my opponent leave Bridgeport...?"

When Fiorello H. LaGuardia first ran for mayor of New York against Jimmy Walker, he lost badly. Walker's campaign plan called for him to ignore LaGuardia completely. But he found he couldn't. "The Little Flower" kept attacking Walker on the radio, and the attacks were hitting home.

At last Walker could take no more. He decided to recognize LaGuardia and then demolish him. Walker's campaign manager made a suggestion. "Just ask LaGuardia one question," he said. "Ask him why he left Bridgeport in 1915."

Mayor Walker looked concerned. "Why did he?" he asked.

"I don't know," the campaign manager replied. "But ask him."

And so he did. At the end of that evening's address, Walker said, "My opponent has been making many wild statements in the course of his campaign. I shall not stoop to answer them. But I have a question to put to him. 'Why did he leave Bridgeport in 1915?'"

It was Walker's first mention of LaGuardia, and it was a bombshell. Reporters descended on The Little Flower. Why had he left Bridgeport, they wanted to know.

LaGuardia, visibly upset, shouted, "Why, I don't remember ever being in Bridgeport. What has this got to do with the issues in the campaign?"

But Walker came right back with the same question the next night. He quoted his opponent's answer, adding darkly, "I think the time for evasion has passed."

The newspapers picked it up. "Why did LaGuardia leave Bridgeport?" The public wanted to know. So, presumably, did LaGuardia. It was all bewildering nonsense. Bridgeport? He couldn't believe this was happening to him. He flew into a rage.

"I never left Bridgeport!" he screamed. "I defy the mayor to state any facts he may have."

"Oh, ho," chortled Walker, "so now he never left Bridgeport. At first he couldn't remember ever being there... Let him come clean with the people of this great city. They are entitled to know, 'Why did he leave Bridgeport in 1915?'"

By this time voters were inclined to suspect the worst about LaGuardia. After all, why *had* he left Bridgeport in 1915? Even without any facts in evidence, it sounded unsavory. The public, always alert to scandal, sensed that The Little Flower must be hiding something.

In fact, he wasn't hiding anything except his own frustration. But Jimmy Walker won the election in a landslide.

FDR made his mark in radio....

Politics was transformed by radio and television. The three great Presidential beneficiaries so far have been Franklin D. Roosevelt, John F. Kennedy, and Ronald Reagan. FDR made his mark in radio, JFK in television, while Ronald Reagan, a professional actor, was effective in both.

President Roosevelt gave his first nationally broadcast fireside chat on March 12, 1933, eight days after he took office—and six days after he had closed all the nation's banks.

It was not his first use of radio. As Governor of New York, he had perfected the strategy of simple, direct, and informal radio talks as a way to go over the heads of hostile state legislators and appeal directly to the people.

It worked at the state level. Each talk would be followed by a deluge of letters to members of the legislature. The lawmakers in Albany might hate Roosevelt, but they could hardly ignore their constituents.

It worked at the national level too. At that first fireside chat to the nation, he explained his reasons for the "bank holiday," speaking in the kind of language everyone could understand. He came across as a man worthy of trust. His warm, confident radio delivery helped to restore faith and hope in a country bewildered by economic collapse.

He hit upon the idea of resigning....

Earl Long, Huey's younger brother, was a major force in Louisiana politics after World War Two. He served as governor from 1948 to 1952. According to Louisiana law, a governor cannot succeed himself directly. So Earl waited four years, then ran again in 1956 and won.

As his second term was nearing its close, he had no desire to wait another four years before succeeding himself. He hit upon the idea of resigning in his final days in office, making his lieutenant governor the governor for a short time. Then Earl would run again.

It seemed like a good idea, and the Louisiana Supreme Court, which Earl had in his pocket, liked the plan well enough. But the State Democratic Committee crossed him up. The committee demanded an almost immediate resignation, with seven months still to go in his term of office, if Earl expected to run in 1960.

After sulking for a while, he decided on an alternate strategy. A friend of his named Jimmy Noe would run for governor; Earl would run for lieutenant governor. Immediately after taking office, Noe would resign in favor of his friend. Clearly, Earl Long was determined to serve consecutive terms one way or another.

But he had miscalculated. The voters just wouldn't go for the little-known Jimmy Noe regardless of any backroom deal he might have had with the popular Earl Long. When the votes were counted, Jimmy Noe ran fourth in a five-man race.

Long turned his attention to running for Congress.

"I am sending you all my Christmas cards."

Congressman Leslie Arends of Illinois received this letter from a constituent.
Dear Congressman:
"I understand that you have free mailing privileges.
"I am sending you all my Christmas cards. Would you be good enough to drop them in the mail for me?
"Thank you."

"'Diplomacy,' someone once said...."

"Diplomacy," someone once said, is "the art of saying 'Nice doggie' till you can find a stick."

"I learned that everyone shoots...."

Federal judges are appointed rather than elected, but that doesn't mean there's a merit system in place. Ambitious lawyers have to campaign for federal judgeships. They have to work out a plan of action, one that enlists the aid of at least two U.S. Senators.

In his book called *Judges,* Donald Dale Jackson explains how a clever Illinois lawyer made it to the federal bench. The lawyer's name... make that the judge's name... was J. Sam Perry. His game lay in not being picked as the number-one choice.

Perry asked two U.S. senators to put his name on their lists, but preferably not first. He said, "I learned that everyone shoots at the number-one choice."

The senators obliged. When the sniping started, sure enough, the two front-runners were attacked mercilessly. They fell by the wayside. And as J. Sam noted, there's "no use lying about it, I helped to shoot them off."

J. Sam got his judgeship.

"...Eunice Shriver, who lives in Chicago."

In the days of Camelot USA, the Kennedys were seen as a large, close-knit clan, all of whose members united behind John F. Kennedy to help him win the White House. JFK used to joke about this public perception. During the Presidential campaign of 1960 he said:

"I would like to introduce my sister, Eunice Shriver, who lives in Chicago. I have sisters living in all the key electoral states in preparation for this campaign."

"Let him become a U.S. citizen...."

Jay Leno, the comedian, was speculating on how to handle Panamanian strongman Manuel Noriega. Nothing the U.S. tried had worked, and the Central American dictator seemed to enjoy thumbing his nose at the gringos.

Said Leno: "Let him become a U.S. citizen, let him become a Democrat, and have him run for President... You'd never hear from the guy again."

Quote/Unquote

Voltaire   (1694–1778)

To succeed in chaining the multitude, you must seem to wear the same fetters.

Camillo di Cavour   (1810–1861)

I have discovered the art of deceiving diplomats. I speak the truth, and they never believe me.

Matthew S. Quay   (1833–1904)

If you have a weak candidate and a weak platform, wrap yourself up in the American flag and talk about the Constitution.

Woodrow Wilson   (1856–1924)

If a man is a fool, the best thing to do is to encourage him to advertise the fact by speaking.

Theodore Roosevelt   (1858–1919)

Speak softly and carry a big stick; you will go far.

F. Scott Fitzgerald   (1896–1940)

The easiest way to get a reputation is to go outside the fold, shout around for a few years as a violent atheist or a dangerous radical, and then crawl back to the shelter.

SUCCESS

After serving a single term....

Campaign promises are seldom kept. The public hardly expects most of them to be kept anymore. But there was a time—one Presidential administration—in which all the candidate's major promises were fulfilled.

As noted by historian Thomas Bailey in his textbook, *The American Pageant*, James K. Polk, the twelfth President of the United States, made five main promises in the campaign of 1844:

One: To acquire California from Mexico
Two: To settle the Oregon boundary dispute
Three: To lower the tariff
Four: To establish a subtreasury system
Five: To serve only one term as President

After serving a single term as he had said, Polk left office. He could look back on his Presidency with satisfaction, for he had kept his other four promises as well.

"It is the ability to foretell...."

An interviewer asked Sir Winston Churchill to name the most desirable qualification for a young person wishing to become a politician.

Churchill replied: "It is the ability to foretell what is going to happen tomorrow, next week, next month, and next year. And to have the ability afterward to explain why it didn't happen."

"It ain't enough to get the breaks."

They called him the Kingfish.

Huey Long, the Louisiana farm boy who rose to prominance with his "Share-the-Wealth" program, was one of the great demagogues of American politics. His amazing story forms the basis of Robert Penn Warren's Pulitzer Prize-winning novel, *All the King's Men.*

The Kingfish played all the angles. "It ain't enough to get the breaks," he used to say. "You gotta know how to use 'em."

He knew how.

"Sometimes these guys forget...."

The success of John F. Kennedy in 1960 and the aura of the New Frontier made many people in the new administration a good catch for employers outside the government.

One of these was Dick Donahue, an assistant to Larry O'Brien. Donahue, who had eight kids, let it be known that he was leaving for the private sector because he needed to earn more money.

Ben Bradlee of *Newsweek* reminded JFK that Theodore White in his book *The Making of the President* had called Donahue "corruscatingly brilliant." He wondered if Kennedy wanted to see Donahue go.

JFK laughed and said, "Sometimes these guys forget that 50,000 votes the other way and they'd all be corruscatingly stupid."

"And they raised Kent's salary...."

Salaries in 1965 weren't what they are today, but this story makes its point despite the dollar amounts.

Lester B. Pearson was prime minister of Canada in 1965. He was the Liberal Party leader who had taken over from the Progressive-Conservatives' John G. Diefenbaker.

Pearson announced a war on poverty, similar to Lyndon B. Johnson's in the United States.

Diefenbaker commented on it, saying, "I was impressed. He appointed Tom Kent to run his war on poverty... that was impressive too. And they raised Kent's salary from $12,000 a year to $25,000."

Diefenbaker paused, then added slyly: "He won *his* war on poverty."

Quote/Unquote

Benjamin Franklin   (1706–1790)

Success has ruined many a man.

Napoleon Bonaparte   (1769–1821)

Calculations are useful when one has a choice of means. When one has no such choice, it is bold moves that bring success.

Benjamin Disraeli   (1804–1881)

I have climbed to the top of the greasy pole!

Ambrose Bierce   (1842–1914)

Success: *n*. The one unpardonable sin against one's fellows.

Theodore Roosevelt   (1858–1919)

If I can be right 75 percent of the time, I shall come up to the fullest measure of my hopes.

Lester B. Pearson   (1897–1972)

Not to seek success but to deserve it.

Richard M. Nixon   (1913–   )

Winners get favorable treatment. Losers are scorned.

Morris K. Udall   (1922–   )

I've been a winner and I've been a loser, and believe me, winning is best.

George Bush   (1924–   )

The definition of a successful life must include serving others.

SURPRISE

"...I almost said something once."

During World War One, Alben W. Barkley went to London as a member of a Congressional fact-finding committee. While there he got a ride in a "cloth-and-piano-wire biplane" piloted by an American Air Corps captain.

Barkley asked for a "lively" ride, and the captain obliged. The young aviator took his flimsy aircraft through a series of maneuvers that would have done credit to Baron von Richthofen. Congressman Barkley held on for dear life, praying that the biplane would hold together until they landed.

Back on the ground the captain asked him how he had enjoyed the flight. Barkley, like Lincoln, was forever being reminded of a story. This flight, he said, reminded him of a tale involving a barnstorming pilot at a county fair in Kentucky. The pilot was taking up sightseers at ten dollars a head.

One frugal Kentuckian wheedled the aviator into taking both him and his wife up at the same time for a single fare. The pilot agreed only on the condition that if the man opened his mouth even once during the flight, he would have to pay double. All right, said the man, and up they went.

The pilot proceeded to go through a sequence of hair-raising maneuvers to try to get the man seated behind him to say something. Through loops and spins and nose-dives and wing-overs the passenger never spoke a word.

When they landed, the pilot expressed his amazement. "How could you go through that," he asked, "without calling out?"

"It wasn't easy," the man admitted. "And, to tell the truth, I almost said something once."

"When was that?" the pilot asked.

"The man replied, "When my wife fell out."

Noticing that Lincoln looked bored....

Abe Lincoln was famous for his storytelling. He would launch into a tale to illustrate almost any point. Often he would start by saying, "That reminds me of....." Sometimes the story would hardly seem relevant, but Abe would usually manage to circle back to the original point.

Once a visitor was trying to explain the undercurrent of public opinion. Noticing that Lincoln looked bored, the visitor decided to try an analogy. He noted that the current in the Mediterranean Sea seems to flow in from both the Black Sea and the Atlantic Ocean, something that seems scientifically impossible. A shrewd investigator used a series of floats to discover the truth—which is that only the surface water of the Atlantic Ocean flows into the Mediterranean. Beneath that shallow and misleading surface current, a tremendous countercurrent flows outward.

The visitor paused, well pleased with his illustration.

But Lincoln still looked bored. "Well," he said, "that don't remind me of any story I ever heard of."

She enjoyed *Oliver Twist*, thrilled to *Jane Eyre*...

Queen Victoria was an avid reader. She enjoyed *Oliver Twist*, thrilled to *Jane Eyre*, and laughed over *Alice's Adventures in Wonderland*.

Immediately after reading *Alice*, the Queen asked her private secretary, Sir Henry Ponsonby, to write and compliment the author. Ponsonby was to say that the Queen would be pleased to receive any other book of his.

Lewis Carroll, a university professor of mathematics—and about as flattered as an author can be—sent her a copy of his best-selling previous book: *Syllabus of Plane Algebraical Geometry*.

"I have secured the authorized steel engravings...."

A successful swindle that followed the assassination of President James A. Garfield is considered by connoisseurs of swindles to be a minor classic. About 200 newspapers carried an advertisement for what sounded like a valuable portrait of the slain 20th President. The ad read:

"I have secured the authorized steel engravings of the late President Garfield, executed by the United States Government, approved by the President of the United States, by Congress and by every member of the President's family as the most faithful of all portraits of the President. It was executed by the Government's most expert steel engravers, and I will send a copy from the original plate, in full colors approved by the Government, postpaid, for one dollar each."

Every word in the ad was true. To each person who sent a dollar, the swindler fulfilled his promise. He mailed back the engraving of President Garfield on a five-cent postage stamp.

"I give you this controller, Mr. Mayor...."

New York City's first subway opened for business on October 27, 1904. Mayor George McClellan, son of the famous Civil War general, made a brief speech. August Belmont, a wealthy financier, then handed the Mayor a mahogany case containing an ornamented silver controller.

Belmont said, "I give you this controller, Mr. Mayor, with the request that you put in operation this great road, and start it on its course of success and, I hope, of safety."

Most people at the scene expected McClellan to pose for photographs with the silver controller.

But no. McClellan the Mayor became McClellan the motorman. He pulled the train out of City Hall station as IRT officials watched nervously. He speeded up to 30 miles an hour. He brought the train into station after station.

When Frank Hedley, the IRT general manager suggested that perhaps the Mayor would like to have a transit employee take over for him, McClellan barked, "I'm running this train!"

And so he did, taking it all the way to 103rd Street before relinquishing the controls.

"You fool, those last four words...."

They called him Uncle Joe Cannon. He was Speaker of the House of Representatives back when Ronald Reagan was a baby.

Cannon's handwriting was notoriously hard to read... on a par with most doctors'. One day a colleague approached him and said, "Uncle Joe, that letter you sent me yesterday—it might as well be in code. I showed it to about fifty people. We finally managed to figure out most of it—all but the last four words. We never did get those."

"Here," said Joe testily, "let me see it." With that he grabbed the letter from his colleague and studied it. After a moment he snapped, "You fool, those last four words are 'Top Secret and Confidential.'"

"Hark! The herald angels sing...."

William Everett, a Congressman from Massachusetts in the late 1800s, told the story of a congregation in England that needed new hymn books but lacked the money to pay for them. The churchgoers learned that a large company, a maker of patent medicines, would furnish hymnbooks at a penny each if the books could carry some advertising.

The congregation saw no harm in making that concession, and so they ordered the books. The new hymnals arrived at the church on the day before Christmas.

On Christmas morning, the pastor announced "Hymn number 138." The good Christians turned to the hymn, and in a few seconds were aghast to find themselves singing:

Hark! the herald angels sing
Beecham's pills are just the thing.
Peace on earth and mercy mild;
Two for man and one for child.

"Finding an imperishable phrase...."

There's a first time for everything, and sometimes the date is more recent than you might think. Take the phrase "Founding Fathers." When was it first used? It's been around forever, hasn't it?

No, it hasn't. It's been around since February 22, 1918, as Sir Denis Brogan points out in his book *Politics in America*. And the name of the man who coined it is quite a surprise—it's Warren G. Harding.

Yes, on that date in 1918 Warren Gamaliel Harding—still the sentimental favorite as America's worst President—was delivering a Washington's birthday speech to the Sons and Daughters of the American Revolution.

On a dais in Washington, D.C., Senator Harding (his Presidency was three years away) said, "It is good to meet and drink at the fountains of wisdom inherited from the founding fathers of the republic."

Nobody ever seems to have put those two words together before that moment. Apparently Harding knew he was on to a good thing because he used it again in his inaugural address as president in 1921. He said, "... I must utter my belief in the divine inspiration of the founding fathers."

Now, Warren G. Harding is known mostly for his bad habits, bad associates, and bad prose. But there you have it. He invented not only the words "bloviating" and "normalcy" but also the phrase that now describes his illustrious predecessors.

Richard Hanser, writing an article for *American Heritage,* rediscovered the origin of the phrase. He could hardly believe it. As he said, "Finding an imperishable phrase in a Harding speech was an unexpected as finding a pearl in a meatball...."

"I'm just interested in a certain obituary."

A whole generation of Republicans thought of President Franklin D. Roosevelt as the devil incarnate. Wall Street types in particular disliked the four-term President.

One such Wall Streeter, who commuted from Westchester, would stop every day at the newsstand in Grand Central Station. He'd grab the *Times*, glance at the front page, and toss it back on the pile.

Finally, the news dealer asked him why he never looked inside the paper.

The financier snapped, "I'm just interested in a certain obituary."

"But, sir," the dealer said, "the obituaries are inside the paper, near the back."

The man from Wall Street snarled, "The one I'm looking for will be on page one."

"Well... I was resident of the University...."

While playing basketball for the New York Knicks, Bill Bradley was thinking about his future beyond sports. Politics appealed to him, and a friend of his, Willie Morris, arranged a lunch for him with Senator J. William Fulbright of Arkansas.

Fulbright was the man Senator Joe McCarthy had labeled Senator Halfbright. But, in fact, Fulbright was one of the best and most intelligent officeholders of his day.

At the lunch the New York Knick star seemed a little awed by the Senator from Arkansas. He asked Fulbright how he had gotten into politics. Such questions can lead to pontifical, self-serving answers, and Bradley may have been expecting one. If so, he was surprised.

"Well," Fulbright drawled, "I was president of the University of Arkansas and got into a dispute with the Governor, and he fired me—so I ran for the House of Representatives."

...a notable Democratic prankster....

Every Presidential campaign has its share of dirty tricks. Back in 1960 Republican candidate Richard Nixon was making a whistle-stop tour of California. Dick Tuck, a notable Democratic prankster, dressed himself up as a railway trainman. While Nixon was in the middle of a campaign speech, Tuck waved the train out of the station.

"As George Bernard Shaw once said...."

Morris K. Udall, Congressman from Arizona and one-time Presidential hopeful, offers a cornucopia of political stories in his book, *Too Funny to Be President*.

One of them concerns Robert F. Kennedy's quest for the Presidency in 1968. It seems that RFK had a standard closing for his stump speech—a quotation from George Bernard Shaw. As soon as the reporters heard that line, they'd head for the bus, train, plane, or whatever else was carrying them to the next campaign stop.

But one day Kennedy unintentionally left off his standard closing. The reporters stood around baffled as the RFK campaign train pulled out of the station. When they caught up with the candidate, reporters asked him to please keep that standard closing as part of his speech, and not to forget it. They needed their cue.

So at the next stop, RFK gave the reporters their wish, at the same time confusing his local audience. He ended his speech with the words, "As George Bernard Shaw once said, run for the bus."

As the band played "Hail to the Chief"....

President Gerald Ford had a hard time shaking his klutz image. Supposedly, the image stemmed from Lyndon Johnson's remark that "Jerry Ford is so dumb he can't walk and chew gum at the same time." The truth was that Ford had graduated in the top third of his class at Yale Law School, and although he did take some pratfalls and make a few misstatements as President, he was hardly the clumsy idiot that many journalists seemed to think.

Johnny Carson got a lot of monologue mileage out of Ford's mishaps. But the comedian who launched a career on them was "Saturday Night Live's" Chevy Chase. When Ford's press secretary Ron Nessen first saw Chase going through his stumbling, bumbling portrayal of the President, he was so fascinated he ordered a videotape. And he made it a point to watch Chevy Chase on future "Saturday Night Live" shows.

President Ford and Chevy Chase sat next to each other at an annual broadcasters' banquet in Washington in 1976. As the band played "Hail to the Chief," Chase began his impersonation. He lurched to the microphone, bumped his head on the rostrum, and made various moronic remarks. Jerry Ford laughed at the comedian's performance.

As it happened, the President was ready with his own secretly rehearsed act. He stood up, and immediately got tangled up with the tablecloth. Silverware and a coffee cup flew off the table. Ford moved to the microphone, dropping what was supposedly his script. The papers scattered on the floor.

The audience loved it. They got an even bigger kick out of it when Ford delivered his opening line.

He said, "Mr. Chevy Chase, you are a very, very funny suburb."

"I'm really very, very flattered."

Americans tend to forget the name of their Vice President a few weeks after a Presidential election. To be honest, the Vice Presidency isn't a very important job.

So imagine Walter Mondale's surprise when, as Jimmy Carter's Vice President, he found a large crowd on hand at the airport in Lewiston, Maine, to watch him leave for Washington.

He turned to one of his local hosts and said, "I'm really very, very flattered. There must be about two thousand people here."

The host agreed, but then explained. This was the first time a Boeing 747 had ever landed or taken off at Lewiston's airport. In his Down Eastern twang the host delivered this unsettling line: "Everyone turned out to see if it'll take off okay, or crash."

"...I've never had my opinion polled...."

This story comes from John Bendix, Professor of Political Science at Lewis and Clark College. It's a quotation from a speech given by Charles Kennedy when he was running for reelection to Parliament from Scotland's Ross and Cromarty County and the Isle of Skye. A young man asked Kennedy why his campaign seemed to be struggling in the polls.

"There's a cautionary note about opinion polls," Kennedy began. "Dr. George Gallup, who set up the Gallup organization, was once giving a lecture in the United States about how good opinion polls were, particularly the Gallup opinion polls, and it came to questions and answers like this, and a lady stood up in the audience and she said:

"'Dr. Gallup, if your opinion polls are so accurate and so sensitive and can predict what's happening in terms of general movements in public attitudes, why is it I've never had my opinion polled, and I've never met anyone who's had their opinion polled?'

"And Gallup replied, 'Well, Madam, you must understand that the probability in the United States of having your opinion polled by the Gallup organization is about the same as the probability of being struck by lightning.'

"And she said, 'But Dr. Gallup, I've been struck by lightning twice!'"

"Today... I am pleased to announce...."

Jim Robinson, chief speechwriter for California Governor George Deukmejian, tells this satisfying tale of a speechwriter's revenge.

The speechwriter's boss was a U.S. senator with no redeeming virtues. He made impossible demands on his staff, reveled in his own success, and gave no credit to anyone or anything beyond his towering genius.

The speechwriter was longing for a chance to get even.

One day the senator came to him in a panic. He said: "I've got to make a speech on energy on the Senate floor in one hour. I need a 20-point energy plan and a compelling speech by then. Bring it to me down on the floor."

The speechwriter did it. He delivered the speech. The senator, with no time to review the stack of four-by-six cards, plunged into his introduction.

"Today," he said, "I am pleased to announce a 20-point plan to free this great nation from the clutches of foreign oil dependency. Let me now outline my program."

He flipped to his second card. Point one was nowhere in evidence. Instead the card read, "Okay, you SOB, you're on your own."

Quote/Unquote

Ernest Bevin   (1881–1951)

If you open that Pandora's Box, you never know what Trojan 'orses will jump out.

Charles de Gaulle   (1890–1970)

Since a politician never believes what he says, he is surprised when others believe him.

T

TACT

"As the Governor of North Carolina...."

Tact.

"As the Governor of North Carolina said to the Governor of South Carolina, it's a long time between drinks."

Hold on: Where does that quote come from? Next question: What on earth does it mean?

Naturally, it's been well researched. And the story does seem to show the virtues of tact. The Governor of North Carolina, one John Motley Morehead, was apparently trying to soothe the hot temper of the Governor of South Carolina, James H. Hammond. The time was the early 1840s.

This is what happened. Maybe.

A resident of North Carolina committed some sort of crime in South Carolina. Seeing no advantage in waiting around to be arrested, he took off for his home state of North Carolina. It was a wise decision, because the Governor of North Carolina, for whatever reason, refused to extradite him.

This incensed the Governor of South Carolina. In fact, it made him so angry that he set off with his staff for North Carolina. He was determined to bring the criminal back with him.

North Carolina could hardly be inhospitable under these circumstances. The Governor of North Carolina received the South Carolina group graciously. He served refreshments. Some friendly conversation ensued.

And then, all of a sudden, it wasn't so friendly anymore. The Governor of South Carolina couldn't forget why he was there. He tried to control his temper, but his sense of injury prevailed. He burst out with an ultimatum:

"If you don't give that rascal up, I'll call up my state militia and take him by force of arms. What do you say to that?"

The Governor of North Carolina was taken aback. This was heavy stuff. But he was a politician, not a warrior, and he answered, "I say it's a long time between drinks."

The Tarheel Governor signaled for more refreshments, which were brought posthaste. Soon the Governor of South Carolina began to see that he had been too hotheaded. There were solid arguments on both sides.

And, as the Governor of North Carolina now realized, it was a mistake to be stingy with the convivial bottle.

The two Governors parted on friendly terms. It isn't clear what happened to the felon who caused all the ruckus. But a saying had been born. Ever afterwards, whenever a dispute threatened to get out of hand, the tactful host could say, "As the Governor of North Carolina said to the Governor of South Carolina, it's a long time between drinks."

"You can't use tact...."

When Henry Adams went to Washington, D.C., in 1868 after many years abroad, he pursued journalism briefly. Since he was a member of the famous Adams family, he already knew some of the prominent politicians there.

Adams was struck by the lack of respect that newspapermen, not to mention Senators and cabinet officers, had for members of the House of Representatives. One day he suggested to a cabinet officer that it might pay to use more patience and tact with Congressmen.

The cabinet officer snarled. "You can't use tact with a Congressman! A Congressman is a hog! You must take a stick and hit him on the snout!"

"Repent of your sins—more or less...."

Tact can easily shade into equivocation. Vice President Alben Barkley used to tell this story:

"Once a delegation of Methodist clergymen from the Midwest called on me, and the girls in my office were surprised when rather uproarious laughter came resounding from my office. The girls asked me what I had done to get the ministers to laughing. I explained that the subject of 'equivocation' had come up in our conversation, and I had simply told the clergymen one of my favorite stories about the preacher who was delivering a sermon to a congregation composed of influential parishioners whom he did not wish to offend. He preached on "Sin"—always a reasonably safe subject—and concluded his remarks with the cautious exhortation:

"'And so, I say unto you: Repent of your sins—more or less; ask forgiveness—in a measure; or you will be damned—to some extent!'"

"Senatorial courtesy...."

American schoolchildren may get the facts wrong, but their hearts are in the right place. One child told Art Linkletter, "Senatorial courtesy means to stop calling the other Senators names after the election."

"Excuse me, Excellency, but...."

General John Metaxas, the Greek dictator, had many talents. He was a good pilot, for one thing, and when he was invited to try out a new seaplane, he took the controls himself.

Metaxas flew well, but his host was horrified when he saw the general about to land the seaplane at an inland airport. He spoke up:

"Excuse me, Excellency, but it would be more suitable to come down in the sea since this is a seaplane."

The general laughed. "But of course. What am I thinking of?"

He then headed out to sea and set the plane down perfectly on the water. Turning to his host, he said, "I must compliment you on the tact with which you handled the incredible blunder I almost made."

So saying, the general got up from his seat and stepped out into the sea.

Quote/Unquote

Benjamin Franklin (1706–1790)

A spoonful of honey will catch more flies than a spoonful of vinegar.

Benjamin Disraeli (1804–1881)

Without tact you can learn nothing. Tact teaches you when to be silent.

Abraham Lincoln (1809–1865)

Tact: the ability to describe others as they see themselves.

THOUGHTFULNESS

"'Ah, my brother,' said a royalist general...."

You don't usually think of thoughtfulness in connection with a major battle. But it occurred at the Battle of Ayacucho, Peru, on December 9, 1824.

Simón Bolívar was engaged in fighting his war of liberation in South America. Bolívar's trusted lieutenant, Antonio Sucre, was about to engage a much larger royalist force in Peru.

General Juan Antonio Monet of the royalist forces asked to talk with one of Sucre's generals. He said that some of the royalist soldiers had relatives in the patriot army. They would like to be allowed to meet with them before the battle.

Fine, said the patriot chieftain. Whereupon about fifty men from each side (out of the 15,000 ready to fight) walked to a point between the lines. They were given a half hour to exchange greetings.

"Ah, my brother," said a royalist general, "how sorry I am to see you covered with ignominy."

His brother, a patriot lieutenant colonel, was incensed. "I didn't come here to be insulted," he said. The lieutenant colonel turned on his heel and walked away. But the general ran after him, embraced him, and they both wept.

After their half hour of talking, both armies ate breakfast. Then, a little later, General Monet walked to the patriot lines again and said, "General, are we ready for battle?"

They were—the patriots more so than the royalists. General Sucre's troops routed the much larger royalist army. The battle won Peruvian independence from Spain. Beyond that, it marked the victory of revolutionary forces throughout South America.

"I will pardon Jeff Davis...."

As John Wilkes Booth leapt to the stage after shooting Lincoln in Ford's Theatre, he shouted, *"Sic semper tyrannis!"*—"Thus ever to tyrants."

Booth thought he was avenging the South. Instead he was guaranteeing a harsh peace. Consider the case of Jefferson Davis, the President of the Confederacy. After the war Davis was arrested, clapped in irons, and imprisoned in Fortress Monroe for two years.

Just three days before Lincoln died, he sent a note to a friend that said, "I will pardon Jeff Davis, if he asks for it."

"I've got to punish you."

Fiorello H. LaGuardia was a man with a heart. As Mayor of New York he endeared himself even to the tough-minded residents of that city.

Hizzoner was also a bundle of enthusiasm. One bitter cold night he decided to preside over a night court. An old woman was brought before him, charged with stealing a loaf of bread. She admitted the theft of the bread, but said her family was starving.

"I've got to punish you." LaGuardia said in that high-pitched voice of his. "The law makes no exceptions. I must fine you ten dollars."

The Mayor reached into his pocket, took ten dollars from his wallet, and said, "Here's the ten dollars to pay your fine."

Then he looked around the court and added, "Furthermore, I'm going to fine everyone in this courtroom fifty cents for living in a town where a person has to steal a loaf of bread in order to eat. Bailiff, collect the fines and give them to this defendant."

The hat was passed, and when the astonished woman left the courtroom, she was clutching $47.50.

"These are just middle-aged men out of a job."

There were few heroes in the incident that historian Arthur M. Schlesinger, Jr., called the "Battle of Anacostia Flats." Although it was less a battle than a cruel eviction, the affair cast a pall over the administration of Herbert Hoover and, briefly, over the impressive career of General Douglas MacArthur.

During and after the First World War, Herbert Hoover was a humanitarian figure to Europe's suffering millions. MacArthur had a reputation for benevolence in the Philippines. But it turned out that the most thoughtful and caring person in the Anacostia affair was the Chief of Police of Washington, D.C. a retired brigadier general named Pelham D. Glassford.

It started with a "Bonus March." The United States, mired deep in the Great Depression, had an unemployment rate approaching 25 percent. Many of those out of work were World War One veterans, who had been promised bonuses to be paid in 1945. It occurred to some of them that it would help to get those bonuses early, and so was born the "Bonus Expeditionary Force." A group of unemployed veterans would march—or hop freight trains—from Portland, Oregon, and other places to Washington, D.C. There they would demand immediate payment.

They marched. They assembled in the nation's capital. They built shanty villages and prepared to wait for Congress to pay up.

The man charged with keeping the peace in Washington was Police Chief Glassford. And he did. Riding a big Harley-Davidson motorcycle among the marchers, he helped them find places to camp, raised cash contributions to help out, fed them from National Guard field kitchens, and kept his police from harassing the new arrivals.

Were these shack-dwelling veterans dangerous? No, said Glassford. "These are just middle-aged men out of a job."

But they were an embarrassment to the federal government. Their shacks were unsightly. And the presence of the unemployed veterans did nothing for Hoover's Presidential image. The administration tried a number of things to get the vets to leave. But many stayed, even after the bonus bill failed in Congress.

At last the District Commissioners decided on a "get tough" policy. They bypassed the compassionate Glassford and asked for federal troops, which they got.

General Douglas MacArthur took the field on the afternoon of July 28, 1932. Along with him were Major Dwight D. Eisenhower and an up-and-coming officer named George S. Patton. Four troops of cavalry swung into action, sabers raised, with six tanks and a column of infantry behind them.

At first many of the veterans cheered. They thought it was a great show.

But it was more than a show. The troops swept systematically through the camps, forcing people out, setting fire to their jerry-built houses. The veterans fled. The Bonus March was over, the marchers (and in some cases their wives and children) dispersed to the countryside.

Glassford played no part in the "battle." The ex-general, the man responsible for law and order in the District, stood by and watched. "You'll be made the goat," someone told him. And indeed he was, losing his job soon afterwards. But Glassford remained philosophical. He said, ". . . if I'm to be the goat, I prefer it to be with my conscience clear."

"That was in the Depression days...."

Ronald Reagan's critics never understood how he could square his genuine liking for people... all people... with programs that hurt the most vulnerable among them. In fact, he couldn't quite square it.

As the newly elected Governor of California, Reagan discovered that his economy-minded administration was about to eliminate 3,700 jobs in California's mental hospitals. This layoff bothered him, and he questioned his cabinet about it. They defended its necessity.

Reagan said to his cabinet, "I'd like to hide... it reminds me of my father who got his slip on Christmas Eve. That was in the Depression days, and my imagination is still that of a little kid who gets up and cries."

But Reagan was now Governor of California, not a little kid, and he continued: "On the other hand, if you fellows tell me that we don't need these employees, I don't see what else we can do. I still like the phasing out better than giving them the slip. And we should help them as much as we can."

TRUTH

"Grandma, how could you...?"

Queen Victoria loved her grandchildren, but she was brutally honest in her judgments about them. She once said, "They are such miserable, puny little children (each weaker than the preceding one)."

When Marie Louise, the daughter of Princess Helena, was two years old, she spent some time with her grandmother, the Queen. To reassure the parents, Victoria sent them a wire that said: "Children very well, but poor little Louise very ugly."

In later years Louise learned of this message and asked, "Grandma, how could you have sent such an unkind telegram?"

Queen Victoria answered bluntly: "My dear child, it was only the truth."

"He understands, with a perception...."

The two candidates for Congress, Republican and Democrat, were scheduled to speak on the same day in a small town in Kentucky. Their schedules were tight, and there was only one large auditorium available. The two hopefuls agreed to appear on the same stage on the same night.

It was the local sheriff's job to introduce the opposing candidates. He stood up and began: "Ladies and gentlemen, I give you a man who has always stood tall for Kentucky, a man who cares deeply about each and every citizen of this glorious state. He understands, with a perception rare among political figures, the problems and, yes, the opportunities facing us in the world today. He is a man of great learning, a man who has immersed himself in foreign affairs, in economics, in education...."

Then the sheriff turned toward the candidates and asked: "Which one of you polecats wants to talk first?"

"You know, Fala is Scotch...."

Negative campaigning works—that's what everybody says. The charges leveled against your opponent don't even have to be true. That's the prevailing view.

Well, it didn't work back in the 1944 Presidential campaign when Franklin D. Roosevelt was running for a fourth term and Thomas E. Dewey of New York was his challenger.

Certain Republican Congressmen began circulating the story that upon FDR's return from Alaska, his dog Fala had inadvertently been left behind. Learning of this, Roosevelt sent a destroyer back to Alaska to pick the dog up. Naturally, the trip cost millions of taxpayers' dollars—the estimates ranged from two to twenty million. The anti-Roosevelt newspapers played this story for all it was worth. It seemed like good negative campaigning.

The tale was completely untrue, though, and Roosevelt vowed revenge. He wrote into his next campaign speech a now-famous paragraph about the incident. Here it is:

"These Republican leaders have not been content with attacks on me, or my wife, or on my sons. No, not content with that, they now include my little dog, Fala. Well, of course, I don't resent attacks, and my family doesn't resent attacks, but Fala *docs* resent them. You know, Fala is Scotch, and being a Scottie, as soon as he learned that the Republican fiction writers in Congress and out had concocted a story that I had left him behind on the Aleutian Islands and had set a destroyer back to find him—at a cost to the taxpayers of two or three, or eight, or twenty million dollars—his Scotch soul was furious. He has not been the same dog since. I am accustomed to hearing malicious falsehoods about myself.... But I think I have a right to resent, to object to libelous statements about my dog."

An angry Tom Dewey, who believed that the best defense was a good offense, tried to contain the damage, but the Fala speech hurt him badly. Dewey's free-swinging attacks only compounded his problem.

The gleeful publicity director for the Democratic National Committee wrote: "We have a new slogan in headquarters now—the race is between Roosevelt's dog and Dewey's goat."

Of course, the obscure archduke....

After World War One, many people came to the conclusion that it had been a pointless war. No one wanted it, no one benefitted from it, and the bitterness over it led directly to World War Two.

In the 1920s a Berlin newspaper put on a contest for the best headline. The winner was: "Archduke Franz Ferdinand Alive—World War for Nothing."

Of course, the obscure archduke whose assassination had touched it all off was dead enough. But the second part of the headline was accurate.

"I Aim At the Stars...."

Wernher von Braun is listed in standard reference books as an American rocket expert. That's technically true, because von Braun became a U.S. citizen in 1955.

But he didn't start his career at White Sands Proving Grounds in New Mexico. He started at the University of Berlin and later worked for many years at Hitler's rocket research center in northern Germany. Von Braun helped develop the liquid fuel for the deadly V-2 rocket.

Immediately after the war von Braun joined the American space program. Over the years he rose to a high position in NASA. When the moviemakers caught up with him, they called his story, *I Aim At the Stars.*

An unfriendly film critic suggested that the title told only half the truth. The critic said the movie should have been called, *I Aim At the Stars—But Sometimes I Miss and Hit London.*

"If that's the way the record is...."

A few recent politicians could take a lesson from President Dwight D. Eisenhower.

When Eisenhower was working with his research assistant, William Bragg Ewald, Jr., on the manuscript of *Mandate for Change*, the President remembered something he had done while in the White House. He insisted that it go in the book.

Ewald disputed the President's memory, showing him documentary evidence that he hadn't done what he thought he had. Eisenhower countered that he recalled very clearly having done it. At last, his face reddening, he got up from his chair and stalked out of the room.

The young research assistant was convinced that his job was about to be terminated. After all, it was possible, although unlikely, that the record was wrong and Ike was right.

Ewald was still thinking along those lines when Eisenhower strode back into the room.

"If that's the way the record is," Ike said, "that's the way it's got to read."

"They promise to build a bridge...."

Charles DeGaulle and Nikita Khrushchev could hardly have been more unlike one another. Yet both had a similar—and cynical—view of politicians' promises.

DeGaulle said, "In politics it is necessary to betray one's country or the electorate. I prefer to betray the electorate."

And Khrushchev, putting it in more earthy language, said, "Politicians are the same all over. They promise to build a bridge even when there is no river."

"What's the matter with these people?"

Former House Speaker Tip O'Neill tells the story of John (Up-Up) Kelly, an advance man for James Curley, the Boston mayor and one-time Massachusetts governor. Up-Up got his nickname for his habit of yelling "Up, up, the governor!" whenever Curley entered the hall where he was to speak. Kelly could really charm an audience, and people would leap to their feet at the "Up, up" command.

One day Curley had been scheduled to speak to a deaf audience. A translator would stand with him on the platform and relay Curley's message in sign language.

That was fine, but Up-Up Kelly knew nothing about it. Figuring it was just another audience, the advance man went through his brief routine. When Curley arrived in the hall, Up-Up shouted, Up, up, the governor!"

No one moved.

Kelly stared out at them in disbelief. Had his patter been that bad?

When Curley got to the platform, Up-Up asked, "What's the matter with these people? Are they all deaf?"

There was no time to go into detail. Curley said simply, "Yes, John, they are."

"...this is the operative statement."

Ron Ziegler, press secretary to President Richard Nixon, had a tough assignment. He had to keep repeating the White House version of the Watergate story, which began to sound more and more like a fairy tale. Ziegler did his job well, but the White House denials of any involvement in the Watergate cover-up were finally exposed as lies.

On April 17, 1973, Ziegler faced a press conference and admitted some of the truth. He said, "...this is the operative statement. The others are inoperative."

How the press corps jumped on that! As Hugh Rawson put it in his *Dictionary of Euphemisms,* Ron Ziegler, "in one glorious gulp, ate practically every word he'd said about Watergate for the previous 22 months."

And Ziegler's phrase about "inoperative statements" seems likely to become one of those classic bits of doubletalk that live on through the years.

Quote/Unquote

Sir Philip Sidney   (1554–1586)

Above all things, tell no untruth, not even in trifles, for there cannot be a greater reproach than to be accounted a liar.

John Dryden   (1631–1700)

Truth is the foundation of all knowledge and the cement of all societies.

Francis Bacon   (1561–1626)

No pleasure is comparable to the standing upon the vantage ground of truth.

John Locke   (1632–1704)

It is one thing to show a man he is in error, and another to put him in possession of the truth.

Horace Mann   (1796–1859)

If any man seeks for greatness, let him forget greatness and ask for truth, and he will find both.

Wendell Phillips   (1811–1884)

You can always get the truth from an American statesman after he has turned 70, or given up all hope of the Presidency.

Winston Churchill   (1874–1965)

Men occasionally stumble over the truth, but most of them pick themselves up and hurry off as if nothing had happened.

The truth is incontrovertible. Panic may resent it; ignorance may deride it; malice may distort it, but there it is.

H.L. Mencken   (1880–1956)

The public... demands certainties; it must be told definitely and a bit raucously that this is true and that is false. But there *are* no certainties.

Harry S Truman   (1884–1972)

I never give them hell. I just tell the truth, and they think it is hell.

Adlai Stevenson   (1900–1965)

Let's talk sense to the American people. Let's tell them the truth, that there are no gains without pains.

John F. Kennedy   (1917–1963)

For the greatest enemy of the truth is very often not the lie—deliberate, contrived, and dishonest—but the myth—persistent, persuasive, and unrealistic.

UNDERSTANDING

"Men are most apt to believe...."

Montaigne was an essayist who in his early years spent some time in the French civil service. Actually, as you probably know, he was quite a bit more than that. He was the inventor of the essay, a keen observer of human behavior, and the only writer whose book (*Essais*) Shakespeare is known to have owned.

From what Montaigne had seen of life, he drew his shrewd conclusions. His writing was lighthearted, but his thoughts were profound. How many politicians have built careers and reputations, good or bad, on this ten-word aphorism from Montaigne: Quote: "Men are most apt to believe what they least understand?"

"Is man an ape or an angel?"

Charles Darwin's theory of evolution has vexed politicians from the beginning. William Jennings Bryan, who was violently anti-Darwin, all but wrecked his reputation at the Scopes Monkey Trial in 1925. He had been the Democratic nominee for President four times before he ran aground on creationism.

Many decades earlier, Benjamin Disraeli, in a speech at Oxford, had handled the Darwin question better. He remarked that the discoveries of science seemed at odds with the teachings of the church. He went on to ask: "What is the question now placed before society with a glib assurance the most astounding? The question is this—Is man an ape or an angel? My Lord, I am on the side of the angels."

Disraeli's knowledge of science may have been no stronger than Bryan's, but his understanding of the public mood was clearer. Laughter greeted his remarks.

Punch, the British humor magazine, published a cartoon showing an apelike Dizzy in white robes and large angel wings. The future Prime Minister's views on creationism were passed off as a pleasant joke.

"How did the reporter know that?"

Lord Dufferin, the Governor General of Canada, gave a speech in Greek at the University of McGill College. Sir John A. Macdonald and Sir Hector Langevin, both prominent statesmen of the day, were with him on the dais.

Next day Macdonald and Langevin read the report of the speech, which declared, "His Lordship spoke in the purest ancient Greek without mispronouncing a word or making the slightest grammatical solecism."

That surprised Sir Hector. "Good heavens," he said. "How did the reporter know that?"

"I told him," said Sir John.

That surprised Sir Hector even more. "But you don't know Greek," he said.

"True," Sir John replied, "but I do know men."

"We're cast wrong."

Whittaker Chambers set off a political bombshell when he accused Alger Hiss of spying for the Russians. Hiss had been a high-ranking official in the State Department and had served as an adviser at many international conferences. People who knew him could not believe the allegations. "I will not turn my back on Alger Hiss," said Secretary of State Dean Acheson.

Nevertheless, a jury found that Hiss had lied when he denied the changes, and Hiss went to jail. His friends still could not believe it. Whittaker Chambers, an ex-Communist and a writer for *Time* magazine, came under heavy attack for his charges, his testimony, and later his autobiography, entitled *Witness*.

Bennett Cerf, president of Random House, came under fire, too, for publishing *Witness*. To try to clear the air, Cerf gave a dinner party at which his friends who doubted Chambers would have a chance to question the author directly.

Chambers answered all questions promptly and seemed to convince many of the guests he was telling the truth. He showed a clear understanding of why his image was so negative.

"You know what the trouble with this case is?" he asked. "We're cast wrong. I look like a slob, so I should be the villain. Hiss, the handsome man who knows all the society people, is the born hero. It's bad casting."

And so it was. Chambers was pudgy and sloppy, a kind of Peter Lorre gone to lard. But, contrary to appearances, he was not the villain in this late 1940s melodrama.

Quote/Unquote

Abraham Lincoln   (1809–1865)

A universal feeling, whether well- or ill-founded, cannot safely be disregarded.

Anatole France   (1844–1924)

His instinct told him that it was better to understand little than to misunderstand a lot.

Adlai E. Stevenson   (1900–1965)

I think that one of our most important tasks is to convince ourselves and others that there is nothing to fear in difference; that difference, in fact, is one of the healthiest and most invigorating of human characteristics....

Dag Hammarskjöld   (1905–1961)

The longest journey
Is the journey inwards
Of him who has chosen his destiny.

WISDOM

"Tim was so learned...."

Wisdom is knowledge plus insight. Knowledge alone isn't enough. According to Ben Franklin in *Poor Richard's Almanack,* "Tim was so learned that he could name a horse in nine languages—so ignorant that he bought a cow to ride on."

The argument was far from settled....

When Lincoln gave his "House Divided" speech at the Illinois Republican State Convention, it attracted national attention. Lincoln's views hadn't always been held in such high regard, though. A few years earlier, as a lawyer on the circuit, he got into an argument one night with Judge T. Lyle Dickey over the slavery question.

Judge Dickey maintained that slavery was written into the Constitution and could not be tampered with. Lincoln objected. He said that slavery would eventually be eliminated. The argument was far from settled when they finally went upstairs to bed.

Lincoln and Judge Dickey shared a room. They argued long into the night. At daybreak Dickey awoke and saw Lincoln half sitting up in bed.

"Dickey," Lincoln said, "I tell you this nation cannot exist half slave and half free."

The judge was more in the mood for rest than for oratory.

"Oh, Lincoln," he said, "go to sleep."

"The lamps are going out...."

When a person is caught up in the events of the day, it can be hard to see what those events mean for the future.

One man who saw the implications of World War One clearly was Edward, Viscount Grey of Fallodon. As Lord Grey stood at the window of his room at the British Foreign Office on an August evening in 1914, the "Great War" had just begun in Europe. The war would cost millions of lives and settle nothing. Yet, as at all such times, patriotism ran high.

Lord Grey stood and watched the lamplighters at work below his window. They were extinguishing the lights in St. James's Park, London.

He turned to a companion and said, "The lamps are going out all over Europe; we shall not see them lit again in our lifetime."

"I'm busy planting iris...."

The news of the day seems important at the time, but the long view of history is sometimes preferable.

In 1939 the novelist Virginia Woolf was listening to the radio while her husband, Leonard, worked in the garden. Suddenly, she called out to him, "Come, listen—Hitler is on the wireless."

Leonard replied, "I shan't come. I'm busy planting iris, and they will be flowering long after he is dead."

"Two paths lie ahead of you...."

Senator Bill Bradley of New Jersey sometimes offers this amusing bit of advice to his listeners:

Woody Allen once said: "Two paths lie ahead of you; one leads to utter despair and the other to total extinction. May you have the wisdom to choose wisely."

The old man stood up at one.

The old man on the park bench had a world-weary look about him. He was taking in the spring sunshine and watching the pigeons, alone but contented.

A younger man sat down beside him. They said nothing for quite a while. Finally, the younger man looked sadly at the other and heaved a long and profound sigh.

270

The old man stood up at once. "That's it," he said. "If you're going to talk politics, I'm leaving.

Quote/Unquote

Francis Bacon (1561–1626)

Nothing doth more hurt in a state than that cunning men pass for wise.

Alexander Pope (1688–1744)

Old politicians chew on wisdom past,
And totter on in business to the last.

Benjamin Franklin (1706–1790)

Here comes the orator with his flood of words and his drop of wisdom.

Thomas Carlyle (1795–1881)

I do not believe in the collective wisdom of individual ignorance.

Abraham Lincoln (1809–1865)

It is said an Eastern monarch once charged his wise men to invent him a sentence, to be ever in view, and which should be true and appropriate in all times and situations. They presented him the words: "*And this, too, will pass away.*" How much it expresses! How chastening in the hour of pride!—how consoling in the depth of affliction.

Konrad Adenauer (1876–1967)

The good Lord set definite limits on man's wisdom, but set no limits on his stupidity—and that's just not fair!

Felix Frankfurter (1882–1965)

Wisdom too often never comes, and so one ought not to reject it merely because it comes late.

Sam Ervin, Jr. (1896–1985)

Age has many handicaps, but I think the only way you can get wisdom is through experience, and you can't have very much experience when you're very young.

Eric Sevareid   (1912–   )

Wisdom is needed in a President; the appearance of wisdom will do in a candidate.

SPEAKER'S 366-DAY CALENDAR OF POLITICAL EVENTS

January

January 1, 1863: Abraham Lincoln signed the Emancipation Proclamation, freeing all slaves in areas that were "in rebellion against the United States." (See story on page 167)

January 2, 1647: Nathaniel Bacon was born into an artistocratic family at Suffolk, England. Following his education at Cambridge and Gray's Inn, Bacon moved to the United States, where he became the champion of disgruntled Virginians on the frontier. Bacon's Rebellion gained some striking successes, but in October 1677 he died suddenly, and his revolt collapsed.

January 3, 1959: It had been 47 years since Arizona was admitted to the Union as the 48th state. In a 1958 referendum the people of Alaska voted five to one for U.S. statehood, and on January 3, 1959, Alaska officially became the 49th state.

January 4, 1948: The British and a Burmese army commander, Aung San, reached an agreement on full independence for Burma, outside the British Commonwealth of Nations. Despite the assassination of Sang in July 1947, the agreement went into effect on schedule. January 4 is Independence Day in Burma.

January 5, 1928: On this date in the village of Ceylon, Minnesota, was born the man who foolishly promised the American people a tax increase upon his election as President in 1984. The people showed their displeasure by giving Ronald Reagan an overwhelming victory in the Electoral College. Former Vice President Walter Mondale thereupon faded from view.

January 6, 1941: In his annual message to Congress, President Franklin D. Roosevelt called for what soon became known as the "Four Freedoms." (See story on page 100)

January 7, 1800: When comedians are in need of an obscure American President to poke fun at, they often choose Millard Fillmore. The 13th President, born on January 7, 1800, was elected to the Vice Presidency in 1848. Fillmore took over as chief executive when Zachary Taylor died in 1850. Passed over by his own party in 1852, he joined the Know-Nothing party.

January 8, 1884:   Barbed wire was threatening to close the open range and end the long cattle drives. Bitter fence-cutting "wars" broke out in Texas and elsewhere. On January 8, 1884, the Texas legislature was called into special session to deal with one such war. William Wallace, a Texan known as "Bigfoot," said later: "Bob wire played hell with Texas."

January 9, 1867:   On this date Emperor Meiji ascended the throne of Japan. He was 15 years old. When the shogun fell from power a year later, the emperor, filling the vacuum, regained a position of dominance and status. This became known as the Meiji Restoration—a turning point in the history of Japan, for it meant the end of feudalism and the forging of a modern nation.

January 10, 1920:   The ill-fated League of Nations first met in Geneva, Switzerland, on this date. Although the League was Woodrow Wilson's special dream, an obstinate Senate kept the United States from participating. The U.S. did join the United Nations, of course. On January 10, 1946—26 years after the League's opening, the UN General Assembly first met in London.

January 11, 1755:   Alexander Hamilton, the first U.S. Secretary of the Treasury, was born on this date on the island of Nevis in the Leeward Islands. He came to New York in 1772, entered King's College (now Columbia University) in 1773, and soon enlisted in the Revolutionary cause. (See story on page 75)

January 12, 1729:   A critic of English stupidity toward Ireland, a staunch defender of the American colonies, Edmund Burke, born on January 12, 1729, was an influential statesman and political philosopher of the eighteenth century. Even though he said, "You can never plan the future by the past," Burke is regarded as one of the great conservative voices of history.

January 13, 1889:   The high point of the Cimarron County Seat War came on January 13, 1889, when a dozen gunfighters galloped into Cimarron, Kansas, hell-bent on stealing the county records and carting them off to Ingalls. (See story on page 104)

January 14, 1784:   Ratification Day gets less attention than Sadie Hawkins Day, but there *is* such a day, and it commemorates an important event. On January 14, 1784, the Senate ratified the peace treaty with Great Britain that ended the Revolutionary War. The treaty had actually been signed on September 3, 1783, but the Senate's okay was needed.

January 15, 1559:   On this date Elizabeth I was crowned Queen of England in Westminster Abbey by Owen Oglethorpe, Bishop of Carlisle. Several other bishops had refused to crown her, since they regarded her as a heretic. Elizabeth reigned during a brilliant period of English exploration and literary achievement.

January 16, 1883: President Chester A. Arthur, a Republican Stalwart, signed the Pendleton Act creating the Civil Service. A year and a half earlier President Garfield had been shot by a crazed office-seeker, who shouted, "I am a Stalwart and now Arthur is President!" Garfield was elected as a reformer, but it was ex-spoilsman Arthur who shook up the spoils system.

January 17, 1961: President Dwight D. Eisenhower delivered his farewell address to the American people. He warned: "In the councils of government we must guard against the acquisition of unwarranted influence... by the military-industrial complex." Ike, one of the great military leaders in U.S. history, was wary of gullible civilian policymakers.

January 18, 1919: The Paris Peace Conference opened on January 18, 1919, to draft what became the Treaty of Versailles, ending World War One. President Woodrow Wilson had called for "open covenants... openly arrived at." But England's Lloyd George and France's Clemenceau had less idealistic, more vindictive ideas.

January 19, 49 B.C.: Caesar crossed the Rubicon, an act that had a profound effect on world history—not to mention spawning a phrase that is used to this day to connote bold action. (See story on page 47)

January 20, 1962: Barry Goldwater, hero of conservative Republicans in the 1960s, delivered a self-parodying speech at the Alfalfa Club in Washington, D.C. It didn't disarm any liberal journalists, but it did show that Goldwater was a lot less stuffy than old William McKinley, for instance, who campaigned from his front porch in Canton, Ohio. (See story on page 66)

January 21, 1950: The first jury had failed to reach a verdict, but on January 21, 1950, a second jury found Alger Hiss guilty of perjury. In a spy case that involved ex-communist Whittaker Chambers, future President Richard Nixon, and some microfilm hidden in a pumpkin, the truth seemed, and still seems, elusive. (See story on page 266)

January 22, 1905: On this date, "Bloody Sunday," the Russian Revolution of 1905 began when troops fired on unarmed workers who were marching to the Winter Palace in St. Petersburg to petition Tsar Nicholas II. More than a thousand marchers were killed. "What the bullets riddled on that day," wrote a Russian historian, "was faith in the Tsar."

January 23, 1737: This is John Hancock's birthday. Hancock, President of the Continental Congress and a leader in the American Revolution, is probably best known for his large, bold signature, which heads the list on the Declaration of

Independence. After signing, Hancock said, "There, I guess King George will be able to read that."

January 24, 41:   As Emperor of Rome he made his horse a consul and showed in other less amusing ways that he was insane. Torture and execution were two of Caligula's hobbies. Finally, on this date a member of the Praetorian Guard murdered him. Caligula was succeeded by Claudius of *I, Claudius* television fame.

January 25, 1533:   King Henry VIII of England had a major problem. He wanted Pope Clement VII to annul his marriage to Catherine of Aragon. The Pope refused. Henry went ahead anyway, and on this date he secretly married the enchanting though plain Anne Boleyn. This unsanctioned marriage led to the separation of the Church of England from the Roman Catholic Church.

January 26, 1784:   Benjamin Franklin's choice for the national emblem of the United States was the wild turkey. In a letter to his daughter dated January 26, 1784, Franklin attacked the bald eagle as "a bird of bad moral character" and praised the turkey as a "true original native of America." Franklin lost this one.

January 27, 1977:   On this date, the fourth anniversary of the signing of the Vietnam peace pacts in Paris, President Jimmy Carter pardoned most Vietnam draft evaders.

January 28, 1986:   The big news story of January 28, 1986, was not political, although it had political implications. The space shuttle *Challenger* exploded moments after liftoff, killing six astronauts and Christa McAuliffe, a New Hampshire teacher. Pressure to maintain schedules, according to investigators, had caused NASA to abandon "good judgment and common sense."

January 29, 1861:   Kansas was admitted to the Union as the 34th state. This was not a routine event. When the Kansas-Nebraska Act repealed the Missouri Compromise back in 1854, all hell broke loose in Kansas. Instead of coming in peaceably as a free state, Kansas was up for grabs. Proslavery and anti-slavery forces fought it out in "Bleeding Kansas" for years.

January 30, 1649:   Branded as "tyrant, traitor, murderer, and public enemy of the good people" of England, King Charles I was beheaded on January 30 in front of his palace at Whitehall. On the same day in 1948 Mahatma Gandhi fell to a Hindu fanatic's bullets in New Delhi. In 1835, also on the same day, an attempt was made on the life of President Andrew Jackson. It failed when the assassin's two pistols misfired.

January 31, 1945:   An insignificant but sad incident became a *cause célèbrè* upon the publication in 1954 of a book called *The Execution of Private Slovik.* As a five-star general almost a decade earlier, Dwight D. Eisenhower had signed the order that sent Eddie D. Slovik, an army deserter, to die before a firing squad on January 31, 1945, the only deserter executed since 1864.

February

February 1, 1860:   The Speaker of the House of Representatives is usually an experienced old pro like Sam Rayburn or Tip O'Neill. But on February 1, 1860, after nearly two months of wrangling between proslavery and antislavery members, the House finally settled on William Pennington of New Jersey as their new Speaker. He was a freshman Congressman with two months' service.

February 2, 1653:   On this date New Amsterdam became the first city in the nation to receive a charter of self-government. The city's first burgomaster returned to Holland, but the second, Martin Cregier, a tavernkeeper and captain of the burgher guard, lived comfortably for many years at 3 Broadway.

February 3, 1945:   "We can gain no lasting peace," said President Franklin D. Roosevelt, "if we approach it with suspicion and mistrust—or with fear." In that spirit he met with Winston Churchill and Joseph Stalin at Yalta, a small resort city on the Black Sea. At the much-criticized Yalta Conference, Roosevelt, in failing health, was too optimistic about Stalin's intentions.

February 4, 1947:   George Bush's Vice President, P. Danforth Quayle, was born on this date. Quayle may not have said after a trip to Latin America that it made him wish he had studied Latin in school, but he did provide the public with plenty of other howlers.

February 5, 1985:   On February 5, 1985, 2,131 years after the start of the Third Punic War, the mayors of Rome and Carthage met in Tunis to sign a treaty of friendship. This act officially ended a war that was fought from 149 B.C. to 146 B.C., reaching its climax when a Roman army under Scipio devastated Carthage.

February 6, 1911:   Sixteen years to the day after heavy-hitter Babe Ruth was born, the political heavy-hitter of the 1980s—Ronald Reagan—first saw the light of day. Reagan was born in Tampico, Illinois. A movie actor before finding his true calling, he served two terms as Governor of California and two more as President of the United States. (See story on page 195)

February 7, 1478:   Sir Thomas More, "A Man for All Seasons," was born in London, England. When More refused to take an oath supporting King Henry VIII's constitutional theory, arguing that the law of God was still part of the law of England, his fate was sealed. He was beheaded on July 6, 1535.

February 8, 1587:   Mary Stuart, better known as Mary, Queen of Scots, was executed at Fotheringhay Castle in Northamptonshire, England. (See story on page 190)

February 9, 1950:   On this date Senator Joseph McCarthy gave the speech in Wheeling, West Virginia, that kicked off his anti-Communist crusade (or, if you prefer, witch-hunt). (See story on page 170)

February 10, 1897:   Page one of *The New York Times* has carried the slogan "All the News That's Fit to Print" ever since February 10, 1897. The *Times* offered a $100 prize to anyone who could come up with a better slogan of ten words or less. No one did.

February 11, 660 B.C.:   The Japanese people celebrate National Foundation Day, formerly Empire Day, on February 11. According to tradition, Jimmu Tenno, a semi-legendary emperor claiming descent from the Sun Goddess, founded the Imperial Family on this date.

February 12, 1809:   Abraham Lincoln was born in a log cabin in Hardin County (now Larue County), Kentucky. Generally regarded as our greatest President, he was often criticized while in office. He said: "If the end brings me out all right, what is said against me won't amount to anything. If the end brings me out wrong, ten angels swearing I was right would make no difference." (See story on page 108)

February 13, 1635:   "If a nation expects to be ignorant and free," wrote Thomas Jefferson in 1816, "it expects what never was and never will be." Nearly 200 years earlier the Puritans believed the same thing. On February 13, 1635, they established the Boston Latin School, one of the first free public schools in the United States. Many famous Americans, including five signers of the Declaration of Independence, attended the school.

February 14, 1949:   Chaim Weizmann, scientist and Zionist leader, was a true citizen of the world. Born in Russia and educated in Germany, he taught in Switzerland, then spent much of his working life in England, where he made important scientific contributions in both world wars. On February 14, 1949, Weizmann became the first President of newly independent Israel.

February 15, 1898:   On this date the U.S. battleship Maine blew up in Havanna Harbor. William Randolph Hearst sent artist Frederic Remington to cover the story in Cuba. When Remington found little happening there, he asked about coming home. Hearst wired back: "Please remain. You furnish the pictures and I'll furnish the war." He was as good as his word.

February 16, 1878:   Does anyone remember "the Crime of '73"? No, not the Watergate affair. The Crime of '73 occurred in 1873. The supposed offense was that the 1873 mint law made no provision for coining silver dollars. Cheap-money advocates and silver producers hopped all over Congress. The result was the Bland-Allison Act, signed on February 16, 1878, that brought back silver dollars.

February 17, 1909:   People are forever proclaiming the end of an era. But when the remarkable Apache Indian leader Geronimo died on this date at Fort Sill, Oklahoma, it really did close out a chapter in American history. The "Indian question" did not go away, but the last great Indian warrior was gone.

February 18, 1857:   When a prophet or prophetess has a vision, the rest of the trible should be wary. That was the lesson learned by the Gealeke Xhosa tribe of South Africa after a 14-year-old girl proclaimed, "All our livestock must be slaughtered on or before February 18, 1857." They were, and the tribe perished. (See story on page 187)

February 19, 1861:   The Edict of Emancipation, issued by Tsar Alexander II of Russia, freed all Russian serfs. Serfdom had grown steadily more oppressive in the 16th cetury, until the distinction between serfs and slaves disappeared entirely. Alexander II's edict of February 19, 1861, promised land to the freed serfs, but the system of distribution proved a failure.

February 20, 1962:   Russia's launching of the space satellite *Sputnik I* in late 1957 threw American politicians into a tizzy. The space race was on. On February 20, 1962, U.S. space scientists sent the first American astronaut into orbit. He was Lieutenant Colonel John Glenn, whose Mercury capsule *Friendship 7* helped carry him all the way to the U.S. Senate.

February 21, 1972:   President Richard M. Nixon arrived in Beijing (then Peiping, or Peking) on a "journey for peace." It lasted eight days and brought Nixon the most favorable press notices of his administration. The U.S. and China issued a joint statement promising efforts toward "a normalization of relations."

February 22, 1918:   On this anniversary of George Washington's birthday, President Warren G. Harding was "bloviating," as he liked to say, and, wonder of wonders, he came up with an original phrase. It's one that's been used many times since—the term "Founding Fathers." (See story on page 249)

February 23, 1927:   The Federal Radio Commission came into being on this date. Seven years later it was replaced by the Federal Communications Commission, or FCC. Just how much or how little regulating this commission should do has been the subject of continuing controversy.

February 24, 1803: We take it for granted that the U.S. Supreme Court can declare an act of Congress unconstitutional. But back in 1803 the powers of the Constitution were still being worked out. On February 24, 1803, the Supreme Court decided in the case of Marbury v. Madison, with Chief Justice John Marshall presiding, that it indeed had this power.

February 25, 1919: Six years to the day after the 16th Amendment to the Constitution ratified a federal income tax, the state of Oregon came up with an idea of its own for raising revenue—a tax on gasoline. Other states liked the idea, and before long they too climbed on the bandwagon.

February 26, 1815: The nations that had defeated Napoleon Bonaparte were still discussing terms of peace at the Congress of Vienna when startling news arrived. On February 26, 1815, Napoleon escaped from his exile on the island of Elba and set out to reclaim his empire. Less than four months later Napoleon's army was utterly crushed at Waterloo.

February 27, 1812: George Gordon, Lord Byron achieved fame as a Romantic poet and a man who had a way with the ladies. But he also had a serious side. On February 27, 1812, Byron delivered his maiden speech in the House of Lords, a stirring talk in defense of the "framebreakers"—workers who had wrecked textile machines because they feared unemployment.

February 28, 1854: A few miles southwest of Oshkosh, b'gosh, lies the small city of Ripon, Wisconsin. On this date in 1854 a local political meeting in Ripon chose the name "Republican" to describe a proposed new party combining the Whigs and the Free Soilers. The name was formally adopted later in the year at a meeting in Jackson, Michigan.

February 29, 1288: In an early outbreak of women's liberation, Scotland made it legal for a woman to make a proposal of marriage to a man.

March

March 1, 1914: On this date Americans had to file their first-ever federal income tax return. Taxpayers anted up one percent of their annual income above $3,000. The highest tax rate was seven percent, payable on income above $500,000 a year. A very small number of people—fewer than one in a hundred—earned even the minimum income. So most Americans paid no income tax at all.

March 2, 1836: A convention meeting at Austin declared Texas's independence from Mexico, creating the Republic of Texas. Military victory at San Jacinto made independence a fact. Sam Houston became the Republic's first

President. In 1845 the United States concluded a treaty of annexation, which specified that the new state could in the future, if it chose, divide itself into as many as five states.

March 3, 1931: By Act of Congress on March 3, 1931, "The Star-Spangled Banner" was designated the National Anthem. Military bands had played it regularly since 1916, and the song itself went back to the War of 1812. Francis Scott Key's verses are sung to the difficult tune of "Anacreon in Heaven." Attempts to make "America the Beautiful" the National Anthem have failed.

March 4, 1829: Andrew Jackson's inauguration as the seventh President of the United States was followed by the wildest White House reception of all time. Jackson supporters swarmed into the White House trying to reach Old Hickory, their hero, who had to be guarded by a circle of friends. Tubs of punch finally lured them to the White House lawn, but not before they had wrecked furniture and smashed dishes in their enthusiasm.

March 5, 1946: In an address at Westminster College in Fulton, Missouri, Winston Churchill said, "An iron curtain has descended across the Continent." It was the first use of the term "iron curtain" to refer to the Soviet Union's foreign policy following World War Two. Less than a year after the shooting war ended, the Cold War was on.

March 6, 1933: Two days after President Franklin D. Roosevelt's Saturday inauguration, his "bank holiday," proclaimed on Sunday afternoon, took effect. The American banking system was in chaos—most banks were already closed— and FDR wanted to give Congress time to enact emergency banking legislation. A special session of Congress convened on March 9, marking the start of the New Deal's "Hundred Days."

March 7, 1850: Senator Daniel Webster delivered his Seventh of March speech, backing the passage of the Compromise of 1850 and ensuring his political doom. (See story on page 40)

March 8, 1965: This might be called Conscientious Objectors Day. On March 8, 1965, the Supreme Court ruled unanimously that a conscientious objector who believes in a nontraditional Supreme Being may be excused from combat training and service. Six years later, on March 8, 1971, the Court held that a conscientious objector must oppose all wars, not just a specific war, in this case Vietnam.

March 9, 1796: Napoleon Bonaparte married Josephine Beauharnais on this date. The marriage seems to have been based mainly on Napoleon's assessment of its potential influence on his career. Desiree Clary, his former mistress, was heartbroken. (See story on page 161)

March 10, 1971: By a vote of 94-0 the U.S. Senate voted to approve a Constitutional Amendment lowering the voting age to 18 in all elections. The House approved by a 400-19 vote on March 23, and the 38th state ratified it on June 30. The 26th Amendment, like the 19th, which provided for women's suffrage, brought no striking changes in voting patterns.

March 11, 1938: A month earlier the Austrian Chancellor, Kurt von Schuschnigg, had been summoned to meet Adolph Hitler at Berchtesgaden. As Schuschnigg admired the mountain scenery, Hitler snapped, "We did not come here to discuss the view and the weather." The Austrian Chancellor signed Hitler's ultimatum, then repudiated it, then resigned on March 11, 1938. The next day German troops marched into Austria.

March 12, 1933: Franklin D. Roosevelt had begun his "fireside chats" on radio while Governor of New York. As President, he delivered his first national radio chat on March 12, 1933. His warm, confident voice and clear explanation of the banking crisis made his informal talk a stunning success. Many fireside chats followed.

March 13, 1881: The grim failure of terrorism was never more evident than in the years following the assassination of Tsar Alexander II of Russia. Alexander II was the reformer who freed the serfs. On the morning of March 13, 1881, the Tsar signed a proclamation promising certain other reforms. That afternoon a terrorist threw a bomb under his carriage. Alexander II died. A quarter century of brutal tsarist repression began.

March 14, 1883: On March 14, 1883, Karl Marx, the theorist behind modern socialism and communism, passed to his presumably just reward. Marx's diagnosis of the ills of capitalism had some validity, but his prognosis was all wrong. Economist John Maynard Keynes wondered how Marxism gained "so powerful and enduring an influence over the minds of men, and, through them, the events of history."

March 15, 44 B.C.: "Caesar, beware of Brutus; take heed of Cassius; come not near Casca; have an eye to Cinna; trust not Trebonius; mark well Metellus Cimber...." Yes, March 15th—the Ides of March—proved to be Julius Caesar's dying day more than two millennia ago. (See story on page 185)

March 16, 1792: On this date King Gustavus III of Sweden was shot at a masked ball in Stockholm's Royal Opera House. A gifted author and patron of the arts, Gustavus had angered the feuding Swedish gentry with his craftiness and extravagance. A group of aristocrats plotted against him, and one of them wounded him fatally at the ball. He died 13 days later.

March 17, 1776: Boston seethed under the military occupation of General William Howe and his British troops. Then one morning Howe looked out and saw new breastworks and behind them the rebel troops of General George Washington. On March 17, 1776—Evacuation Day—the British soldiers, along with a thousand Boston Tories, left Boston on 170 ships of the British fleet.

March 18, 1782: John C. Calhoun, champion of states' rights and Southern unity, was born on this date on the South Carolina frontier. Calhoun, along with Henry Clay, Daniel Webster, and Thomas Hart Benton, served in the U.S. Senate at a time when political pygmies, by comparison, were being elected to the White House. (President Grover Cleveland was born on this day in 1837.)

March 19, 1697: On this date Peter the Great of Russia began his European tour, a journey of discovery that was to affect the future of tsarist Russia. (See story on page 91)

March 20, 1852: Certain books are political events. One of them was *Uncle Tom's Cabin* by Harriet Beecher Stowe, first published on March 20, 1852. The book, and later the stage production, played a major role in the antislavery movement. Said Lincoln when he met Mrs. Stowe, "So you're the little woman who wrote the book that made this great war!"

March 21, 1806: Benito Juárez, one of the great heroes of Mexico, was born on this date. An Indian, he opposed the privileges of the church and the army. As President of Mexico, he helped to transfer power from the creoles to the mestizos. Juárez defended his nation against the French empire of Maximilian, and helped to imbue Mexicans with a sense of national pride.

March 22, 1887: In an era of deregulation, the Interstate Commerce Commission may seem like a throwback. But when the first five commissioners were appointed on March 22, 1887, most Americans felt the need for them. Laissez-faire had allowed the big railroads of the day to set excessive and discriminatory rates. The ICC, the first regulatory agency in U.S. history, was established to cure the abuses.

March 23, 1775: On this date Patrick Henry made his famous speech to the Virginia convention in Richmond ending with the words, "...give me liberty or give me death!" (See story on page 130)

March 24, 1788: A majority of Rhode Island voters were convinced that the new U.S. Constitution threatened liberty and democracy. In a popular referendum on March 24, 1788, they rejected it by a vote of 2,708 to 237. A state convention later ratified the Constitution, but only after Providence had seceded from Rhode Island and threatened to remain separate pending ratification.

March 25, 1894: As the Panic of 1893 worsened, Jacob Coxey of Massillon, Ohio, decided to do something about it. A self-made businessman, he came up with a scheme to end the depression. When President Grover Cleveland and Congress refused to listen, Coxey said he would "send a petition to Washington with boots on." And he did. "Coxey's Army" never numbered more than 500, but it conveyed a sharp message of unrest.

March 26, 1930: This is Sandra Day O'Connor's birthday. O'Connor, who was born in El Paso, Texas, took the oath as an Associate Justice of the U.S. Supreme Court on September 25, 1981. An appointee of President Reagan (on July 7, 1981), she was the first woman ever to be nominated or to serve on the highest court of the land.

March 27, 1306: On or about March 27, 1306—sources differ—Robert I was crowed King of Scotland at Scone. Most people remember Robert Bruce (or Robert *the* Bruce), as he is usually called, because of the "spider story." Legend has it that a resolute spider led to Robert's resolve to ascend the Scottish throne. (See story on page 178)

March 28, 193: The Roman Emperor Pertinax was assassinated on this date— just 86 days after taking office. According to the historian Gibbon, Pertinax was an excellent prince. But excellence wasn't enough. The Praetorian Guard despised Pertinax, whose reforms they saw as a threat. They stabbed him to death, mounted his head on a lance, and carried it to their camp. The imperial guardians thus became the masters of Rome.

March 29, 1790: John Tyler, the tenth President of the United States, was born on March 29, 1790. He is best remembered as the tail end of the Whigs' 1840 campaign slogan, "Tippecanoe and Tyler too." The election focused on Tippecanoe—which is to say, on William Henry Harrison. It featured hard cider and a log-cabin theme. Harrison won, served one month and died in office. Tyler, a Democrat, finished his term and went home.

March 30, 1981: On this date John W. Hinckley, Jr., a disturbed 25-year-old drifter who wanted to show movie star Jodie Foster his own star quality, tried to assassinate President Ronald Reagan. (See story on page 45)

March 31, 1968: Lyndon B. Johnson's "Great Society" Presidency had fallen on evil days largely because of his escalation of the Vietnam War. On March 31, 1968, LBJ announced on television that he would not be a candidate for reelection. It was one of the dramatic TV moments in American politics. Johnson, a landslide winner against Barry Goldwater in 1964, retired to his Texas ranch.

April

April 1, 1908: Consider the odds against rising from a log cabin childhood to the Presidency of the United States. Then think how hard it must be to rise from the Untouchable class in India to a position of power and prestige. Yet that is what Jagivan Ram did. Born an Untouchable on April 1, 1908, Ram served in various Indian cabinet positions and twice ran for Prime Minister. He died at New Delhi on July 6, 1986.

April 2, 1792: A bill passed Congress on this date stating that "the money of account of the United States should be expressed in dollars or units, dismes or tenths, cents or hundredths...." Coins authorized ranged from the gold eagle, worth ten dollars, down to the copper half-cent. The first coin to be struck under the new law was a half-disme.

April 3, 1860: Trying to win a U.S. Mail contract, three entrepreneurs set up the Pony Express—190 way stations at ten-mile intervals from St. Joseph, Missouri, to San Francisco. Mail-carrying riders galloped their horses for ten miles at top speed, then grabbed fresh horses. Each letter cost $38 to carry—but ten-day delivery was a big feature. The first rider left St. Joseph on April 3, 1860.

April 4, 1968: On April 4, 1968, the Rev. Martin Luther King, Jr., was assassinated on the second-floor balcony of his motel in Memphis, Tennessee. King had won a Nobel Peace Prize in 1964 for his leadership of the nonviolent civil rights movement. His birthday (January 15) is celebrated as a federal legal public holiday.

April 5, 1930: "I am thinking furiously night and day," said Mahatma Gandhi early in 1930. The result of his thinking was a march to the sea to extract salt—a protest against the British government's salt tax. It was a triumphant procession that attracted supporters as it advanced. The 24-day march ended on April 5, 1930. Gandhi's taking of a few grains of untaxed salt had tremendous symbolic impact.

April 6, 1199: At the moment of his death, England's King Richard the Lionhearted proved himself a true hero of chivalry. Mortally wounded in combat on April 6, 1199, he breathed a word of forgiveness for his foe. Richard Cœr de Lion appears fictitiously in Sir Walter Scott's *Ivanhoe*.

April 7, 1831: Emperor Pedro I of Brazil abdicated on this date and soon returned to Portugal, carrying with him, wrote one historian, "as much of the Brazilian treasury as was within reach." This is often called the Revolution of

April 7. Dom Pedro left behind his six-year-old son as emperor—and the Brazilians accepted him, although a three-member regency ruled temporarily.

April 8, 1826:   Senator John Randolph of Virginia often gave brilliantly abusive speeches. His wording got him into *Bartlett's*, but in his own day it also got him into duels. One of the most famous occurred on April 6, 1826, when Randolph faced off against Secretary of State John Clay. Both men fired twice, but the only damage done was to Randolph's coat.

April 9, 1865:   On Palm Sundy, April 9, 1865, the Confederate States of America came to an end (for all practical purposes) when General Robert E. Lee surrendered his Army of Northern Virginia to General Ulysses S. Grant at Appomattox Court House, Virginia. Officers and men of the Confederacy could go home "not to be disturbed by the United States authorities" so long as they obeyed the laws.

April 10, 1864:   Napoleon III of France saw the American Civil War as his chance to install a puppet regime in Mexico. He convinced Archduke Maximilian of Austria, a bold, artistic dreamer, to take the Mexican throne. On April 10, 1864, Maximilian agreed. Four days later he and his lovely wife Carlotta embarked for Veracruz and misfortune. Maximilian died before a Mexican firing squad on June 19, 1867.

April 11, 1974:   American-educated Golda Meir resigned as Prime Minister of Israel on this date. (See story on page 225) Also, on April 11, 1951, President Harry S Truman removed General Douglas MacArthur from his Korean command for making unauthorized policy statements.

April 12, 1861:   Decades of political conflict over states rights, secession, and slavery came to a head on the morning of April 12, 1861, with the firing of the first shot of the Civil War. This shot, a signal from a Confederate mortar at Fort Johnson, exploded directly over Union-held Fort Sumter in the harbor of Charleston, South Carolina.

April 13, 1743:   On this date Thomas Jefferson was born in Albemarle County, Virginia. Author of the Declaration of Independence, founder of the University of Virginia, and third President of the United States, the brilliant and practical Jefferson was also an inventor and an architect. (See story on page 3)

April 14, 1986:   President Reagan sent U.S. warplanes to bomb the Libyan cities of Tripoli and Benghazi. He had been fuming for some time over the actions of Col. Muammar al-Qaddafi, Libya's strongman. Reagan blamed Libyan terrorists for the April 5 bombing of a West Berlin discotheque. The American bombing raid killed Qaddafi's young daughter, but Qaddafi himself escaped uninjured.

April 15, 1865: "Except for that, how did you like the play, Mrs. Lincoln?" Time makes it possible to joke about even the most tragic events. On the evening of April 14, 1865, while watching the play *Our American Cousin* at Ford's Theatre in Washington, D.C., President Abraham Lincoln was shot by John Wilkes Booth, an actor. Lincoln died on the morning of April 15. Booth was shot dead on April 26.

April 16, 1917: In one of the key events of the Bolshevik Revolution, Vladimir Ilyich Lenin returned to Russia from Switzerland. The Germans, although at war with Russia, permitted Lenin to cross their country in a sealed railway car. They reasoned, correctly, that Lenin's success in Russia would benefit the German cause.

April 17, 1973: As the Watergate scandal began to unfold, President Nixon's press secretary, Ron Ziegler, was trapped in a tangle of lies. On this date he made his famous "inoperative statement" statement. (See story on page 263)

April 18, 1775: Listen, my children, and you shall hear
Of the midnight ride of Paul Revere.
On the eighteenth of April in Seventy-five;
Hardly a man is now alive.
Who remembers that famous day and year.

Next day the American Revolution began when Minutemen fired on British troops at Lexington. (See story on page 131)

April 19, 1951: General Douglas MacArthur, stripped of his command in Korea by President Harry S Truman, gave his "Old soldiers never die" speech to a joint session of Congress.

April 20, 1889: The man whom Winston Churchill called "the repository and embodiment of many forms of soul-destroying hatred" was born on this date. Adolf Hitler, the illegitimate son of Maria Anna Schicklgruber, rose to become not the Austrian artist he had hoped but the German Führer, the Nazi architect of the Second World War and the Holocaust.

April 21, 1960: Moving the capital of Brazil inland from Rio de Janeiro had been discussed since the 1820s. The name for the new capital, Brasilia, was suggested during the reign of Dom Pedro I. But it took a dynamic President in the 1950s, Juscelino Kubitschek, to make the dream a reality. On April 21, 1960, the capital was formally transferred to the new, still uncompleted city.

April 22, 1889: A map of the United States from 1885 shows the state of Oklahoma as "Indian Territory." And so it was—the home of 22 tribes. But the prize was too rich to leave entirely to the Native Americans. "Boomers," as they were called, pushed for white settlement. Finally, a date and a time were set: high noon, April 22, 1889. Within a few hours, whites had settled the 1,920,000 acres of the new "Oklahoma District."

April 23, 1791: This is President James Buchanan's birthday. Buchanan, the 15th President, was the only bachelor in the office and the only President from Pennsylvania. He proved an inspiration to neither bachelors nor Pennsylvanians. Well out of his depth in the crisis preceding the Civil War, he wrote, "I shall carry to my grave the consciousness that I at least meant well for my country."

April 24, 1916: Richard Brinsley Sheridan called Ireland "the land of happy wars and sad love songs." One of the wars, if not a happy one, was the Easter Rebellion, which started on April 24, 1916. It was led by members of the Sinn Fein movement who hoped to set up an independent Irish Republic. Like earlier rebellions, this one was crushed by English troops. Its leaders were executed. But Sinn Fein's popularity and influence grew.

April 25, 1959: On this date the St. Lawrence Seaway opened. The Seaway permits all but the largest ocean-going ships to go as far as Duluth, Minnesota, at the western end of Lake Superior—more than 2,300 miles from the Atlantic Ocean.

April 26, 1983: The National Commission on Excellence in Education issued its report indicating that the United States was "a nation at risk." It called elementary and secondary schooling in the U.S. "mediocre" and recommended a number of reforms.

April 27, 1822: This is Ulysses S. Grant's day four times over. Grant was born on April 27, 1822. The groundbreaking for his famous tomb in New York City occurred on April 27, 1891; the cornerstone was laid on the same day in 1892; and Grant's Tomb, located on Riverside Drive at 123rd Street, was dedicated on April 27, 1897.

April 28, 1965: There was a time not so long ago when American troops were routinely dispatched to trouble spots in the Caribbean and Central America. On April 28, 1965, President Lyndon B. Johnson sent some 400 U.S. Marines to the Dominican Republic to protect American citizens threatened by civil war. Within a week the U.S. had committed nearly 12,500 soldiers and 7,000 Marines.

April 29, 1975: U.S. civilians were evacuated from Saigon on this date, as Communist forces completed their takeover of South Vietnam.

April 30, 1803: While negotiating with the French for the purchase of New Orleans and western Florida, U.S. diplomats were stunned when France offered to sell the whole Louisiana territory—an area equal in size to the rest of the United States of that day. Jefferson doubted his Constitutional authority to make the purchase, but he went ahead anyway, signing the purchase agreement on April 30, 1803.

May

May 1, 1851:   Queen Victoria and her ever-faithful Albert were on hand for the opening of the Great Exposition of 1851 in London, which featured the gleaming Crystal Palace. (See story on page 151)

May 2, 1729:   The German princess who rose to become Czarina Catherine II of Russia was born on this date. Catherine the Great, as she is now called, was an energetic letter-writer, and her correspondence with Voltaire, Diderot, and others helped to build her reputation as an enlightened monarch. (See story on page 1)

May 3, 1791:   Influenced by the ideas and events of the French Revolution, the Four Year Diet, or Polish "Great Parliament," approved the Constitution of the Third of May 1791. The anniversary of this milestone event is still celebrated in Poland. By the terms of the Constitution the Polish nobles gave the rising burgher class equal access to public offices and to Parliament.

May 4, 1970:   Student protest against the Vietnam War was at fever pitch when, on May 4, 1970, National Guardsmen fired on demonstrators at Kent State University, Ohio, killing four and wounding nine. Less than two weeks later, city and state police fired on student demonstrators at Jackson State College, Mississippi, killing two.

May 5, 1925:   A Tennessee law made it a crime to teach the theory of evolution in the state's public schools. John T. Scopes of Dayton, Tennessee, broke the law. He was arrested on May 5, 1925. The subsequent "Monkey Trial," which pitted William Jennings Bryan and his fundamentalist doctrine against Clarence Darrow, the famed "attorney for the damned," is the subject of the stage play and movie *Inherit the Wind*.

May 6, 1626:   Peter Minuit arrived on "Manhattes" Island on May 4, 1626, as Director General of New Netherland. Two days later—wasting no time—Minuit purchased the island from the Indians for 60 guilders worth of trinkets, or roughly $24.

May 7, 1915:   The Imperial German Embassy warned travelers on May 1, 1915, that "vessels flying the flag of Great Britain ... are liable to destruction...." They were serious. On May 7, after an uneventful voyage from New York, the Cunard liner *Lusitania* was torpedoed by a German submarine off the Irish coast. Many Americans were among the nearly 1,200 who died. Public opinion condemned Germany.

May 8, 1987:   Revelations about Presidential hopeful Gary Hart, Miami model Donna Rice, and the good ship *Monkey Business* forced Hart to withdraw from the race for the 1988 Democratic nomination. He reentered the campaign later, but his support had evaporated.

May 9, 1933:   Four and a half months after Adolf Hitler became Chancellor of Germany, a torchlight parade of thousands of students ended at a square opposite the University of Berlin. There, a little after midnight on May 10, torches were put to a pile of subversive books written by such authors as Thomas Mann, Albert Einstein, Jack London, Helen Keller, Sigmund Freud, and Marcel Proust.

May 10, 1940:   On May 10, 1940, Winston Churchill replaced Neville Chamberlain as Prime Minister of Great Britain. Leopold Amery, a Conservative M.P., expressed the national mood perfectly a few days earlier when he turned to Chamberlain in Parliament and said—borrowing a line from Cromwell—"Depart, I say, and let us have done with you. In the name of God, go!" (See story on page 128)

May 11, 1812:   The only Prime Minister of England ever assassinated met his fate on this date, nearly two centuries ago. His name, Spencer Perceval, does not loom large in the annals of British history. (See story on page 141)

May 12, 1975:   On the morning of May 12, 1975, Cambodia seized the U.S. merchant ship *Mayaquez* in the Gulf of Siam. Thirty-nine Americans were on board. President Jerry Ford, smarting from the humiliating U.S. retreat from Cambodia and South Vietnam, reacted promptly. He sent 1,100 Marines to the scene. Confronted by force, Cambodia released the ship and crew, but not before 38 Americans had died in the mission.

May 13, 1918:   Airmail made its debut in the United States with the issuance of the first airmail stamps on May 13, 1918. The stamps came in denominations of 6 cents, 16 cents, and 24 cents. Scheduled airmail service began two days later with flights between New York City and Washington, D.C.

May 14, 1948:   With the departure of the British high commissioner for Palestine, the state of Israel was proclaimed at Tel Aviv on this date. The United States extended immediate recognition. On the same day, armed forces from the Arab states of Syria, Lebanon, Jordan, Egypt, and Iraq invaded Israel. Far from losing their new homeland as a result of this Arab assault, the Israelis gained territory.

May 15, 1972: George Wallace's quest for the Democratic Presidential nomination ended abruptly on May 15, 1972. At a campaign appearance in a shopping mall in Laurel, Maryland, 21-year-old Arthur Bremer fired five shots at Wallace, who was shaking hands with the crowd. One of the bullets paralyzed the Alabama Governor from the waist down.

May 16, 1868: On this date Senator Edmund G. Ross of Kansas cast the key vote that acquitted President Andrew Johnson at his impeachment trial. The vote infuriated Ross's Congressional Republican colleagues and cut short his political career. (See story on page 42)

May 17, 1954: It was one of the landmark judicial decisions of the 20th century—Brown v. Board of Education of Topeka, Kansas. The U.S. Supreme Court by a unanimous vote overturned the separate-but-equal doctrine of Plessy v. Ferguson and outlawed public school segregation in the United States. The Court called for "all deliberate speed" in integrating the nation's schools.

May 18, 1852: Massachusetts enacted the first effective school attendance law. The law required all children between the ages of eight and 14 to attend school at least 12 weeks a year. Not only that, but six of the weeks had to be consecutive.

May 19, 1777: Button Gwinnett died of dueling wounds on May 19, 1777. The most memorable thing about Gwinnett is that he signed the Declaration of Independence and very little else. (See story on page 164)

May 20, 1862: On May 20, 1862, in the midst of the Civil War, Abraham Lincoln signed the Homestead Act. Southerners had blocked it before the war, fearing that the 160 acres of public land it offered settlers would attract antislavery farmers to the territories. It did, but it also attracted ranchers, who needed up to 50,000 acres each, not 160.

May 21, 1832: The Democratic-Republican Party held a nominating convention in Baltimore on this date. It adopted its new, and present, name: the Democratic Party. It nominated Andrew Jackson for a second term as President and Martin Van Buren to run for Vice President. This was the first time a major party chose its candidates at a nominating convention.

May 22, 1807: The trial of Aaron Burr for treason began on this date before a United States Circuit Court in Richmond, Virginia. Burr had been Vice President of the United States under Jefferson when he first began scheming to carve some territory for himself out of the Southwest, or perhaps it was Mexico. The jury acquitted Burr of treason, as the crime was defined by Chief Justice John Marshall, presiding.

May 23, 1909: Catastrophic health insurance and national health care are continuing topics of discussion in the United States. Unlikely as it may seem, Winston Churchill advocated national health insurance for the people of Great Britain in a speech he gave way back on May 23, 1909. (See story on page 205)

May 24, 1819: Queen Victoria, who reigned for 64 generally prosperous years, was born in London on this date. She ascended the throne at the age of 18. (See story on page 27) Victoria's marriage to a German princeling, Albert of Saxe-Coburg-Gotha, angered many Britons, but was deeply satisfying to Victoria. They had nine children. (See story on page 139)

May 25, 1940: Leon Trotsky, a co-founder with Lenin of the Soviet state, lost out in a power struggle with Joseph Stalin. Banished from the Soviet Union, Trotsky took up residence in Mexico City. Although his house was fortified and under heavy guard, Stalin's hit men could not be deterred. The first attempt on Trotsky's life occurred on May 25, 1940. (See story on page 169)

May 26, 1660: King Charles II landed in England on this date to reclaim his throne. By then the English were ready for a restoration of the monarchy, which had ended ten years earlier with the beheading of Charles I. Common people went to their knees in the street to honor their king—"which," wrote diarist Samuel Pepys, "methinks is a little too much."

May 27, 1911: This is the birthday of Hubert H. Humphrey, a liberal Mayor of Minneapolis and later U.S. Senator from Minnesota. As Vice President under Lyndon B. Johnson, Humphrey felt obliged to defend the President's Vietnam policy. This loyalty did him little good with voters. He lost the Presidential election of 1968 to Richard Nixon.

May 28, 1830: On this date Congress passed the Indian Removal Act, the purpose of which was to move Native Americans from their homes east of the Mississippi to lands in the West. Congress regarded this as a humane policy, but tribes such as the Cherokees, Creeks, Croctaws, Chickasaws, and Seminoles were bitterly opposed. Results were sometimes tragic, as in the Cherokee "Trail of Tears," a forced removal from Georgia.

May 29, 1917: Everyone who is old enough to remember knows where he or she was on the day John F. Kennedy was shot. Few know where they were on the day he was born. This is that day. To his "brief, shining moment" JFK, the first Catholic President, brought Camelot, charisma, and confrontation with Cuba. His charm was widely admired.

May 30, 1922: "In this temple, as in the hearts of the people for whom he saved the Union, the memory of Abraham Lincoln is enshrined forever." Those words are engraved in marble behind the imposing statue of Lincoln by Daniel Chester

French that stands in the Lincoln Memorial in Washington, D.C. The shrine was dedicated on May 30, 1922.

May 31, 1962:   Adolf Eichmann claimed to be simply a technician, but the Israeli court that tried him for crimes against humanity, thought otherwise. As chief of the Gestapo's Jewish section, the meek-looking Eichmann directed the deportation and murder of millions of Jews between 1938 and 1945. Israeli agents abducted him from Argentina in 1960. He was hanged on May 31, 1962.

June

June 1, 1958:   Charles André Joseph Marie de Gaulle was named Premier of France in the wake of a military and civilian revolt in Algeria. He became President in 1959 and dominated French politics for the next ten years. Always an egotist, de Gaulle loved glory and grandeur. This made him difficult to deal with. Winston Churchill once said: "Of all the crosses I have borne since 1940, none is so heavy as the Cross of Lorraine."

June 2, 1953:   On this date Queen Elizabeth II was crowned. During World War Two, Elizabeth had served as a junior subaltern—a second lieutenant—in the British women's services. She became a pretty good truck driver and mechanic, skills that were needed in the war effort but probably fell into disuse at Buckingham Palace.

June 3, 1861:   Stephen A. Douglas, the Little Giant, and Abraham Lincoln's most familiar political opponent, died on June 3, 1861. Douglas's deathbed advice to his sons underscored his patriotism. (See story on page 175)

June 4, 1940:   On this date, in England's darkest hour of World War Two, Winston Churchill delivered perhaps his most inspiring speech: "...we shall fight on the beaches, we shall fight on the landing grounds...." (See story on page 218)

June 5, 1968:   Robert F. Kennedy had just won the California Presidential primary and was about to leave the Ambassador Hotel in Los Angeles. Shots rang out, and RFK fell to the floor of the hotel's serving pantry, mortally wounded. His assassin, a Palestinian refugee, screamed, "I can explain... I did it for my country...." The time was 12:15 a.m. on June 5, 1968. Kennedy died the next day.

June 6, 1978:   In a sense, the Reaganomics era began on this date, the anniversary of D-Day in World War Two. Californians, fed up with increasing taxes, and armed with initiative and referendum, voted decisively for Proposition 13, which put arbitrary and severe limits on state and local taxes. Thus began the "tax revolution" and along with it "supply-side economics" and a soaring national debt.

June 7, 1905:   For most of the 19th century Norway and Sweden were joined in an uneasy union. Finally, on June 7, 1905, the Storting, or national parliament of Norway, declared the end of the union and the end of allegiance to Sweden's King Oscar II. When a vote showed that Norwegians favored separation almost unanimously, Sweden let Norway go.

June 8, 1886:   A medical report signed by five doctors on this date certified that Mad King Ludwig II of Bavaria was indeed mad. A few days later he and his psychiatrist drowned in Lake Starnberg. The exact circumstances of their deaths remain a mystery. In happier times, Ludwig's infatuation with the mature but spendthrift Richard Wagner led the mad king to pay off the opera composer's huge debts.

June 9, 1851:   San Francisco was a wide-open town in the days of the California gold rush. Saloons and gambling dens lined Portsmouth Square. Crime ran rampant. On June 9, 1951, Sam Brannan and others met to form the country's first Vigilence Committee. Two days later one John Jenkins, who had stolen a small safe, was hanged from a gable of the old Customhouse.

June 10, 1943:   World War Two cost the U.S. a great deal of money. To help fund the war, President Franklin D. Roosevelt wanted to put income taxes on a pay-as-you-go basis. Congress agreed, and on June 10, 1943, FDR signed the bill that required employers to withdraw taxes from their employees' wages. The arrangement is with us yet.

June 11, 1861:   When Virginia voted to secede from the Union in April 1861, a group of disgruntled unionists led by John S. Carlile of Clarksburg called for a two-part division of the state. Although the Second Wheeling Convention on June 11, 1981, didn't create the State of West Virginia immediately, it did lay the groundwork.

June 12, 1924:   George Herbert Walker Bush, 41st President of the United States, was born on this date in Milton, Massachusetts—just a few miles up the road from the birthplace of Olympia Dukakis and her brother Michael. By the time Bush's father, Prescott, ran for the U.S. Senate, George was already out in West Texas on the trail of oil.

June 13, 1971:   One of the big news stories of 1971 was the publication of the top-secret "Pentagon Papers," excerpts of which began appearing in *The New York Times* on June 13. The full title of the 47-volume government study was *History of the U.S. Decision-making Process on Vietnam Policy*. The government's criminal case against Daniel Ellsberg, who had leaked the papers to the *Times*, was dismissed.

June 14, 1777: On this date the Second Continental Congress, meeting at Philadelphia, adopted a resolution that "the flag of the United States be 13 stripes, alternate red and white; that the union be 13 stars, white in a blue field, representing a new constellation." There is no record of an original flag law implementing the resolution and clarifying the format of the Stars and Stripes.

June 15, 1775: George Washington went to sessions of the Second Continental Congress wearing his military uniform. But he wasn't lobbying for command of the continental army. Far from it. He knew that "the resources of Britain were... inexhaustible... and that her troops had harvested laurels in every quarter of the globe." Nonetheless, on June 15, 1775, Congress voted unanimously to make George Washington commander-in-chief of the continental army.

June 16, 1858: The Republican Party in Illinois chose Abraham Lincoln to run against Stephen Douglas for the U.S. Senate. In accepting the nomination, Lincoln gave his famous "House Divided" speech on this date in Springfield. Although Lincoln lost the election to the Little Giant, their brilliant series of debates made Lincoln a national figure.

June 17, 1972: In the early morning of June 17, 1972, five men were arrested for breaking into the headquarters of Democratic National Chairman Larry O'Brien in the Watergate complex in Washington, D.C. The climax of the drama would come 26 months later with the first Presidential resignation in American history. (See story on page 115)

June 18, 1873: On this date a judge in Canandaigua, New York, fined Susan B. Anthony $100 for "knowingly, wrongfully, and unlawfully voting" in the 1872 election. Her offense was that she was a woman. The judge refused to allow Ms. Anthony to testify on the grounds that, as a woman, she was incompetent to speak for herself.

June 19, 1934: The 73rd Congress adjourned on June 18, 1934, passing a host of New Deal bills that arrived on President Franklin D. Roosevelt's desk the next morning. On that day FDR signed into law, among other things, an act that created the National Archives (see story on page 2) and another that established the Federal Communications Commission (FCC).

June 20, 1837: Eighteen-year-old Victoria ascended the British throne on this date to begin her 64-year reign. (See story on page 27)

June 21, 1756: Rudyard Kipling wrote about "lesser breeds without the law." That kind of naive imperialism led 18th-century Britons to regard the Black Hole of Calcutta as a grim example of Indian barbarity and British heroism. It *was* pretty horrible—64 or so British prisoners jammed into a tiny room on the night of June 20. Next morning, June 21, 1756, only 21 of them came out alive.

June 22, 1870:   In the early days of the Republic, the Attorney General had very little to do. He argued government cases in the Supreme Court. But there weren't many such cases, so the Attorney General spent much of his time in private practice. However, California land cases and then Civil War lawsuits added to his duties. The act of June 22, 1870, establishing the Department of Justice, recognized that fact.

June 23, 1967:   The summit meeting between President Lyndon B. Johnson and Soviet Premier Alexei Kosygin was a spur-of-the-moment thing. With Kosygin in New York to address the UN, the idea of a summit came up. Johnson suggested Washington; Kosygin favored New York; they compromised on Glassboro, New Jersey, where they met at the home of the President of Glassboro State College. (See story on page 206)

June 24, 1813:   Preachers in American politics go back a long way. Consider the Reverend Henry Ward Beecher, born on June 24, 1813. Sinclair Lewis called him "a combination of St. Augustine, Barnum, and John Barrymore." Some people thought him "the greatest preacher since St. Paul." Beecher was neither the first nor the last spellbinding clergyman to mix politics-plus-sex with sermonizing. (See story on page 126)

June 25, 1950:   On Saturday, June 25, 1950, President Harry S Truman was relaxing at his home in Independence, Missouri. The telephone rang. The caller was Secretary of State Dean Acheson. "Mr. President," said Acheson, "I have very serious news. The North Koreans have invaded South Korea."

June 26, 1893:   Seven years after the event, Governor John P. Altgeld of Illinois pardoned the three surviving men convicted of throwing a bomb in Chicago's Haymarket Riot. It was an act of rare political courage. (See story on page 112)

June 27, 1846:   This is the birthday of Charles Stewart Parnell, the great Irish nationalist leader—a man who, until scandal broke over him, was often called "the uncrowned king of Ireland."

June 28, 1914:   Historian Barbara W. Tuchman quoted Bismarck to the effect that "some damned foolish thing in the Balkans" would ignite the next year. She wrote, "The assassination of the Austrian heir apparent, Archduke Franz Ferdinand, by Serbian nationalists on June 28, 1914, satisfied his condition." (See story on page 261)

June 29, 1956:   President Dwight D. Eisenhower realized a long-held dream when he signed into law the Federal Highway Act, setting in motion what was officially called the National System of Interstate and Defense Highways. The ten-year building program that the Act provided for is still in progress.

June 30, 1800: It doesn't mean much today, but on June 30, 1800, a Baltimore newspaper reported that Thomas Jefferson, who was then seeking the Presidency of the United States, had died after a brief illness at his Monticello home. The obituary came 26 years ahead of time. (See story on page 151)

July

July 1, 1867: Canadians celebrate their Fourth of July on the first of July. They call it Dominion Day, and it commemorates the uniting of Canada West (now Ontario) and Canada East (now Quebec), along with New Brunswick and Nova Scotia.

July 2, 1776: John Adams wrote, "The Second day of July, 1776, will be the most memorable Epocha in the History of America." Adams assumed that the day Richard Henry Lee's resolution for independence was passed would be the day celebrated, rather than the date on which the Declaration of Independence was adopted, two days later.

July 3, 1962: France recognized the independence of Algeria on July 3, 1962, ending seven years of bitter fighting. Nearly a million European colonists, many of them born in Algeria, had emigrated prior to independence.

July 4, 1825: On this date—the 50th anniversary of the Declaration of Independence—the second and third Presidents of the United States, John Adams and Thomas Jefferson, died within a few hours of each other. (See story on page 174)

July 5, 1811: After long debate on the wisdom of remaining loyal to Spain's King Ferdinand VII, a congress assembled in Caracas declared the independence of Venezuela. Not all the provinces agreed to the separation, and it took nearly 20 years of struggle for a truly independent nation to emerge.

July 6, 1964: Early July seems to be a time of national liberation. On this particular date the small southeastern African country of Malawi gained its independence from Great Britain. Before that it was the British protectorate of Nyasaland. Trivia quiz: Name Malawi's capital and its largest city. (The capital is Lilongwe; the largest city is Blantyre.)

July 7, 1865: Less than three months after the assassination of Abraham Lincoln, four conspirators swung from a single gallows in the courtyard of the

Arsenal Penitentiary in Washington, D.C. One of those hanged was a woman, Mrs. Mary E. Surratt. Four other conspirators were sent to prison at desolate Fort Jefferson in the Dry Tortugas.

July 8, 1896: On July 8, 1896, Williams Jennings Bryan made his electrifying "Cross of Gold" speech at the Democratic national convention in Chicago. The speech led straight to his nomination for the Presidency. (See story on page 104)

July 9, 1575: The Earl of Leicester knew how to throw a party. The 19-day soiree he put on at Kenilworth for Queen Elizabeth I of England cost the deep-pocketed Earl something in the neighborhood of three million dollars. (See story on page 8)

July 10, 1953: The Soviet Union under Joseph Stalin was a gangster regime, and Lavrenty Pavlovich Beria was its brutal enforcer-in-chief. Beria headed the secret police, called the NKVD in his day—later the KGB. Beria's ambition, not his murderous cruelty, led to his termination, which was announced in *Pravda* on this date.

July 11, 1804: A duel at Weehawken, New Jersey, between two political head-liners of the early American Republic, Alexander Hamilton and Aaron Burr, ended in the death of Hamilton. The duel took place on July 11, 1804; Hamilton died the next day. (See story on page 75)

July 12, 1856: It's hard to imagine an American of today storming into Central America and becoming President of one of the countries. But that's exactly what William Walker, a 19th-century adventurer from Nashville, Tennessee, managed to do. (See story on page 8)

July 13, 1787: The Ordinance of 1787, often called the Northwest Ordinance, was passed on this date. It established guidelines for the settlement, government, and admission to the Union of the Western territories. A burst of activity followed. Late in 1787 advance parties of the Ohio Company set out for the West, and in the spring started to build the town of Marietta.

July 14, 1853: Although July 14 is best known as Bastille Day (1789), it has another distinction as well. On July 14, 1853, Admiral Matthew Perry landed in Japan at Kurihama, a small village at the entrance to Tokyo Bay. Perry's subsequent treaty opened the door to trade with Japan, a nation that had been cut off from Western contact for many years.

July 15, 1863: Three days of draft riots came to an end in New York City on this date. Irish laborers resented the fact that a man with $300 could buy his way out of service in the Civil War. $300 was a huge sum back then, nearly a year's wages. Also, the Irish were fearful that freed slaves would come North and take their jobs. The Mayor's house was attacked; streetcar tracks were torn up; scores of blacks were murdered.

July 16, 1918: On the night of July 16, 1918, Tsar Nicholas II of Russia, his wife, four daughters, and a son were murdered in a ground-floor room of a house in Ekaterinburg. The entire family died without warning in a hail of bullets fired by a dozen or so Bolshevik executioners. Next day their bodies were burned and thrown down a mine shaft a few miles from town.

July 17, 1917: In the words of a German nobleman, "The true royal tradition died on that day in 1917 when, for a mere war, King George V [of England] changed his name." Quite true. During World War One, there was a strong British reaction against anything German—including the German name of the royal family: Saxe-Coburg-Gotha. On July 17, 1917, the name was changed to the House of Windsor. (See story on page 118)

July 18, 1969: The Presidential ambitions of Senator Edward Kennedy were snuffed out on the night of July 18–19, 1969, along with the life of Mary Jo Kopechne. She was the young woman in the car that Ted Kennedy drove off a narrow bridge on Chappaquiddick Island, Martha's Vineyard.

July 19, 1984: On this date, the anniversary of the women's rights convention at Seneca Falls in 1848, Geraldine Ferraro accepted the Democratic nomination for Vice President of the United States. She and Walter Mondale were defeated, but her nomination was a historic milestone. (See story on page 189)

July 20, 1969: The U.S. reached a goal set by President John F. Kennedy when astronauts Neil Armstrong and Buzz Aldrin landed their lunar excursion module Eagle on the moon, near the Sea of Tranquillity. Armstrong's statement as he first stepped on the moon is often misquoted (because the "a" he put before "man" was illogically edited out of the tape): "That's one small step for a man, one giant leap for mankind."

July 21, 1898: This day belongs to Guam. On July 21, 1898, to the accompaniment of a 21-gun-salute, the American flag was formally raised over Guam for the first time, ending Spanish rule. Forty-six years later to the day, U.S. forces hit the beach, prepared to free Guam from Japanese occupation. The bitter campaign, lasting 21 days, ended Japanese rule there.

July 22, 1871: When *The New York Times* began publishing hard evidence of the Tweed Ring's plunder of the New York City's treasury, the career of William Marcy Tweed, Tammany Hall chieftain, went downhill in a hurry. Thomas Nast's cartoons in *Harper's* magazine added to Tweed's woes. (See story on page 88)

July 23, 1945: Marshal Henri Pétain, head of the French Vichy government during World War Two, went on trial for treason. It was a sad day even for his detractors. The old man, now nearly 90, had become a national hero for his defense of Verdun in World War One. Then came Hitler, collaboration, and disgrace. (See story on page 72)

July 24, 1783: Simón Bolívar, liberator of half a dozen South American countries, was born on this date. He lived only 47 years and died a deeply frustrated man. His deathbed comment was, "If only my death can help where my life has failed." But of course he had not failed. His name and deeds are honored throughout South America and beyond.

July 25, 1952: On July 25, 1952, Puerto Rico officially became a commonwealth of the United States. The anniversary is called Constitution Day, or Commonwealth Day, or Occupation Day. Some Puerto Ricans doubt that commonwealth status is a permanent condition. Some look to statehood, others to independence.

July 26, 1952: Colonel Gamal Abdel Nasser of Egypt overthrew King Farouk in a coup d'etat. A number of army officers wanted to execute the corpulent and corrupt Farouk. "Let us spare Farouk," Nasser said, "and send him into exile. History will sentence him to death."

July 27, 1953: "I shall go to Korea," promised Dwight D. Eisenhower late in the Presidential campaign of 1952. Ike was willing to settle for a stalemate in the Korean War, a willingness that eventually brought an armistice agreement, signed on July 27, 1953, between Communist North Korea and U.S.-backed South Korea. Casualties in Korea were slightly higher than those in the Vietnam War.

July 28, 1932: The "Bonus Expeditionary Force," a group of unemployed veterans demanding money, had camped in shantyvilles not far from the Capitol in Washington, D.C. On July 28, 1932, federal troops led by General Douglas MacArthur drove the veterans away and wrecked or burned their dwellings. (See story on page 258)

July 29, 1883: This is the birthday of Benito Mussolini, Il Duce, organizer of the blackshirt Fascist party in Italy and partner in crime of Adolf Hitler. Having brought his nation to ruin in World War Two, this "Sawdust Caesar" (as an American novelist called him) died before a firing squad of his own angry countrymen. (See story on page 114)

July 30, 1619: One year before the Pilgrims landed at Plymouth, the first legislative assembly met at Old Church, Jamestown, Virginia. Called the House of Burgesses, it could pass whatever laws it wished, but these laws required the approval of the Virginia Company, the London sponsors of the settlement.

July 31, 1948:   On this date President Harry S Truman dedicated New York's International Airport at Idlewild Field. Idlewild, many times the size of LaGuardia Airport, was renamed John F. Kennedy International Airport following the assassination of the 35th President.

August

August 1, 1914:   World War One was imminent. The German Chancellor, Bethmann-Hollweg, issued a statement that ended, "If the iron dice roll, God help us." A German ultimatum to Russia expired at noon on August 1, 1914, without a reply. At five o'clock a policeman outside the Kaiser's palace in Berlin announced mobilization—Germany and Russia were at war. The iron dice had rolled.

August 2, 1790:   On this date the United States government began counting its citizens. Since the country was largely rural, many of the enumerators set out on horseback. Some people were suspicious of the government's motives, which in fact were benign. The U.S. Constitution requires a census every ten years, apportioning seats in the House of Representatives based on it.

August 3, 1981:   Only two large labor unions supported Ronald Reagan for President in 1980. One was the Professional Air Traffic Controllers Organization, or PATCO. Imagine everyone's surprise, then, when PATCO called a strike against the new administration. President Reagan responded in kind. He fired the strikers, crushed the union, and sent it into bankruptcy.

August 4, 1962:   Nelson Mandela, black South African leader, was arrested on August 4, 1962. Although acquitted of treason in 1961, he was tried again and sentenced to five years in prison. While there, he was charged with sabotage, high treason, and conspiracy to overthrow the government—and resentenced to life imprisonment. To the black South African majority, Mandela became a symbol of both injustice and hope.

August 5, 1884:   On August 5, 1884, Americans laid the cornerstone for the pedestal of the Statue of Liberty. The statue—all 225 tons of it—arrived the next year from France in 214 packing cases. The year after that, on October 28, 1886, President Grover Cleveland dedicated the finished statue.

August 6, 1945: "Let there be no doubt about it," wrote President Harry S Truman. "I regarded the [atomic] bomb as a military weapon and never had any doubt that it should be used." On this date it was used against the Japanese city of Hiroshima. World War Two ended nine days later, after the awesome new weapon had been used once more, on Nagasaki (See story on page 48)

August 7, 1964: On this date the U.S. House and Senate signed a blank check for escalating the war in Vietnam. The Gulf of Tonkin Resolution, passed unanimously by the House, gave the President almost unlimited power to send troops to Southeast Asia. In the Senate only Wayne Morse of Oregon and Ernest Gruening of Alaska voted against the Resolution. History suggests that these two lone dissenters were right.

August 8, 1540: England's King Henry VIII called Catherine Howard his "rose without a thorn." She was his fifth wife, replacing Anne of Cleves. On August 8, 1540, Henry acknowledged her as his Queen. But Catherine's lack of thorns proved to be an illusion. She had entertained a number of lovers before marriage and one, Thomas Culpeper, during it. Her head soon fell to the ax.

August 9, 1974: As *Air Force One* winged its way toward California, Richard M. Nixon sipped a martini, and at noon on August 9, 1974, became the first American President ever to resign from office. Done in by the Watergate cover-up, faced with certain impeachment and probable conviction, R. Milhous checked out of the White House and into early retirement.

August 10, 1498: Talk about princely rewards! England's King Henry VII felt he owed something to explorer John Cabot. After all, Cabot had discovered and claimed for England what is now Canada. With the explorer back at court, Henry VII meditated on a suitable bonus, reached into the nation's coffers, and on this date presented John Cabot with... ten pounds.

August 11, 1902: President Theodore Roosevelt appointed Oliver Wendell Holmes, Jr., to the U.S. Supreme Court. At the age of 61 the "Great Dissenter" began his nearly 30 years of service on the nation's highest court. (See story on page 224)

August 12, 1676: American Indians were at a disadvantage in dealing with white settlers. Often exploited, they were prone to fight back with tomahawks. An early instance was King Philip's War, a struggle in which a Wampanoag sachem (King Philip) struck fear into the hearts of New England frontiersmen. The Indian cause was already doomed when on August 12, 1676, an Indian in the colonists' service shot King Philip dead. The sachem's head was mounted on a pole in Plymouth.

August 13, 1961: On this date the Berlin Wall was thrown up overnight, first as a barbed wire fence, to keep East Germans from fleeing to the West. Five days later construction began on a concrete wall, a 13-foot-high barrier that came to be a stark symbol of the Cold War. Over the next 28 years, 200 people were killed and 4,000 arrested while trying to breach the wall.

August 14, 1935: That most hardy of all entitlements, immune even to Reaganomics, came into being with the passage of the Social Security Act on August 14, 1935. The Act itself was flawed, but the Social Security Board proved to be a highly efficient government bureau. Social Security, more than any other New Deal scheme, changed the relationship between the federal government and the private citizen.

August 15, 1769: August 15 (1945) is V-J Day, signaling the Allied victory over Japan in World War Two. August 15 (1769) is also the birthday of Napoleon Bonaparte. Both events had world-shaking consequences.

August 16, 1924: The Dawes Plan for German reparations for World War One was accepted on this date. It earned a Nobel Peace Prize for Charles G. Dawes— an unlikely recipient. "Hell-and-Maria" Dawes, who served as Vice President under Calvin Coolidge, was as brash as Silent Cal was reticent.

August 17, 1960: African colonies were usually the last to gain independence. On August 17, 1960, Gabon, a nation the size of Colorado, became a republic, free from French rule. Gabon is best known to Westerners as the long-time home of Albert Schweitzer, the theologian, musician, and medical missionary at Lambarene. In his day, Gabon was French Equatorial Africa.

August 18, 1914: President Woodrow Wilson hoped to keep the United States out of World War One. When Europe erupted in conflict, Wilson issued a proclamation of neutrality dated August 18, 1914. He asked that the U.S. "be neutral in fact as well as in name ... impartial in thought as well as in action...." British propaganda and German U-boats made it impossible.

August 19, 1934: President Paul von Hindenburg of the Weimar Republic had been a great hero in the Great War. He died on August 2, 1934, at the age of 87. A plebescite on August 19 endorsed Adolf Hitler as President as well as Chancellor of Germany, with 89.9 percent of voters approving. Der Führer—a title he preferred to the other two—thus took complete control of Germany's future.

August 20, 1778: With a name like Bernardo O'Higgins, how could he miss? Still, as the liberator of Chile and its first "supreme director," O'Higgins had more military talent than political skill. He admitted his limitations, having once said, "The career to which I seem inclined by instinct and character is that of laborer." He was too modest. If not quite a Bolívar or a San Martin, he belongs in their company.

August 21, 1968: There is a whole book called *August 21st*. Its subtitle is *The Rape of Czechoslovakia*, and there you have it in all its pre-glasnost grittiness. On the night of August 21, 1968, troops from five Warsaw Pact countries invaded Czechoslovakia to put down the increasingly liberal and pro-Western government of Alexander Dubček. Tanks rolled through the streets of Czech cities, Dubček was arrested, and a pro-Soviet regime installed.

August 22, 1939: On August 22, 1939, the British cabinet issued a communique strongly reiterating Great Britain's treaty obligations to Poland. If Hitler invaded Poland, a general European war would result. The long months of appeasement were over. Nine days later, having observed that "further successes are impossible without the shedding of blood," Hitler loosed his blitzkrieg across the Polish border.

August 23, 1814: Dolley Madison fled from the White House in the face of advancing British troops. By her timely flight on this date the First Lady saved some valuable papers and a priceless painting. (See story on page 221)

August 24, 1949: The North Atlantic Treaty Organization (NATO) was born on this date. Joining NATO were the United States, Canada, and ten Western European nations. An attack against any of these nations was to be considered an attack against all. President Harry S Truman wrote later that "the peace of the world would best be served by a Europe that was strong and united...."

August 25, 1945: On this date John Birch, a U.S. soldier and intelligence officer, was killed by Chinese Communists ten days after V-J Day—the first American casualty of the Cold War. His name would be lost to history except for the fact that Robert Welch, an extreme right-wing businessman, formed the John Birch Society to fight subversives, Social Security, the graduated income tax, and Red dupes (in his view) such as Dwight D. Eisenhower and John Foster Dulles.

August 26, 1698: Peter the Great of Russia had traveled through western Europe and seen its modern ways. He liked what he saw, and being a man of action, he decided to do something about it. In Western Europe, men were clean-shaven. So Peter assembled his court and on this date began personally to clip the old-fashioned beards and mustaches from the astonished boyars.

August 27, 1858: The second of the Lincoln-Douglas debates was held at Freeport, Illinois, on August 27, 1858. Abraham Lincoln forced Stephen Douglas to admit that slavery could not exist in a territory if the residents agreed to prohibit it. This commonsense admission helped Douglas win his Senate seat, but outraged Southerners, who considered it a sellout.

August 28, 1963: On August 28, 1963, a quarter of a million people came to Washington by plane, train, bus, and automobile. They gathered in front of the Lincoln Memorial to show their support for the civil rights movement. The last speaker of the day was the Reverend Martin Luther King, Jr., whose powerful "I have a dream" speech is an American classic.

August 29, 1786: Times were hard in western Massachusetts after the Revolutionary War. Debtors demanded relief, and beginning at Northampton on August 29, 1786, they used force to gain their ends. Daniel Shays, a veteran of the Revolution, came forward as a leader—thus the name Shays' Rebellion. Militia led by General Benjamin Lincoln finally put down the revolt. The incident led to demands for a stronger federal government.

August 30, 1963: So-called "hot lines" are everywhere today, but on August 30, 1963, *the* hot line came into existence. John F. Kennedy was in the White House. Nikita Khrushchev was in the Kremlin. Henceforth they (and their successors) could reach one another at a moment's notice—just in case.

August 31, 1949: This date marks the final National Encampment of the Grand Army of the Republic. An organization of Union veterans of the Civil War, the GAR reached its greatest size—409,000 members—in 1890, and then gradually declined. In 1949 six of the 16 surviving veterans met in Indianapolis at the 83rd annual Encampment, and that was it. The last GAR member, Albert Woolson of Duluth, Minnesota, died in 1956 at the age of 109.

September

September 1, 1932: New York's Mayor in the late 1920s was Jimmy Walker. A one-time songwriter, he was dapper, debonair, and corrupt. *Outlook* magazine said, "Jimmy translates the problems of municipal government... into simple musical comedy terms that the average person understands." The Depression and the law caught up with him, and on September 1, 1932, he resigned.

September 2, 1789: Congress established the Treasury Department on this date. The act authorized the President to appoint a Secretary of the Treasury, which he did. George Washington chose Alexander Hamilton of New York for the job.

September 3, 1189: On September 3, 1189, at Westminster Abbey, King Richard I, "the Lion-hearted," was crowned King of England. An unfortunate incident marred the ceremony. Richard had ordered that no women or Jews be admitted. Some London Jews, determined to show their loyalty, arrived bearing gifts. They were thrown out, a riot ensured, and many Jews were killed.

September 4, 1957:   Governor Orville Faubus of Arkansas asked President Eisenhower to cooperate with him in trying to prevent integration at Central High School, Little Rock. Ike replied by telegram: "The only assurance I can give you is that the federal Constitution will be upheld by me by every legal means at my command." Three weeks later Ike sent federal troops to Little Rock to enforce the court order requiring integration.

September 5, 1755:   On or about this date British troops forced 6,000 Acadians to leave their homes and flee south. Their sad exodus from Nova Scotia is the background of Longfellow's long poem *Evangeline*, a charming narrative that a British critic of the day called "one of the decisive poems of the world."

September 6, 1901:   Leon Czolgosz told a friend he had decided to protest the sorry state of American society by killing a priest. His friend replied, "Why kill a priest? There are so many priests...." The would-be assassin thought it over, journeyed to Buffalo, New York, and on September 6, 1901, fatally shot William McKinley, the President of the United States.

September 7, 1988:   On this date George Bush, campaigning for the Presidency, startled his American Legion audience by referring to "today" as Pearl Harbor Day. Bush, a World War Two veteran, quickly corrected his error.

September 8, 1935:   In the book *All the King's Men* Robert Penn Warren named him Willie Stark. In real life they called him "The Kingfish." He was Huey Long, an immensely powerful Louisiana Governor and Senator. Naturally, Long had his enemies. One of them was Dr. Carl A. Weiss, who on September 8, 1935, for reasons unknown, shot and killed the Kingfish in the corridor of the state capitol.

September 9, 1919:   When the police of Boston tried to unionize, their Police Commissioner said no. The cops when out on strike, and robberies and riots followed. Governor Calvin Coolidge sent in the Massachusetts militia. (See story on page 48)

September 10, 1742:   Faneuil Hall in Boston, a market and public building that Bostonians call the "Cradle of Liberty," was completed on this date. Boston's Revolutionary leaders gave ringing speeches in Faneuil Hall. When they wrote to the local newspapers, on the other hand, they were more circumspect, signing their letters Populus or Bostonian or Determinatus.

September 11, 1906:   Racial tension in South Africa is nothing new. In 1906 all Indians who lived there were ordered to register, he fingerprinted, and agree to carry identification certificates with them. On September 11 in the Imperial Theater, Johannesburg, Mahatma Gandhi asked his audience to take a vow pledging nonviolent resistance to the order. All 3,000 Indians in the hall took the pledge.

September 12, 1953: It was the social event of the season—the marriage of Senator John F. Kennedy of Massachusetts to Jacqueline Bouvier of New York, East Hampton, and Newport, Rhode Island. The site of the reception was Hammersmith Farm, Newport, where Jackie had earlier made her debut. After a wedding night at New York's Waldorf-Astoria, the couple flew off to Acapulco for their honeymoon.

September 13, 1971: "Call the Governor," they used to mutter in those 1930s movies when the convicts got restless. Well, in 1971 they did call the Governor—Nelson Rockefeller of New York—after the inmates took over Attica Prison. The Governor said forget it; his presence wasn't needed. From Albany he approved an assault on the prison. Forty-three people, including many hostages, died in the September 13 attack.

September 14, 1814: By "the dawn's early light" of September 14, 1814, Francis Scott key finished writing the words of "The Star-Spangled Banner." The flag Key saw during the bombardment of Fort McHenry is now on display at the Smithsonian Institution in Washington. It has 15 stars, since Kentucky and Vermont had by then joined the original 13 states.

September 15, 1794: On this date James Madison married Dorothea D.P. Todd, better known as Dolley. Dolley took snuff and was rumored to use rouge, but few were offended. She was a popular First Lady and a renowned hostess. Before Madison became President, Dolley served as official hostess in widower Thomas Jefferson's White House.

September 16, 1485: King Henry VII of England needed protection from his enemies. To that end he established the Yeomen of the Guard, an elite corps of veteran soldiers. From that day to this the Yeomen have worn the elegant red and gold costume of the Tudor period. The Yeomen Warders at the Tower of London wear a similar outfit. Both groups are called "Beefeaters."

September 17, 1978: On this date President Jimmy Carter looked on approvingly at the White House as Menachem Begin of Israel and Anwar Sadat of Egypt signed the Camp David accord. This historic reconciliation, worked out in 13 days of meetings at the President's Maryland retreat, took great courage for both Sadat and Begin, given the historic and bitter Arab-Israeli conflict.

September 18, 1961: The plane that carried UN Secretary-General Dag Hammarskjöld crashed on this date in Northern Rhodesia. Hammarskjöld, a complex and thoughtful Swedish statesman, greatly increased the prestige of the United Nations. In one of his early speeches as Secretary General he quoted a Swedish poet, saying, "The greatest prayer of man does not ask for victory, but for peace."

September 19, 1796: George Washington never delivered his famous Farewell Address publicly. It first appeared in print in the Philadelphia *Daily American*

Advertiser on this date. Washington did not use the term "entangling alliances" in his speech, but he did warn against "the insidious wiles of foreign influence." He also advised against the establishment of political parties.

September 20, 1926: In the musical comedy *Guys and Dolls* one of the shady-looking gamblers describes himself as a scoutmaster from Cicero, Illinois. In the 1920s Cicero was a mob-controlled town. Al Capone operated out of its well-guarded Hawthorne Inn, a bastion that rival gangsters attacked in force on September 20, 1926. (See story on page 183)

September 21, 1981: On this date the Senate voted 99 to 0 to confirm Sandra Day O'Connor as an Associate Justice of the U.S. Supreme Court. On September 25, 1981, she became the 102nd member of the high court—and the first woman to serve on it.

September 22, 1957: When the people of Haiti elected Francois Duvalier as their President on this date, they hoped for social and economic reform. Instead they got corruption and terror. Papa Doc, as he was called, ruled Latin America's poorest nation with brutal repression—and made it poorer.

September 23, 1944: This is a day for the dogs. On September 23, 1944, President Franklin D. Roosevelt made his renowned "Fala" speech. (See story on page 260) Not to be outdone, on September 23, 1952, Richard M. Nixon, Ike's choice as a running mate, answered the charges raised against him in his equally famous "Checkers" speech.

September 24, 1869: There have been a number of "black" days on Wall Street. This was one of them. Jay Gould and Jim Fisk, two scalawags of the Gilded Age, had contrived to corner the gold market. They almost succeeded—and they did succeed in creating a financial panic. (See story on page 84)

September 25, 1963: This is a dog-bites-man story, which is to say no story at all. On September 23, 1963, Senator Everett Dirksen, known as the "Wizard of Ooze," was asked about possible passage of a civil rights bill. His answer drifted from its moorings and floated aimlessly away. (See nonstory on page 16)

September 26, 1971: In a historic visit, Emperor Hirohito of Japan met with President Nixon in Anchorage, Alaska. The aging Emperor then took off on a 17-day tour of Europe. This trip abroad—the first ever for a reigning Japanese emperor—made headlines at the time, but it failed to make Nixon's memoirs.

September 27, 1964: The Warren Commission report was released on this date. President Lyndon Johnson's blue-ribbon panel, having investigated the events surrounding the assassination of President Kennedy, concluded that Lee Harvey Oswald had acted alone. Criticism of the report began immediately and has continued ever since. The critics have posed various conspiracy theories.

September 28, 1839:   Francis Willard, born on September 28, 1839, in Churchville, New York, devoted her life to fighting the demon rum. She served for 20 years as President of the Women's National Christian Temperance Union. The WCTU, based in Evanston, Illinois, became a powerful political force. Willard also helped to organize the Prohibition Party.

September 29, 1862:   Otto von Bismarck, the new Prime Minister of Prussia, spoke to the lower house of Parliament on this date. As one writer put it, he "foretold the bloodstained history of the coming 80 years in words that echoed through the world like the clash of steel upon steel": "The great issues of the day," said Bismarck, "will not be decided by speeches and majority resolutions... but by blood and iron."

September 30, 1938:   Britain's Prime Minister Neville Chamberlain is famous for the remark he made on September 30, 1938, after returning from Munich. He believed that his appeasement of Hitler had bought "peace for our time." Winston Churchill had no use for this abject accommodation. In a speech to the House of Commons Churchill said, "The German dictator, instead of snatching the victuals from the table, has been content to have them served to him course by course." (See story on page 71)

October

October 1, 1940:   During FDR's Presidency, Pennsylvania had its own "Little New Deal." One of its accomplishments was the building of the Pennsylvania Turnpike. This prototype of all later freeways, expressways, and thruways was opened to traffic between Middlesex (near Harrisburg) and Irwin (near Pittsburgh) on October 1, 1940.

October 2, 1967:   President Lyndon B. Johnson appointed the first black to the U.S. Supreme Court. He was Thurgood Marshall, the son of a Pullman car steward, who took his seat on October 2, 1967. Marshall had been chief counsel in the landmark Brown v. Board of Education case, which overthrew the separate-but-equal doctrine for America's public schools.

October 3, 2333 B.C.:   Everyone wants to pin down dates exactly. The people of Korea are no exception. According to legend, Tangun, the mythological first king of the Koreans, began his reign on this date. Accurate or not, October 3 is celebrated as Korea's National Foundation Day.

October 4, 1957:   At the height of the Cold War, the USSR threw Americans into a panic with the launching of Sputnik I, an unmanned space satellite. Launched on October 4, 1957, it circled the globe until it fell to earth three months later. The U.S. commenced a frantic game of catch-up.

October 5, 1877:   American Indians had very little success in negotiating fair land agreements with the U.S. government. Chief Joseph of the Nez Percé nation was no exception. Like other Indian chiefs, Joseph became embroiled in war. He was a brilliant tactician who won many battles, but it all ended for him and his people on October 5, 1877, when he surrendered to General Nelson A. Miles.

October 6, 1976:   On this date President Gerald Ford, debating candidate Jimmy Carter, insisted that Eastern Europe was not under Soviet domination. The slip may have cost him the election. (See story on page 149)

October 7, 1888:   Henry A. Wallace, born on this date, served as FDR's Vice President for one term. Wallace's fondness for Soviet Communism during the Second World War caused FDR to pick Harry S Truman as his Vice Presidential running mate in 1944. It's well he did. Truman became President upon FDR's death, and Wallace embarked on a peculiar, left-wing quest for the Presidency.

October 8, 1871:   Fire overshadowed politics on this date. An abnormally dry summer led to many small fires. Then on October 8, 1871, Mrs. O'Leary's cow kicked over a lantern, setting off the great Chicago fire. Three hundred people died; 90,000 were left homeless. On the same day, the great Peshtigo forest fire began in northeastern Wisconsin. It was the deadliest of all American fires, killing 1,182 people.

October 9, 1962:   On this date Uganda became independent of Great Britain. The young nation has had a troubled history, most notably under the savage dictatorship of President Idi Amin. (See story on page 120)

October 10, 1973:   Vice President Spiro Agnew, while under criminal investigation, resigned from office on October 10, 1973. Agnew thought that President Nixon, who was in plenty of trouble himself, seemed eager for his Veep to go. Agnew went, moving to Rancho Mirage, California, becoming an international business consultant, writing a novel, then following up with a book of self-defense, which he dedicated to his friend Frank Sinatra.

October 11, 1890:   If you're a lineal female descendent of someone who aided or served in the American Revolution, and you're over 18 years old, you're eligible to join the DAR—the Daughters of the American Revolution. The national organization was founded on October 11, 1890, in Washington, D.C. Its patriotic mission often involves it in politics.

October 12, 1960:   On Columbus Day, 1960, Soviet Premier Nikita Khrushchev pounded his shoe on the table at a UN meeting in New York. (See story on page 163)

October 13, 1947: The largest flag ever flown was displayed at dawn on October, 13, 1947, from the New Jersey tower of the George Washington Bridge. The flag, 60 by 90 feet, required 19 men, four machine winches, and 5,000 pounds of guy ropes to raise it into place. The Port of New York Authority promised to fly the flag on other holidays if the wind velocity was low.

October 14, 1912: A would-be assassin shot Theodore Roosevelt in the chest on this date. Roosevelt, deathly pale, went ahead and delivered a speech anyway. (See story on page 44)

October 15, 1964: On October 15, 1964, Nikita Khrushchev lost his political position in the USSR. Overnight the Soviet Premier went from being one of the most powerful men on earth to being almost a nonperson. (See story on page 23)

October 16, 1793: She never said "Let them eat cake" in response to the bread famine in France. But Queen Marie Antoinette did lack sympathy with the French Revolution, especially after her husband, Louis XVI, was beheaded on January 21, 1793. Nine months later, on October 16, 1793, the "Widow Capet," as she was jeeringly called, followed her husband to the guillotine.

October 17, 1777: Gentleman Johnny Burgoyne wrote plays, served in Parliament, and won a major battle during the Seven Years War. He and Lord George Germaine laid military plans in London that they felt sure would defeat the rebellious American colonists. Burgoyne went to America. His campaign went awry. On October 17, 1777, Gentleman Johnny, outnumbered and cornered, surrendered his troops at Saratoga in upstate New York—the first great American victory of the Revolution.

October 18, 1867: When Americans learned that Secretary of State William Seward wanted to buy Alaska, they were scornful. They called it "Seward's Folly," "Seward's Icebox," and "Walrussia." But the deal went through. On October 18, 1867, the Russian flag was lowered in front of the Governor's residence in Sitka, and the flag of the United States raised in its place.

October 19, 1216: In the early morning hours of October 19, 1216, King John died. Sometimes called John Lackland or John Softsword, he was one of England's worst monarchs. Of the man who was forced to sign the Magna Carta, a rhymester wrote:

"With John's foul deeds all England is stinking,
As does hell, to which he is now sinking."

October 20, 1973: John Dean and his wife were watching a TV variety show, when ... *"We interrupt this program for a special announcement."* NBC reporter Carl Stern appeared on the screen. President Nixon, said Stern, had fired Special Prosecutor Archibald Cox. Attorney General Elliott Richardson had resigned. Deputy Attorney General William Ruckelshaus had been fired. It was the Saturday Night Massacre! The dirty linen of Watergate was coming unraveled, and Nixon's Presidency was unraveling along with it.

October 21, 1940:   Hitler threatened to invade Great Britain in World War Two, but never made it. During a radio broadcast on October 21, 1940, Prime Minister Winston Churchill jibed, "We are waiting for the long-promised invasion. So are the fishes."

October 22, 1836:   On this date Sam Houston was sworn in as President of the Republic of Texas. Near the end of his inaugural address, he took off his sword—"this emblem of my past office," he said—promising to put it on again if his country demanded it. Meanwhile, he saw to it that Texas began building a seven-ship navy.

October 23, 1956:   The Cold War turned briefly hot in Hungary. On October 23, 1956, an anti-Communist revolt broke out. A coalition government headed by Imre Nagy declared Hungary neutral and asked the UN for aid. However, a counter-government under János Kádár turned to the USSR for military support—and got it. In brutal fighting, Soviet forces put down the revolt and kept Hungary in the Communist bloc.

October 24, 1945:   Vidkun Quisling, a Norwegian Fascist, made his last name a synonym for "traitor." He collaborated with Hitler during World War Two, urging German occupation of Norway. When the Allies won the war, Quisling's days were numbered. He was executed by a firing squad at Akershus Castle, Oslo, on October 24, 1945.

October 25, 1983:   "Grenada," President Reagan told the American people, was supposed to be "a friendly island paradise for tourism. Well," he continued, "it wasn't. It was a Soviet-Cuban colony being readied as a major military bastion to export terror and undermine democracy. We got there just in time"—just in time being October 25, 1983, with enough U.S. Marines and Rangers to pacify the island nation of 87,000 people.

October 26, 1676:   In the midst of leading a fairly successful rebellion in colonial Virginia, Nathaniel Bacon died of a fever on this date. A member of the House of Burgesses, he had the royal governor, Sir William Berkeley, on the run for a time. Bacon's followers hated taxes and feared Indian uprisings, but what they planned to do about them is unclear. With Bacon gone, Berkeley restored order and executed 23 of the rebels.

October 27, 1904:   New York City celebrated this day with foghorns sounding in the harbor and bells pealing in St. Patrick's Cathedral. The occasion was the completion of New York's first subway, the IRT from City Hall to 145th Street, Harlem. (See story on page 247)

October 28, 1886:   President Grover Cleveland dedicated the Statue of Liberty Enlightening the World—its full name—on October 28, 1886. A gift from the people of France, the statue stands on what until 1956 was known as Bedloe's Island. Cleveland said, "We will not forget that Liberty has here made her home...." But whether that "here" is actually in New York State or in New Jersey has been a subject of controversy.

October 29, 1954:   Herblock's famous "sewer cartoon" of Richard Nixon first appeared in newspapers. (See story on page 36)

October 30, 1735:   John Adams, one of America's Founding Fathers, was born on this date in Braintree, Massachusetts. Adams, who thought of himself as "puffy, vain, conceited," had the tough task of following George Washington in the Presidency. As the first President to live in the White House, Adams prayed, "May none but honest and wise men ever rule under this roof."

October 31, 1864:   News of the Comstock Lode brought a rush of settlers to the Nevada region of the Utah Territory. Congress made Nevada into a territory in 1861 and into a state three years later. So eager were Nevadans to see their territory admitted to the Union that they telegraphed their entire constitution to Washington, a deed that cost the steep sum of $3,416.77. Nevada was admitted on October 31, 1864.

November

November 1, 1979:   On this date the Jimmy Carter administration proposed a $1.5 billion loan guarantee to Chrysler Corporation to prevent the bankruptcy of the auto company. The bailout, which saved Chrysler, involved a U.S. President, Congress, 452 banks, the governments of four states and three foreign countries, 1,500 suppliers and dealers, and six labor unions.

November 2, 1930:   The Empress Zauditu died in April, and Tafari Makonnen succeeded her the next day. But it was not until November 2, 1930, after a decent period of mourning (and the passing of the rainy season) that Makonnen was crowned as His Imperial Majesty Haile Selassie, Conquering Lion of the Tribe of Judah, Elect of God, Emperor of Ethiopia.

November 3, 1936:   Jim Farley, President Roosevelt's campaign manager, predicted that FDR would win reelection in 1936 by an electoral college margin of 523 to 8. Most people scoffed, but election day, November 3rd, proved that Farley was right. (See story on page 188)

November 4, 1979:   Just after 3:00 a.m. Washington time on November 4, 1979, the U.S. State Department learned that a mob of Iranian students had overrun the American Embassy in Teheran. The Iranians took 62 Americans as hostages, holding them for the next 444 days—until Ronald Reagan took the oath of office as President, succeeding Jimmy Carter.

November 5, 1605:   November 5th is Guy Fawkes Day, celebrated in Great Britain with firewords and bonfires. It is the anniversary of the arrest of Guy Fawkes and others in the Gunpowder Plot of 1605. The Plot was a conspiracy by a small group of English Catholics to blow up the Parliament and King James I with 36 barrels of gunpowder stored in a cellar under the House of Lords.

November 6, 1936:   On November 6, 1936, the Loyalist government of Spain evacuated Madrid and fled to Valencia. Generalissimo Francisco Franco, a man the American ambassador to Spain had called "a bit academic," was nearing Madrid at the head of a professional army. Franco, who had the support of Hitler and Mussolini, won out despite the valiant defense of the city by a hastily recruited militia.

November 7, 1962:   This is the date of Richard Nixon's "last press conference"—a whining, vindictive attack on the press after his loss to Pat Brown in the California gubernatorial race. It's true that the journalists didn't like Nixon, but as later events proved, they had their reasons. *Time* Magazine editorialized: "Barring a miracle, Nixon's political career has ended." Six years later came the miracle.

November 8, 1966:   Edward Brooke, a Massachusetts Republican, won a seat in the United States Senate on this date. Brooke was the nation's first popularly elected black Senator. He served two terms.

November 9, 1989:   In a move that stunned the world, East Germany removed the border restrictions imposed after World War Two. The next day sections of the Berlin Wall, a grim symbol of the Cold War, began coming down. Happy East Germans poured into West Germany to sightsee and to shop. Talk of reunification of the two Germanys began at once.

November 10, 1961:   It can be hard to keep up with the names of cities in Russia. Under the tsars there was a city on the Volga named Tsaritsyn. Naturally, the Bolsheviks couldn't live with that. So in 1925 it was renamed Stalingrad. Then came Nikita Khrushchev and his anti-Stalin campaign. On November 10, 1961, the city became Volgograd, which it is today.

November 11, 1918: The World War One armistice was signed on this date. Until 1954 the nation celebrated Armistice Day; now we call it Veterans' Day. One of Art Linkletter's kids-who-say-the-darndest-things defined it: "Armistice Day is when many countries signed a treaty and said that they would never fight again, but they did."

November 12, 1923: On this date, following the Nazis' Beer Hall Putsch in Munich, Adolf Hitler was arrested for high treason. At his trial, Hitler impressed the German people with his eloquence. "The army we have formed is growing from day to day," he told the court—"the old flags will wave again." Convicted and sentenced to five years at Landsberg prison, Hitler began dictating the chapters of his book, *Mein Kampf*.

November 13, 1927: After seven years of construction, the Holland Tunnel carried its first public traffic on November 13, 1927. The tunnel, a joint enterprise of New York and New Jersey, linked Canal Street, Manhattan, with Jersey City, New Jersey. When it opened, the Holland Tunnel was the longest underwater tunnel anywhere. A book published for the occasion called engineer Clifford M. Holland's project *The Eighth Wonder*.

November 14, 1889: This is the birthday of Jawaharlal Nehru, the man who led India through the difficult early years of independence. A lawyer educated at Harrow and Cambridge, he became a fervent nationalist after British troops shot thousands of demonstrators at Amrishtar. Prior to becoming Prime Minister in 1947, Nehru spent much of his time in jail.

November 15, 1777: It's easy to forget that the highly successful Constitution of 1787 was preceded by an unworkable document—the Articles of Confederation, adopted by Congress on November 15, 1777. The Articles gave the central government very little power. George Washington dismissed the Articles as "the shadow without the substance" and was among those who favored a Constitutional Convention.

November 16, 1776: An American vessel, the *Andrew Doria*, fired a ritual salute as it entered port at the small Dutch island of St. Eustatius in the West Indies on November 16, 1776. The guns of Fort Orange answered the salute. It was the first official foreign greeting for the new red-and-white striped flag of the Continental Congress—the first recognition that a new nation had emerged on the world stage.

November 17, 1973: When a newspaper editor in Orlando, Florida, raised a question about President Nixon's tax returns, the President decided to come clean. "I welcome this kind of examination," he said, "because people have got to know whether or not their President is a crook." He then tried to remove their doubts by adding, "Well, "I'm not a crook.""

November 18, 1307:   William Tell, a legendary Swiss patriot, refused to remove his hat before a stake on which the hat of the local Austrian bailiff was mounted. The Austrian bailiff decreed as punishment that Tell would have to shoot an apple off his small son's head. On November 18, 1307 (according to legend) the steady archer William Tell did just that. Tales of the event led to a play by Schiller and an opera by Rossini.

November 19, 1863:   On this date, a few months after the Battle of Gettysburg, President Abraham Lincoln delivered his famous Gettysburg Address. He was dedicating the new national cemetery on the Civil War battlefield. (See story on page 108)

November 20, 1789:   The Bill of Rights—the first ten amendments to the Constitution of the United States—did not create any new rights. Freedom of speech, freedom of the press, freedom of religion, and the rest already existed in the 13 states. The Bill of Rights simply declared that the Federal government had no authority to take them away. On November 20, 1789, New Jersey became the first state to ratify the Bill of Rights.

November 21, 1864:   Abraham Lincoln's moving letter to Mrs. Bixby in Boston is dated November 21, 1864. Lincoln seems to have been misinformed—Mrs. Bixby did not actually lose five sons in battle—but his letter is so magnificently worded that it has appeared in literature anthologies ever since.

November 22, 1963:   Jacqueline Kennedy thought at first it must be a motorcycle backfiring. But the hunters in the John F. Kennedy motorcade in downtown Dallas recognized the sound right away. It was rifle fire. When it ended, the 35th President of the United States was dead, the tentative promise of Camelot erased in an instant.

November 23, 1804:   Does anyone today know who was once called the "Young Hickory of the Granite Hills"? No? He was Franklin Pierce, 14th President of the United States, a Jacksonian Democrat from New Hampshire, born on this date. Pierce tried without success to smooth over the slavery issue. History has not treated him kindly. In fact, it has hardly treated him at all.

November 24, 1929:   France's Georges Clemenceau, called "the Tiger," had a stormy political career. A staunch defender of Alfred Dreyfus in the Dreyfus Affair and twice Premier of France, Clemenceau harbored fears of German military resurgence after World War One. (See story on page 36)

November 25, 1921:   On November 25, 1921, Hirohito was made Regent of Japan, succeeding his father, Taisho, as Emperor five years later. Hirohito helped to persuade the Japanese government to accept unconditional surrender at the end of World War Two. A student of marine biology, Hirohito remained Emperor—though no longer divine—after the war. He died in 1989.

November 26, 1783:   Annapolis, Maryland, served briefly as the capital of the United States, starting on this date. Congress had been moving around since 1776, so other cities can also claim to have been the nation's capital—Baltimore, Lancaster, York, Princeton, Trenton. At Annapolis, Congress received George Washington's resignation as Commander-in-Chief.

November 27, 1759:   The Reverend Francis Gastrell, Vicar of Frodsham, was living in William Shakespeare's old house at Stratford-upon-Avon. One day he cut down a 150-year old mulberry tree that the Bard himself had planted. Outraged, the town corporation brought an action of ejectment against him. The Reverend was ejected from Stratford "amid the ragings and cursings of its people, a citizen well lost."

November 28, 1919:   On this date Lady Astor, the American-born wife of British politician Waldorf Astor, won election to the British House of Commons. She took the place of her husband when he became a viscount. Lady Astor was known for her sharp tongue. Once when Winston Churchill was causing some difficulty, an exasperated colleague said, "We just don't know what to make of him." Said Lady Astor, "How about a nice rug?"

November 29, 1908:   This is Adam Clayton Powell, Jr.'s birthday. For many years Powell was the only black Representative in Congress. Because of his flamboyance and his excesses, people tended to overlook Powell's genuine contributions to the black cause. A Congressman from Harlem for more than two decades, he was not merely a high-living junketeer. He also had a legislative record of some significance.

November 30, 1874:   Winston Churchill, the inspiring leader of Britain's opposition to Nazi Germany, was born on this date. He seemed to know he was destined for greatness. In a conversation with Lady Asquith when she was 19 and he was 32, Churchill growled, "Curse our mortality. How cruelly short is the allotted span for all we must cram into it." Then he added, "We are all worms. But I do believe that I am a glowworm."

December

December 1, 1955:   On this date Rosa Parks, a black woman in Birmingham, Alabama, was ordered to move to the rear of a city bus. She refused. She was arrested—and a black boycott of Birmingham city buses followed. December 1, 1955, marks the beginning of the modern civil rights movement that led to the passage of the Civil Rights Act of 1964.

December 2, 1823:   The Monroe Doctrine, proclaimed on December 2, 1823, is still a lively topic of conversation. President James Monroe wanted to prevent further European intervention in the Americas. More than 80 years later President Theodore Roosevelt extended the doctrine to permit U.S. intervention in the affairs of unruly Latin American Nations (the "Roosevelt Corollary"). The Monroe Doctrine is not international law, but it exerts a powerful influence on American diplomatic thinking.

December 3, 1948: On December 3, 1948, Senator Karl Mundt of South Dakota revealed the existence of the so-called "pumpkin papers." Actually, they were rolls of microfilm rather than paper. They had been squirreled away in a hollow pumpkin on Whittaker Chambers's farm in Maryland. When developed and put into evidence, they helped convict Alger Hiss of perjury. (See story on page 266)

December 4, 1867: Oliver Kelley, a clerk in the Post Office Department in Washington, D.C., founded the Patrons of Husbandry, better known as the Grange, on this date. At first the National Grange was a social and educational organization for farmers, but as the number of local Granges grew and as farmers' grievances against the railroads increased, the Grangers turned to politics, with some success.

December 5, 1933: In 1919 the 18th Amendment to the U.S. Constitution brought national prohibition. Deaths from alcoholism went down, but the crime rate soared, for along with prohibition came speakeasies and roadhouses, rum runners and racketeers. The 21st Amendment, ratified by the 36th state on December 5, 1933, ended what Herbert Hoover called a "great social and economic experiment, noble in motive...."

December 6, 1884: Americans had wanted a monument to George Washington for a long time—101 years to be exact. Finally, on December 6, 1884, they got it. (See story on page 179)

December 7, 1787: On Pearl Harbor Day (a century and a half earlier) Delaware became the first of the original 13 states to ratify the Constitution of the United States. In gaining the honor of being the First State, Delaware beat out Pennsylvania by five days and New Jersey by eleven.

December 8, 1987: Proving that talk of disarmament was not all talk, Soviet President Mikhail Gorbachev and U.S. President Ronald Reagan met in Washington, D.C., and signed an agreement to dismantle all intermediate range nuclear missiles—1,752 of them belonging to the United States, 859 belonging to the USSR. Reagan chided critics who feared that "war is inevitable."

December 9, 1824: On this date General Antonio Sucre's patriot forces won a victory over royalist forces at the Battle of Ayacucho, Peru. The victory ensured Peruvian independence from Spain and marked the triumph of revolutionary forces throughout South America. (See story on page 256)

December 10, 1869: Legislators in Cheyenne may have thought it was something of a joke to give women the right to vote in the wild west Wyoming Territory back on December 10, 1869. But it wasn't, as events soon proved. (See story on page 168)

December 11, 1936: Romantics throughout the world swooned on December 11, 1936, when King Edward VIII announced on radio that he was giving up the British throne to marry the woman he loved—Wallis Warfield Simpson, a divorcee from Baltimore. The next person in line for the monarchy, his younger brother, was the able and sensible King George VI, a decided improvement.

December 12, 1871: Wild Bill Hickok represented law and order as marshal of Abiline, Kansas. Cowtown Abiline and straight-shooting Wild Bill were at the height of their notoriety. On a night in early October the marshal was playing poker when he heard a shot outside. He raced out, confronted a rowdy Texan, and shot him dead. Hearing another man running toward him, Hickok wheeled in the darkness, fired, and brought down his own deputy. On December 12, 1871, the town fathers fired him.

December 13, 1769: "It is a small college, but there are those who love it." So said Daniel Webster in arguing the Dartmouth College Case before the U.S. Supreme Court. This landmark case declared private-corporation charters to be contracts. The charter in question, that of Dartmouth, was dated December 13, 1769.

December 14, 1897: Margaret Chase Smith, one of the most noteworthy women in American politics, was born on this date. A Republican from Maine, she served four terms in the U.S. House of Representatives and four in the U.S. Senate. Highly respected, she sought the Republican Presidential nomination in 1964. However, the GOP was not yet ready for a woman standard bearer, or even for a Vice Presidential nominee.

December 15, 1890: Sitting Bull died on this date. He was a remarkable Sioux chief. His long-time white foe, General Nelson Miles, said of him, "Since the days of Pontiac, Tecumseh, and Red Jacket, no Indian had had the power of drawing to him so large a following of his race...." An able leader of a hopeless cause, Sitting Bull was shot and killed while being placed under arrest by Lieutenant Bullhead of the Indian police.

December 16, 1773: The British, hoping to unload some surplus tea on the American colonists—and to collect a tax on it as well—succeeded only in uniting all factions against them. "The Tea that bainfull weed is arrived," wrote Abigail Adams. On the night of December 16, 1773, several hundred men disguised in Indian paint and feathers dumped 342 chests of the "bainfull weed" into Boston Harbor. It was the Boston Tea Party.

December 17, 1925: After two major air disasters, General Billy Mitchell accused the War and Navy Departments of "incompetence, criminal negligence, and almost treasonable administration of our national defense." He wasn't one to mince words. But those particular words led to a famous court-martial. Mitchell was convicted on this date and sentenced to five years' suspension from the Army. Twenty years later the U.S. Senate awarded him posthumously the Congressional Medal of Honor.

December 18, 1913: West German Chancellor Willy Brandt (his original name was Karl Herbert Frahm) was born on December 18, 1913. Forced to flee—and change his name—when the Nazis came to power, he returned home from Sweden after the war. Elected Mayor of West Berlin in 1957, he watched the Berlin Wall go up. As Chancellor from 1969 to 1974, he sought to improve relations with East Germany and the USSR. Brandt received the Nobel Peace Prize in 1971.

December 19, 1974: There's a book called *"I Never Wanted To Be Vice-President of* Anything!" It's a biography of Nelson Rockefeller, and the title—a quote from Rocky—is the simple truth. Nonetheless, on December 19, 1974, Nelson Rockefeller was sworn in as the 41st Vice President of the United States. He was the second nonelected Vice President in U.S. history. Jerry Ford, the President who chose him, was the first.

December 20, 1989: As Panama strongman Manuel Noriega continued to thumb his nose at the United States, President George Bush lost patience. On December 20, 1989, U.S. armed forces invaded Panama, toppled the Noriega government, and surrounded the Vatican Embassy where "Pineapple Face," as the press liked to call him, was holed up. He surrendered in early January.

December 21, 1976: On November 21, 1976, an inept would-be spy named Edwin Gibbons Moore tossed a package of documents into the Russian Embassy in Washington. What ensued was a comedy of errors. (See story on page 73)

December 22, 1894: On this date a French court-martial found Captain Alfred Dreyfus guilty of treason and sentenced him to Devils Island for life. Thus began the Dreyfus affair, which divided France for more than a decade. Dreyfus, a wealthy Alsatian Jew, had been framed. When evidence of this came to light, political power in France shifted from the royalist right to the socialist left.

December 23, 1913: The Owens-Glass Act of December 23, 1913, set up the Federal Reserve System—12 regional banks coordinated by a seven-member central Board of Governors in Washington, D.C. The regional banks are "banker's banks." The Fed is charged with maintaining credit and monetary conditions favorable to sound business activity. It also issues currency. Nearly all American paper money today consists of Federal Reserve Notes.

December 24, 1814: On this date the Treaty of Ghent was signed in Ghent, Belgium, ending the War of 1812 between the United States and Great Britain. But wait. The news took days to reach the United States, and by the time it did, General Andrew Jackson had routed the British at the Battle of New Orleans, January 8, 1815. His victory had no effect on the peace terms, but it vaulted Jackson into political prominence.

December 25, 1776: On Christmas night, 1776, George Washington embarked on a venture of crucial importance to the new nation. It was military, not political, but like many military engagements it had political consequences. On this date General Washington crossed the ice-choked Delaware near Trenton, New Jersey, fell on the mostly Hessian troops quartered there, and defeated them. Washington's victory helped to keep the flickering American Revolution alive.

December 26, 1931: The musical comedy *Of Thee I Sing* opened on this date at the Music Box Theatre in New York. Featuring Presidential nominee John P. Wintergreen and Vice-Presidential hopeful Alexander Throttlebottom, this clever lampoon of U.S. politics won a Pulitzer Prize. (See story on page 66)

December 27, 1948: Jozsef Cardinal Mindszenty of Hungary, a strong foe of Communism, was arrested on December 27, 1948, on charges of espionage and treason. His public trial was staged—he confessed to the charges, but he had warned before his arrest that any confession would be coerced. Mindszenty was eventually released. He left Hungary for the Vatican, then moved to Vienna.

December 28, 1930: On this date fire destroyed the State Capitol building of North Dakota in Bismarck. The state responded by constructing a skyscraper Capitol, a 19-story "slender shaft of modernity" rising from the prairie. The usual reasons for a skyscraper, high land values and population density, were absent from Bismarck, North Dakota. Impressiveness was the aim and, in a modest way, the consequence.

December 29, 1845: Ending its brief fling as an independent nation, Texas entered the Union on December 29, 1845, as the 28th state. For the next century no other state could match it in area, but then in 1959 Alaska came in to relegate Texas to the number two spot.

December 30, 1853: The United States and Mexico signed a treaty of sale on this date. For $10 million the U.S. bought nearly 30,000 square miles of land south of the Gila River in what today are Arizona and New Mexico. This was the Gadsden Purchase, named for the U.S. minister to Mexico who conducted the negotiations. The Gadsden Purchase completed the present outline map of the 48 contiguous states.

December 31, 1948: If the Kennedys of Massachusetts once looked like an American dynasty, how about the Longs of Louisiana? On this date Russell Long was sworn in as a United States Senator. His father and mother had both preceded him in the Senate—Huey Long from 1932 to 1935 and Rose McConnell Long in 1936. Huey's brother George served in the U.S. House of Representatives for three terms, while another brother, Earl, was a three-term Governor of Louisiana.

BIBLIOGRAPHY

This is a list of books consulted in compiling the Speaker's Treasury. Only books are included, not periodicals, newspapers, or other published or unpublished sources that provided information for a number of entries.

Abels, Jules. *In the Time of Silent Cal: A Retrospective History of the 1920's.* New York: G.P. Putnam's Sons, 1969.

Abels, Jules. *The Parnell Tragedy.* New York: The Macmillan Company, 1966.

Adams, Henry. *The Education of Henry Adams.* Boston: Houghton Mifflin Company, 1918.

Adler, Bill, with Norman King. *All in the First Family: The Presidents' Kinfolk.* New York: G.P. Putnam's Sons, 1982.

Adler, Bill. *The Churchill Wit.* New York: Coward-McCann, 1965.

Adler, Bill. *The Kennedy Wit.* New York: The Citadel Press, 1964.

Adler, Bill. *More Kennedy Wit.* New York: The Citadel Press, 1965.

Allen, George E. *Presidents Who Have Known Me.* New York: Simon and Schuster, 1950.

Ambrose, Stephen E. *Eisenhower: Volume Two, The President.* New York: Simon and Schuster, 1984.

Andrews, Wayne, ed. *Concise Dictionary of American History.* New York: Charles Scribner's Sons, 1962.

Archer, Jules. *Twentieth Century Caesar: Benito Mussolini.* New York: Julian Messner, 1964.

Asimov, Isaac. *Isaac Asimov's Treasury of Humor.* Boston: Houghton Mifflin Company, 1971.

Bailey, Thomas A. *A Diplomatic History of the American People,* 4th ed. New York: Appleton-Century-Crofts, Inc., 1950.

Baker, Nina Brown. *Robert Bruce: King of Scots.* New York: The Vanguard Press, 1948.

Baker, Russell, *Poor Russell's Almanac.* Garden City, NY: Doubleday & Company, 1972.

Barkley, Alben. *That Reminds Me—*. Garden City, NY: Doubleday, 1954.

Bartlett, John. *Familiar Quotations,* 13th, 15th eds. Boston: Little, Brown and Company, 1955, 1980.

Bauer, Fred, ed. *Ev: The Man and His Words.* Old Tappan, NJ: Hewitt House, 1969.

Becker, Carl A., and Kenneth S. Cooper. *Modern History.* Morristown, NJ: Silver Burdett Company, 1977.

Bernardete, Doris, ed. *Mark Twain: Wit and Wisecracks.* Mount Vernon, NY: The Peter Pauper Press, 1961.

Bierce, Ambrose. *The Devil's Dictionary.* Owings Mills, MD: Stemmer House, 1978.

Billington, Ray Allen. *Westward Expansion: A History of the American Frontier.* New York: The Macmillan Company, 1960.

Bingham, Colin. *Men and Affairs: A Modern Miscellany.* New York: Funk & Wagnalls, 1967.

Block, Herbert. *Herblock Special Report.* New York: W.W. Norton & Company, Inc., 1974.

Blunt, Wilfrid. *The Dream King: Ludwig II Of Bavaria.* New York: The Viking Press, 1970.

Bohle, Bruce, ed. *The Home Book of American Quotations.* New York: Dodd, Mead & Company, 1967.

Bolitho, Hector. *Albert: Prince Consort.* Indianapolis: The Bobbs-Merrill Company, 1964.

Boller, Paul, ed. *Presidential Anecdotes.* New York: Oxford University Press, 1981.

Bowen, Catherine Drinker. *Yankee from Olympus: Justice Holmes and His Family.* Boston: Little, Brown and Company, 1944.

Boykin, Edward C. *The Wit and Wisdom of Congress.* New York: Funk & Wagnalls, 1961.

Bradlee, Benjamin C. *Conversations with Kennedy.* New York: W.W. Norton & Company, 1975.

Braider, Donald. *Solitary Star: A Biography of Sam Houston.* New York: G.P. Putnam's Sons, 1974.

Braude, Jacob M. *Speaker's and Toastmaster's Handbook of Anecdotes by and About Famous Personalities.* Englewood Cliffs, NJ: Prentice-Hall, 1971.

Brendon, Piers. *Eminent Edwardians.* Boston: Houghton Mifflin Company, 1980.

Browne, Arthur, Dan Collins, and Michael Goodwin. *I, Koch: A Decidedly Unauthorized Biography of the Mayor of New York, Edward I. Koch.* New York: Dodd, Mead & Company, 1985.

Browne, Ray B., ed. *Lincoln-Lore: Lincoln in the Popular Mind.* Bowling Green, OH: Popular Press, 1974.

Brundage, James A. *Richard Lion Heart.* New York: Charles Scribner's Sons, 1974.

Buck, Paul H. *The Road to Reunion, 1865-1900.* Boston: Little, Brown and Company, 1937.

Buckley, William F., Jr. *The Unmaking of a Mayor.* New York: The Viking Press, 1966.

Burchell, S.C., and the Editors of Time-Life Books. *Great Ages of Man: Age of Progress.* New York: Time-Life Books, 1966.

Burns, James MacGregor. *The Deadlock of Democracy*. Englewood Cliffs, NJ: 1963.

Burns, James MacGregor. *Roosevelt: The Lion and the Fox*. New York: Harcourt Brace Jovanovich, 1956.

Bush, George, with Victor Gold. *Looking Forward: An Autobiography*. New York: Doubleday, 1987.

Byrne, Robert. *The 637 Best Things Anyone Ever Said*. New York: Atheneum, 1982.

Cannon, Lou. *Reagan*. New York: G.P. Putnam's Sons, 1982.

Carano, Paul, and Pedro C. Sanchez. *A Complete History of Guam*. Rutland, VT: Charles C. Tuttle Company, 1964.

Carruth, Gorton, and Associates, ed. *The Encyclopedia of American Facts and Dates*. 6th ed. New York: Thomas Y. Crowell Company, 1972.

Carruth, Gorton, and Eugene Ehrlich. *The Harper Book of American Quotations*. New York: Harper & Row, 1988.

Carter, Jimmy. *Keeping Faith: Memoirs of a President*. New York: Bantam Books, 1982.

Castelot, Andre, trans. by Guy Daniels. *Napoleon*. New York: Harper & Row, 1971.

Catton, Bruce. *Never Call Retreat*. Garden City, NY: Doubleday & Company, 1965.

Catton, Bruce. *This Hallowed Ground*. Garden City, NY: Doubleday & Company, Inc., 1956.

Cerf, Bennett. *Bennett Cerf's Bumper Crop*. Vols. 1 and 2. Garden City, NY: Garden City Books, 1956.

Cerf, Bennett. *The Laugh's on Me*. Garden City, NY: Doubleday & Company, 1959.

Chambers, William Nisbet. *Old Bullion Benton: Senator from the New West*. Boston: Little, Brown and Company, 1956.

Chapman, Colin. *August 21st. The Rape of Czechoslovakia*. Philadelphia: J.B. Lippincott Company, 1968.

Chase's Annual Events: Special Days, Weeks & Months in 1989. Chicago: Contemporary Books, 1988.

Chidsey, Donald Barr. *The Great Conspiracy: Aaron Burr and His Strange Doings in the West*. New York: Crown Publishers, 1967.

Clark, Sir George. *English History: A Survey*. London: Oxford University Press, 1971.

Clissold, Stephen. *Bernardo O'Higgins and the Independence of Chile*. New York: Frederick a. Praeger, 1969.

Cobb, Irvin, S., *A Laugh a Day Keeps the Doctor Away*. Garden City, NY: Garden City Publishing Co., 1923.

Colombo, John Robert, ed. *Colombo's Canadian Quotations*. Edmonton: Hurtig Publishers, 1974.

Conkin, Paul K. *Big Daddy from the Pedernales: Lyndon Baines Johnson*. Boston: Twayne Publishers, 1986.

Conlin, Joseph R. *The Morrow Book of Quotations in American History*. New York: William Morrow, 1984.

Conrad, Barnaby. *Famous Last Words.* Garden City, NY: Doubleday & Company, 1961.

Cook, Fred J. *American Political Bosses and Machines.* New York: Franklin Watts, 1973.

Cook, Roy J. *One Hundred and One Famous Poems.* Chicago: The Cable Company, 1928.

Coons, Hannibal, ed. *Dere Mr. President: The Hilarious Letters They Write to the President.* Garden City, NY: Doubleday & Company, Inc., in arrangement with Key Publishers, Inc., 1971.

Coote, Colin, and Denzil Batchelor, eds. *Maxims and Reflections of the Rt. Hon. Winston S. Churchill, C.H., M.P.* Boston: Houghton Mifflin Company, 1947.

Copeland, Lewis and Faye. *10,000 Jokes, Toasts & Stories.* New York: Doubleday, 1965.

Cronin, Vincent. *Catherine: Empress of All the Russias.* New York: William Morrow and Company, 1978.

Davidson, James West, and Mark H. Lytle. *The United States: A History of the Republic.* Englewood Cliffs, NJ: Prentice Hall, 1984.

Davis, Burke. *The Billy Mitchell Affair.* New York: Random House, 1967.

Davis, John H. *The Kennedys: Dynasty and Disaster, 1848-1984.* New York: McGraw-Hill Book Company, 1984.

Dean, John III. *Blind Ambition.* New York: Simon & Schuster, 1976.

Dirksen, Everett McKinley, and Herbert V. Prochnow. *Quotation Finder.* New York: Harper & Row, 1971.

Dudden, Arthur Power. *American Humor.* New York: Oxford University Press, 1987.

Dunaway, Philip, and George DeKay, eds. *Turning Points: Fateful Moments that Revealed Men and Made History.* New York: Random House, 1958.

Eaton, Clement. *Henry Clay and the Art of American Politics.* Boston: Little, Brown and Company, 1957.

Editors of *Reader's Digest. The Reader's Digest Treasury of American Humor.* New York: American Heritage Press, 1972.

Editors of *Reader's Digest. The Reader's Digest Treasury of American Quotations.* New York: Reader's Digest Press, 1975.

The Eighth Wonder. Boston: B.F. Sturdevant Company, 1927.

Eisel, Deborah Davis, and Jill Swanson Reddig, eds. *Dictionary of Contemporary Quotations.* n.p.: John Gordon Burke Publisher, 1981.

Elliott, Lawrence. *Little Flower: The Life and Times of Fiorello LaGuardia.* New York: William Morrow, 1983.

Elson, Robert T., and the Editors of Time-Life Books. *World War II: Prelude to War.* New York: Time-Life Books, 1976.

Erickson, Carolly. *Great Harry: The Extravagant Life of Henry VIII.* New York: Summit Books, 1980.

Erickson, Paul D. *Reagan Speaks: The Making of an American Myth.* New York: New York University Press, 1985.

Ervin, Sam J., Jr. *Humor of a Country Lawyer.* Chapel Hill: University of North Carolina Press, 1983.

Evans, Bergen. *Dictionary of Quotations.* New York: Delacorte Press, 1968.

Ewald, William Bragg, Jr. *Eisenhower the President: Crucial Days, 1951-1960.* Englewood Cliffs, NJ: Prentice Hall, 1981.

Fadiman, Clifton, ed. *The Little, Brown Book of Anecdotes.* Boston: Little, Brown and Company, 1985.

Farley, James A. *Jim Farley's Story: The Roosevelt Years.* New York: Whittlesey House/ McGraw-Hill Book Company, 1948.

Federal Writers Project. *North Dakota: A Guide to the Northern Prairie State.* New York: Oxford University Press, 1938, 1950.

Felton, Bruce, and Mark Fowler. *Felton & Fowler's Best, Worst, and Most Unusual.* New York: Thomas Y. Crowell, 1975.

Felton, Bruce, and Mark Fowler. *Felton & Fowler's More Best, Worst, and Most Unusual.* New York: Thomas Y. Crowell, 1976.

Ferraro, Geraldine A., with Linda Bird Francke. *Ferraro: My Story.* New York: Bantam Books, 1985.

Ferrell, Robert H., and John S. Bowman, eds. *The Twentieth Century: An Almanac.* New York: World Almanac Publications, 1984.

Fischer, Louis. *The Life of Mahatma Gandhi.* New York: Harper & Brothers, 1950.

Fischler, Stan. *Uptown, Downtown: A Trip Through Time on New York's Subways.* New York: Hawthorn Books, 1976.

Flexner, Eleanor. *Century of Struggle: The Woman's Rights Movement in the United States.* Cambridge, MA: Harvard University Press, 1959.

Flexner, James Thomas. *Washington: The Indispensable Man.* Boston: Little, Brown and Company, 1974.

Ford, Gerald R. *A Time to Heal: The Autobiography of Gerald R. Ford.* New York: Harper & Row, 1979.

Fowler, Gene. *Beau James: The Life & Times of Jimmy Walker.* New York: The Viking Press, 1949.

Frankland, Noble. *Imperial Tragedy: Nicholas II, Last of the Tsars.* New York: Coward-McCann, 1961.

Frew, Andrew W. *Frew's Daily Almanac: A Calendar of Commemorations.* Jefferson, NC: McFarland & Company, 1984.

Frost, David. *Book of the World's Worst Decisions.* New York: Crown, 1983.

Garraty, John A., with Aaron Singer and Michael J. Gallagher. *American History.* New York: Harcourt Brace Jovanovich, 1982.

The Galaxy of Wit. Upper Saddle River, NJ: Literature House/Gregg Press, 1969 (reprint of 1830 edition in two vols.).

Gardner, Gerald C. *The Quotable Mr. Kennedy*. New York: Abelard-Schuman, 1962.

Gibbon, Edward. *The Decline and Fall of the Roman Empire*. Vol. 1. New York: The Modern Library, n.d.

Green, Jonathon. *Morrow's International Dictionary of Contemporary Quotations*. New York: William Morrow and Company, 1982.

Green, Mark, and Gail MacColl. *Reagan's Reign of Error*. New York: Pantheon Books, 1987.

Griffith, Elisabeth. *In Her Own Right: The Life of Elizabeth Cady Stanton*. New York: Oxford University Press, 1984.

Halberstam, David. *The Best and the Brightest*. New York: New York: Random House, 1972.

Halecki, O. *A History of Poland*. New York: David McKay Company, 1976.

Hanna, Edward, Henry Hicks, and Ted Koppel, eds. *The Wit and Wisdom of Adlai Stevenson*. New York: Hawthorn Books, 1965.

Hardy, Alan. *Queen Victoria Was Amused*. New York: Taplinger Publishing Company, 1977.

Harris, Leon A. *The Fine Art of Political Wit*. New York: E.P. Dutton, 1964.

Haskins, James. *Adam Clayton Powell: Portrait of a Marching Black*. New York: The Dial Press, 1974.

Hayes, Paul M. *Quisling: The Career and Political Ideas of Vidkun Quisling, 1887-1945*. Bloomington: Indiana University Press, 1972.

Henry, Lewis C. *Humorous Anecdotes About Famous People*. Garden City, NY: Halcyon House, 1948.

Hershfield, Harry. *Laugh Louder, Live Longer*. New York: Grayson Publishing Corp., 1959.

Hibben, Paxton. *Henry Ward Beecher: An American Portrait*. New York: The Press of the Readers Club, 1942 (reprint of 1927 edition)

Hilton, George S. *The Funny Side of Politics*. New York: G.W. Dillingham Co., 1899.

Holbrook, Stewart. *The Age of the Moguls*. Garden City, NY: Doubleday & Company, 1953.

House, Jack, ed. *Winston Churchill: His Wit and Wisdom*. London: Collins, 1965.

Huie, William Bradford. *The Execution of Private Slovik*. New York: Delacorte Press, 1954.

Humes, James C. *Podium Humor: A Raconteur's Treasury of Witty and Humorous Stories*. New York: Harper & Row, 1975.

Humes, James C. *Speakers' Treasury of Anecdotes about the Famous*. New York: Harper & Row, 1978.

Jefferson, Louis. *The John Foster Dulles Book of Humor*. New York: St. Martin's Press, 1986.

Jessel, George. *The Toastmaster General's Favorite Jokes*. New York: Hawthorn Books, 1973.

Kelen, Emery. *Hammarskjöld*. New York: G.P. Putnam's Sons, 1966.

Kelen, Emery. *Peace in Their Time*. New York: Alfred A. Knopf, 1963.

Kennedy, Charles O'Brien, with David Jordan, eds. *American Ballads: Naughty, Ribald and Classic*. New York: Fawcett Publications, 1952.

Kennedy, John F. *Profiles in Courage*. New York: Harper & Row, 1956.

Komroff, Manuel. *Talleyrand*. New York: Julian Messner, 1965.

Kouwenhoven, John A. *The Columbia Historical Portrait of New York*. New York: Harper & Row, 1953, 1972.

Kramer, Michael, and Sam Roberts. *"I Never Wanted To Be Vice-President of Anything!": An Investigative Biography of Nelson Rockefeller*. New York: Basic Books, 1976.

LaFollette, Robert M. *LaFollette's Autobiography*. Madison: The University of Wisconsin Press, 1963 (reprint of 1911 edition).

Lane, Hana Umlauf, ed. *The World Almanac Book of Who*. New York: World Almanac Publications, 1980.

Langer, William. *An Encyclopedia of World History*, 4th ed. Boston: Houghton Mifflin Company, 1968.

Leamer, Laurence. *Make-Believe: The Story of Nancy & Ronald Reagan*. New York: Harper & Row, 1983.

Levin, Murray B, with George Blackwood. *The Compleat Politician: Political Strategy in Massachusetts*. Indianapolis: The Bobbs-Merrill Company, 1962.

Lewin, Leonard C., ed. *A Treasury of American Political Humor*. New York: Delacorte Press, 1964.

Lieberman, Gerald F. *3.500 Good Quotations for Speakers*. Garden City, NY: Doubleday, 1983.

Liebling, A.J. *The Earl of Louisiana*. New York: Simon and Schuster, 1961.

Linkletter, Art. *A Child's Garden of Misinformation*. New York: Bernard Geis Associates, 1965.

Linkletter, Art. *I Wish I'd Said That! My Favorite Ad-libs of All Time*. Garden City, NY: Doubleday, 1968.

Lloyd, Alan. *The Maligned Monarch: A Life of John of England*. Garden City, NY: Doubleday & Company, 1972.

Lombardi, John V. *Venezuela: The Search for Order, the Dream of Progress*. New York: Oxford University Press, 1982.

Lord, Walter. *The Good Years: From 1900 to the First World War*. New York: Harper & Row, 1960.

Lowell, Juliet. *Dear Mr. Congressman*. New York: Duell, Sloan and Pearce, 1960.

Lundberg, Ferdinand. *Scoundrels All*. New York: Lyle Stuart, 1968.

MacArthur, Douglas. *Reminiscences*. New York: McGraw-Hill Book Company, 1964.

McCarthy, Eugene. *Up 'Til Now: A Memoir*. New York: Harcourt Brace Jovanovich, 1987.

McGinniss, Joe. *The Selling of the President 1968*. New York: Trident Press, 1969.

McKee, John Hiram. *Coolidge Wit and Wisdom: 125 Short Stories About "Cal."* New York: Frederick A. Stokes Company, 1933.

McLeave, Hugh. *The Last Pharoah: Farouk of Egypt*. New York: The McCall Publishing Company, 1969.

McLellan, Diana. *Ear on Washington*. New York: Arbor House, 1982.

McPhee, Nancy. *The Book of Insults*. New York: St. Martin's Press, 1978.

Manchester, William. *The Death of a President: November 20-November 25, 1963*. New York: Harper & Row, 1967.

Mandel, Morris. *A Complete Treasury of Stories for Public Speakers*. Middle Village, NY: Jonathan David Publishers, 1974.

Matthiessen, F.O., ed. *The Oxford Book of American Verse*. New York: Oxford University Press, 1950.

Mattingly, Garrett. *The Armada*. Boston: Houghton Mifflin Company, 1959.

Maurois, Andre. *Disraeli*. New York: D. Appleton and Company 1928.

Mirkin, Stanford M. *What Happened When: A Noted Researcher's Almanac of Yesterdays*. New York: Ives Washburn, 1966.

Missen, Leslie. *Quotable Anecdotes*. London: George Allen & Unwin Ltd, 1966.

Montaigne. *The Selected Essays of Montaigne*. Edited and with an Introduction by Lester G. Crocker. New York: Pocket Books, 1959.

Montapert, Alfred Armand. *Distilled Wisdom*. Englewood Cliffs, NJ: Prentice Hall, 1964.

Morison, Samuel Eliot. *The Oxford History of the American People*. New York: Oxford University Press, 1965.

Morrow, Ian F.D. *Bismarck*. London: Duckworth, 1943.

Mosely, Leonard. *Haile Selassie: The Conquering Lion*. Englewood Cliffs, NJ: Prentice Hall, 1964.

Murphy, Edward F. *The Crown Treasury of Relevant Quotations*. New York: Crown Publishers, 1978.

Nenarokov, Albert P. *Russia in the Twentieth Century*. New York: William Morrow & Company, 1968.

Nessen, Ron. *It Sure Looks Different from the Inside*. New York: Playboy Press, 1978.

Nevins, Allan. *Grover Cleveland: A Study in Courage*. New York: Dodd, Mead & Company, 1932.

Nichols, Roy Franklin. *Franklin Pierce: Young Hickory of the Granite Hills*, 2nd ed. Philadelphia: University of Pennsylvania Press, 1958.

Nixon, Richard. *Leaders*. New York: Warner Books, 1981.

Nizer, Louis. *Thinking on Your Feet*. New York: Liveright Publishing Corporation, 1940.

O'Kill, Brian. *Exit Lines: Famous (and not-so-famous) Last Words*. Burnt Hill, Harlow, Essex: Longman, 1986.

O'Neill, Thomas P., Jr., with William Novak. *Man of the House: The Life and Political Memoirs of Speaker Tip O'Neill*. New York: Random House, 1987.

The Oxford Dictionary of Quotations, 3rd ed. London: Oxford University Press, 1979.

Partnow, Elaine. *The Quotable Woman: 1800-1981*. New York: Facts on File, 1982.

Payne, Robert. *The Life and Death of Trotsky*. New York: McGraw-Hill Book Company, 1977.

Pearson, Hesketh. *Merry Monarch: The Life and Likeness of Charles II*. New York: Harper & Brothers, 1960.

Peters, Charles. *How Washington Really Works*. Reading, MA: Addison-Wesley, 1980.

Pile, Stephen. *The Incomplete Book of Failures*. New York: E.P. Dutton, 1979.

Plato, *The Republic*, trans. by Francis Macdonald Cornford. New York: Oxford University Press, 1945.

Platt, Suzy, ed. *Respectfully Quoted: A Dictionary of Quotations Requested from the Congressional Research Service*. Washington, DC: Library of Congress, 1989.

Pringle, Henry F. *Theodore Roosevelt*. New York: Harcourt Brace Jovanovich, 1931.

Prochnow, Herbert V., and Herbert V. Prochnow, Jr. *A Treasury of Humorous Quotations*. New York: Harper & Row, 1969.

Pusey, Merlo J. *Charles Evans Hughes*. New York: The Macmillan Company, 1952.

Putnam, Peter Brock. *Peter, the Revolutionary Tsar*. New York: Harper & Row, 1973.

Rawson, Hugh. *A Dictionary of Euphemisms and Other Doubletalk*. New York: Crown, 1981.

Ridley, Jasper. *Elizabeth I: The Shrewdness of Virtue*. New York: Viking, 1987.

Ringo, Miriam. *Nobody Said It Better*. Chicago: Rand McNally, 1980.

Riordon, William L., ed. *Plunkitt of Tammany Hall*. Mattituck: MY: Amereon House, 1982 (reprint of 1905 edition)

Robinson, James W. *Better Speeches in Ten Simple Steps*. Rocklin, CA: Prima Publishing and Communications, 1989.

Rose, Kenneth. *King George V*. New York: Alfred A. Knopf, 1984.

Roseboom, Eugene H. *A History of Presidential Elections*. New York: The Macmillan Company, 1957.

Rosenman, Samuel I. *Working with Roosevelt*. New York: Harper & Row, 1952.

Rovere, Richard H. *Senator Joe McCarthy*. New York: Harcourt, Brace and Company, 1959.

Roy, Jules. *The Trial of Marshal Pétain*, trans. by Robert Baldick. New York: Harper & Row, 1968.

Russell, Francis. *The Shadow of Blooming Grove: Warren G. Harding in His Times*. New York: McGraw-Hill Book Company, 1968.

Schlesinger, Arthur M., Jr. *The Age of Roosevelt: The Crisis of the Old Order, 1919-1933*. Boston: Houghton Mifflin Company, 1957.

Schutz, Charles E. *Political Humor: From Aristophanes to Sam Ervin*. Rutherford, NJ: Fairleigh Dickinson Press, 1977.

Seldes, George. *The Great Quotations*. New York: Lyle Stuart, 1960, 1966.

Shaw, Archer H., ed. *The Lincoln Encyclopedia: The Spoken and Written Words of A. Lincoln Arranged for Ready Reference*. New York: The Macmillan Company, 1950.

Shenkman, Richard, and Kurt Reiger. *One-Night Stands with American History*. New York: William Morrow, 1980.

Shirer, William L. *The Rise and Fall of the Third Reich.* New York: Simon and Schuster, 1960.

Sifakis, Carl. *The Encyclopedia of American Crime.* New York: Facts on File, 1982.

Simpson, James B. *Contemporary Quotations.* New York: Thomas Y. Crowell, 1964.

Smith, Mrs. Chetwood. *History's Most Famous Words.* Boston: Lothrop, Lee & Shepard, 1926.

Smith, Page. *John Adams,* Vol. II. Garden City, NY: Doubleday & Company, 1962, 1963.

Spinrad, Leonard, and Thelma Spinrad. *Complete Speaker's Almanac.* Englewood Cliffs, NJ: Prentice Hall, 1984.

Steinberg, Alfred. *Sam Johnson's Boy: A Close-up of the President from Texas.* New York: The Macmillan Company, 1968.

Sterling, Bryan B. *The Best of Will Rogers.* New York: Crown Publishers, 1979.

Stevenson, Burton, ed. *The Macmillan Book of Proverbs, Maxims, and Famous Phrases.* New York: The Macmillan Company, 1948.

Sullivan, Frank. *Legend: The Only Inside Story About Mayor Richard J. Daley.* Chicago: Bonus Books, 1989.

TerHorst, J.F., and Col. Ralph Albertazzie. *The Flying White House: The Story of Air Force One.* New York: Coward, McCann & Geoghegan, 1979.

Toland, John. *Adolf Hitler.* Garden City, NY: Doubleday & Company, 1976.

Tomlinson, Gerald. *Speaker's Treasury of Sports Anecdotes, Stories, and Humor.* Englewood Cliffs, NJ: Prentice Hall, 1990.

Trefousse, Hans L. *Ben Butler: The South Called Him BEAST!* New York: Twayne Publishers, 1957.

Troyat, Henry, trans. by Joan Pinkham. *Peter the Great.* New York: E.P. Dutton, 1987.

Truman, Harry S *Memoirs by Harry S Truman: Volume One, Year of Decisions.* Garden City, NY: Doubleday & Company, 1955.

Truman, Harry S *Memoirs by Harry S Truman: Volume Two: Years of Trial and Hope.* Garden City, NY: Doubleday & Company, 1956.

Tuchman, Barbara W. *The First Salute.* New York: Alfred A. Knopf, 1988.

Tuchman, Barbara W. *The Guns of August.* New York: The Macmillan Company, 1962.

Twain, Mark. *Adventures of Huckleberry Finn.* New York: Harper & Bros., 1884.

Udall, Morris K. *Too Funny to Be President.* New York: Henry Holt and Company, 1988.

Unitarian Universalist Association, Washington Office for Social Justice. *A Congressional Directory & Action Guide.* Washington, DC: UUA, 1989.

Untermeyer, Louis, ed. *Story Poems: An Anthology of Narrative Verse.* New York: Washington Square Press, 1957.

Urdang, Laurence, ed. *The World Almanac Dictionary of Dates.* New York: Longman, 1982.

Wagner, Phyllis Cerf, and Albert Erskine, eds. *At Random: The Reminiscences of Bennett Cerf.* New York: Random House, 1977.

Wallace, George, Jr., as told to James Gregory. *The Wallaces of Alabama.* Chicago: Follett Publishing Company, 1975.

Warren, Charles. *Odd Byways in American History.* Cambridge, MA: Harvard University Press, 1942.

Wecter, Dixon. *The Hero in America: A Chronicle of Hero-Worship.* New York: Charles Scribner's Sons, 1941.

White, Theodore H. *The Making of the President 1960.* New York: Atheneum, 1961.

Wicker, Tom. *A Time to Die.* New York: Quadrangle, 1975.

Williams, John Alexander. *West Virginia: A History.* New York: W.W. Norton & Company, 1984.

Williams, Neville. *Elizabeth the First: Queen of England.* New York: E.P. Dutton & Co., 1968.

Williamson, Hugh Ross. *Historical Whodunits.* New York: The Macmillan Company, 1955.

Wittlin, Thaddeus. *Commissar: The Life and Death of Lavrenty Pavlovich Beria.* New York: The Macmillan Company, 1972.

Wise, Bill M. *The Wisdom of Sam Ervin.* New York: Ballantine Books, 1973.

Worcester, Donald E. *Bolivar.* Boston: Little, Brown and Company, 1977.

Worcester, Donald E. *Brazil: From Colony to World Power.* New York: Charles Scribner's Sons, 1973.

The World Almanac and Book of Facts, 1990. New York: Pharos Books, 1990.

Wyden, Peter. *The Unknown Iacocca.* New York: William Morrow & Company, 1987.

Zall, P.M., ed. *Abe Lincoln Laughing: Humorous Anecdotes from Original Sources by and about Abraham Lincoln.* Berkeley, CA: University of California Press, 1982.

Index

A

Abernethy, Arthur Talmadge, 65–66
Acheson, Dean, 120, 266, 298
Acton, Lord, 185
Adams, Abigail, 321
Adams, Gridley, 140
Adams, Henry, 58, 111, 236, 255
Adams, John, 87, 174, 184, 299, 315
Adams, John Quincy, 186
Addison, 70
Addison, Joseph, 4, 101
Adenauer, Konrad, 270
Adler, Bill, 235
Agnew, Spiro T., 32, 34, 118, 120, 312
Albert, Prince, 22, 139, 152, 204, 291, 294
Aldrin, Buzz, 301
Alexander II, Tsar (Russia), 281, 284
Alexandra, Tsarina (Russia), 180
Allen, George E., 124, 209–210
Allen, "Private" John, 51, 234
Allen, Woody, 269
Allison, W.B., 134
Altgeld, John P., 112–113, 298
Amery, Leopold, 292
Ames, Fisher, 50
Amin, Idi, 120, 312
Anthony, Susan B., 165, 297
Anne of Cleves, 304
Antony, Marc, 31
Antigonus, 211
Apponyi, Count, 109
Arbuthnot, John, 182
Arends, Leslie, 241
Aristides, 35
Aristotle, 50, 125, 158, 182
Armstrong, Neil, 301
Arthur, Chester A., 277
Ashurst, Henry, 194
Asquith, Lady, 319
Astor, Lady, 215–216, 319

Astor, Waldorf, 319
Atlee, Clement, 92
Atwater, Lee, 126
Augustine, Saint, 298
Aung San, 275
Austin, Warren, 6

B

Bacon, Francis, 263, 270
Bacon, Nathaniel, 275, 314
Bailey, Pearl, 13
Bailey, Thomas, 243
Baker, Edwin D., 4
Baker, Russell, 107, 204, 207
Balfour, Arthur, 15–16, 96
Balzac, Honoré de, 19
Barkley, Alben W., 20, 115, 170, 213, 219, 246, 255
Barnum and Bailey, 65–66
Barnum, P.T., 204–205, 298
Barrymore, John, 298
Beame, Abraham, 24
Beard, Charles A., 230
Beauharnais, Josephine, 161, 283
Beecher, Henry Ward, 61, 127, 298
Beefeaters, 309
Begin, Menachem, 37, 309
Bellingham, John, 141–142
Belmont, August, 247–248
Bendix, John, 252
Ben-Gurion, David, 220
Bennis, Warren G., 129
Benton, Thomas Hart, 103, 227, 233–234, 285
Beresford, Charles, 229
Beria, Lavrenty Pavlovich, 300
Berkeley, Sir William, 314
Bernhardt, Sarah, 31